Alastair MacKenzie comes from a military family of long standing and he served as an officer in the New Zealand infantry in South Vietnam and in the special forces of South Africa, Oman and the UK, where for four years he was troop commander in the 22nd Special Air Services Regiment. After his retirement as a full-time Army officer he enjoyed a successful commercial career with Royal Ordnance and British Aerospace before setting up his own consultancy firm. In civilian life he retained an involvement with the Territorial Army as an SAS officer and retired with the rank of Lieutenant Colonel in 2001. He obtained his PhD in Politics in 2005 and is the author of a number of articles for military journals.

Special Force

The Untold Story of 22nd Special Air Service Regiment (SAS)

Alastair MacKenzie

I.B. TAURIS

LONDON · NEW YORK

Published in 2011 by I.B.Tauris & Co Ltd
6 Salem Road, London W2 4BU
175 Fifth Avenue, New York NY 10010
www.ibtauris.com

Distributed in the United States and Canada Exclusively by Palgrave Macmillan,
175 Fifth Avenue, New York NY 10010

ISBN: 978 1 84885 017 2

A full CIP record for this book is available from the British Library
A full CIP record is available from the Library of Congress

Library of Congress Catalog Card Number: available

Designed and Typeset by 4word Ltd, Bristol, UK
Printed and bound in Sweden by scandbook AB

Dedication

I could not have completed this work without the support and assistance of my dear late wife, Cecilia. After 38 years of 'following the colours' with me, from Vietnam to Northern Ireland, Southern Africa and the Middle East, she willingly relived those experiences in the pages of this book.

My daughter, Juliette, and son, Andrew, who is now a 'pilgrim' himself, had complete confidence in me and I am eternally grateful for their continuing acceptance of my challenges throughout their lives.

My late parents, Lieutenant Colonel Archibald and Mary MacKenzie – despite being a military family with service including Dunkirk, D-Day, Palestine, Cyprus and the Malayan Emergency – were always a little bemused by my service in special forces and my academic commitments but, nevertheless, consistently offered me encouragement from afar.

The incentive for this work was the time I spent with the 'pilgrims' of the Special Air Service Regiment whose support on active service operations was given without question and upon whom the Nation can have complete confidence in any hour of need. These Centurions remain unrecognised by the world at large but to them I offer my thanks – in particular to – Brad; George; 'Gonz'; 'Mac' (RIP); Pete Mac; 'Minky'; 'Playboy' (RIP); 'Rusty'; 'Tak'; Jim et al. I am particularly indebted to 'DC'; 'Nasty Neil'; Roy; 'Snapper'; 'Valdez'; and Dave. Similarly, I am especially grateful to the late Colonel JW MBE MC, as one of the founding fathers of the post-war SAS, for sharing his experiences with me, as I am to other SAS stalwarts who have assisted me but have requested to remain anonymous. This 'band of few' has the vision to realise that research on the Special Air Service Regiment can only be healthy in contrast to the reactionaries who continually fret over what academic research may reveal.

'We are the Pilgrims, Master...'

Dr Alastair R.F. MacKenzie Lt Col (Ret)
Tara Bay
NEW ZEALAND

Author's Disclaimer

The concealment of selected names in this book by the use of initials or by random letters was made at the request of the UK Ministry of Defence for personal security reasons, although some details of individuals mentioned in the book are already in the public domain.

CONTENTS

PART FOUR – COUNTERING TERRORISM, AND INTERNATIONAL HUMANITARIAN OPERATIONS

PART FIVE – CONCLUSION

ABBREVIATIONS

ANZAC   Australian and New Zealand Army Corp
ATO   Ammunition Technical Officer
BAOR   British Army on the Rhine
BATT   British Army Training Team
CAD   Civil Aid Department
CCO   Clandestine Communist Organisation
CDS   Chief of the Defence Staff
CGS   Chief of the General Staff
CinC   Commander-in-Chief
CPU   corps patrol unit
CQB   close-quarter battle
CRW   counter-revolutionary warfare
CT   counter-terrorist
DLF   Dhofar Liberation Front
DMO   Director of Military Operations
DSF   Director Special Forces
DZ   dropping zone
FARELF   Far East Land Forces
FCO   Foreign and Commonwealth Office
FO   Foreign Office
FRA   Federal Regular Army
FRU   Field Research Unit
GHQ   General Headquarters
GOC   General Officer Commanding
GPMG   General Purpose Machine Gun
GPS   global positioning system
GSG9   Grenzschutzgruppe 9

HQ	headquarters
IIBG	Imperial Iranian Battle Group
INLA	Irish National Liberation Army
IO	international operations
IRA	Irish Republican Army
JCO	Joint Commission Observers
JWS	Jungle Warfare School – Kota Tinggi, Johore Bahru
KLA	Kosovo Liberation Army
LRDG	Long Range Desert Group
MAWT	Mountain and Arctic Warfare Team
MCP	Malay Communist Party
MoD	Ministry of Defence
MPAJA	Malay People's Anti Japanese Army
MRF	Mobile Reconnaissance Force
MRLA	Malay Races Liberation Army (formerly MPAJA)
NATO	North Atlantic Treaty Organisation
NCO	non-commissioned officer
NEO	non-combatant evacuation operations
NGO	non-government organisation
NI	Northern Ireland
OA	offensive action
OOTW	operations other than war
OP	observation post
OR	other ranks (i.e. not commissioned)
ORBAT	order of battle
PDRY	People's Democratic Republic of Yemen
PFLO	Popular Front for the Liberation of Oman
PFLOAG	Popular Front for the Liberation of the Arabian Gulf
PIRA	Provisional IRA
PMC	Private Military Company
PRO	Public Records Office
REME	Royal Electrical and Mechanical Engineers
RFA	Royal Fleet Auxiliary
RM	Royal Marines
RSM	regimental sergeant major
RTU	return to unit
RUC	Royal Ulster Constabulary
RV	rendezvous
RWW	Revolutionary Warfare Wing
SADF	South African Defence Force
SAF	Sultan's Armed Forces (Oman)
SAS	Special Air Service

SB	Special Branch (police)
SBS	Special Boat Service
SEAC	South-East Asia Command
SEP	surrendered enemy personnel
SF	special forces
SIS	Secret Intelligence Service
SNCO	senior non-commissioned officer
SOCOM	Special Operations Command (US)
SOE	Special Operations Executive
SOF	special operations forces
SOP	standard operational procedure
SOVF	Special Operations Volunteer Force
SRR	Special Reconnaissance Regiment
SRS	Special Raiding Squadron
SSF	Sultan's Special Force
SSRF	Small Scale Raiding Force
STS	Special Training School
TA	Territorial Army
TNKU	North Kalimantan National Army
UAE	United Arab Emirates
UDA	Ulster Defence Association
UDI	Unilateral Declaration of Independence
UDR	Ulster Defence Regiment
UFF	Ulster Freedom Fighters
UKLO	United Kingdom Liaison Officers
UN	United Nations
UNPROFOR	United Nations Protection Force
UVF	Ulster Volunteer Force

APPENDICES

PART ONE

BACKGROUND

Chapter 1

INTRODUCTION

The British Government maintains a requirement for a small specialist force to be used in direct or indirect military actions focused on strategic or operational objectives. This force requires combinations of trained specialised personnel, equipment and tactics that exceed the routine capabilities of conventional military forces. The special operations carried out by the force are politically sensitive, so only the most proficient forces can be deployed in order to avoid detection and possible failure resulting in damage to British national interests and reputation.

Since 1945 there have been two organisations providing the nation with a special forces ability. The first and larger of the two is an Army-based organisation, and the one upon which this book is based, the SAS. The other organisation is a Royal Navy organisation based upon the Royal Marines and known as the Special Boat Service (SBS).[1] Until very recently, the SBS has had little operational involvement in special forces operations and therefore their activities are not assessed in any detail in this study.

In this book the involvement of the SAS as part of UK defence and foreign policy from 1950 to 2000 is reviewed and assessed in order to establish how it has fitted into the UK's overall national strategy during this period and how effective its contribution has been.

The book examines the activities of the SAS from the end of the Second World War up until the start of the twenty-first century and covers the modern development of the SAS from its almost accidental re-birth at the end of the war to the present, where the SAS has been used in every deployment of British military forces. I examine just how effective the SAS has been in its campaigns in Malaya, South Arabia, Oman, Borneo, Oman, the Falklands, the Gulf War, Northern Ireland and in international operations (IO) such as Bosnia, Kosovo and Sierra Leone.

The role of British special forces has never been fully clarified throughout the post-war period under review. After 1945 it was difficult to pin down the political and the military leaders and get them to specify what special forces were actually for. As this all-important specification was ignored, it left the special forces with conundrums of strategy and operations, and clearly the procurement of weapons and the formulation of training policies were a very hazardous process. British strategy after 1945 was Janus-faced, and this remained the case until the late 1980s with the dual areas of possible or real commitments to the European continent and the defence of, or retreat from, Empire.[2]

Even in periods of prolonged peacetime no sustained or convincing British special forces philosophy has emerged. This is one of the striking features of the period reviewed. During these years the British Army, for the first time in its history, maintained a commitment to the defence of continental Europe. Simultaneously, the British Army waged numerous colonial and 'low intensity' operations during its retreat from the Empire. In conducting its postcolonial campaigns, the Army fell back on its old 'small wars' traditions – traditions which did not include the use of special forces. Under the circumstances, it is not surprising that no coherent view of special forces application evolved.

There has been little strategic analysis of the activities of the SAS since the end of the Second World War; nor has there been any analysis of their effectiveness, or otherwise, when they have been deployed. Professor Colin Gray considers that 'the literature on SAS is vast but generally arid', adding:

> There is a great deal of tactical doctrine for Special Forces but virtually no relevant strategic theory or history.[3]

As Gray has stated, there are numerous publications describing in detail the heroic activities of participant authors in the various SAS deployments that have taken place, worldwide, since the end of the Second World War. As he also states, there are few publications that provide any academic and credible analysis of the effectiveness of post-war SAS operations. The question is raised of how effective the SAS has been in operations since the end of the Second World War, and whether it remains an effective political and/or military tool. This leads to the separate question of whether, with the changing face of warfare, the SAS is going to be a necessary requirement for the future.

Gray provides clarity to the oft-overlooked relationship between special forces operations and foreign policy aspirations:

> It is useful to define special operations as being conducted 'in support of foreign policy'. Special operations forces are a national grand-strategic asset; they are a tool of statecraft that can be employed quite surgically in support of diplomacy, of foreign assistance (of several kinds) as a vital adjunct to regular military forces, or as an independent weapon.[4]

British Post-War Foreign and Defence Policy

The maintenance of great power status was of paramount importance to British leaders immediately after the Second World War. At the root of Britain's aim of upholding its great power status, and central to an understanding of the nature of the world order being constructed, lay a desire to use the world economic resources for its own benefit. Any general withdrawal by the United Kingdom on political and military fronts would have an adverse effect on its economic position. While British foreign policy in the post-war period until the collapse of the Soviet Union is invariably portrayed by commentators as responses to Soviet designs and as part of the so-called Cold War, the primary threats to Britain's interest in the Third World arose from independent nationalist movements, from within states.

The British Army continued to be responsible for imperial policing after the end of the Second World War. During 1950–2000, the period under review, it was involved in numerous military operations; peacekeeping in Palestine at the end of the UN mandate; Korea; the Malayan Emergency; Suez; the EOKA terrorist campaign in Cyprus; the Mau Mau uprising in Kenya; withdrawal from Aden; the Confrontation in Borneo; the Sultanate of Oman; the Falklands War; the first Gulf War; Bosnia; and Yugoslavia.

At the end of the Second World War there was no lack of British military commitments. The liquidation of occupation responsibilities took time and the process was not finally completed until the mid-1950s. In the Middle East, the British presence was an elaborate and expensive one. The great Suez base was the cause of friction with the Egyptians; the Palestinian mandate, which was originally acquired in part for strategic reasons, had become an arena in which the British were caught in the crossfire between Jew and Arab.

Neither the Brussels Treaty of 1948 nor the establishment of NATO on 4 April 1949 had any radical effect upon British defence policy,[5] but these arrangements had some influence on NATO planning. Strategic bombing would be the responsibility of the United States, as the only Western nuclear power, and the only possessor of modern long-range bombers. The European states, and especially France, would provide the bulk of the ground forces.

The paramount considerations in guiding British defence policy in 1955 were a desire to create an effective nuclear capability; the belief that in Europe the Soviet threat might be lessening but that elsewhere, and especially in the Middle East, it might increase; and the conviction that the current defence programme was still beyond the nation's resources.

The era in which Britain engaged unilaterally in military interventions, colonial wars and coups to pursue its first-order objectives largely passed in the 1960s. Since then the priorities have been pursued chiefly by lending diplomatic, and sometimes material, support to the foreign policy and aggression, abroad, of the United States. The decline of Britain's global power was evidenced above all in the Middle East: in the failed invasion of Egypt in 1956 and, as a consequence of budgetary pressures at home, in the military withdrawal from the Gulf in 1971.

> Our most painful experience of the country's reduced circumstances was the failure of the Suez expedition in 1956. This was the result of political and economic weakness rather than military failure, because the Government withdrew a victorious force from the Canal Zone in response to a 'run on the pound' encouraged by the US Government. Whatever the details of this defeat, however, it entered the British soul and distorted our perspective on Britain's place in the world. We developed what might be called the 'Suez Syndrome': having previously exaggerated our power, we now exaggerated our impotence.[6]

Though Britain retained a foothold in the region to maintain close relationships with one important oil producer, Kuwait, and traditionally close allies, Oman and Jordan, the Western ability to control events in the Middle East lay primarily with the United States.

The break-up of the Soviet Empire in Eastern Europe shifted the focus of attention to Germany. Triumphs like the successful war to regain the Falklands had made it momentarily possible to believe in a return to Britain's role of the late 1940s and early 1950s. However, in 1989 Britain was once again seen for what she was, a middle-ranking European state forced by her geographic position and her economic problems to sit on the sidelines.

> Foreign policy is not made in a political vacuum but is shaped by domestic factors (such as public opinion), globalising pressures (such as communications technologies), integrative tendencies (especially within the European Union) and transnational forces (such as lobbying from NGOs). The logic underlying the UK's foreign policy process, however, has changed remarkably little over the past century.[7]

Britain's whole defence position in the 1990s reflected confusion about her future world role. Britain's chief structural weaknesses stem from the fact that the United Kingdom is small in area and densely populated, and that her share of mineral resources is severely limited both quantitatively and qualitatively. There is insufficient arable land to feed more than approximately half the population and the only substantial domestic source of energy is coal in an age which gives priority to petroleum. Britain has some domestic sources of iron but hardly any of the other important minerals. The well-known consequences of these and other shortages is the overwhelming importance of foreign trade to her economic prosperity with all that extensive foreign trade necessarily implies: fragility of the economy as a whole, a chronic and probably in-eradicable balance of payments problems, and a very high degree of governmental sensitivity to the economic aspects of policy questions, both domestic and external, in all spheres of administration.

Defence planning in the 1990s could only respond to the notion of cuts and not to clear strategic initiatives. By 2000 Britain occupied a position in the world very different from that in 1945. The Empire had gone and she had accepted the inevitable and entered Europe but still seemed the least enthusiastic member of the union, even under the 'new' Labour Government. Despite the long years of imperial decline, Britain was still an important player on the world scene, lying at the centre of several interlocking groupings of nations. She was America's closest partner in NATO, one of the big four in the European Union, a Permanent Member of the UN Security Council and still the mother of the Commonwealth. She was a genuinely world-orientated country in a way that no other Europe in-state could claim to be. A remarkable revival of the British economy in the late twentieth century also enhanced her importance. By 2000 she was once again the fourth largest economy in the world, having over-taken France. Perhaps at long last the United Kingdom had recov-ered from those devastating effects of the Second World War.

So how is British defence policy made? The first thing that should be acknowledged is that it is extremely difficult to define defence policy. It is an aspect of security policy, intimately linked – and becoming even more intimately linked – with diplomatic and other general government policies. British defence policy is found in the twin classic principles of the balance of power and collective security. For a small country such as the United Kingdom there can be no realistic alternative to collective security. The political and economic survival of the United Kingdom is closely bound up with those of her allies in Europe and North America, and its continued security freedom cannot be seen in isolation.

British defence policy, not surprisingly, revolves around the defence of the UK and its dependent territories; major alliance activities to resist aggression; and then a range of possibilities from a disaster relief through peacekeeping and peace enforcement, to the possibility of an engagement like the first Gulf War, which could require early action. These are all likely to require mobility and the ability to sustain British forces for months rather than weeks. They are unlikely to require the UK to deploy any significant amount of specific kinds of heavy forces. As regards ground forces, either the essential needs will be for infantry with some combat support and combat service support, or a judgement about what the UK needs in order to be politically credible.

What are British Special Forces?

In discussing the SAS it is useful to try and establish an acceptable definition of the terms 'special force' and 'special force operations'. There are a number of definitions used by historians, academics and writers of military journals and publications.[8] Kiras states:

> Special Operations are not merely unconventional in character.
> ... special operations fill a void that is unachievable convention-
> ally and there is an elevated political or military risk associated

with their failure. In addition, special operations should be defined according to their intended effect: improving conventional military performance.[9]

Gray, a mentor of Kiras's, examines the matter in some detail and reluctantly accepts a somewhat unsatisfactory definition that special operations are whatever special operations forces do, or are trained to do. But noticeably the historical range of special operations embraces such a vast array of activities that he agrees this definition is somewhat pointless. He looks at the terms 'irregular' and 'unconventional' warfare as an alternative but suggests that these terms retain 'unhelpful historical baggage'. He also compares the term 'elite' with regard to special operations forces but considers that elite, as a quality, refers to a standard of selection and not operational activity. It then follows, he says, that special operations forces must be elite, but that elite forces, generally, are not special operations forces. At the risk of entering a battle of semantics, certain terms and definitions will be used in this research to define and differentiate between various 'special' organisations within the British Armed Forces.

The British Armed Forces have several organisations that could be called 'special'. Special,[10] as defined by the Concise Oxford English Dictionary, being of a particular kind, for a particular purpose. This includes the Parachute Regiment in the Army and the Royal Marines in the Navy and it is tempting, generically, to define these organisations as 'special forces'. Both the Parachute Regiment and the Royal Marines have a selection process and both have unique methods of delivery to the battlefield. Also included under the term 'special' must be the SAS and the SBS. These two organisations, particularly the SAS, have an extremely arduous selection and training process and so it could be considered that they should be placed on a higher plane of 'special'. I consider that a highly selective and difficult selection course for personnel entering specialist organisations is the critical essential for recognition as a special force. This is where the term 'elite'[11] could be used to assist in the differentiation between the types of 'special' organisations in the British Army. This somewhat convoluted defining process is necessary due to common utilisation of the term 'special forces', to describe almost any organisation that wears a brightly coloured beret, camouflaged uniforms and aggressive badges. In the interests of accuracy, within the British Armed Forces, the SAS are the elite of the special forces.

In order to further clarify matters prior to proceeding, I provide several other acceptable definitions. The first and most obvious requirement is to define 'special operations' in order to provide some parameters on the military agencies to be researched. Gray[12] provides the following definitions.

> *Special operations* – Special operations have as their core identity the overt or covert conduct of a desperately dangerous raid by relatively few elite fighting men for high operational or more strategic stakes.[13]

> A *clandestine operation* is one which attempts to conceal its very existence.

> A *covert operation* is one which tends to conceal its true authorship.

> An *overt operation* does not attempt to conceal either the action or its perpetrators.[14]

Another important distinction that is required to be made is between 'tactical' and 'strategic' operations. Luttwak[15] provides the following comprehensive definitions:

> *Strategy* – The art of developing and using military and other resources in order to achieve objectives defined by national policy. The conventional distinction between strategy and tactics is that the first deals with the development and deployment of military forces – including the selection of the form of warfare and of the 'battlefield' – whereas the latter deals with the use of armed forces within the context set by strategic decisions.

> *Tactics* – The 'art' of using armed forces in battle; more generally, elements of knowledge or belief applied to decisions over armed forces deployed in a particular setting or 'theatre' determined by a strategic decision.[16]

However, in the interests of common usage and common understanding, the term British special forces, in this research, will only refer to the SAS and the SBS. Moreover, British special forces can be defined as forces selected, trained, organised and equipped specifically to conduct special operations. Special operations will be defined as those operations carried out by special forces to achieve national political and military objectives by conventional or unconventional means. This stance avoids the folly of those studying special forces who continually agonise over establishing an acceptable definition of special forces which will satisfy all the pundits.

Before considering the role of SAS troops it is necessary to specify certain principles or factors which must influence their employment. The employment of SAS troops, especially in the planning stage, will be strategic more often than tactical. SAS activity should, therefore, be an integral part (however small) of the main plan rather than a diversionary role allotted at a later stage. In this connection a clear charter exists for SAS troops where there are important tasks which cannot conveniently or economically be tackled by regular formations and, more particularly, which lie far behind the enemy lines or present particular difficulties of access. Areas in which SAS operations may take place are graded:

> Red areas – The country is occupied and dominated by the enemy and with untrustworthy civilians.

> Green areas – The country is sparsely occupied or loosely controlled by the enemy with a reliable civilian population.[17]

Intervention by SAS troops must have a strategic or tactical effect on operations. The degree of risk that should be accepted depends on importance of the task. It is invidious to state that such a task is or is not an SAS role, but it is essential to consider whether the task allotted cannot be carried out with greater chance of success by other military units or other branches of the services. This applies particularly to diversionary tasks or attacks on specific pinpoints in a tactical area. The very high degree of individual and collective SAS training makes it possible to operate in smaller parties with equal or greater effect than troops not specially trained for this role. When troops are operating behind the enemy lines, they should be scattered in as many small parties as possible, but having, where possible, good communications with a small central base. Good signal communications are essential and only under very exceptional circumstances is it operationally sound to land parties without some form of communications. Parties must have firm plans for eventual withdrawal, however vital the target. SAS troops can rarely achieve their objective if landed in the face of immediate and alerted ground opposition. They must retain the initiative as long as possible by operating in an offensive manner. The psychological importance of keeping morale high – the morale both of the troops and of the local partisans and civilians who may be assisting them – is enormous. Surprise should be achieved and exploited fully and for this reason operations are normally carried out at night. Casualties can and should be kept at a low percentage, bearing in mind that all personnel captured may be shot.

SAS troops are trained to operate in such numbers as most suitable for the task in hand, after initial landing by sea, air or land infiltration. They can be employed in either a strategic or tactical role. Strategic employment gives more scope for small parties to fulfil the first essential of any detachment, which is to contain a larger force of enemy than the detachment concerned. For SAS troops to pay proper dividends their role must be tied up with the main strategic plan. In strategic areas it is easier to select suitable terrain where enemy troops are not so thick on the ground; the time factor is not likely to be so vital; the selection of suitable DZs (dropping zones),[18] or landing points, is simplified and resupply by air is also easier unless enemy aircraft or air defences are very active. The difficulties in coordinating plans with one's own front-line troops does not arise. However, withdrawal may prove more difficult if the parties cannot be overrun by own troops within a specified time.

It is obviously more difficult for small parties to achieve surprise and operate successfully in the immediate battle area, where enemy troops are normally numerous, and a period of operating must, therefore, be short and depend on accurate timing and employment at the opportune moment. The selection of suitable DZs for airborne operations will be more difficult owing to enemy and own anti-aircraft fire. The necessity of terrain being suitable becomes an even more important factor. It is unlikely that parties will have many worthwhile targets during a static period, but far greater opportunities occur when the position is fluid. It is unlikely that if enemy opposition is strong a small SAS party could successfully attack and hold any pinpointed target such as a headquarters, artillery unit, or bridge. At the same time, however, the threat of possible landings of SAS parties will tie up a considerable number of enemy troops, and any landing of small SAS parties in a tactical area is likely, for a short period, to be mistaken for a major airborne landing and to have an exaggerated effect.

The employment of SAS troops in a large scale withdrawal has not yet been tested. Their role would likely be very similar to that allotted to HQ auxiliary units in England, Wales and Scotland during the Second World War,[19] when a German invasion was contemplated. They could undoubtedly achieve similar results in delaying enemy spear heads by harassing his comparatively unprotected lines of communication, carrying out demolitions and in supplying information. The problem of withdrawing them would be difficult.

The British SAS Regiment since the mid-1970s has built up an almost mythical reputation. It is the prime ingredient for a regular fare of heroic exploits of almost superhuman dimensions in the British tabloid press. This press obsession increased enormously following the dramatic 1980 hostage rescue at the Iranian Embassy siege in London, which was seen live on television.

The misinformation and myth surrounding the SAS have been exacerbated by government secrecy in all matters related to the regiment as well as by a good deal of government propaganda relating to the SAS, released in discreet press briefings resulting in much speculation about the regiment's activities and deployments.

Blurring the line between fiction and fact are a number of supposedly factual accounts which, some allege, are in reality highly dramatised and based very loosely on actual events. Perhaps the most well-known examples are two books written under pseudonyms by two ex-SAS soldiers who served together on a patrol into Iraq in the first Gulf war of 1991.[20] Both of these works have been subsequently criticised as being highly embellished dramatisations of actual events with only a tenuous relation to reality by authoritative sources, including the RSM (regimental sergeant major) of 22 SAS at the time of the first Gulf War. There is even the surprisingly common phenomenon of individuals attempting to bask in the reflected glory of the SAS by claiming to have served with the regiment, when in reality they have had little or even no connection whatsoever with the SAS. This 'wanna-be' phenomenon also occurs in relation to other special force units, both British and foreign, as well as with war veterans such as those from Vietnam.

Despite the alleged embellishments, these books sold very well and consequently started a publishing frenzy by ex-SAS soldiers cashing in on this public appetite for 'Boys' Own' tales. The British government has since moved to prevent this in future by insisting that all who serve with the regiment sign an agreement not to publish details of their service.

As a result of the plethora of exaggeration, myth and plain falsehood put out as fact in relation to the British SAS, and its methods of operation, anything written about the SAS should perhaps be treated with a great deal of caution and some scepticism. This is all, perhaps, indicative of aspects of the human condition and psychology and tells us something about the birth of myth and legend.

Assessing Effectiveness

How is the effectiveness of a special force measured? Julian Thompson believes it can be achieved by assessing its value in terms of 'return' against 'investment'.[21] The investments are the best manpower; training time and effort; research and development; expense; and the use of supporting ships, submarines and aircraft. Thompson believes that the 'return' is the strategic, operational or tactical effect on the battlefield, campaign or even a war. There is, also, the propaganda impact upon an enemy. In the Second World War, for example, Churchill formed the commandos to 'get back at the enemy'[22] not to cause damage, although that was a useful by-product, but to bolster public morale. The operational or tactical effects are provided by conventional forces. If they have to be provided by special forces then, it is my contention, those special forces are being misemployed.

However, Gray believes there is little need to differentiate the meanings with regard to special forces operations with the key requirement being to achieve 'significant' results.

> Many of the most thoughtful commentators on special operations insist upon strategic rather than a tactical or operational role for such endeavours.[23]

At the close of the Second World War, Britain's special forces were disbanded with unseemly haste but have become the present weapon of choice and a political force multiplier. As described by the commanding officer of 22 SAS:

> We, as a Regiment have ... been at the cutting edge of all the major and minor conflicts that have occurred during Her Majesty's reign.[24]

If we accept that special forces, if they are formed, need to do certain things that provide a strategic or political return – or both – then we need to understand how SAS have evolved from the post-war situation, from deployment in the Malayan Emergency (where its impact was neither strategic nor political) through the various campaigns and conflicts since the Second World War (with varying degrees of military, strategic or political impact) to its present place as the panacea of all problems military and political. Whether this is for strategic and/or political reasons, or whether it is merely because the country has the forces and so feels the need to use them, also requires analysis.

SAS are also involved in counter-terrorism, which has marked a fundamental change in its role. The introduction of the counter-terrorist, or 'black role' (as opposed to the 'green role' of conventional soldiering), after the events in Munich on 5 September 1972[25] has provided new demands upon UK special forces. Counter-terrorism is essentially portrayed as a unique type of warfare played out in an urban environment observed by the world at large through a variety of media outlets. The counter-terrorist 'assault' on an aircraft or a building is the culmination of a series of events which have taken the subject nation or host nation by surprise. There is also an anti-terrorist role. This is less clear and less easy to define, but anti-terrorism is the covert deployment to locate and neutralise terrorists in a global environment. Thus there are a number of elements in the generic term 'counter-terrorism'. These elements are blurring the previously clear distinction between black roles and green roles. The SAS is currently seeking confrontations with such regionally or ideologically sponsored terrorists as Al Qaeda.

Inevitably, this book includes an assessment of 'personalities' within the SAS who have sometimes assisted, and sometimes hindered, SAS development. The accuracy of this assessment has frequently been obscured by myth and legend – good and bad. My research has also identified a number of documented situations involving what I will describe as 'moral dilemmas'. These may well prompt future analysis to assess the source of such internal conflicts and determine whether this is a unique recent phenomenon within the SAS and/or a consequence of certain personalities within the modern SAS.

> An almost universally observed characteristic of elite units is their lack of formal discipline – and sometimes a lack of substantive discipline as well. Also, a prolonged decline of formal discipline within an elite unit seems conducive, at least, to an erosion of obedience to political authorities.[26]

It is relevant to quote Brigadier Michael Calvert, the outstanding Chindit and SAS commander, who is alleged to have remarked:

The main job of the soldier is to kill people. As a guerrilla you
don't achieve anything by just being present. No regular force of
any nation in the world is really frightened of guerrillas unless
they can see the results in blown bridges, their friends being
killed, or trucks being ambushed. There were cases in Burma, and
elsewhere, for example in Europe, where missions just existed,
were supplied by the RAF at great risk, and did nothing.[27]

The lack of a major conflict since the Second World War has,
inevitably, not provided a source of freethinkers to assist in defining
the role of the SAS and their position in the new world order. The
SAS have become more and more the political 'instrument of choice'
for reasons of media coverage rather than for reasons of strategic
necessity. The SAS, and in particular SAS deployments, seem to be
a first option in any conflict situation, and these deployments are
publicised to provide maximum political effect. Recent examples are
Kosovo, Sierra Leone, Afghanistan, and the two Gulf Wars.

What are Special operations? They are unorthodox coups, that is,
unexpected strokes of violence, usually mounted and executed
outside the military establishment of the day, which exercise a
startling effect on the enemy; preferably at the highest level.[28]

So what is it that the British government and the Ministry of
Defence want the SAS to do? Current British military doctrine[29]
defines special forces as strategic troops who are selected, trained,
equipped and organised to special levels and are usually employed in
the pursuit of national objectives. They operate in support of conventional forces, or independently. Politico-military considerations
often shape SAS operations; they offer potentially high gain but at
comparatively high risk. They rely on technology and high degrees of
training, but usually require detailed pre-mission preparation to be
most effective. Special forces organisations have been raised for specific campaigns, but it is more usual to employ regular established
formations. It is to be remembered that their activities are likely to
be politically sensitive; they are scarce in number and take a long
time to regenerate.

There are various levels of operation into which SAS are likely to
be deployed. These levels provide an enormous variation in the type
of tasks available to carry out. Each task will require certain specific
training and equipment, although it is accepted that some roles may
have certain areas of commonality. The levels are:

Strategic SAS operations. Strategic SAS operations are aimed at the enemy's long-term capacity and the will to sustain hostilities and at key strategic targets. The use of SF for information reporting and offensive action during the first Gulf War allegedly helped prevent Israel's involvement in the war. However, subsequent battlefield analysis has indicated negligible actual successful results.

Operational-level SAS operations. At the operational level, SAS extend the conflict in depth. Their operations will be designed to fix the enemy, to break his cohesion and prevent him controlling the tempo of the conflict. SAS operations directly support theatre objectives and create opportunities for operations by conventional forces. In Borneo in 1965 (Operation CLARET), SAS conducted deep operations into Indonesian Kalimantan to interdict the deployment of Indonesian forces and to collect and interpret information about enemy dispositions, intentions and morale. During the Falklands War, SAS and SBS patrols were the only source of such information for the weeks prior to the main landings as well as attacking and interdicting high operational level targets (such as the Argentinean tactical helicopter lift capability).

Tactical-level SAS operations. SAS operations at the tactical level are possible, but should be avoided. SAS lack the combat power, tactical mobility, sustainability, and responsiveness to be at their best in direct support of tactical operations. However, on Jebel Akhdar in Oman, the SAS were used in an operational campaign at a tactical level due to a political, not a military, need. In the Radfan and during the Falklands campaign there were a number of examples of the use of SAS in tactical roles that had little effect on the campaign as a whole and should have been carried out by other forces, such as Royal Marines or Paras.

Operations other than war. In operations other than war, SAS are a discrete, low-visibility asset with particular value in preliminary operations. They can demonstrate national resolve, provide a presence, support governments and non-governmental groups, and improve the military capability of allied or friendly forces. In conjunction with other agencies they can undertake protracted operations to gain and sustain public support, or provide the striking element to the fixing operations of conventional forces. In Dhofar, Oman (Operation STORM), the SAS was involved in undermining the insurgency against the Sultan by assisting with many of the social and economic reforms the population were seeking as well as providing intelligence, civil aid and working with the Sultan's Armed Forces and indigenous forces – the Firqat. SAS groups can also be utilised in limited intervention operations, namely those operations which have limited objectives such as the rescue of hostages, security of non-combatants, or re-establishment of law and order. Invariably, they would be planned to be of short duration and specific in objective and scope. They may be mandated by the Security Council of the United Nations or legitimised under international law and mounted unilaterally or multi-nationally.

Non-combatant evacuation operations (NEO). British forces, including SAS, may be required either to conduct or participate in operations to evacuate UK or other specified nationals from a conflict area. Certain preconditions should ideally be present, including the agreement of the local government to the evacuation, the provision of logistic facilities, the availability of suitable airfields in the host country, or a neighbouring country, and the availability of reliable intelligence. In any event, the deploying force must be prepared to provide not only for its own security but also for the physical security of the evacuees from their point of assembly in country to their final departure from the area of conflict. Such operations will invariably be 'joint' and be planned, commanded and executed in the same way as any other intervention operation.

The principal roles of SAS on the ground continue to be reconnaissance, including information reporting and target acquisition; offensive action, which includes direction of air, artillery and naval gunfire; designation for precision-guided munitions; use of integral weapons and demolitions; and military assistance. SAS also provide the UK immediate-response counter-terrorism teams. Their roles are relevant to all levels of war and to any theatre of operations. SAS capabilities are flexible and versatile, and although their method of operation may differ according to circumstance and mission the basic principles governing the employment of SAS should be enduring.

It is generally accepted among SAS operatives that there are four key principles that *should* govern the employment of SAS:

1. *Employment on high-value tasks.* SAS must be employed with care and precision, exploiting their potential while husbanding

their limited availability. SAS are discrete and responsive and capable of protracted operations. Importantly, it has been historically demonstrated that they are particularly valuable early in a campaign after which their considerable initial usefulness may frequently diminish. Therefore, their employment requires constant review, and circumstances may dictate their withdrawal and re-tasking. There are several post-war examples when this did not occur and they remained in an operational theatre after their roles had expired. SAS missions have integral phases which include infiltration, approach, execution, resupply, exfiltration and extraction.

2. *Command at the highest appropriate level.* SAS should always be commanded at the highest appropriate level compatible with ensuring the necessary tactical coordination between their operations and those of conventional forces. In practice this usually means at the level of command concerned with the overall operational deployment. This will normally be the theatre level; at a minimum, SAS should have direct access to theatre command. Their operations will nevertheless need management with those operations by tactical commanders, although the latter may not be aware of the purpose of the management. Historically, since the Second World War, this has been poor in SAS deployment, NI being the worst example when SAS troops were actually under tactical command of infantry battalion commanders.

3. *Access to the highest-level intelligence.* The importance and sensitivity of SAS operations demand particular precision in targeting. It follows that SAS require access to the best available intelligence, which they may then need to develop further by reconnaissance. This may itself carry risk of compromise and needs fine judgement. In NI, for some time after their deployment into South Armagh in 1976, the SAS was not permitted to liaise directly with Special Branch (SB). The reason for this remains a mystery and smacks of petty politics between the Ministry of Defence and the RUC.

4. *Security.* Special forces have relatively limited combat power, tactical mobility and sustainability once deployed. They therefore rely heavily on strategic and tactical surprise. The secrecy surrounding SAS operations enhances their psychological impact, but their compromise can have disproportionately serious penalties. This is compounded by naturally intense media and public

interest. A sensible policy is to neither confirm nor deny SF activity. Unfortunately, an over-reaction can have an opposite effect and increase media and public interest. This was demonstrated after the action in Sierra Leone, Operation BARRAS,[30] involving the SAS and the PARAs, which was reported in the Army's *Soldier Magazine* – a well-respected military house journal.[31] The SAS has been very poor in its media management in recent years, since the exposés after the first Gulf War – which followed the example set by General DLB when he wrote two books on his experiences with the SAS.[32]

These principles have been gained through operational experience over time, particularly during the Second World War. The correct utilisation of these principles has provided a template for successful special forces deployment. However, analysis of the application of these principles in SAS operations since 1950 demonstrates clearly that politicians have had little, if any, knowledge or appreciation of these principles and, more disturbingly, nor have military planners.

There is a fifth possible principle, but it may be neither politically nor militarily acceptable, and that is the requirement for 'access to the highest political authority'. If SAS are to be increasingly involved in sensitive operations, and in that I assume *legally* sensitive operations, with high political repercussions then there is surely a requirement for an 'organic' link to political authority. The unlikelihood of this suggested principle being adopted is based upon the inevitable concern by the military hierarchy of a potential 'third force' operating outside the formal parameters of the military chain of command and on politicians' deep-seated wariness of being personally exposed in the event of a military, political or psychological disaster.

> Elite unit prominence occurs only during a politico-military crisis,
> for it is then that the public searches for heroes and politicians
> look for panaceas.[33]

The concept of an SAS that is directly tasked by the government and operates without referral to the military is worthy of further exploration outside this study. As an analogy, the South African Special Forces were a separate entity within the South African Defence Force (SADF). The SADF was composed of the Army, Navy, Air Force, medical services, and the special forces. This structure made political direction and authority easier to apply.

The methodology adopted for this book was, to a certain degree, dictated by the accessibility and availability of primary material to define and substantiate the great deal of general material available about the SAS. The time frame for the period of research, 1950–2000, was based upon two factors. The first was that the period covered a wide variety of SAS operations carried out during a variety of major British political changes and foreign policy contortions. During this time Britain withdrew from its colonies and vacated a substantial presence in the Middle East. It was also during this period that Britain suffered the embarrassment of the Suez expedition and received a severe 'reality check' regarding its international relationships, especially with the USA.

Secondly, the SAS became embroiled with terrorism both in Northern Ireland and internationally, as well as in international humanitarian and peacekeeping operations in the Balkans and Kosovo.

Also, involvement in two conventional campaigns, one in the Falklands and one in the Gulf, did not show the SAS in a good light and demonstrated, to a degree, that maybe all was not well internally.

The final event of note during the period concerned was the operation in the former colony of Sierra Leone. In this exceedingly brief but successful operation, the SAS, combined with elements of the Parachute Regiment, each carrying out separate roles, rescued British military personnel who had been kidnapped by an armed gang. This concluded a period of fifty years that started and ended with the SAS involved in counter-insurgency operations.

Having established the time frame to be covered in this book, the task was then to research the substantial amount of secondary material available and, having identified areas of core interest, locate and obtain primary material. The amount of definitive primary material regarding political influence and foreign policy direction given to the SAS is minimal. This rather surprising fact is due to the lack of strategic awareness, by politicians, of the skills and capabilities of the SAS. This, to a certain degree, has been assisted by the policy of the Ministry of Defence (MoD) in ensuring that the special forces in general, and SAS in particular, remain firmly locked within the control of the military mandarins and they are considered, in any strategic deployments, as 'merely' one of the tools in the MoD's toolbox. This philosophy, a somewhat understandable one, ensures that the SAS does not become the Praetorian guard of any particular political master, or some sort of third force composed of 'shadow warriors' working independently for, or with, the security services.[34]

Certain, but limited, primary material is available in the Public Records Office (PRO) at Kew as well as at King's College, London but, despite the limitations of the present government's ability, or intentions, to release new information to the public there is adequate corroborative information which relates specifically to the SAS and its interrelationship with foreign and defence policy matters. The material that is available has been more than sufficient to develop the aim of this book and to enable firm conclusions to be reached. The availability of new research material following the Freedom of Information Act on 1 January 2005 was investigated in January 2005 but only one new document of interest, at the PRO, has become available.[35] Other documents were requested for advanced release after 1 January 2005 but are not available to be released at present due to 'asbestos contamination'.[36]

The penultimate part of the research process was to carry out a series of interviews with key personnel who had been involved in SAS operations during the period of research. The particularly pleasing part of this phase of the research was the frank and open manner in which the interviewees responded to the questions and queries presented to them. The recorded responses of the interviewees have been reproduced *verbatim* in order to maintain their authenticity, but this has meant that some quotations may not be syntactically or grammatically correct. In order to respect the identity and security of the interviewees they have been identified by a three-letter code.

Conclusion

I have chosen to measure the effectiveness of the SAS during 1950–2000 based upon the answers to several questions:

* Why were the SAS there and what were they to achieve?

* Did they achieve what was expected of them either politically, militarily – or both?

* Could the tasks they carried out have been completed just as effectively by other non-specialist organisations?

The period from 1950 to 2000 has a number of almost stand-alone campaigns, and the involvement of the SAS in these enterprises has been relatively simple to encapsulate and identify. The areas of counter-terrorism – which includes anti-terrorism and, of course, Northern Ireland – are more difficult to pigeon-hole as they remain on-going. As referred to previously, asymmetric counter-terrorism is becoming an adjunct to general warfare and more and more the SAS are becoming involved in general deployments against terrorists to such places as Afghanistan and Iraq. The division between classic, embassy-storming, counter-terrorist actions and multiple squadron anti-terrorist deployments is becoming more blurred as events progress following the 'Twin Towers'.

Using the parameters explained this book will assess how the SAS has performed during the last fifty years examining links, if any, with British foreign and defence policy of the times. There is ample evidence to doubt whether the legendary key strategic influence of the SAS on campaigns and operations during 1950–2000 is backed up by reality. There is also a concern that urban legends and fact have become confused in the eyes of both the public and politicians.

In summary, the book researches the post-war re-birth of the SAS and assesses under what criteria it was established and how those criteria may have changed as the SAS operated in different areas of the world. Analysis of SAS operations exposes the fact that these operations had little, if any, strategic impact on the different foreign and defence policy requirements of the government at the time. For example, was the employment of SAS in Malaya, during the insurgency at the end of the Second World War until 1957, of any strategic value and what degree of tactical value? Would events have differed whether they had been deployed or not? What was the impact of the introduction of Rhodesians,[37] New Zealanders[38] and the Parachute Regiment Squadron?[39] In statistical terms, for example, the Suffolk Regiment[40] was a great deal more successful than the SAS and was in Malaya for a shorter time. Did the experience of Malaya assist or hinder SAS in later years? For example, its experiences may have helped it in Borneo, but hindered it in Northern Ireland.

The book examines the actions of the SAS since the Second World War relating, wherever appropriate, to the defence and foreign policy needs of the times. The research assesses the SAS's effectiveness, or otherwise, as well as the key personalities involved and their impact on the development of the SAS during the time analysed. This book will assist readers in making an objective judgement as to the strategic and political direction of the SAS and its likely progression in the next century.

> Elite units of the guerrilla, counter guerrilla, and commando type offer politicians in democracies both a tool of policy and a source of fantasy.[41]

The author on operations in Southern Africa in 1980.

Chapter 2

THE ORIGINS OF THE SAS

Background

Before examining the roles and effectiveness of SAS since the Second World War it is important to examine the activities of British special forces in that war in order to provide a certain benchmark on which to gauge their later activities.

In the Second World War British Commandos and parachute soldiers were originally conceived as:

> specially trained troops of the hunter class, who can develop a reign of terror down these coasts [German-occupied Europe], first of all on the 'butcher and bolt' policy ... leaving a trail of German corpses behind them.[42]

The SAS grew from the Commando movement. In June 1940 Lieutenant Colonel Dudley Clarke,[43] a General Staff Officer, prepared a memo for Sir John Dill, Chief of the Imperial General Staff, outlining a concept for a small, mobile, offensive fighting force. This was based upon Clarke's observations in Palestine in 1936 where he had seen how small hit-and-run units, such as Wingate's Special Night Squads,[44] could tie down large forces while inflicting damage both physical and psychological. Wavell[45] makes illuminating comments about Clarke and Wingate[46] in the Introduction to Clarke's book.[47]

Winston Churchill gave his approval by mid-June, instructing that units be raised from volunteers in existing organisations. By the end of June, 180 officers and men had been assembled and the trial unit was called '11 Commando'. Led by Dudley Clarke they carried out a minor, but successful, cross-Channel raid and, as a result, the

establishment of further units was approved. These units were originally started under the title of 'Special Service Battalions'.

The initial successes of the British Commandos led to increased
raids against the Continent – contrary to the limited nature of
Dudley Clarke's original proposal. Churchill advocated large numbers of raids despite indications that these operations were keeping
the enemy alert rather than harming him as well as leading to
German reprisals against the local population. He wanted to keep
up public morale by demonstrating Britain's ability to 'strike back'.

Churchill also ordered the widening of the Commando concept
to include the training of a corps of parachutists. By July 1940,
Special Service troops of 2 Commando commenced parachute training at Ringway Aerodrome near Manchester. On 21 November, 2
Commando was renamed '11 Special Air Service Battalion'.[48] On 10
February 1941, X Troop from 11 SAS Battalion was parachuted into
Southern Italy to destroy an aqueduct over the Tragino River in the
first British para-commando raid. This raid is understandably attributed to the SAS though, in fact, it has no connection, having been
carried out by troops from No 2 Commando.[49] The raid, Operation
COLOSSUS, had limited success and all the party were captured.[50]

As a result of the successful German airborne offensive in Crete,
which started on 8 May 1941, it was decided to establish an airborne army to be delivered by either parachute or glider. Two British
parachute brigades were to be formed, one in the UK and one in the
Far East. As a result 11 SAS Bn became 1 Parachute Bn as part of
1st Parachute Brigade.[51] The 50th Indian Parachute Brigade was
formed in October 1941 at Willington Airport in New Delhi.[52]

'Layforce'[53] was a Commando Brigade formed in the UK at the
end of 1940 to assist operations in North Africa. This force was the
brainchild of Lieutenant Colonel Robert Laycock[54] and consisted of
7 Commando formed in August 1940; 8 Commando formed in June
1940 from the Brigade of Guards, Royal Marines (RM) and Somerset
Light Infantry; 11 Commando, a Scottish unit formed in late 1940;
the Special Boat Section formed in Arran,[55] Scotland and sent to the
Middle East with 8 Commando; and 50 and 52 Commando raised in
the Middle East in early 1941 from RM and Army personnel.

The formation of these Commando forces was being closely
monitored by Churchill himself.

> I wish the Commandos in the Middle East to be reconstituted as
> soon as possible ... The Middle East Command have indeed mal-
> treated and thrown away this invaluable force.[56]

Formation of the SAS

GHQ Middle East had insufficient ships to use Layforce in its sea-borne raiding role.[57] Lieutenant David Stirling serving with 8 Commando thought that delivery by parachute might be an option and with Laycock's permission he, Lewis[58] and six others carried out parachute training in Mersa Mutrah airfield using the parachutes originally destined for India.[59] Stirling was injured in one of these descents and, while convalescing, expanded on paper his ideas for airborne commando operations. He considered the current concept of a surprise landing of some 200 men from the sea ineffective because the size of the force meant a large proportion was needed to secure the landing area. He believed that a force of about 60 men, parachuted in small groups of four men into the desert, close to their objectives, could conceal themselves until dark and then carry out sabotage raids. After the raids these forces would move back into the desert and rendezvous with transport back to Allied lines.

By using subterfuge Stirling took his plan to the Deputy Commander of HQ Middle East Command, General Ritchie, and then to the Commander-in-Chief, Gen Auchinleck. John Newsinger describes the events in his brutally sceptical book about the SAS:

> How was a mere lieutenant to bring his ideas to the attention of the commander-in-chief, General Sir Claude Auchinleck? In the British Army it is certainly not the custom for senior officers to entertain proposals from young lieutenants.[60]

Newsinger is not convinced by the conventional and accepted view of the birth of the SAS:

> Lieutenants did not get to put proposals to generals unless they came from suitably elevated backgrounds – and this Stirling most evidently did. Clearly it was this background that secured Stirling a hearing and permission to establish the SAS.[61]

Newly appointed Auchinleck was under pressure from Churchill to carry out an offensive, and Stirling's concept of operations[62] would assist in easing this pressure until he was ready to launch an offensive.

> Three days later Stirling was summoned to meet Auchinleck and received permission to raise a small raiding force consisting of six

officers and 60 other ranks. This force would be known as 'L Detachment' of the Special Air Service.[63]

Stirling's new unit was under the fictitious Special Air Service Brigade, but meanwhile the paratroops in the UK continued to be called 11 Special Air Service Battalion. The first operation planned for this new unit was a parachute attack on five German forward airfields to assist Auchinleck's offensive in November 1941. The plan involved dropping 62 men near their target airfields to rendezvous (RV) with the Long Range Desert Group (LRDG)[64] for ferrying back to Allied lines on the completion of their raid. High winds and a lack of moon completely disrupted the parachute drop and the operation on the night of 16 November was a disaster:

> Out of the fifty five men and seven officers who had taken part in the venture only eighteen men and four officers were left. This operation was not merely a failure: it was a debacle.[65]

Stirling abandoned the idea of parachuting and planned greater cooperation with the LRDG, who would be tasked to provide transport and navigation to and from targets. In November 1941 General Ritchie, now Commander-in-Chief of the 8th Army, approved the move of L Detachment to Jalo Oasis to operate with a squadron of the LRDG.[66] The members of the LRDG became experts at living and navigating in the desert.[67] Its primary means of transport was the 30-cwt Chevrolet truck. During December a number of successful airfield raids were carried out resulting in some 90 enemy aircraft being destroyed. Lewis was killed on one of these raids.[68]

Stirling was promoted to major in January 1942 and was directed to enlarge, re-organise and re-equip L Detachment. With the approval of General Ritchie, Stirling formalised the identity of his SAS with the well-known unit insignia.[69]

In August 1942, the Special Boat Section[70] of Middle East Commando came under SAS control, and Earl Jellicoe and Fitzroy McLean organised within the SAS what would become the SAS Special Boat Squadron. SBS members were full members of the SAS, qualified to wear the wings and the 'sand' beret. McLean was transferred to other duties and his 'M' Detachment was taken over by Ian Lapraik, with the other detachments being 'L' Langton and 'S' Sutherland.[71]

In October 1942, the title L Detachment was changed to 1st Special Air Service, now with a strength of some 390 personnel. In

November it was joined by another 100 personnel when Middle East Commando was disbanded.[72]

In January 1943, David Stirling was, somewhat ignominiously,[73] captured by the dentist of a German unit[74] and command was taken over by Blair 'Paddy' Mayne.[75] April 1943 brought a reorganisation of the North African SAS. The French Squadron returned to Britain and 1 SAS was split into two.[76] The 250 men of B Squadron under Lord Jellicoe became the Special Boat Squadron, absorbing the Special Boat Section and also the Small Scale Raiding Force (SSRF).[77] The former A Squadron became the Special Raiding Squadron (SRS), led by Paddy Mayne. It played a spearhead role in the July 1943 invasion of Sicily, Operation HUSKY. SRS, with 3 Commando and 40 RM Commando suffered heavy losses in October 1943, at Termoli against the German 1st Parachute Division.

A second SAS regiment officially came into existence in May 1943, formed out of 62 Commando in North West Africa, and commanded by David Stirling's brother, William. It was based in Philippeville in Algeria and raided Sardinia, Sicily and mainland Italy. However, William Stirling did not consider that 2 SAS was being used for the job for which it was trained, believing that small sabotage groups parachuted behind enemy lines would be more effective.[78]

At the end of 1943, after a brief but effective existence, SRS reverted to 1 SAS and, with 2 SAS, it was pulled out of its commando role and placed under command of 1st Airborne Division, Lieutenant General Miles Dempsey,[79] Commander of 13 Corps, under whose command the SRS had operated since landing in Sicily.

Dempsey, although not from a special forces background very effectively summarised the requirements for special forces to be effective and how they should be used by commanders to best effect. The reasons he gave may well have been forgotten by today's UK Special Force's commanders, but they still hold good for current Special Force operations. His words remain as appropriate now as they were in 1943, and those involved in deploying current special forces would be wise to revisit them (see Appendix 1).

In January 1944, an SAS Brigade was approved, and 1 and 2 SAS returned to Britain.[80] These two British units had been joined by a Belgian SAS squadron and two French battalions of SAS – the 3rd and 4th. This rapid expansion into a brigade group had been carried out to enable the troops to meet anticipated heavy commitments in the forthcoming Second Front in Europe.

By March 1944 all components of the SAS Brigade, some 2,000 men, were assembled[81] in Ayrshire under command of Brigadier Roderick 'Roddy' McLeod.[82] At this stage, William Stirling, commanding officer of 2 SAS, resigned[83] because he felt the SAS was again being misused and their original concept of operations ignored. He was replaced by Lieutenant Colonel Brian Franks.

Neither SHAEF, nor 21st Army Group, who were responsible for the OVERLORD operations, were prepared to take direct command of the SAS despite the brigade's vast experience. 21st Army Group actually blocked the use of the SAS until after OVERLORD had begun.[84]

The SAS was given a very limited role of preventing German reserves from reaching the front lines. Only half the brigade was initially committed, with the rest being held in reserve. Early operations involved both clandestine penetration of the front line and air drops into enemy occupied country. Bases were set up in remote wooded countryside and all re-supply was by air. Audacious use of the armed and armoured jeep achieved some good successes[85] through the element of surprise, but often with the result of bringing about severe enemy reaction upon themselves or the civil populace.

On operations, the SAS Brigade had to liaise with a number of different headquarters – 1st Airborne Division, 46 or 38 Gp RAF, and SOE HQ (Special Forces). The SAS was not committed to action until the invasion of Normandy in June 1944 and so this amazing force with such a combined wealth of combat expertise was unemployed operationally for some three months.

> Even after the SAS had been active for nearly two and a half years, there were few military men in positions of authority who understood how they should be employed.[86]

The effectiveness of the SAS in France was almost negated by the limitations of their own 'organic' firepower, the speed of the Allied advances, and the enormous destruction caused by the Allied bombing campaign. Moreover, the German military had great experience of being harassed by partisans on the Eastern Front, and so the efforts of the SAS and the French Resistance, while involving some events of great courage and personal bravery, and exciting to read about, did not cause the Germans great angst.

Late in 1944, members of 2 SAS were parachuted into Italy in Operation TOMBOLA[87] to work with Italian partisans and remained with them until the end of the war in Italy. The remainder of the

SAS Brigade worked with local resistance groups in a series of operations which took them into France, Belgium, Holland and Germany.

In March 1945, Brigadier McLeod was posted to India and his place was taken by Brigadier Mike Calvert,[88] a former Chindit commander with Major General Orde Wingate. Calvert was an expert on guerrilla warfare and long-range penetration operations but his seems to have been a less than popular appointment – probably because Calvert had no SAS, desert or European war experience.

When the war in Europe ended on 8 May 1945, the SAS Brigade had suffered some 330 casualties. In May, 1 and 2 SAS was sent to Norway to supervise the surrender of 300,000 German troops. The Belgian 5 SAS was tasked with counter-intelligence work in Denmark and Germany. A small number of SAS personnel continued serving as part of a unit to identify German war criminals who had been responsible for the murder of SAS personnel in France and Germany. This group's existence was short and it had no operational role.[89]

In 1945, after being liberated from the German prison camp in Colditz Castle, David Stirling came back to the SAS, and, under Mike Calvert, had some pertinent ideas on roles for the SAS regiments in the continuing conflict in the Far East.[90] In the second week of May 1945, 1 and 2 SAS returned to the UK to prepare for new tasks. Stirling's scheme for operations included the use of SAS regiments to stiffen a guerrilla army in northern China as well as making attacks on Manchurian railways carrying not only military forces, but also vital raw materials for the Japanese as they prepared for a war of attrition. These tasks were considered especially appropriate as the former commander of the SAS Brigade, Brigadier McLeod, was currently the Director of Military Operations at GHQ in New Delhi and wanted to use the SAS in Asia. These aspirations finished with the surrender of the Japanese on 12 September 1945.

Conclusion

The end of the Second World War left all three of the major victors, the Soviet Union, the United States and Great Britain, in possession of armed forces vastly greater than were required by political and military necessity. In Britain's case, the armed forces were much larger than could be afforded by its massively indebted economy. The country had lost one quarter of its entire national wealth during the war.

British demobilisation began in the summer of 1945, even before the defeat of Japan, as various classes and categories of wartime conscripts began their journey home. Whole battalions, brigades and divisions were eliminated from the regular order of battle (ORBAT) as the army shrank down to a size commensurate with the perceived peacetime tasks it faced. Among the many casualties of this process was the SAS.

The SAS never caught the popular imagination in the way the Commandos did. For one thing, they fought mainly in North Africa, remote from the British homeland and Europe. Secondly, they never expanded as the Commandos did, mainly because they did not have the institutional support that the Combined Operations Headquarters offered the Commandos.

Orde Wingate's views on the disbandment of his penetration forces after their success in Ethiopia in 1941 can be equated to the demise of the SAS at the end of the Second World War.

> To dissipate such a military organisation after it had been created, and while the need for it still exists, or to suppose that you could get equal results from the employment of equal numbers in sporadic operations, this is the mark of the military ape.[91]

The contribution of special forces to the Allied victory is hard to measure. It cannot be calculated solely in terms of enemy killed and the amounts and numbers of equipment and vehicles destroyed, but in other ways such as building up the morale of one's own side by stirring actions, and eroding the enemy's. Churchill, himself, was very aware there was also a disadvantage to the publicity surrounding the actions of special forces – when conventional units considered that their actions were being overlooked or ignored.

> The idea that large bands of favoured 'irregulars', with their unconventional attire and free-and-easy bearing, should throw an implied slur on the efficiency and courage of the Regular battalions was odious to men who had given all their lives to the organised discipline of permanent units. The Colonels of many of our finest regiments were aggrieved. 'What is there that they can do that my battalion cannot? This plan robs the whole Army of its prestige and of its finest men'.[92]

Also, one has to seek answers to questions such as what will be the effect of not mounting special forces operations against the enemy in a particular theatre or campaign?

The extreme view among those critical of special forces, whether of the behind-the-lines variety or not, is typified by a general who said to John Verney, who served in Lord Jellicoe's Special Boat Squadron, that:

> ... they [special forces] contributed nothing to Allied victory. All they did was to offer a too-easy, because romanticised, form of gallantry to a few anti-social irresponsible individualists, who sought a more personal satisfaction from the war than of standing their chance, like proper soldiers, of being bayoneted in a slit trench or burnt alive in a tank.[93]

Of the British special forces in the Second World War, the LRDG must surely rate as the most cost-effective British Special Force, and one that fully adapted to the circumstances of the theatre in which it operated. It was not expensive in resources. Its record bears repeating: during the five years of its existence, the LRDG carried out more than two hundred operations behind enemy lines, and throughout those five years there were only two periods of five months when no patrols were operating behind enemy lines. The unit was in existence and on operations the longest and made a considerable contribution to Allied victory.[94]

The SAS, especially in North Africa, was cost-effective. The SAS efforts materially helped to tilt the balance of air power in the Mediterranean theatre. In 1941–42, the Special Air Service, which at that time consisted of fewer than two hundred combat soldiers (and had started with fewer than seventy), was responsible for the destruction, on the ground, of approximately three hundred aircraft of the Italian and German forces based in North Africa. The number of aircraft destroyed personally by the SAS far outweighed the personal score achieved by any aircrew, whose training was both long and costly, and who attacked in expensive aircraft maintained by a large number of ground crew.

There is, of course, an opposite view of the growth of special forces. This view is that the desert campaign was won by General Montgomery's relentless use of British superiority in men and material and by the Allied exploitation of 'ULTRA'[95] to prevent supplies crossing the Mediterranean. The SAS attacks on Axis airfields were a sideshow with a marginal impact, at best, on the course of operations and with some militarily expensive forays on the abortive, larger, Special Force and Commando raids.

The contribution of the Special Boat Squadron (SBS) was particularly valuable in the Aegean, but less so in the Adriatic. Much of the reconnaissance work carried out by SBS was absolutely indispensable to the success of the amphibious operations, particularly the Normandy landings carried out by the Allies.

On the whole, between 1940 and 1945 the SAS was not managed well. There were faults with those who encouraged proliferation, and those who failed to coordinate the various special force activities. These faults wasted time and precious talent. This failure manifested itself in various ways. There was often duplication of effort with units crowding each other, resulting in squabbles over 'real estate'. For example, in the Middle East, the SAS jeopardised LRDG road watch operations by attacking enemy positions nearby. There was sometimes self-generation of tasks and invention of roles on the part of commanders of special units. (There have been some glaring examples of this in more recent times, such as during the Falklands War, and these are examined in more detail later.) The personality of the commander of a force was often a deciding factor in prolonging a special unit's existence well beyond its useful operational life. This encouraged the cult of the personality, of which David Stirling[96] was perhaps the supreme example.

Two things stand out clearly from the experience gained in operating SAS troops in the Second World War:

> a. The dividends paid by introducing small parties of well-trained and thoroughly disciplined regular troops to operate effectively behind the enemy lines can be out of all proportion to the numbers involved.

> b. The operations of these uniformed troops are quite distinct from special non-regular parties such as Secret Service or political parties introduced behind the enemy lines.

Field Marshal Slim, arguably one of the greatest field commanders on either side in the Second World War, said, with regard to his operations in Burma:

> It was not until the activities of all clandestine bodies operating in or near our troops were co-ordinated, and where necessary controlled through a senior officer on the staff of the commander of the area, that confusion, ineffectiveness, and lost opportunities were avoided.[97]

At the completion of hostilities, the British General Staff could see no future role for the SAS. When 1 and 2 SAS returned from

Norway, where they had been disarming some 300,000 Germans, they were disbanded. They and the Brigade HQ finally closed down on 8 October. The Belgian regiment had transferred to the Belgian Army's command the previous month and the French regiment had formally transferred to their national army on 1 October.

> It is a persistent theme of post-war histories of the Special Air Service that there was a determination on the part of the War Office to get rid of the SAS at the end of the war. In 1945, a decision was made to disband the SAS Brigade, together with 1 and 2 SAS Regiments, pending the outcome of a study into the use of unconventional units during the war and any further requirement that the British Army might have for them.[98]

Calvert wrote a paper[99] in October 1945 which he sent to all his officers outlining his views on the future of the SAS and urging his staff to respond to the War Office request for contributions to the consultative paper on the future of the SAS.[100] In 1946, the War Office, prompted by Calvert, Franks and other senior officers who had served in the SAS, set up an enquiry by the Tactical Investigation Committee which examined possible roles for the SAS in the future.[101]

The recommendation to reform a regular unit was rejected and the formation of a territorial regiment was approved.[102] The new regiment was initially named 21 SAS Regiment but was later affiliated with the Artists Rifles. Subsequent SAS regiments, 22 and 23, have continued numerically

Churchill was convinced of the strategic value of special forces and was a firm advocate for their usage throughout the war. At the highest political level he had identified the need for military organisations which could carry out tasks that others could not. Prior to the landings in Normandy in June 1944 he was concerned that expertise should be garnered from the SAS, and instructed that training be provided by members of 2 SAS currently in the Middle East.

> General Montgomery speaks of his need to have ten Commando units for 'Overlord' and has only seven. Pray let me know whether this request could be met. What arrangements have been made for bringing home some of the specialised personnel for teaching purposes of the 2nd Special Air Service Regiment?[103]

He had a firm grasp of the strategic utility of special forces but this understanding did not continue in political circles nor military circles following the cessation of the Second World War hostilities. Nor was an understanding apparent in the fifty years following the end of this war.

The Second World War concluded with the disbandment of the SAS forces, despite the best efforts of their Brigade Commander, Calvert. Former SAS personnel re-surfaced in Palestine, Greece and Malaya immediately after the war using their hard-earned talents in counter-insurgency operations.[104] However, this was no longer a global war, and some of the SAS unconventional techniques and skills employed in the previous international conflict were no longer seen as appropriate by the army as a whole. Prejudices against elite organisations maintained by 'regular' officers during the war resurfaced as the career officers re-established themselves in the new peace-time military. Britain's existence was no longer at threat. Effective and robust covert fighting skills were no longer wanted by the likes of Montgomery and the War Office.

The War Office was content to have a territorial Special Force unit but the intention to form a regular unit did not exist at this time. However, the combination of a communist insurgency in Malaya and the raw personality of Calvert played a key role in the regeneration of the regular SAS regiment.

Chapter 3

THE STRUCTURE AND MANAGEMENT OF THE SAS

Now, as I say, the soldiers [in the SAS] are the best you will ever meet. Nonetheless, within your troops too you have got men who will lie in their teeth, who will deliberately falsify accounts in order to make money for themselves, who will seduce their comrades' wives while they are overseas, who will steal and who will even carry out armed robbery, and in case you think I am exaggerating all those things have been done by soldiers of this Regiment in the last two years. Nor should you be surprised. You don't train tigers and expect them to sing like canaries and these men are highly individual and highly active.[105]

In making any sort of assessment of the post-war SAS it is important to have an understanding of the structure and management of the organisation. The detailed structure of the SAS and information about the selection process is contained in numerous publications about the SAS, both authorised as well as unauthorised.[106] However, for the purposes of this book an overview is provided here but one of the key facts to be aware of, and which has implications in all the activities of the SAS since 1950, is the small size of the unit. If fully recruited, the 'badged'[107] strength of 22 SAS is only some 450 operatives – comparable to a single, under-strength infantry battalion. As a comparison, the US Special Operations Command (SOCOM), which includes Army, Navy and Air Force special operations groups, has some 46,900 personnel.[108]

The British SAS is composed of one Regular Army Regiment, 22 SAS, based in Hereford and two Territorial Army Regiments, 21 SAS and 23 SAS. 21 SAS is based in London with sub-units in the South of England and 23 SAS is based in the north of the country with sub-units in the Midlands, Northern England and Scotland. 22 SAS also used to have a Territorial Army unit attached to it in Hereford called R Squadron. R Squadron was mainly composed of 22 SAS personnel who had recently left the Regular Army and was occasionally called upon to supplement 22 SAS. R Squadron has now been disbanded.

Members of the Territorial SAS are part-time soldiers but carry out a similar selection process to 22 SAS. They are required to attend a certain number of training nights and training weekends each year as well as attending a two-week 'annual camp'. Despite being highly motivated and committed the Territorial SAS are not able to reach the standards of the full time SAS due to their limited training time and lack of operational experience.

The structure of the modern SAS is based upon patrols of four men and this evolved from the original size of jungle patrols during the Malayan Emergency.[109] Within each patrol there is specific individual tradecraft. The key skill was, and still is, that of signaller. The signaller was required to send messages in Morse code on high-frequency radios, normally at night to utilise better atmospheric conditions. The signaller would carry the classified codes. Recently, communications have become more sophisticated with the use of 'burst'[110] transmissions, to minimise the time available to enemy radio-direction finding equipment,[111] as well as satellite communications. The other members of the patrol are the patrol commander, who will not necessarily be the most senior in rank but the most senior in experience in a particular environment; the linguist; and the patrol medical specialist. The linguist is frequently also a demolitions expert. In most patrols there is a duplication of skills. Four patrols make up a troop and a squadron has four troops. Each troop is commanded by a Captain with a Sergeant or Staff Sergeant as deputy and each squadron is commanded by a Major. A shortage in suitable officers has often meant that troops are commanded by experienced non-commissioned officers.

> I think that the 4x4 (men in patrol, patrols in a troop, troops in a squadron, squadrons in the Regiment) worked very well during my time. Whenever the task required it we would juggle around with numbers to make it work. If it was possible to increase recruitment to fill a fifth squadron, it could ease some of the strain on the Regiment and make skill retention better. When the Regiment is fully committed or stretched, the various troop skills go out the window and we have to re-invent the wheel all over again.[112]

Each troop has specialist skills which are based upon providing a diverse number of infiltration techniques. These techniques are reflected in the generic skills of each troop. i.e. freefall, mobility, boat and mountain troop. There is a feeling among a number of SAS operatives that some of these skills are anachronistic and relate more to image than operational necessity. Freefall training,[113] for example, requires a large number of air assets and high-value equipment and yet, up until 2000, the SAS has only once ever carried out an operational freefall descent and that had a fatality. A senior member of the regiment believes:

> After 40 odd years freefall has still to prove itself. Why not change the role to surveillance? The present structure is over 40 years old, the world has changed and the SAS structure needs to reflect that.[114]

The regular SAS currently has four squadrons, A, B, D and G. One, squadron G, has an additional Arctic warfare capability, and during the Cold War was to be deployed on the northern flank of NATO.

> When I first joined the Regiment I was surprised to find that we had two TA Regiments and a Group Headquarters in London. I thought then and still think now that TA and SAS are an apparent contradiction to each other. SAS being a way of life and something you are fully committed to. TA being something that you do for two weeks in the year and one weekend in four.[115]

21 SAS is based in London and 23 SAS is based in Leeds. These two units had a Cold War role as the British corps patrol units (CPU) and would dig deep, nuclear-proof hides to observe along the expected routes of a Soviet advance through Central Europe and, in war, would call in artillery fire, aircraft support or even tactical nuclear weapons onto identified high-value targets. After the demise of the Soviet Union these two SAS units, to a degree, replicated the role of the regular SAS and, in times of operational deployment, have supplemented the regular soldiers. The SAS units are commanded by a Lieutenant Colonel and they, in turn, report to a brigadier – Director Special Forces (DSF) – in London.

> To justify a Group headquarters with a Brigadier in charge you probably needed such a structure with three Regiments even though two are TA. Now that it's Group SF with the SBS, you

may even be able to push for a Major-General in charge. We were always good at building monsters![116]

There is little about the unit's structure that is revolutionary, or even controversial or contentious and merely confirms that the SAS is a normal unit detailed in the British Army's order of battle. However, this may well be a normal structure but the SAS is not composed of 'normal' individuals.

Recruits to the SAS, who can come from all three Services,[117] have to successfully complete an arduous selection course[118] on which only 10 per cent of aspirants will succeed. Officers also have to complete a separate phase in which their leadership skills are assessed by a panel of both SAS officers and NCOs. The TA SAS recruits used to have to complete a separate selection course spread over a number weekends to fit in with their work commitments but they must now attend the regular SAS selection course. Personnel from the SBS who want to join the SAS must also complete the SAS selection course. The original selection and training of recruits for 14 Intelligence and Surveillance Company (14 Int)[119] was carried out by SAS personnel but this was gradually taken over by operationally experienced 14 Int operatives. This led to senior 14 Int operatives being permitted to transfer to the SAS without completing a selection course. This has been seen by SAS personnel as a 'back-door' entry to the regiment and, not surprisingly, has caused a great deal of friction.

Successful completion of the selection course is then followed by lengthy continuation training, which ensures that all recruits, either NCOs or officers, reach the same standards of individual soldier skills be they a paratrooper or a driver. This is an ambitious exercise and has prompted criticism as to the level of basic soldiering skills of non-infantry SAS soldiers or officers. The preponderance of Parachute Regiment soldiers serving in the SAS provides a certain Parachute Regiment elitism. A 'badged' SAS operator from a non-airborne parent unit, particularly a technical unit, can expect to be discriminated against or criticised by former members of the Parachute Regiment for lacking in infantry skills.

> SAS soldiers who come from a non-infantry organisation cannot be expected to have the necessary infantry skills for operations. The way around this lack of experience would be for non-infantry SAS personnel to spend some time with an infantry battalion.[120]

The continuation training concludes with training and robust exercises in escape and evasion, and resistance to interrogation followed by a static line parachute course.

Any NCO joining the SAS is required to drop his current rank and work his way through the SAS promotion ladder.[121] However, the loss of rank and its associated status is more than compensated for by the generous special forces pay increment each operative receives on posting to the SAS.[122] A senior non-commissioned officer (SNCO) who has served in all the post-war SAS campaigns does not consider this has had a beneficial impact on the quality of the modern operatives:

> The SAS changed after the Iranian Embassy not due to the adulation but the pay rise. Money and career became more important than the good of the SAS.[123]

Not surprisingly, once the selection and training is completed and the recruit is 'badged'[124] there is often a feeling of superiority and a dismissal of other lesser mortals in the army and other services.

> I was never a great lover of the SAS. I rated soldiers in Patrol Company [the organic reconnaissance groups of Parachute Regiment battalions] better than SAS. In my opinion, based on my observations of the SAS soldiers I met, they had poor soldier skills. They were arrogant and looked down on other soldiers.[125]

Contrary to popular belief, officers do not get promoted on passing selection and joining the SAS but retain their normal rank. An officer will complete two to three years as a troop commander and then will return to the regular Army, normally back to his parent unit, before returning, if selected, some three to four years later as a squadron commander. Non-commissioned soldiers are able to remain in the organisation as long as they maintain the necessary standards of skill and fitness.

A number of SAS NCOs can obtain commissions in the regiment. This used to be kept to a deliberately low number but for a number of years more NCOs have been promoted to assist with the ongoing officer shortage. This is not a healthy trend and provides some SAS personnel with the opportunity to see themselves as a Praetorian guard, answerable to themselves and not the army. The commissioning of SAS NCOs was a matter which those who established the SAS after the war were very anxious to control.

But it was actually in the days of Dare Newell that it was applied
with a great deal of precision and correctness and I felt, when I
saw it breaking down, that it was a very bad thing for the SAS
and was going to undermine the flexible thinking of the SAS and
make them feel that they were something separate from the rest
of the Army, and better than the rest of the Army. This is what
one always tries to avoid doing – maybe they were better than
the rest of the Army but, they had to prove it, not talk about
it.[126]

The differences between officer and NCO terms of service in the
SAS has led to a two-tier system and one in which there is a growing perception by NCOs that the SAS does not need officers and the
NCOs can run the organisation perfectly well without them. This
perception by NCOs of the utility, or lack of utility, of officers is
fully exposed in the virulent and vitriolic references to officers which
feature in most books written by former SAS NCOs. The disparag-
ing references to the stupidity of 'Ruperts'[127] are a common theme
of these recent books.

Internally the problem with management of the SAS is the
perennial one of Ruperts [sic] and ORs [other ranks – not com-
missioned]. The Ruperts, especially middle management, are
never told they have a future career within the Regiment and
therefore cannot plan accordingly. Many either therefore leave
the Army or move away from SF. This leads to shortfalls in the
management filled by last-minute selection of non-badged personnel or unqualified ORs.[128]

A young officer, on completing SAS selection and being posted as a
troop commander to a Squadron, has a difficult task establishing the
correct balance between the formal discipline of the regular Army
and the relaxed informality of the SAS.

... you are too concerned about short term popularity at the
expense of long term respect. Some of you have got yourself into
a relationship where you could not give an unpopular decision if
you wished to.[129]

This informal manner is manifested in a certain accepted lack of discipline and formality that would be totally unacceptable in other military units. This difficult situation is often deliberately compounded

and exacerbated by those NCOs who consider that an officer is an inconvenience and an impediment and actively work to erode the status of the officer.

> During the 'Storm' [Operation Storm, Dhofar, Oman 1970–76] years DLB [Lt Col DLB, CO of 22 SAS during Operation STORM] issued a directive to Squadron Commanders that all new Troop Commanders were to take charge of their troops from day one. The tried and tested system on ops [operations] was to let them stay in the background for a period and with the help of the Troop Sergeant slowly bring them on. SNCOs have a duty to help and assist troop commanders and see that they get the best possible chance to develop and eventually take control of the troop. You want the good ones back as squadron commanders. Where some of the troop commanders took control too early[130] it resulted in disasters and in some cases death.[131]

A young officer in the SAS is torn between the desire to be 'accepted' by his troop, especially the more senior members, many of whom have operational experience, and maintaining those standards that he knows are correct. If the officer gets the balance wrong, to a certain degree, anarchy prevails.

> Some of you do not command your troops, you are commanded by your troop sergeants.[132]

This can also happen when officers return as squadron commanders and, again, wish to be 'accepted'. If the officer was weak as a troop commander he will be just as weak as a squadron commander. He will be easily manipulated by those of his senior NCOs with strong personalities. This is exactly what happened with B Squadron prior to Operation MIKADO, the proposed raid onto mainland Argentina during the Falklands War. The weak squadron commander allowed himself to be manipulated by several SNCOs in the squadron who were apprehensive about the operation.

> Well, you see you've got this officer and NCO thing again – you have got a weak CO [OC] and strong NCOs, and the NCOs start muttering amongst themselves, gathering up a level of fear if you like, which is then transmitted to the CO [OC] who wasn't capable of controlling it – he wasn't strong enough ... all mutinies were basically evolved during the time when NCOs had superiority

over the officers. This is a similar sort of thing. I suppose you
can argue it was a mutiny.[133]

For the SAS NCO, however, the ideal officer was a warrior – a
fighter engaged in violence himself rather than a manager directing
the employment of violence by others. This 'them' and 'us' attitude
and the divergence between the officers' mess and the sergeants'
mess has been the cause of a number of situations within the SAS
which, in normal military organisations, would have led to a number
of courts martial, but in the SAS was concealed within the organisation in order not to cause regimental or national embarrassment.

> The SAS is great at suppressing these things. Perhaps they ought
> to come out in the open a bit more than they have.[134]

The suggested source of this internal antipathy towards officers is
explained by two well-respected SAS NCOs:

> SNCOs and Ruperts [sic] is a class thing. In a normal Regiment
> ORs resent the privilege and 'divine rights' of the Officer Class
> [sic] but cannot hope to articulate their anger. In the SAS they
> have room to express themselves. I can say that I did not serve
> with bad Officers, just Officers who were slower to adjust to life
> with SAS troops.[135]

> I think that there are several things going on here. Firstly the
> 'them and us' thing, Bosses vs. the workers etc. With some there
> is a bit of jealousy which creeps in. Both these first two are com-
> pounded if you have to work with an officer who is not up to
> scratch or one who believes in the divine right to lead. Wisdom
> often comes through experience and it is very hard for someone
> without the experience to jump in and lead those who have the
> experience. What's the answer? I think something radical.[136]

The SAS is an unusual unit and it contains unusual people. Its
members have completed a gruelling selection and a demanding
training process before they could join the ranks of the very 'special'.
Once someone has arrived in an operational patrol and troop his difficulties are only just beginning, particularly if he is an officer.

The SAS is a military unit in the British Army order of battle – it
is not MI6, MI5 or a third force composed of 'Shadow Warriors'.
Unfortunately, a number of its members have started believing their

own propaganda with inflated ideas of their own abilities and, more disturbingly, inflated ideas of their own importance in the new world order.

> The majority of [SAS] SNCOs were living life inside the pages of a book as opposed to real experience. The first Gulf War showed how rank with inexperience[137] can lead to disaster.[138]

The less than impressive results of the SAS involvement in events in Dhofar, the Falklands, and the first Gulf War demonstrated quite clearly that, despite vigorous attempts by the SAS and some politicians to show the contrary, the SAS has not been performing well or effectively.

In recent years, after 2000, the other recognised 'special forces' in UK, the SBS and 14 Intelligence and Surveillance Company (14 Int), have come under the command structure of DSF. This uncomfortable amalgamation has come about after many years of rivalry and animosity. James Rennie, a former officer in 14 Int,[139] comments on the SAS:

> Since the televised assault on the Iranian Embassy Siege in 1980, the SAS had revelled in the well-deserved mystique that surrounded their every action. That was fine, but the appetite of the press is insatiable once whetted and, as more and more detail was, wittingly or otherwise, released over the years, so the silver began to tarnish and the carpets began to fray a little in their Hall of Fame. In some ways the climax of this painful decline in esteem was the disastrous (and now very fully recounted) tale of the Bravo Two Zero patrol in the Iraqi desert during the Gulf War.[140]

Former members of the SBS who served in 14 Int make similar observations:

> On certain levels, relationships between 14 Int and the SAS were deteriorating with each passing year. This was mainly due to the SAS heavy-handedness and the cock-ups they were continuing to make.[141]

> Most military units came out of the Falklands War with standing enhanced. The reverse was true of 22 SAS.[142]

Once a Special Forces outfit like the SAS starts believing its own mythology, it's in trouble.[143]

This 'competition' between the various 'specialists' is not one-sided and Connor has a view on the SBS:

In Special Forces terms, the SBS are not very professional.[144]

As the myth of the SAS regiment as grown, it has become an increasingly introspective organisation, beset by the contradictions between its past and present values and by bad feeling within its ranks. Regimental officers have seen their authority undermined by the potent working-class ethos of their soldiers.

In summary, the SAS contains aggressive and committed personnel who would not fit into other units or organisations, but who are ideal for those high-risk/high-value operations that need to be carried out as a part of key foreign-policy decisions and international-influence projections.

This book identifies that the utilisation of these special troops has not been at an appropriate political or military level. The strategic use of this exceedingly small, elite group of specialists has been based more upon the personal drive of relatively low-level officers than upon national necessity.

The author on operations in the jungles of South Vietnam in 1970 as a platoon commander with the New Zealand infantry.

PART TWO

IMPERIAL POLICING

Chapter 4

Malayan 'Emergency', 1948–1960

... in Malaya they wearily stalk guerrillas through FSC's jungles.[145]

Introduction

From 1948 to 1960, the British government was involved in a counter-insurgency campaign in Malaya. In 1950, the SAS, known initially as the Malayan Scouts, became involved in the campaign and remained there until 1958. This was the rebirth of the SAS from its post-war demise and it was also the catalyst that enabled the SAS to gain itself a permanent position in the UK forces order of battle. It was a very difficult birth due to the various personalities involved and post-war resentment against special forces by 'proper soldiers', and because of the limited effectiveness of this newly formed unit against an elusive jungle enemy.

This time was one of the most complex in the post-war period for the SAS. Not only was the SAS reformed but it was the longest time that it had been involved in a conflict, as well as involving the largest number of SAS troops deployed in one campaign since 1945. At one stage between 1950 and 1958 the SAS had five squadrons deployed, A, B, D, the Independent Parachute Regiment Squadron (1955–57), and the New Zealand SAS Squadron (1955–57). C (Rhodesia) Squadron had operated with the SAS from 1951 to 1953. Britain's other Special Force unit in existence at the time, the SBS, did not carry out any independent operations in Malaya during the Emergency.

Background

Malaya is a peninsula about the size of the United Kingdom. The land mass divides the South China Sea from the Bay of Bengal and it occupies a strategic position in South East Asia. The city-state of Singapore is at the southern most tip of the peninsula, is about 220 square miles in area and is joined to the mainland by a causeway three-quarters of a mile long, which at the beginning of the Emergency in the mid-1940s, carried both a road and railway line. Communications in the peninsula consisted of one main road and railway running north to south, with poor lateral communications. On both sides of most roads, rubber and oil palm estates extended outwards for up to three miles before reaching dense jungle.

The indigenous Malay is easy-going, and lacks any great interest in commerce; they contrast strongly with the extremely industrious Chinese and the imported Indian labour.

On 8 December 1941 Japanese troops landed at Kota Bahru, in NE Malaya and began to advance down the peninsula. In Singapore, a special jungle and sabotage training centre, which had existed in a dormant embryonic form for some time, known as the 101st Special Training School (101st STS), was quickly made ready to train volunteers from the Malay Communist Party (MCP) to fight the Japanese. 101 STS was commanded by Lieutenant Colonel FSC.[146]

> It was agreed that the MCP would provide as many young Chinese as we could accept at 101 Special Training School (STS) and that after the training they could be used against the Japanese in any way we thought fit.[147]

Before Malaya was overrun by the Japanese, the STS was able to train some 200 Chinese Communists in sabotage and guerrilla training.[148] These students would form the basis of organised resistance, the Malay People's Anti Japanese Army (MPAJA), during the Japanese occupation. Some British officers stayed with the MPAJA and others, part of the Special Operations Executive (SOE), Force 136, were parachuted into Malaya and Thailand.

In early 1944 the Allies SEAC (South-East Asia Command), agreed to provide supplies, money and training facilities to the MPAJA on condition that they would cooperate with the Allies against the Japanese. The allied invasion of Malaya, which was scheduled for September 1945, never occurred as the Japanese surrendered on 16

August, and a ceasefire came into effect the following day. Although working with the MPAJA, the Force 136 officers very seldom became involved in any operational activities and so had little opportunity to observe MPAJA attacks or tactics. Nor were they informed of the locations of camps and weapons caches.

The Japanese surrender left a largely communist force in Malaya, armed, equipped and organised, as the British returned. Led by Lai Tek,[149] the MCP and the MPAJA believed they could follow the success of other communist-led insurgencies that were being waged against colonial governments, as well as the success of the Chinese Communist Party. In the meantime, the British hurriedly landed more Allied troops and formally took control of Malaya. A British Military Administration was quickly established to govern the country until a civilian one could be restored.

In January 1946 the British government published a White Paper proposing the establishment of a Malayan Union of 11 states, and a colony of Singapore to which the ruling Sultans agreed, although with some reluctance due to the loss of their traditional feudal powers. Militant Communism seemed to be on the rise, and the MCP saw no reason why it should not be successful in opposing the British-backed regime in Malaya and Singapore.

In 1947, Lai Tek failed to appear for a meeting of the Central Executive Committee of the MCP. His successor was Chin Peng,[150] the second-in-command, in effect, until Lai Teck's disappearance.[151] He was elected Secretary-General of the MCP. Born in Malaya, he had fought against the Japanese during their occupation of Malaya, had been in frequent contact with British officers[152] and Allied personnel, and was a confirmed communist. He was 27 years old in 1948 and had been awarded the OBE for his services during the occupation (the award was later revoked). He spoke English, Malay and several Chinese dialects.

The 'Emergency'

It *was* a war, but there was a curious reason why it was never called one. It was a war – though out of regard for the London insurance market, on which the Malayan economy relied for cover, no one ever used the word. This misnomer continued for twelve years, for the simple reason that insurance rates covered losses of stock and equipment through riot and civil commotion in an emergency, but not in a civil war.[153]

Malaya possessed valuable minerals such as coal, bauxite, tungsten, gold, iron ore, manganese and china clay, but its main riches were rubber and tin. Apart from rubber, in 1950, the tin mining industry of Malaya was the biggest dollar earner in the British Commonwealth. The chief problem with the insurgency was it threatened British control and disrupted the dollar earning exports of the rubber and tin industries. In 1948 Malaya was the most important source of dollars in the colonial empire and it would gravely worsen the whole dollar balance of the Sterling area if there was serious interference with the Malayan exports. Even if the insurgents did not score any military or political successes they could easily wreck the economy of Malaya. Existing deposits of tin were being quickly used up and, owing to communist activities in the jungle and on the jungle fringe, no new areas were being prospected for future working. If no new prospecting were to be resumed over a large area, tin mining could cease in about 10 to 12 years. The situation regarding rubber was no less difficult, with the fall in output largely due to the direct and indirect effects of communist sabotage.

The threat of communism represented by the Malayan insurgents was perceived by British planners as real. Britain's primary interest in Malaya was economic, and it wished to continue to use the resources of that country for the benefit of British business interests. Communism in Malaya simply posed a threat that Britain would lose control over these economic resources. There was never any question of the military intervention in Malaya by either the USSR or China. Nor, indeed, was any material support ever proffered by either the USSR or China to the insurgents in Malaya; the problem was a purely internal affair.

The murder of three European planters on 16 June 1948 near the small town of Sungei Spur, in Perak, brought matters to a head and resulted in the High Commissioner, Sir Edward Gent, declaring an emergency in parts of Perak and Johore, which was extended to the whole of the country the following day. This was the beginning of the period known as the Malayan Emergency.

In Malaya on the declaration of the Emergency the British and Malay armed force amounted to five British, two Malay and six Gurkha battalions. The RAF had 100 aircraft in the country, and in mid-1948 started to strafe guerrillas' locations and bomb suspected guerrilla camps and locations. The Federation Police numbered 10,223, nearly all Malays.

The Military was commanded by the General Officer Commanding (GOC), Major General Charles Boucher, GOC Malayan District.

Boucher, and the Commander-in-Chief (CinC), Far East Land Forces (FARELF), General Sir Neil Ritchie,[154] were both familiar with recent counter-insurgency operations in Greece, Boucher having been there himself, and Ritchie's chief of staff having also served there immediately prior to his posting to the Far East. Two British battalions, also recently in Greece, were transferred to Malaya in mid-1948.

In 1948, the Malay Races Liberation Army (MRLA), as the MPAJA was now known, was insufficiently organised and incapable of directly engaging British armed forces. It continued to attack small village police stations, which usually had fewer than a dozen Malay policemen to defend them. Also, they continued terrorist activities against civilians and sabotage attacks on machinery, plantations and communications.

Early Special Operations

Former British officers of Force 136, many of them now planters, and a number of serving and former servicemen, established a small organisation which was designed to seek out the guerrillas so they could be attacked by the main security forces.

> In late July, in order to relieve some of the pressure on infantry battalions, a temporary unit was formed for country-wide operations. Known as Ferret Force, it was made up of a Force Headquarters and four Groups. A Group consisted of four infantry sections, each commanded by an ex-member of either Force 136 or Wingate's Chindits.[155]

This unique organisation, which demonstrated the flair and imagination that had been missing from operations so far in Malaya, had a brief, but effective, life. Regular units resented losing trained men to this new force – a frequent criticism of special forces ever since Churchill's 'commandos' were formed in 1940.

> The secondment of men to Ferret Force, however, left the rifle companies less than fifty strong.[156]

The Ferret Force teams travelled as light as they could and only essential rations were parachuted to them as they tried, as much as possible, to live off the land, minimising the possibility of their presence being detected by the CTs (Communist Terrorists).[157]

The purpose of this long-range jungle group was to go and live in the jungle, to establish good relations with the aborigines and locate and destroy the guerrillas either by themselves or in conjunction with regular forces.[158]

Lieutenant Colonel Walter Walker,[159] a highly decorated Burma veteran, was chosen to command Ferret Force. Walker's own study of communist terrorist strategy and tactics convinced him that he would be dealing with an increasingly powerful and cunning enemy. Walker had been training the Ferret Force teams for only about a month when he was told that he was going to take over as Commandant of the new jungle-warfare training school (JWS). This new school was to prepare British soldiers to fight the terrorists on their own ground. During his time at the JWS, Walker wrote the definitive Anti-Terrorist Operational Manual.[160] Without military sponsorship or Walker's drive and enthusiasm Ferret Force survived only a matter of weeks after his departure.

Even in its short life, there were disagreements between Army and Police officers over Ferret Force methods and its use.

For various reasons which included administrative problems; the dislike of the services for 'private armies'; and the change in composition from that originally envisaged, the four Ferret groups were ending their operations by November.[161]

The brief life of Ferret Force was not wasted. It not only helped inspire the future deep-penetration operations of the SAS at a later stage of the campaign, but also enhanced the routine jungle patrolling techniques used by infantry platoons, which would otherwise have seemed hopelessly beyond the capabilities of European soldiers. Other initiatives included Chinese jungle squads.

If it had been possible, John Davis's[162] proposal of the experiment of a Chinese jungle squad might have paid the greatest dividends. Their role was part intelligence gathering, part agent provocateur.[163]

Later, in mid-1953, the Special Operations Volunteer Force (SOVF) was created. This force was composed of surrendered enemy personnel (SEP) and other volunteers. It had 180 ex-communists grouped into 12 platoons of 15 men each. These men volunteered for 18 months' service, lived in police compounds, received similar salaries to the lowest-ranking policemen and went back into the jungle to persuade their erstwhile colleagues to surrender, or to kill them.

After the declaration of the Emergency in 1948, there were a number of important developments. The High Commissioner of Malaya, Sir Edward Gent, was killed in an air crash in the UK and in September Whitehall appointed a successor, Sir Henry Gurney. Gurney had been Chief Secretary to the Administration in Palestine during the last two years of the British mandate.

> It was Gurney who quietly devised a classical strategy for eventual victory.[164]

Gurney was a man who, even if he did not have the power to win the war, had the foresight to know how it should be won. His tenure of office lasted two years to the day before ending in tragedy.

> Gurney's first historic decision was, briefly, that on no account, must the armed forces have control over the conduct of the war. This, he argued, was a war of political ideologies.[165]

The British authorities had already indicated that they would give Malaya its independence and this took away the mainstay of the MCP's role – that of removing the colonial power. Gurney was very conscious that he needed a director of operations, and finally, in April 1950, Whitehall appointed Lieutenant General Sir Harold Briggs as:

> Director of Operations 'to plan, to co-ordinate, and direct the operations of the police and fighting forces'.[166]

Briggs was to act as the executive to the High Commissioner, Gurney. Briggs had retired to Cyprus in 1948 after a distinguished military career which included commanding the 5th Indian Division in Burma from 1942 to 1945, and he had much experience in jungle warfare.

As well as undermining the political direction of the MCP, Gurney realised that the key to destroying the CTs was removing them from their source of food, information and recruits. These were mainly being provided by the squatters, of Chinese origin, who lived on the outskirts of all the villages and towns in Malaya. The CTs' support group, or Min Yuen, provided assistants either willingly or under threat. If the CTs and the Min Yuen could be separated, this would make the military task of destroying the terrorists easier. The only way to do this would be to move the squatters into controlled villages from which movements of both food and personnel could be monitored by the police and the army.

On 6 October 1951, a terrorist platoon of 38 CTs carried out a successful ambush of Sir Henry Gurney as he was travelling to the Fraser's Hill 'change of air station'. This was a major coup by the CTs, even though the ambush had not been directly targeted against Gurney.

> Suddenly a door of the Rolls opened and out stepped Gurney.
> Almost leisurely he banged the door shut, and started to walk
> towards the high bank – and the shooting.[167]

Gurney's death caused a severe drop in morale[168] within the political, civilian and commercial communities and was a major blow to the campaign.

On 21 October 1951 Winston Churchill became Prime Minister and he was immediately concerned about the situation in Malaya. By 1951–52 British troops in Malaya numbered about 25,000 with a further 10,000 Gurkhas. Total security forces equalled about 300,000 in 1953. Even so, progress against guerrillas, who never numbered more than 8,000, was painfully slow. It was much more than just a military operation. Briggs had been in communication with Churchill and he had recommended there should be one man in control of both military and civil affairs. Churchill gave the appointment to General Sir Gerald Templer.

> 54 year-old General Sir Gerald Templer was every inch a soldier
> – and looked it ...[169]

General Templer, departing from Britain in earlier 1952 to become High Commissioner in Malaya, declared that the political, economic and social policies would be decisive. Briggs completed his tour and returned to UK in that same year.

Involvement of the SAS

> It should be remembered that the situation in Malaya was bad
> and getting worse in 1950.[170]

The involvement of the Special Air Service (SAS) in the Emergency was at a time when, immediately prior to the establishment of the unit, there was a complicated and convoluted military and political situation. The complex picture at the time is exacerbated by the fact that the SAS in Malaya was, literally, being started from scratch.

The success of Ferret Force, albeit brief, demonstrated that the most effective military operations were by small units of platoons, sections and even sub-sections undertaking deep-penetration patrols into the jungle.

General Sir John Harding, Commander-in-Chief Far East, decided he needed independent advice from an expert in jungle warfare to combat the communist insurgents. He called in Major 'Mad' Mike Calvert,[171] who had considerable experience of jungle warfare in Burma during the Second World War and, by the end of the war, was commanding the SAS brigade. Calvert had also been one of the prime movers in ensuring the SAS ethic had not died out at the end of the war. Calvert, having been demoted to the rank of major, as had most wartime officers of brigadier rank, had a staff appointment in Hong Kong as G1 Air, training troops bound for Korea in the use of air support.

Once given this task, Calvert tackled it with his normal aggression and drive and he travelled throughout Malaya[172] with an open brief to assess the current situation. His fact-finding trips, working with both police patrols and military patrols, covered over 1,500 miles of enemy-occupied territory.

> For the next six months I travelled extensively all over Malaya. I visited ornate palaces and asked the views of wealthy sultans. I went to brothels and picked up the gossip of the gutter. I had myself put in jail in disguise and rubbed shoulders with captured Communists. I went on tours of the jungle on my own and I joined anti-rebel patrols of British troops in the jungle.[173]

Not all Calvert's advice was received with good grace and this was made particularly clear when he was visiting an infantry unit in the field.

> I suggested that they go out on patrols, not in a section or platoon, but just a few men at a time. The battalion commander listened to this and suddenly he blew up and said, 'My Regiment was raised and trained to fight in Europe and I am not going to change my organisation and training just to chase a few bare-arsed niggers around South East Asia'.[174]

Calvert made a number of significant observations about the quality of the troops involved in the campaign at the time and their methods of operations.

> Most of the troops were national servicemen with little or no jungle experience. Many of the officers had no experience of jungle fighting; they had been taken prisoner of war at places like Dunkirk and Singapore and were released at the end of the war.[175]

Calvert delivered the results of his survey direct to Briggs.

> When the six months were up I made my official report, which comprised ten or twelve points. A number of these were included in what became known as the Briggs Plan, put forward by General Briggs, the Director of Operations at that time.[176]

Calvert recommended separating the terrorists from their support element; training a deep-penetration patrol unit to locate CT encampments and either destroy them or to lead conventional forces to the area; and to separate the CTs from the jungle aborigines, who, it was believed, were assisting the CTs. The task was to interdict the CTs' food and intelligence supply by denying them support and freedom of movement.

Calvert recommended that the Police should stop sending patrols into the jungle and concentrate on the protection of civilians and the expansion of Special Branch. In connection with this it was essential to move scattered settlements of Chinese, known as squatters, into new villages where they could be concentrated and protected. Calvert firmly believed that only once these proposals were adopted should a Special Force be formed to operate in the deep jungle.

Calvert's recommendations struck a chord and he was provided with the opportunity to re-establish the SAS.

> This suggestion was approved and I was told to form a force. The name I chose for the new unit was the Malayan Scouts (Special Air Service Regiment) and its role was to operate in deep jungle areas not already covered by other security forces, with the object of destroying guerrilla forces, their camps and sources of supply.[177]

This was the area, key to the future of the SAS, where Calvert had identified a niche for a new force. However, it was stressed by

General Ritchie that it would be only for the duration of the emergency, under Far East Command, and with nothing to do with the SAS Territorial Army set-up in Britain.

Calvert worked to establish the unit that he had recommended but, to a certain degree, he had been handed a poisoned chalice. He was only able to recruit personnel from the Far East land forces and his choice of officers was limited. Frequently commanding officers would send him their worst men. Moreover, he was not provided with a suitable administrative infrastructure.

> Another cause of the bad start in Malaya was the woeful inadequacy of the administrative and field staff. Malaya Command should have known that a strong staff of A [Administration] and Q [Quartermastering] was essential but they had failed to appoint one and Mike Calvert did not insist on replacements.[178]

He was tasked with setting up the unit as quickly as possible and as a result he received a certain amount of criticism about his command and discipline.

> Perhaps the strongest and most justified criticism of the Malayan Scouts was poor discipline in and out of the jungle.[179]

The absolutely critical role that Calvert played in the formulation of the Briggs Plan is often given only passing acknowledgement, and often ignored. Without Calvert's recommendation, it is unlikely that the SAS would have been resurrected.

At this point, it is useful to identify key 'personalities' in the fledgling SAS. An assessment of British Special Forces (BSF) during and since the Second World War shows that elite forces have a number of identifiable individuals who, through extreme bravery, original thought, vision, administrative tenacity, or opportunism feature throughout the years. These individuals may be liked or disliked by the organisation they belong to, or they may be liked or disliked by the military fraternity as a whole, but they cannot be ignored. The early days of the SAS in Malaya have several key personalities who will re-appear throughout this book. Individuals identified at this stage are Calvert himself, JW, Newell, Sloane, Deane-Drummond and DLB. This is not meant to mean that others were not important or critical but these particular individuals are very relevant at this stage.

The development of the Briggs Plan[180] was critical for the future of the SAS. Without Calvert's initial input, the Briggs Plan might not have been produced. Moreover, without Calvert's insistence to Briggs that there was a need for a force to be specifically tasked with deep-penetration patrolling, the SAS would not have been regenerated.

Calvert's initial step was to search for volunteers but, under the pressures to start operations as soon as possible, he could not be as particular as he would have liked over the standard of recruits. Moreover, he was only permitted to recruit in the Far East. This first recruiting search produced 100 men. Gaining approval for the new unit was a far easier task than raising the new organisation. This was in many ways due to the very big anti-Chindit element among the former Indian Army officers, dating back to the Burma campaign days.

The new formation was called the Malayan Scouts (SAS)[181] and the first recruits to the new unit were formed into A Squadron, The Malayan Scouts.

These first recruits included volunteers[182] who – like Major CE ('Dare') Newell – had served with SOE in Malaya in 1945. Newell, as well as some other recruits, had also been in Ferret Force. Importantly, Calvert also brought together in Johore an intelligence section of men experienced in jungle operations from the time seven years earlier when they had worked with him in Burma, including Hong Kong Chinese to act as interpreters. The head of this 'int' Section was JW, Dorset Regiment. JW had joined the army as a private in 1941. A linguist, he had served for two years as an interpreter with the Russians. Calvert was impressed with JW.

> One of my better acquisitions was Captain JW who was serving as G3 Intelligence to 40th Infantry Division in Hong Kong.[183]

Calvert was under pressure to get results quickly and in his inimitable fashion drove things on with determination.

> There are far too many officers afraid to make a decision, looking for the bloody rules before they do anything. An officer who never makes a mistake is not doing anything, he's useless – but don't make the same mistakes twice. We've got to get a move on with our training, people want to see results from us, and they put a lot of faith in us. There isn't time to 'do a Monty'. We can't afford to wait until everything is ready before we begin operations.[184]

The second source of recruits was the group of wartime SAS, now reservists, known as M Squadron of 21 SAS and commanded by Major Anthony Greville-Bell, who had been formed to fight in Korea. Re-designated B Squadron of the Malayan Scouts, they were under the command of, and trained by, JW.

The new arrivals from Britain, now B Squadron, were not impressed with what they saw and sent back reports to 21 SAS in UK of indiscipline and heavy drinking, which obviously marred the reputation of A Squadron, and its founder, Calvert. Calvert based some of his operational procedures on his wartime experiences but this was now a different army and these were different times.[185]

Calvert made time to widen his search for suitable men, visiting Rhodesia where his staff was able to select some 120, most of whom had wartime experience, to form C Squadron. As there was this opportunity to be selective, 'C' would prove one of the most professional of the SAS Squadrons, serving in Malaya from 1951 to 1953.

> They were, many of them, very big, strong and physically robust men and indeed, of course later on, they or their successors in the Rhodesian SAS had put up a terrific show in the fight against independence for Rhodesia.[186]

Two of the squadron were killed in action before it returned to Rhodesia (modern Zimbabwe). There it was later to become the nucleus of the Rhodesian SAS Regiment, although it continued to be known as C Squadron for many years.

> The Rhodesian squadron in 1951 had a three weeks training exercise before operations advised only by me and one NCO, with perhaps nine months jungle experience between us – it was a case of the blind leading the blind. This squadron with a high percentage of potentially outstanding SAS soldiers never realised its full potential in Malaya. Through no fault of its own, but because it was never properly trained, the same mistake was not made with the New Zealand SAS squadron, when it joined in 1955.[187]

Meanwhile, A Squadron, a hundred strong, was completing its training course. This included throwing grenades and diving for cover in the deep monsoon drains running through their camp area, one of several lessons with live ammunition that disregarded the normal safety rules for field firing ranges. Since there was neither the time nor facilities for such routines, all training – much in the way

Calvert had known it in 1940[188] – had to take place on football pitches and other clear spaces around the camp. This and A Squadron's hard drinking were criticised at the time by the more prosaic officers of B and C Squadrons, and would be a lingering criticism of SAS standards for the next ten years. In 1981, JW felt compelled to write a letter[189] as a result of lingering criticisms of the Malayan Scouts.

> Calvert was under pressure to get results and get them quickly. Calvert's comparison was that a building site can be a rough and mucky place until construction is finished.[190]

However, not all the observations of A Squadron were critical and the newly arrived Rhodesians were somewhat overawed and impressed by the 'hard men' of the original A Squadron.

> Despite their shortcomings, they did have some very good jungle soldiers and fine officers, and the Rhodesians would be impressed with the way some men could use themselves around the jungle.[191]

What was not realised by the more critical officers were Ritchie's directions to Calvert about the Malayan Scouts being a 'one-off' unit, as well as Calvert's quite different concept of the Scouts as an ad hoc unit. Such units – Calvert argued – could be formed and disbanded more readily than squadrons drawn entirely from a British regiment.

While conflicts with the enemy were few, the Malayan Scouts learned vital lessons about jungle warfare. JW, however, has some withering comments to make about A Squadron's operations:

> The lack of success of these first big operations was certainly not due to any 'lack of determination or will'. It was also a fact that 'A' Squadron was not up to scratch ... prolonged failure to make contact with the enemy led to 'a slackening of battle procedures', the troopers becoming 'extremely careless, very noisy and rather bored, going round the jungle in a slaphappy way with big fires at night, dropping sweet papers or ration tins around the place and not hiding them.'[192]

Calvert had driven his troops hard, and himself even harder. Even a man with his iron constitution could not keep going forever and, not surprisingly, ill and exhausted he had to withdraw from operations. He was hospitalised in Malaya and then Singapore before being medically evacuated back to Britain. He describes the situation himself:

> In June 1951, I found myself in the British Military Hospital in Kinrara for 12 days, suffering from 'Hepatomegaly' [sic] of unknown origin. On 22nd June I was flown to the British Military Hospital in Singapore and thence to the UK as a Class 'A' invalid to the Queen Alexandra Military Hospital in London.[193]

A little under six months after Calvert's medical evacuation, on 22 December 1951, his success was articulated by General Headquarters, Far East Land Forces (GHQ, FARELF), which wrote a comprehensive report to the Under Secretary of State at the War office about the employment of the Malayan Scouts. In this report, the role of the Malayan Scouts was defined as to operate in the deep jungle areas not already covered by other Security Forces with the object of destroying 'bandit' forces, their camps and their sources of supply. The report stated that no other units in Malaya were sufficiently organised or equipped for this task, which was vital for bringing the bandits to battle. The result, the report stated, was that the unit was becoming a 'Corps d'Elite' in deep jungle operations and a most valuable component of the armed forces in Malaya. This report, prepared only some 18 months after Calvert had been given the task to establish a Special Force but with virtually no assets, was a comprehensive vindication of his vision and commitment against the odds. Moreover, the report recommended that the Malayan Scouts title be amended to 22 Special Air Service Regiment and added to the Army's permanent order of battle.[194]

Calvert remained a key supporter of the SAS but his departure from Malaya marked the high point of his military career. He had, personally, re-established the SAS, but like a catalyst in any chemical action, he was 'destroyed' in the process and played little further part in any future SAS decision-making process. Sadly, his efforts have been less than appreciated by the majority of the newer generations of SAS who, through ignorance, are not aware of his importance to the sophisticated organisation that the SAS has now become.

> I am sorry to say that I think people's views of Mike Calvert had been affected by his heavy drinking initially, and I am afraid also that the fact that he was convicted on a homosexuality charge in

1953 or 1954 in Germany, after he had left the SAS. I think that
tends to influence people's view of him.[195]

On 27 July, Lieutenant Colonel John Sloane, Argyll and Sutherland
Highlanders, fresh from Korea and an infantry officer, with neither
special forces experience nor jungle experience, took over from
Calvert.

> He took but a short time to assess the situation he found himself
> in and made a number of far-reaching decisions. His feelings and
> tentative ideas are shown in a letter[196] he wrote soon after
> assuming command.[197]

He brought in more conventional measures of discipline and 'normal
military order'. Sloane pulled the squadrons out of the jungle and
instituted a period of solid retraining for all personnel in late 1951
and early 1952. Newell and several other officers, who were considering returning to conventional soldiering, were persuaded to stay
with the unit.

> It is a pity that so little recognition has been made to [sic] Lt.
> Colonel Sloane, who started the administrative and disciplinary
> improvements continued by Colonel Oliver Brooke in the early
> 50s.[198]

In 1952 the designation 'Malayan Scouts' was dropped and 22 SAS
Regiment came into being, albeit at this time wearing the red beret
of the Parachute Regiment – adopted with the SAS cap badge.

JW went back to England to start a selection process for new
aspirants to the SAS.[199] JW had a unique manner of teaching his
soldiers the sort of skills necessary to successfully defeat a wily jungle enemy – some of his methods are legendary.

> There is a rather silly story that I gave a man a grenade without the
> pin in for a week whereas the true facts of that is that a man was
> put out on sentry just out of sight from the camp with a grenade
> only and it obviously had the pin in – but it was ready to throw. I
> once discharged a rifle negligently too and had to fine myself dou-
> ble. On a training exercise, when I came back to patrol base on an
> exercise, the sentry there who should not have had live ammuni-
> tion, fired a shot which missed me narrowly and I did charge him
> for missing – that was just a stunt to amuse the troops.[200]

When JW returned to Malaya to command D Squadron after a short tour at Regimental Headquarters in England he left behind a properly established selection set up at Dering Lines in Brecon. JC, one of the original members of the wartime SAS, took over B Squadron. A young lieutenant who was to feature regularly in the regiment's activity over the forthcoming years, DLB, also joined the regiment at that time.

DLB[201] had some reservations about his first acquaintances with the SAS, and some particularly harsh comments about Mike Calvert's methods:

> ... to join such a shoddy organisation would finish my career prospects in one quick move – a kind of sudden death.[202]

It is worth examining some of the observations that DLB makes during his work with the SAS in Malaya because they can be linked with activities with which he is involved later during his lengthy and varied career in the SAS.[203]

DLB also describes the difficulties he had as troop commander with his new troop in B Squadron – the same squadron he had difficulties with in another war on the other side of the world in 1980.

> Yet physical difficulties were small in comparison with the problems I had in controlling my troop. Not for nothing was B Squadron known as 'Big-Time B'.[204]

As previously mentioned, DLB's initial introduction to the SAS was not particularly impressive and he was removed from the operational area and deployed in the base area. The reason for his removal from operations seems to have been somewhat of a mystery to him; however, his new position in the Operations Room actually placed him in an excellent position to be firmly involved in the next campaign the regiment was to become involved in.

One of the main problems with the SAS's adopted role of deep penetration patrolling of the jungle hinterland was the time and energy spent actually walking into the main operational area. This was before the regular availability of troop-carrying helicopters. A new tactic of parachuting into the high trees which covered the landscape was instituted, and although there were frequent casualties, it continued until the end of the war. DLB describes the process as an 'exceedingly hazardous procedure'.[205]

Lieutenant Colonel Sloane handed over command of 22 SAS in 1953 to Lieutenant Colonel Oliver Brooke[206] and, towards the end of that year, the Rhodesian C Squadron departed for Rhodesia.

> The Rhodesians' commitment lasted almost two years. Malaya had been a valuable experience and they had learned the elementary principles of counter-insurgency warfare.[207]

Always ready to make an observation, Dare Newell commented on the Rhodesian's contribution to the Emergency.

> Of course we owe them a debt of gratitude. Their numbers swelled our ranks at a time when we desperately needed them and they had some very fine soldiers. There are criticisms, of course, I don't think they were as at ease with the aborigines as the Brits but that is understandable given the background and they had a lot of trouble with jungle diseases.[208]

Newell's comments, which are often repeated in books and journals about the early days of the SAS in Malaya, are certainly at odds with the view the Rhodesians had, particularly regarding their ability to relate to the aboriginals. Cole's comprehensive book about the Rhodesian SAS offers a quite different view.

> Off-duty, the Rhodesians became the best of friends with the black Fijians, making nonsense of some claims that the Rhodesians in Malaya were a shade too colour conscious. The truth was the Rhodesians with their background were better orientated towards mixing with blacks and coloureds than the average British troopie [sic] who seldom associated with them.[209]

The Rhodesian's Malaya experience would prove invaluable when they fought encroaching terrorist threats in their own homeland. One young trooper in C Squadron was Ron Reid Daly, who would raise and command Rhodesia's Selous Scouts.

The former Rhodesians still maintain their connection to the British SAS and C Squadron still remains vacant in the 22 SAS order of battle today, and this strong affiliation between 22 SAS and its Rhodesian colleagues remains. Interestingly, when the Unilateral Declaration of Independence (UDI) was declared by Ian Smith's government in Rhodesia on 11 November 1965, it is alleged that the Wilson government considered using the British SAS in Rhodesia but primary sources to this effect have not been located. If this is true, Wilson, who also deployed the SAS to Northern Ireland in 1976, is one of the very few post-war prime ministers who could understand the strategic and public relations value of correctly utilising the SAS. According to Connor, the possible use of troops from 22 SAS against Rhodesia caused a great deal of disquiet. Again according to Connor, there was a strong possibility of dissent if 22 SAS had been directed to carry out offensive operations in Rhodesia against former colleagues. Connor alleges a secret poll was conducted among SAS troopers.

> If the order to go to Rhodesia is given, would you be willing to fight? A substantial majority said 'No!'[210]

The requirement for the services of the SAS was increasing substantially and in October 1953, following the departure of the Rhodesians, D Squadron was formed.

> They (The Rhodesians) were quickly followed by what became 'D' Squadron, made up of volunteers who 'had spent a few weeks at the Airborne Forces Depot in Aldershot[211] where they were not parachute-trained but simply used as heavers of coal and hewers of wood – not the best preparation for joining the Malayan Scouts.' JW became 'D' Squadron's first commander,[212] leading them for six months before his first tour in Malaya ended.[213]

The Director of Operations in Malaya, General Sir Geoffrey Bourne, suggested that a replacement squadron should be formed from volunteers from The Parachute Regiment. Bourne's suggestion was not received with the greatest of enthusiasm by the SAS, but

> ... at the time the SAS was desperately short of recruits, officers particularly: the Regiment's reputation stood so low that the commanding officers of other units were making it difficult for their people to go on the selection course.[214]

The Parachute Regiment and the SAS are different creatures and quite a few of the members of the SAS had less than favourable memories of their treatment at the Airborne Forces Depot in Aldershot before travelling to Malaya.

There was much hostility for the SAS from Airborne Forces, bitterly resented by us at the time, but in most respects it was
deserved. Parachute training was not undertaken by our recruits
until they were in the Regiment and this lack of that special viril-
ity symbol of 'parachute wings' was one reason for the scorn and
derision. The other reasons were that the World War II record of
the SAS was little known even in the Army and the post-war
record non-existent. The standard of recruit was not high and
used as fatigue men, discipline and morale soon worsened at the
Airborne Depot. In later years up to 1962 or so, attempts were
made to absorb the SAS into Airborne Forces. Fortunately, I
think for both sides these were not successful. The presence of
the SAS in Airborne Forces would have been disruptive. I was a
Company Commander in 3 Para for a year in 1959, and the
qualities of the Para were best maintained, then and as now, by
dominant commanders, not at that time by the SAS methods of
discussion and self-criticism.[215]

However, primarily influenced by the need for additional manpower,
the Independent Parachute Regiment Squadron was formed and
added to the SAS strength at the end of 1955. Commanded by
Major Dudley Coventry, it comprised men from all three Parachute
battalions.[216]

The Parachute Regiment squadron was quite well trained – it
was not up to the standard reached by the SAS squadrons at the
time in Malaya but only because it was trained, I think, by the
jungle warfare school, which trained the infantry whose operations in Malaya were very different to the SAS operations.
However, they did do a good job and, one of the reasons that
Dare Newell and I and others in the SAS was so pleased to see
them there, was because it completely changed the attitude of
the Parachute Regiment towards the SAS.[217]

In 1955, a squadron of SAS was raised in New Zealand and after
rigorous selection and basic training arrived in Malaya towards the
end of the year, where they carried out their parachute course. The
total strength of the squadron was 140, a third of whom were
Maoris who found it particularly easy to work with the aborigine
tribesmen. Major Frank Rennie commanded the squadron. After a
brief preparation period they went on to make a valuable contribution to the campaign.

> The New Zealand squadron trained in the jungle areas of New
> Zealand before it came out and when it came, the Commander
> was attached to my squadron and we got on very well on a per-
> sonal level, and they were an outstandingly good squadron – they
> were at least as good as any of the British squadrons – one might
> perhaps say better. They were really high-class troops.[218]

JW, in an interview in later years, commented on the contribution of
the Parachute Regiment, and the New Zealanders. His observations
on the non-'organic' SAS units are of particular interest:

> ... there is no doubt that the healthy competition provided by
> Frank Rennie's Kiwis and Dudley Coventry's chaps from the
> Parachute Regiment did the 22nd far more good than many of
> the old hands were prepared to admit at the time.[219]

A normal pattern for a squadron was two months in the jungle, two
weeks of leave, two weeks retraining and then back to the jungle. As
an example, on Operation SWORD, the SAS suffered three dead as
a result of a parachute drop into the jungle in Kedah in January
1954. But in July all three operational squadrons dropped into Perak
with only negligible injuries. These encouraging results led to a series
of major offensives. The most important of these was Operation
TERMITE in July 1954, the largest combined operation to that point
in the Emergency. The target was two CT camps in the Kinta and
Raia valleys east of Ipoh in the state of Perak, which had long been
one of the 'blackest' areas in Malaya. More than 50 aircraft
(Lincolns, Hornets and Valettas) and helicopters, 200 SAS paratroopers, and ground forces from the 2nd Company, West Yorkshire
Regiment, the 1/6th Gurkhas, the Royal Scots Fusiliers, the
Singapore Royal Artillery and the Police Field Force were deployed in
a coordinated attack on the CT hide-outs. Five RAAF Lincolns and
six RAF Lincolns were briefed to make two separate but virtually
simultaneous attacks (30 seconds apart) on the camps. As soon as
the bombing had ceased (each Lincoln carried 14 1,000-pound
bombs), Valettas were to drop two squadrons of the 22nd SAS
Regiment as close as possible to the main target, with helicopters following with the 'tail' of each SAS headquarters. The SAS had many
casualties from injuries received during the parachuting decent into
trees.[220]

At the beginning of 1955 Oliver Brooke, who had replaced
Sloane, was injured and replaced by Lieutenant Colonel George

Lea. Lea, some years later, took over operational command in Borneo from the legendary General Walter Walker.

Throughout the Emergency, there was no serious attempt by the SAS or other organisations to develop 'pseudo-gangs' as used with significant success by the British in Kenya against the Mau Mau[221] and by the Rhodesian Selous Scouts in the 1970s.[222] In 1952 a Hong Kong Chinese man called Ip Kwang Lau, who had escaped from Hong Kong to join the Chindits, joined SAS. JW used him in CT uniform to link up with the aborigines with a cover story.[223] There were no major results[224] but a lot of useful information was gained about how the aborigines dealt with the CTs. Lau also did similar work for police special branch (SB) in Sarawak during the Borneo campaign.[225]

Conclusion

The MCP failed because it overestimated the backing it would get from the people and by neglecting to organise an adequate open wing to supply and support its operations. The dispersion of its effort geographically and racially throughout the Federation of Malaya undoubtedly contributed to this failure. Having failed to gain a quick victory in any part of the country, it reorganised for a war of attrition. Its high-handed methods in the early stages, the attitude of the Malays and the progress of the Briggs Plan defeated its efforts to gain any widespread measure of support from the people and it fell back on the hope of intervention from outside the country. This hope faded as the situation in Indo-China and Korea became stabilised.[226]

Despite popular history developed in such books as *Re-enter the SAS*,[227] the SAS had a very ineffectual role in the early days of the Malay Emergency and, in fact, only became of importance in about 1954 when it had become competent in deep-penetration patrolling. Also, the introduction of the helicopter made the insertion of patrols more tactical.

The success of cutting off the CTs from food and intelligence by the removal of the squatter-based Min Yuen meant that the CTs were virtually defeated as a fighting force and had withdrawn deep into the jungles. The SAS had become efficient at carrying out long patrols and, in association with the police forts, were probably the most capable of the units in-country to do this type of work. The SAS had greater flexibility than the regular infantry units and their soldiers, very few of whom were conscripts, and who were generally older than their army counterparts, gave fewer administrative problems, to FARELF headquarters, on long patrols.

> I would think that we had about 6 or 7 National Servicemen in my squadron of about 70 men, and they of course didn't serve for two years of the tour, so whatever was left of their tour probably about one year, and they were, in general, very good. They had been on a selection course from 1952 onwards – everyone went on a selection course, including the National Servicemen – so they probably didn't have much more than a year in the Regiment.[228]

In retrospect, 1951–52 could be seen as the turning point in the campaign. Victory had been denied the terrorists; demoralisation had been averted, and the 'white' areas had inched forward, so the reforms began to make an impact. An independent Western-orientated Malaya became possible. As the security patrols probed deeper into the jungle, the isolation of the guerrillas increased. The first truce overtures were made by the communists in 1955 and 1957 and by then their numbers had fallen to around 2,000. Nevertheless, the magnitude of the security forces' task is well illustrated when it was reported that an average of 1,000 patrol hours were needed to capture a terrorist and no fewer than 1,600 to achieve the kill. Ambushes, dependent upon a good intelligence, were rather more rewarding, with a success for every 350 hours spent in wait. Air support included helicopters, first introduced in 1950, and regularly used from 1953. These proved valuable – increasing troop mobility, making deeper penetration into jungle possible, and improving the soldiers' morale, particularly since they could speedily remove the wounded to medical care. A naval squadron alone carried 10,000 troops and 300 casualties in 1953 and the first months of 1954. The Navy also operated along the coast, further restricting guerrilla mobility and supplies. Finally the army moved into central Malaya and the northern border state of Kedah to try and deny the guerrillas a last refuge. Medical and technical aid helped to win over the local primitive tribesman, and throughout Malaya soldiers did much to win the confidence of the population.

By the end of 1955, the back of the Malayan terrorist campaign had been broken and murder of civilians was down to five or six a month. The CT leadership had fled to Thailand and the policy of rewarding defections had paid off. Low-flying aircraft equipped with loudspeakers made tempting offers of money and food. The SAS campaign wound down during 1956 and 1957. At the end of 1956 the regiment's official 'score' was 89 terrorists killed and nine captured and by the end of 1959 it was a total of 108.

In 1957 deep cuts in the military were made, and the SAS squadrons, depleted already, were made smaller and consolidated – B Squadron was disbanded and its men absorbed by the under-strength A and D Squadrons.

By the end of 1958 and under the command of Lieutenant Colonel Tony Deane-Drummond, DSO, MC, the writing was on the wall for the SAS's future in Malaya. The figures stated at the time were that 6,400 terrorists had been killed with a further 3,000 captured or surrendered. The total number of terrorists killed by the SAS was small when compared to some of the outstanding British infantry battalions, composed mainly of National Servicemen, who rotated through the theatre. In his memoirs, Chin Peng does not mention the SAS at all during the main years of the Emergency and only makes reference to them possibly trying to assassinate him on the Thai border in 1960.[229] This apparent contradiction is explained by JW in a conversation with the author in August 2004.

> As far as I know, he never himself went very deep into the jungle, most of his autobiography is concerned with when he was in Perak, I think, and North Malaya, where he was in fairly close contact with the larger force of terrorists who were based naturally enough near their potential targets – the roads and the railway.

Judged purely in terms of 'kills' the success rate of the SAS Regiment in Malaya was unimpressive. In eight years it was in Malaya the SAS killed 108 terrorists, significantly fewer than outstanding units such as The Suffolks and the Royal Hampshires and some of the Gurkha battalions achieved in two or three years.

> They only killed a 100 plus terrorists but they did a job which would not have been effectively done by infantry battalions.[230]

However, 22 SAS had gained a wealth of experience in long-term, deep-penetration, jungle patrolling.

Compounding this was the effective British, and later, Australian[231] patrolling of deep jungle areas.[232]

The SAS did play an effective role in the collection of intelligence, harassment of the CT lines of communications, and by the investment of their 'safe' areas.

Chin Peng mentions the disruption of courier which was the method of passing orders and instructions and policy matters throughout the whole of the Chinese terrorist organisation, and the disruption of these routes would occur in the deep jungle, largely through the presence of the SAS.[233]

The unit had also gained a certain reputation for dealing effectively and empathetically with the indigenous population such as the Orang Asli. These tribes lived in the vast depths of the jungle and CTs blistered onto them for secure bases providing food and early warning of attack. The SAS task was to disrupt this arrangement. There was the danger of natives betraying or killing SAS, who would always be at a disadvantage however clever they might be in the jungle. In 1951, Sakai aborigines murdered Trooper J.A. O'Leary, who became detached from his patrol and lost in the jungle.[234]

The majority of publications about the conflict and the part played by the SAS refer to the critical importance of these Orang Asli/aborigines to the CTs. Chin Peng makes one small reference to them in his entire biography.

In Kelantan, we had a few small groups in very remote camps working among the Orang Asli.[235]

Either he wishes to play down the part they played in assisting his forces, or the aborigines did not play as an important part in the conflict as we are led to believe.

The SAS played a very small part in the very large campaign in Malaya; they had struggled to survive throughout the conflict and, even by the end, most people had not heard of them.

In these early years a number of key personnel firmly established their relationship with the future of BSF and they continue to appear as the permanency of the SAS becomes firmly established. Calvert has nothing further to do with the SAS in an official capacity but remains a firm supporter of the organisation until his death. JW, Lea, Newell, DLB and JS feature in later campaigns. An

element of cult-following is evident, particularly where personal lobbying is required to ensure SAS participation in future conflicts.

The future of the SAS was certainly not guaranteed by its contribution to the Malayan Campaign. Other issues including major
forces withdrawals and military downsizing were being debated in
Whitehall, and the SAS was not necessarily high on the strategic
agenda. Moreover, some of the staff officers involved in the discus-
sions were not necessarily benevolent to the SAS, particularly if the
future of their own regiments was at risk.

On 31 July 1960, the 'Emergency' finally ended – with a victory
parade in Kuala Lumpur. Britain had achieved all of its aims
in Malaya: the insurgents were defeated, and, with independence in
1957, the country was set upon a course of political and economic
development in which Britain's substantial economic interests were
essentially preserved.

Now, all restrictions were lifted except in the Thai border area,
where a Border Security Council was formed to control the remnants
of the MRLA in remote regions in Perlis, Kedah, Perak and Kelantan
– all that was left of the estimated 12,000 men and women who had
passed through its ranks. Of these, 6,698 had been killed, 2,696 surrendered and 2,819 wounded. About a thousand more had died,
deserted, or had been liquidated by their commanders.

The cost in lives to Malaya, and those who fought for it, had
been heavy. The Security Forces had lost 1,865 killed, 2,560
wounded; 2,473 civilians had been murdered, 1,385 wounded and
810 were missing. It was also a war in which the Police suffered 70
per cent of the total casualties and in which Malays in the special
police squads killed more of the enemy than did the entire British
army.

The impact of the SAS was valuable but certainly not critical and
their absence would not have affected the timing or the outcome of
the campaign. Success in jungle operations is about good training,
not about having elite troops.

> If jungle operations are to achieve success, special training is,
> indeed, necessary but not special men.[236]

The main input the SAS made to the campaign was the contribution
by Mike Calvert to the content of the Briggs Plan and the imple-
mentation of deep-penetration, long-range patrolling.

Calvert was the originator of all the basic SAS tactics in Malaya.[237]

Chin Peng is quite clear about what defeated his forces. In December 1955 his view of the situation was:

> The battlefield outlook for our forces by this time was indeed gloomy. The Briggs Plan with its objective of starving us out of the jungle had been the foundation of a devastatingly effective programme. It had increasingly denied us access to our Min Yuen supporters and lines of supply.[238]

If Calvert made mistakes, JW never had any doubts as to his value as the 'originator of the post-war SAS', whose ideas on the employment of special forces in counter-insurgency were to have a major impact on SAS thinking.

The continuing survival of the SAS was a close-run thing and was, primarily, as a result of a committee of enquiry into the role of special forces, not, the unit's operations in Malaya;

> That the SAS did survive to fight another day during that critical decade before 1957 was the result of a committee of inquiry into the role of Special Forces, headed by a Lieutenant-General. This group soberly evaluated the impact of all the private armies of the Second World War, including the Long Range Desert Group, Lovat Scouts, Popski's Private Army, SAS, PARAs, Commandos ... even, it is jokingly suggested, the Royal Corps of Tree Climbers.[239]

Calvert, the man of unrecognised vision, knew quite clearly that the SAS had a unique role to play in Malaya.

> Be under no illusions about this business. We in this unit are not going to win the war. All that we can do is to play a particular part in it for which other Army units are neither trained nor suited.[240]

A blunt analysis of the effectiveness of the SAS in the Malayan Campaign has to be: would their absence have affected the outcome of the conflict at all – and, if so, how? The answer must be that the contribution of the SAS to the Malayan Emergency did not affect the outcome at all. An SAS troop officer of the time defines his view of the results of SAS activities – with a certain amount of defensiveness:

I can't say that the British would never have won in Malaya if
there had been no SAS, but it would have been a slower and
more difficult process, and the finishing off of it.[241]

A continuing theme is the key part that SAS personalities played in
the usage of the SAS in the Malayan campaign and the minimal
input received from the Ministry of Defence or the government to
direct their utilisation.

But, ironically, the Malayan campaign contributed to the development of the SAS, providing it with a harsh classroom in which it
was able to develop a number of skills and tactical procedures which
were utilised soon after and which continue to be used today.

The experience in Malaya gave a background to developing
counter-guerrilla tactics which, as it turned out, was extremely
fortunate because, only five years after the end of the operation
in Malaya, a much bigger operation took place in Borneo for
which the SAS was very well trained and Malay happened to be
the language again that was required.[242]

However, it was events in Oman, in the Middle East, which provided the unit with a unique, and timely, opportunity to demonstrate
its usefulness.

Chapter 5

Counter-Insurgency in the Mountains and the Desert

Introduction

In the 1950s, British strategic thinking was based around the threat from the USSR with a strategy of escalation from conventional deterrence through limited war to nuclear retaliation. The SAS only became relevant to the Cold War to match the USSR with the development and deployment of the Soviet special forces in the 1960s.[243]

However, in the Middle East, Britain was still the key power. The southern half of this zone was still largely isolated from modern politics. Due to constraints in content, this book, deliberately, does not cover in great detail the macro-politics of the region, about which there is a wealth of comprehensive and detailed literature available.[244] With the settlement of the Iranian oil crisis in 1954, British forces in the Persian Gulf could return to their normal duties, but some account had to be taken of the Buraimi oasis dispute between Saudi Arabia and the British protected Sultan of Muscat and Oman in 1952–55. The British-officered Oman Scouts had been formed in 1951 to assist the local British political agent. Meanwhile Aden, in the neighbouring protectorate, remained a useful stepping-stone to the East, but it was not yet a major base and its protection was entrusted to the RAF.

On 26 July 1956, Nasser nationalised the Suez Canal. The nationalisation evoked great indignation in the British government. Plans were immediately prepared in the Foreign Office (FO) for the overthrow of Nasser, though not for the creation of an alternative regime. But Britain faced a more serious nationalist challenge in a greatly changed international environment. Her own power was too dwarfed by two giants, America and the Soviets, one of which wished to exploit her embarrassment while the other refused to associate with a policy that contained so many echoes of an imperial past. Egypt was led by a politician who was fully conscious of these new currents, who himself represented the aspirations of a growing number of Arabs, and who was equipping his armed forces with modern weapons from the communist bloc. The real defenders of Egypt lay outside her, in the USA especially, and in the world at large. Britain and France in conjunction with Israel sought to reverse this action – though it was successful militarily, the action ultimately failed mostly because of the opposition of the USA and much of the UN: this joint, secretly arranged reaction by France, Britain and Israel was blocked halfway by the USA. On 5 November 1956, 600 British paratroops seized the Gamil airfield without much difficulty, and on the following morning the main Allied forces streamed ashore from the great Anglo-French armada. Organised resistance soon ended in Port Said, but at 6pm on the same day the British Prime Minister announced his readiness to accept the ceasefire at midnight. American financial pressure was the main cause of this decision, since Washington refused to agree to give aid to the faltering Sterling from the International Monetary Fund until a ceasefire had been agreed.[245]

In 1957, yet another strong point was to be lost. The Anglo-Jordanian Treaty of Friendship ended in March and all British troops were withdrawn. Britain, after 1957, was still trying to remain a nuclear and world military power, based on limited resources for which the welfare state and private consumption at home, and various overseas interests, were also competing.

Estimates of the strength needed east of Suez were rudely upset by the concurrent challenges of Arab and Indonesian nationalists, one in the protection of southern Arabia and the other in Borneo. But even without these emergencies Britain had reached the point by 1962–63 when either her commitment to the world had to be cut or her defence spending sharply increased.

Between 1959 and 1967, the SAS fought three 'low-intensity' campaigns of which the British public knew very little. These campaigns, nevertheless, had important implications for SAS and assured the regular 22 SAS Regiment of a permanent place in the British Army. The campaigns were the very short, mountain war of Jebel Akhdar in northern Oman; the bitter mixture of pitiless mountain warfare in the arid Radfan hills combined with urban terrorism in the alleys of Aden city; and the more protracted jungle conflict in Borneo.

This chapter considers the SAS operations against insurgents on the Jebel Akhdar in Oman and then SAS operations in the Radfan and Aden. This is geographically convenient because of the relative proximity of Oman and South Arabia, but not completely correct chronologically, because at the same time as the SAS was operating in Southern Arabia, it was also operating against Indonesian forces in the Borneo 'Confrontation'.

Jebel Akhdar

A signal from the War Office sent me scuttling off on a recon-naissance in the Oman.[246]

Background

The Sultanate of Oman is the largest state in the Persian Gulf or, more correctly, the Arabian Gulf. Formerly known as the Sultanate of Muscat and Oman, it has no political connection with the former 'Trucial Oman'. Trucial Oman, earlier known as the 'Pirate Coast', is a Protectorate of seven sheikhdoms extending from the base of the Qatar Peninsula eastward to the entrance of the Persian Gulf. The defence of Muscat and Oman, as well as Trucial Oman, was, until 1971, the responsibility of the British government.[247] The former Trucial Oman is separated into the seven independent states of the United Arab Emirates (UAE) which include Abu Dhabi and Dubai. Muscat, the capital of Oman was separated by some 1,000 kilo-metres of desert from the main town of Salalah in the mountainous southern provinces of the country. A very basic road connected these two main parts of the country. Oman also includes the Musandam Peninsular, the southern part of the strategic Straits of Hormuz at the entrance to the Arabian Gulf.

The British connection with Muscat dates from the early days of the East India Company in the seventeenth century, though the first treaty between Britain and the Sultan was not signed until 1798.

After the Second World War the two super-powers, Russia and the USA, became increasingly involved in Arabia and the Gulf, the former pursuing an old imperial design, the latter attracted by fresh discoveries of oil, and both had a common interest in reducing the influence of Britain.

Encouraged by the political situation, in 1952, the Saudis suddenly occupied the strategic oasis of Buraimi, owned partly by the Sheikh of Abu Dhabi, one of the Trucial States, and partly by the Sultan of Muscat, Said bin Taimur. The Sultan of Oman gathered a force of between six and eight thousand tribesmen and was about to launch an attack on the Saudis but was dissuaded by the British government. The attack would have expelled the intruders immediately, dealing a sharp blow to Saudi prestige and cementing the loyalty of the Omani tribes. In hindsight, DS believes the intervention of Britain to stop the Oman attack was ill-advised.

> The three year delay had been disastrous for the Sultan for during this time the Saudis had made good use of the time to spread their influence in Oman, suborning the tribesmen with lavish gifts of money and arms.[248]

Talib, the Wali [governor] of Rostaq,[249] a brave, energetic and extremely ambitious leader with considerable military ability emerged as the driving force behind a new insurgency movement. Throughout 1956 Talib was recruiting men from Omani labourers in Saudi Arabia and having them trained, under Saudi instructors, in the use of Bren and Browning machine guns, mortars and mine-laying. Talib's plan was for a revolt in central Oman, led by himself and to begin in May, 1957.

Talib landed from a dhow on the Batinah Coast, north of Muscat, with a force of trained guerrillas. In small groups they made their way through the mountains to the interior and Talib, with his brother, again raised the Imam's white standard in rebellion. In order to consolidate and face the new threats, the Muscat and Oman Field Force was withdrawing from the Jebel area when it was disastrously ambushed and virtually annihilated. Some survivors were brought back by their British officers to safety, but as a fighting force it was finished.

There was now open rebellion on the Jebel. The Jebel Akhdar, which means Green Mountain in Arabic, is a sheer limestone massif between 40 and 50 miles in length, and 20 miles wide; it rises straight out of the desert with a fertile plateau at 6,000 feet and peaks rising to nearly 10,000 feet at the summits. The approaches to the mountain led through narrow ravines which could be held against an army by a few determined snipers. On the main plateau of the Jebel Akhdar there were villages and crops to house and feed the rebels, and caves where they could shelter from aerial bombardment.

Also, they continued to receive arms and other supplies from Saudi Arabia, which were being smuggled into the mountains by sympathetic tribesmen.

The Sultan of Oman had neither sufficient nor effective troops to combat the rebellion so, invoking the country's defence treaties, he requested military assistance from Britain. In 1957, a British infantry brigade from Kenya restored the Sultan's authority at Nizwa,[250] its surroundings and the important communication routes.

> The British Government sent it quickly, before the combined pressures of Cairo Radio, Saudi-American intrigue, and left-wing protest in UK could cause further embarrassment.[251]

Talib and his partners withdrew into the remote heights of the Jebel Akhdar, and the suppression of the rebellion had to be achieved quickly, quietly, and preferably with no casualties, because anti-British sentiment ran high in the Middle East after the 1956 Suez debacle and also within the geopolitics of the United Nations (UN). The Sultan's army was too weak and demoralised after the destruction of the Muscat and Oman Field Force to dominate the Jebel approaches and prevent the influx of weapons and ammunition. It was certainly in no position to assault the rebel forces entrenched on the plateau. In mid-1958 the trouble flared up again. Without any effective operations against them, the rebels gradually built up their strength as well as sending patrols down the mountain onto the plain to lay mines and, frequently, to ambush military convoys.[252]

Involvement of the SAS

In charge of the Sultan's forces at that time was Colonel DS, who took up the appointment as the Chief of Staff in April 1958. DS had served with the SOE in the Second World War and later, after service with the Oman Forces, he operated in covert and clandestine operations on behalf of the British government, in the Yemen. DS played a pivotal role in the Jebel Akhdar campaign but his involvement and influence has been largely unrecognised. DS recalls a meeting with the Sultan soon after his arrival in Muscat in which his appointment was changed:

> 'We shall begin,' he said, 'by changing your appointment from Chief of Staff to Commander. After all, you are not my Chief of Staff; you are the Commander of all my forces – not only of my

army but navy and air force as well, small, though they may be.
You will therefore be called El Caid, 'the Commander.' [253]

DS could see that the only way of ending the present stalemate was
to ask for reinforcements of British troops to assault the Jebel. On
13 June he flew to Sharjah to see Christopher Soames, the
Secretary of State for War, with General Firbank, the Director of
Infantry, who were passing through in the course of a visit to the
Gulf. They promised to do their best, but made it clear that the
whole matter involved a political rather than a military decision, and
that, in any case, the most DS could hope for was two battalions.
DS responded by saying:

> In these circumstances I asked if one of them could be either a
> Royal Marine Commando, parachutists, or a unit of the Special
> Air Service; I doubted whether a normal infantry battalion would
> be fit enough for the assault, at least without a great deal of extra
> training.[254]

DS was aware that 22 SAS was returning home from Malaya later in
the year and thought it might be possible for them to 'spare a
squadron for a few weeks' service in Oman'. DS also asked for:

> ... a whole squadron of Life Guards' Ferrets[255] instead of the two
> troops which were due to replace the 13th/18th Hussars and my
> request was granted. I was particularly pleased because the
> Ferrets had proved to be the most useful of all our vehicles; with
> their armour, machine guns and wireless they were ideal for the
> protection of convoys.[256]

DS received a distinctly chilly reception from the diplomats and it
was clear to him that it was the FO[257] which was objecting to the
use of formed units of British troops in Oman because they feared
repercussions at the UN. At the UN, already, both Saudis and
Egyptians were denouncing British military intervention in Oman,
with grossly exaggerated accounts of the scale of its involvement.
Now the very suggestion that regular British troops might again be
committed to action in Oman made the FO mandarins' 'well
groomed hair stand on end'.[258]

Suppressing the rebellion on the Jebel was not an impossible task
for resolute soldiers, although the terrain and the environment were
particularly harsh.[259] The steepness of the mountains and the limited

routes into the area were of concern. Meanwhile, in the UK, the Director of Military Operations (DMO) in the War Office was studying the Oman problem. One of his officers was FK.[260] In his autobiography, FK details the military situation.[261]

> The military problem of defeating Talib was perfectly straight-forward. In its simplest terms it amounted to devising a method whereby a sufficiently strong Government force could reach the plateau.[262]

The main difficulties surrounding the use of military forces continued to be those imposed by the political and international climate at the time. There was no recognition of the SAS as particularly well-suited to this strategic task to obfuscate the UN and international critics.

FK has recorded that he put forward ideas gleaned from his previous experiences in Kenya, but these plans were rejected as being unsuitable for this desert environment.[263] The difficulty that FK encountered was in getting hold of the right men to start the whole thing off. Then, according to FK, the DMO, for whom FK worked, thought of the SAS.

> General Hamilton reckoned that 22 SAS might provide most of the soldiers needed in our teams, which would be a quicker and more efficient way of getting individuals than collecting them from the army as a whole.[264]

On 17 October 1958, the Chief of Staff (CoS) FARELF received a signal from the DMO in which the DMO asked CoS FARELF to discuss with the commanding officer of 22 SAS the possibility of employing SAS troops to attack rebel positions on the Jebel Akhdar.[265] Meanwhile, in Malaya, DLB became involved in the proceedings:

> Sitting in the Ops Room on the morning of 28 October[266] 1958, I read a highly classified, coded signal from London which set the hair on my neck crawling. It came from Major FK in the Planning Branch at the War Office, and asked the Commanding Officer urgently to appraise the possibility of deploying the SAS into Oman, where rebel leaders had established themselves on top of a mountain called the Jebel Akhdar.[267] I took the message in to Deane-Drummond [the commanding officer], who seized on the opportunity as eagerly as I had, though for different

reasons.[268] He saw this not merely as another operation, but as a chance for the SAS to prove to the world that it could fight effectively in environments other than the jungle. Moreover, many people believed that when the Malayan campaign came to an end, the SAS would be disbanded. As Deane-Drummond at once realised, Oman would give us another chance.[269] In short order, and largely on Deane-Drummond's initiative, the decision was taken that the SAS would deploy a squadron into Oman immediately.

The DMO's scheme was accepted in principle and FK was flown to the Aden for a meeting to be arranged in Aden with Air Vice-Marshal Heath.

> The control of operations in the whole of the Persian Gulf, including Oman, was in the hands of Air Vice-Marshal Heath at Aden. At the time there was a considerable weight of opinion that the domination of the many unruly tribes scattered over thousands of miles in Arabia could best be done from the air with occasional support from the Army.[270]

The meeting included Heath, FK himself and Deane-Drummond. DLB worked closely with Deane-Drummond in Malaya and describes him:

> ... he came to the Regiment with a reputation for outstanding courage, and with a ready-made nickname, 'The Cupboard'. This derived from his astonishing feat, after the Battle of Arnhem in 1944, of hiding for thirteen days in a cupboard in a house full of German soldiers.[271]

Connor, a long-serving SNCO of 22 SAS who joined the regiment some three years after the Jebel Akhdar operations, and who sees himself as the 'mouthpiece' of the 'troopers' in the SAS, describes Deane-Drummond differently:[272]

> An unbending, ramrod-stiff career officer, he was one of a succession of COs (Commanding Officers) who had come to the Regiment to instil discipline and order. He was never entirely at ease with the hard-drinking, hard-fighting, semi-disciplined men under his command and would RTU (Return To Unit) people for the smallest misdemeanour.[273]

Deane-Drummond and FK did not see eye to eye at their first meeting. FK as the co-author of the 'approved' War Office plan for subduing the rebels on the Jebel, and the War Office representative, expected 'his' plan to receive much more attention than it did.

> It cannot be denied that my first impressions of Lieutenant-Colonel Deane-Drummond were unfavourable. He had marched into the Muscat venture that morning without knowing the first thing about it and had immediately set about explaining just how the SAS would deal with the enemy. I wished that the Director of Military Operations had left him in Malaya because I felt sure that he was not going to be much help with regard to the plan.[274]

From his point of view, Deane-Drummond was surprised, but not a little pleased, to be asked for his views on the situation as soon as the meeting commenced.

> I had read summaries of what was happening in Oman, but I was not prepared for the Air Marshal when he asked me straightaway how I thought the SAS might be able to help. I told him that my first requirement was to have a close look at the Jebel Akhdar and see how SAS patrols might be deployed. 'With a bit of luck,' I told him, 'I think there might be a good chance of killing the leaders of the rebellion before the hot weather starts in April. If we do not kill them, I think we could give the rebels a lot of bloody noses, and this could allow successful negotiations to take place.' A general discussion then took place. FK's ideas were received, with considerable scepticism, although they might well have to be tried out in the long term if the SAS had not been given the task. *My plan was strongly favoured by all those present* [emphasis added].[275]

When approval was given by the War Office and FO, Deane-Drummond gave the task to D Squadron, which had a total strength of 70 men. It was ready to move from Malaya by 15 November 1958. Seizing an opportunity, DLB replaced a colleague who was not available and was included in D Squadron, which, commanded by Major JWT[276] arrived in Oman on 18 November. Deane-Drummond was there too. In consultation with DS, plans for patrolling and blocking exits from the Jebel were made.

What is not generally known is that in the second week in November, a patrol from the Sultan's Armed Forces (SAF) commanded by Major Tony Hart, a British contract officer, found a way to the top of the Jebel that was unguarded.[277] This route, known as the Hajar Track, entailed a six-hour climb and included climbing some 80 steps cut by the Persians when they assaulted the Jebel some centuries earlier.[278]

In the ensuing weeks, the troops strengthened their positions on the sides of the Jebel. At the end of December, the Trucial Oman Scouts put a squadron into the village of Hajar, out of which they maintained two troops at a new base on the top to reinforce the existing garrison of the Muscat Regiment and SAS. A platoon from the Northern Frontier Regiment joined them, and, to provide additional fire-power, a dismounted party of 20 Life Guards under a Corporal of Horse carried up eight of their Browning machine-guns.

> We never ceased to bless the authorities for giving us these Life Guards.[279]

DS requested another SAS squadron, realising the task was too much for the relatively small numbers of SAS soldiers already in country. The FO and the military command in Aden agreed to the extra SAS troops, but the FO instructed DS that all British troops must be out of Muscat by the first week in April. The significance of this deadline, apparently, was that the UN was to discuss the Middle East situation soon afterwards, with Oman featuring large on the agenda. Britain did not want to be embarrassed at the UN meeting by an escalating and on-going conflict in Oman.

The next problem for DS was the chain of command. Officially all British troops serving inside the country came under his orders, but Deane-Drummond had to be in a position where he could give orders to his own troops, and so, to avoid complications, DS appointed him as his Deputy Commander. When Deane-Drummond arrived on New Year's Day, 1959, the first decision DS made was to set up a joint headquarters to coordinate the operations of the Sultan's Armed Forces, the SAS, and the Royal Air Force. A tactical headquarters or 'Tac HQ', with a small staff, was installed in Falaj on 9 January.

On 12 January A Squadron, 22 SAS Regiment flew in from Malaya, under Major JC, one of the longest-serving officers in the SAS.[280]

> Dark and thin, with strong, expressive features and a quick
> though short-lived temper, he was a brilliant soldier whose thirst
> for adventure and danger was to bring him under my command
> again in the Yemen.[281]

The April deadline imposed by the FO meant there was only some
three months in which to assault the Jebel. The primary object in all
the planning was to gain a foothold as quickly as possible on the top
of the Jebel, near the rebel headquarters, and hold it for the reception of air supply drops and as a firm base for further operations.
Surprise was obviously essential in order to avoid the heavy casualties that were expected if the assault were opposed.

DS had received strict instructions from Aden that all troops,
Life Guards, Trucial Oman Scouts, and Sultan's Armed Forces, were
to be used only in support of the SAS, and so the two SAS
squadrons would lead the assault. These orders caused some natural
disappointment to the Sultan's forces, who had tried for so long to
reach the top, and who had in fact been the first to get there.
However, these forces had little option but to accept the situation
philosophically, especially as they themselves had important roles to
play: firstly, they would make the diversionary attacks before the
main assault; secondly, they would follow the SAS and take over
successive features as they were captured; and, thirdly, they would
consolidate the top of the Jebel and hold it against attack while the
SAS pressed forward into the main caves.

In order to confuse Talib, DS mounted a series of diversions during the weeks before 25 January in different parts of the Jebel. DS
describes the plans:

> Our plan of attack was necessarily simple, even primitive. The
> operation was essentially a straight slog up the mountain face,
> and everything would depend on whether we achieved surprise;
> even when we postponed it for twenty-four hours because of a
> poor weather forecast – a wise decision, as it turned out – there
> was no need to alter the details.[282]

The attack was a success. Captain ZZ, who was involved in the operation, describes the final assault in his book about Oman.[283] The
SAS suffered the only casualties among the attacking forces of the
entire operation. A bullet hit and exploded a rifle grenade in a soldier's pack. He and the two men following him were badly wounded.
Two of them died within 24 hours.

On 8 February the last of the follow-up searches was called off. SAS troops were initially withdrawn from the Jebel but were then later required to maintain a 'public relations' presence on the Jebel.

> The inhabitants of the plateau were in a wretched state: their villages had been wrecked (by bombing and strafing by the RAF), their fields left untilled. The ancient falaj, or water-conduit, system was in ruins, and the people themselves had been living miserably in caves. For the next three weeks the SAS carried out a programme of flag-marches,[284] trekking all over the jebel in half-troops, each accompanied by a couple of donkeys and an officer from one of the native Regiments.[285]

Many decorations for gallantry, mainly to officers, were awarded to the SAS for this operation. A somewhat disillusioned, but magnanimous, DS describes the events after the successful assault:

> In accordance with the Foreign Office directive, the SAS returned to England in March; the Life Guards rejoined their Regiment in Aden. We were deeply grateful to those units of the British Army and freely recognized that we couldn't have won our war without them – particularly the SAS, whose expert training and modern equipment proved decisive. But I confess I was a little piqued that in the accounts of our operations that appeared in the British Press the SAS received the entire credit for our success; the Life Guards were barely mentioned, and the Sultan's Armed Forces – who had, after all, borne the burden of the preliminary campaign and endured the appalling rigours of the heat and the hazards of mining throughout the summer – were totally ignored, although they had suffered the highest casualties.
>
> The British Government even refused us a campaign medal – perhaps they were unwilling to admit there had ever been such a campaign; but when the Sultan awarded a Jebel Akhdar medal to all his troops and Contract Officers, the War Office forbade the British Seconded officers and attached British troops to accept it.[286]

Conclusion

The main impact of the SAS in the campaign was the politically discreet and cost-effective way in which the operation was managed. This was a lesson that was not lost on the ever cost-conscious War Office.[287]

However, it was accepted by many that the Jebel Akhdar campaign could have been carried out by an infantry unit – as was admitted by Deane-Drummond:

> As it turned out, it might have been a task which could have also been done by any well trained battalion of all regulars with reasonably young and active company commanders.[288]

The successful outcome of the brief campaign influenced the government of the day to adopt a strategy of using military quick-reaction organisations, based in Britain, to protect its interests in the Third World.

> From the point of view of the army as a whole the most important effect of the campaign was that it ensured the continued existence of the Special Air Service.[289]

The success of the campaign also went a long way towards consolidating the SAS permanence, expanding and broadening their reputation from merely a good jungle force whose value was limited to the expiring Malayan conflict.

> The Jebel Akhdar campaign proved a turning-point in the history of the SAS. No word of our involvement in Oman reached the public until April, when *The Times* newspaper[290] broke the secret with an article fed to the newspaper by Deane-Drummond.[291]

Deane-Drummond also wrote an article for the *British Army Review* which included extracts from *The Times*[292] article and was published in September 1959.[293]

In almost every description of the successful domination of the Jebel Akhdar by British Forces the success of the attack is attributed to the extraordinary skills of the SAS.

> ... ascribed to the almost superhuman powers of endurance, military skill and courage of the SAS. A handful of these brave,

resourceful men successfully took a fortress that would otherwise have required a major military operation.[294]

However, reports of the action, almost without exception, ignore the following: the attrition of the rebels caused by the pressure from the Sultan's Army patrolling the base of the Jebel; the artillery's constant shelling of the Jebel and the routes to it; the ambushes of known infiltration routes by both the Sultan's forces and the SAS prior to the assault; and, most importantly, the air bombardment.

> What these accounts leave out is that the Jebel had been under heavy air bombardment for weeks before the SAS arrived. Movement in daylight became virtually impossible and by night extremely dangerous as the inhabitants of the plateau had their homes and crops destroyed and their livestock killed.[295]

Air Chief Marshal Sir David Lees in his account of the campaign[296] gives some idea of the scale of the bombardment. In the week ending September 1957, for example, four-engine Shackleton heavy bombers dropped 148 1,000-pound bombs on the plateau, while roving Venom jet fighters fired 40 rockets and a large quantity of cannon ammunition. Later in the month aircraft from the carrier *HMS Bulwark* joined in the attack with her full complement of Sea Venoms and Seahawks. In one week, 43 offensive sorties against the plateau targets were flown from the ships as well as ten reconnaissance sorties.[297]

This bombardment, within such a small area, and 'against simple agricultural tribes, continuing week after week, was a terrifying experience'.[298] Even before the SAS arrived, the villagers were pleading with the Imam and his brother to surrender:

> One day a woman arrived in Nizwa with a message from the Imam to Sayid Tarik suggesting a truce during which both sides would refrain from hostilities, including bombing and shelling on our part and mine-laying on theirs. Not surprisingly, the terms proposed by the rebels proved unacceptable to the Sultan, and so we went back to war.[299]

Prior to the arrival of the SAS, a major campaign using leaflet drops and voice aircraft was carried out to try and persuade the rebels to surrender. The damage being caused to the simple dwellings and inhabitants of the Jebel by medium artillery and aircraft bombing was causing the FO some concerns. These were expressed by Sir Bernard Burrows, the Political Resident.

> The reports of destruction inflicted on the mountain villages by the medium guns have caused me to give further thought to the problem of what should be done to bring the campaign to a speedy end.[300]

It is of interest to note the full composition of the forces who were available to Deane-Drummond and deployed for the assault on the Jebel:[301]

> Two SAS Squadrons.
> Assault troop of D Squadron, Life Guards.
> Section of British Sappers.
> Two Squadrons of Trucial Oman Scouts.
> The Northern Frontier Regiment.
> 200 Abriyeen Tribal Levies.
> 400 Bani Ruwaha Tribal Levies.
>
> Aircraft on Call
> 12 Venoms from Sharjah.
> 6 Shackletons from Masirah.
> 6 Valettas from Bahrain.
> 2 Light Helicopters based at Nizwa.
>
> Artillery
> 2 x 5.5" guns.
> 2 x 3.5" Screw Guns.
> 2 x 3.75" Howitzers.
> 2 x 4.2" mortars – all well served by Pakistani gun crews.
> Field Surgical Team and associated transfusion unit.[302]

The subjugation of the rebels on the Jebel was a brief operation covering a few months only. In the operation, two squadrons of the SAS, in conjunction with a large number of other ground troops and substantial air resources, carried out a physically demanding assault over very difficult terrain. FK remained adamant that an assault with conventional troops would have been a success.

> The plan, which the Commander of the British Forces in the Arabian Peninsular forwarded from Aden, was therefore based on

a conventional assault using a British battalion in addition to the
Sultan's forces. The operation would be commanded by a British
brigadier and would be preceded by a small parachute drop, if
the weather was favourable. *It was a sound plan and could not
have possibly failed* [emphasis added].[303]

Whether another unit, either Royal Marines or paratroopers as
requested by DS, could have operated just as well, we will not know.
In this case, it is somewhat irrelevant to consider if the SAS was the
right organisation to use in the campaign and to assess whether they
were effective or not. The SAS were the only troops available who
could be moved discreetly to the region. The question of whether
this was or was not a task for special forces is a little more vexing.
When questioned by the author on the use of troops other than the
SAS, JW said:

The alternative was to use a battalion of the Parachute Regiment
or I suppose any other Infantry Regiment perhaps with artillery
support, and it was not possible to move units of the British
Army without attracting public attention, and the SAS on the
other hand had earlier established its ability to move troops in
secret. In other words the soldiers could be trusted not to pass
on the information to local hands, and therefore the whole operation could be carried out without any publicity [so for] the
Government of the day – which was the Conservative Government – Macmillan Government I think – it was an attraction
that the SAS could be used and [it] would not have to come out
– the news wouldn't be made public until it was decided that the
operation was complete.

The SAS was still relatively unknown at this stage in their development, which was politically convenient; but, more importantly, they
were available and without a specific task. Moreover, the SAS knew
that the way they approached this task would be critical in the way
they would be used in the future or, even, in the decision whether
they would be used at all. After all, the unit was only very small,
composed of two squadrons, and its future was certainly not
confirmed.

   The Jebel Akhdar operation was very opportune indeed for the
SAS, and they used the opportunity well, both militarily and as a
public relations exercise. Deane-Drummond, the commanding
officer, marketed the regiment unashamedly, to the extent of writing

in the Army's house journal and to *The Times*. However, the application of the SAS to this task was as a result of individual lobbying and not as a defence or foreign-policy option.

In stark contrast to this campaign, the SAS operations in the Radfan and Aden were badly thought out, and virtually negated all the political benefits gained from the Jebel Akhdar campaign.

The author briefing an armoured personnel carrier (APC) commander before an operation in South Vietnam in 1971.

Chapter 6

RADFAN AND ADEN

In Aden, the very first acquisition of Queen Victoria's Empire, the British left shooting to the last.[304]

It is geographically convenient, due to the relatively close proximity of Oman and Southern Arabia and the similar terrain, to consider the SAS involvement in Southern Arabia, which followed the attack on the Jebel Akhdar, even though the events were separated by several years and occurred in conjunction with the SAS's involvement in Borneo.

Elements of 22 SAS Regiment were involved in fighting in the Arabian Peninsula and the Aden Protectorate at intervals between 1964 and 1967. At the same time, elements of the SAS were deployed into Borneo. The terrain of the two areas, Borneo and South Arabia, could hardly have been more different, yet the troops coped relatively well with both. Many of the serving SAS had also been involved in the battle for the Jebel Akhdar.

Background

The Aden Protectorate, as it was known, lay at the southern tip of Saudi Arabia strategically placed at the entrance to the Red Sea; directly to the north was the Yemen. British interest in the area started at the end of the nineteenth century in the age of the coal-fired warships. When the Suez Canal opened it had considerably shortened the lines of communication from Britain to the colonies in India, the Far East and Australasia. Aden, with its natural harbour, was annexed in 1839 as a colony administered from India. By the turn of the century a large naval base had been established there.

Aden became a crown colony in 1937, when Britain also assumed a protectorate over some 100,000 square miles of the inhospitable volcanic hinterland. In 1959, the status of the latter was changed to that of a federation of Arab emirates and the colony of Aden was added in early 1963. Britain also had important bases in Singapore and Hong Kong, so Aden was a strategic staging-post as well as a port of regional importance. However, Britain intimated that, by 1968, it would pull out and leave Aden as an independent, and stable, state within the Commonwealth. This was not what happened and the withdrawal from the area was a saga of political muddle and incompetence.[305]

Pan-Arab nationalism had come to the fore after the debacle of the Suez invasion in 1956. This rising tide of Arab nationalism was supported by Nasser's propaganda machine, which exhorted Arabs everywhere to revolt against both their colonial masters and their traditional rulers. The nationalism was backed by Soviet support for 'liberation' movements and provoked an anti-colonial guerrilla war in those sheikhdoms whose rulers' credibility depended upon British support.

Involvement of the SAS

In September 1962, a group of left-wing army officers overthrew the Imam, the hereditary ruler of the Yemen. This resulted in the arrival of Egyptian troops in the Yemen together with considerable supplies of weapons. A 'UK Government approved' mercenary force – or, in more modern parlance, a 'private military company' (PMC) – was deployed in support of the Imam. The force included ex-SAS members and was led by Major JC,[306] who had served in the Malayan Scouts and also on the Jebel Akhdar. Also involved was DS,[307] who had been commanding the Oman forces in the Jebel Akhdar campaign. This PMC[308] operated successfully in the ensuing civil war for several years.

Also, in 1962, after completing his first tour with the SAS, DLB was posted to the Yemen, on loan service, as an intelligence officer with the Federal Regular Army (FRA). JW, who had been heavily involved with the original Malayan Scouts, was in the military staff in Aden at the same time. Ever the opportunist, in early

1963, DLB became involved in the covert activities supporting the Imam.[309]

In London, successive governments set targets for self-government and then for a total British evacuation. This was interpreted in South Arabia as abdication. Since the existing local rulers enjoyed no apparent legitimacy, the stage was set for defections from the FRA, and for military defeat. The SAS, like other security forces, was defending a lost cause.

In 1963 trouble had flared up in the Radfan, the mountainous area which lies some 50 miles to the north of Aden itself. Scattered throughout the mountains are villages of stone houses, each one fortified because of the interminable feuds which have been waged between families and tribes. With the exception of Aden itself, which was a British colony, these were administered by the local rulers, under the watchful eyes of political officers, in each state.

The federal government sought more substantial British military help. The government's own ministers, responsible for internal security, had major misgivings about this new involvement and believed the deployment of British troops in so hostile an area would simply exacerbate matters.

> There were many local officials, with a profound knowledge of the Arabs, who believed strongly that any attempt to subdue the tribes by force was doomed to be a waste of time and effort.[310]

The response from the British authorities was to send in FRA units. The FRA, previously known as the Aden Protectorate Levies[311] was a local force previously raised by the British. Between December 1963 and April 1964, the FRA battalions did occupy parts of the Radfan Mountains for a few weeks. These operations achieved some success, but the troops were subsequently withdrawn to perform the even more important task of guarding the frontier.

The tribesmen promptly reoccupied their former hill positions and, once again, began attacking traffic on the road linking Aden and Yemen. The tribesmen, who were supplied with arms by the Egyptians and some of whom had received training in the Yemen, grew bolder and the tempo of attacks increased on convoys using this Dhala Road. Meanwhile, Cairo and its surrogate regime in the Yemeni capital of Sana'a, announced the FRA's withdrawal from Radfan as a resounding defeat for the imperialist British.

It was decided to suppress this latest insurrection by deploying British troops, not FRA troops, to quell the tribesmen. The formation was called Radfan Force, which was shortened to 'Radforce'. The forces allocated to the task were:

> D Squadron, 4 Royal Tank Regiment (armoured cars)
> J Battery, 3 Royal Horse Artillery (105 mm howitzers)
> 2 Troop, 12 Field Squadron, Royal Engineers
> 45 Commando, Royal Marines, with B Company 3 PARA under command
> 1 FRA[312]

In 1964, DLB completed his posting with the FRA, and his extra-curricular activities with DS and JC, and was posted back to the SAS as a squadron commander with A Squadron

> Then I rejoined 22nd SAS at Hereford as commander of 'A' Squadron. ... I felt confident that the future would bring plenty of action.[313]

In May 1964, DLB's squadron was tasked to fly to Aden to carry out desert training prior to deploying to Borneo. On arriving in Aden, as part of the squadron advance party, DLB became aware of the Radforce operation, which was to secure the high ground that dominated the Danaba Basin and the Wadi Taym. Both were tribal strongholds. DLB immediately offered the assistance of his men for the planned operation.

> Here, surely, was an operation in which the SAS might play a useful part – yet there seemed to be no mention of Special Forces in the plans. I went to see the Commander-in-Chief, Lieutenant-General Sir Charles Harington, and suggested that we should not wait for our projected exercise, but should upgrade it into a live operation, and call the SAS deployment forward.[314]

This is another occasion where an SAS commander has 'marketed his wares' to a local commander. The SAS men arrived at Khormaksar, the RAF base in Aden, just two weeks before they were to spearhead the Radfan offensive. Two weeks was also the minimum period normally allowed for troops to acclimatise prior to operating in temperatures up to 150 degrees Fahrenheit. The newly arrived SAS troops, ignoring these well-proven procedures, drove immediately to a hastily prepared base at Thumier, 60 miles from Aden and just 30 miles from the hostile Yemeni border.

> By then things were moving so fast that we had no time to acclimatise.[315]

Somewhat rashly, the same night, the squadron moved into the nearby Radfan Mountains for a 24-hour proving patrol. In the darkness there was an exchange of fire with a group of armed men who were, in fact, British soldiers. One SAS trooper was slightly wounded in the exchange of fire. This overconfidence, and lack of acclimatisation, was to lead to an avoidable tragic conclusion.

The Radforce tactical plan involved the insertion of paratroopers into a dropping zone (DZ) close to key objectives. The job of establishing a DZ was traditionally that of the Paras' own independent pathfinder company, but DLB had been lobbying hard and recommended that the DZ should be marked and secured by a patrol from the SAS. This patrol's job was to travel to the DZ on foot, secure it and then signal in the parachute force.

The operation was a disaster. Not yet acclimatised, and with at least one member of the patrol not fit through ill health, the patrol was compromised at an early stage when spotted during the morning by a tribesman herding goats, whom they killed. The patrol was soon surrounded and pinned down by heavy fire. An attempt was made to fly in a second patrol to relieve them by helicopter, but the machine was so badly damaged by enemy fire that it had to return to base. No other plans seem to have been prepared. The majority of the patrol members were able to withdraw, but Captain RE and Trooper NW were killed and mutilated and their heads displayed in the Yemeni town of Taiz.

There did not appear to have been a contingency plan made to extract the patrol if it was compromised. The basic special forces tenet of planning for contingencies, such as a compromise, seems to have been poorly addressed. There also appeared to be a reluctance by DLB to seek support from outside agencies to assist in the rescue of the SAS patrol members. No elements of the Parachute Regiment, for whom the DZ was being prepared, were requested to assist in any sort of reinforcement planning. The SAS commanding officer was visiting at the time and listened to the original patrol briefing – and agreed with it. When challenged by the author about the apparent lack of any contingency planning he was surprisingly ambivalent about the need for such a plan:

> I don't think an operation by a Troop of 15 should have had special contingency planning – it was always obvious that things

could go wrong on any operation by a troop on any, and every, occasion, and the answer to contingencies that arise suddenly must lie in the hands of the Commander on the spot, and it was up to him to decide whether to stay and fight or to go – he was in radio contact with the Regiment [Squadron Headquarters] and through them with the RAF – he did what he should have – only he could have decided to do, which was the best course of action that was open to him – the fact that two of the men, he and another soldier was killed is no reflection on the operation.[316]

During the Gulf War, when DLB was in command of the British forces, the SAS was deployed on the proviso that they would not require US assets to extract them in the event of problems. This was agreed between DLB and Schwarzkopf. There are certain similarities between the deficient planning of Edward's patrol and that of *Bravo Two Zero* [radio call sign B20] in the Gulf War, which also ended with the deaths of SAS soldiers.

Notes made by another troop commander at the time give an idea of the limited support that was available to rescue the trapped patrol:[317]

One day at the Thumier base, the Troop was resting between ops when I was called over to the ops room. There DLB [Major DLB] explained that 3 Troop, who had been sent out to establish a DZ for 3 Para, had been compromised and were under heavy enemy fire. I was to get the Troop on stand-by in case there was a requirement for some rescue operation as it got dark. It was still early in the morning and I popped over to the ops room several times during the day to hear how things were going. Not too good apparently. Although the RAF were doing a sterling [sic] job keeping up overhead cover throughout the hours of daylight there were more and more *adoo* [enemy] arriving, sensing the kill. The troop commander, RE, was continually targeting the Hunters who brought down fire within 25 yards of 3 Troop sangars.[318]

Unfortunately, the next of kin of the dead were under the impression that they were in the UK on an exercise and heard of the deaths through the media.[319]

Stephen Harper, foreign correspondent of the *Daily Express* was invited to a briefing about the forthcoming operation that was to follow up the initial failed SAS insertion. He noticed an SAS officer, DLB, outside the briefing tent.

One officer, wary of my presence, paused outside the tent to tear an SAS flash from his shoulder.[320]

The general attack on the Radfan had to be somewhat modified and it took several weeks of hard slogging by the main force to impose some sort of control on the area, which was, at best, most tenuous.

SAS patrols had a variety of tasks, laid down by Headquarters, Middle East, in both the Radfan and the Aden hinterland. These included the establishment of forward observation posts (OPs) from which they could direct artillery fire and air strikes on to enemy groups or to intercept columns of arms and supplies as well as ambushing routes from the North Yemen border.

Our orders were to bring in the guns or aircraft on anything that moved. *It proved to be good sport but of questionable value* [emphasis added].[321]

D Squadron arrived in Aden in January 1966, tasked to patrol the Radfan in an attempt to halt the caravans bringing weapons in from the Yemen. Operational patrolling was limited to five days: the limit set by the amount of water one man could carry as well as his weapons and equipment. Sergeant LL described it as a terrible routine.[322] According to LL, the SAS patrol could not achieve anything, as they were not allowed to engage independently and at dusk the patrols were withdrawn.

... What we [the SAS] were doing in Aden remained a mystery to all of us. Ours [was] not to reason why.[323]

Inevitably the war in the Radfan spilled over into Aden town itself.[324] In December 1963, a state of emergency had been declared after a grenade attack on the High Commissioner killed his aide and one other. In October 1964, Harold Wilson's Labour administration swept to power and, in February 1966, the new government announced a total evacuation deadline of the Aden base to coincide with Independence. In March 1967, the evacuation deadline was advanced to November of that year. In the sprawling urban slums of Aden, the Arab Nationalist 'liberators' adopted terrorism methods, including the murder of other nationalists with whom they disagreed.[325]

Yemeni assassination squads infiltrated into Aden city, where they killed local politicians suspected of being friendly towards the

British administration. The SAS became involved, for the first time, in counter-insurgency warfare in an urban setting. Once again, DLB features. Early in 1966, with A Squadron, he was again back in Aden, for desert training. The Squadron set up a clandestine operation, Operation NINA, which involved a group of SAS personnel, disguised as Arabs, going out in small groups into the town, looking to engage armed insurgents and terrorist squads.[326]

> The problem with NINA is that the concept was OK – the management was not – I doubt whether that it was particularly successful at all.[327]

These clandestine operations had been previously used in Palestine and Cyprus, using undercover 'Q' units.[328] These had been started by Roy Farran, and were frequently manned by other former SAS soldiers and officers. Major (later General) FK had been involved in the development and deployment of pseudo-terrorist 'counter gangs', a mixture of former terrorists and loyal tribesmen led by British officers disguised as natives during the Mau Mau campaign.[329] Similar types of operations were also carried out using 'turned' CTs (those CTs who had agreed to work for the security forces) during the Malayan Emergency by the SOVF.

The Operation NINA squad of about 20 men operated from various centres in Aden, where they slipped out in twos and threes to make their way to the Crater and Sheikh Othman districts. Their main target, the assassination teams, were steadily suppressing the meagre Intelligence that was reaching the British authorities by the simple, bloody expedient of killing Special Branch officers and their contacts. Sometimes the SAS men would take with them a comrade dressed in Army uniform, or European civilian clothes, for use as bait in areas where the assassins lurked.

These operations, like most of the intelligence gathering at the time, were poorly coordinated. Also, operations in civilian clothes brought with them the possibility of confusion with the other Army and Police special squads which, not completely surprisingly, were also formed at the same time. On one occasion an SAS patrol fired on some 'disguised', armed, members of the Royal Anglian Regiment, seriously wounding two of the soldiers.

> Similarly, ten different agencies were initially involved in intelligence work. Indeed, it was only in 1965 that a Security Policy Committee was established and only in June that same year that

the GOC Middle East Land Forces was designated security commander and the intelligence agencies brought under a single
army officer, Brigadier TC.[330]

Conclusion

In 1965, Borneo had taken priority over Aden and, while the SAS
still only had two operational squadrons to deploy, as well as the
normal momentum of training to maintain, operations in Aden could
not be continued. However, when B Squadron was reformed and
became operational for Borneo, the SAS did return periodically to
the area for desert training.

In 1966 Britain proclaimed her intention of granting independence to Aden within a new South Arabian federation. This had the
effect of substantially intensifying the terror campaign waged by
Egyptian- and Yemeni-backed radical nationalists in Aden intent on
wresting the political initiative away from the British-backed, conservative South Arabian government, and ensuring their own control of
the territory upon the departure of the British. The Labour government had pulled the rug from under their own troops by announcing
withdrawal far in advance of the proposed dates. In 1964, just two
British servicemen had been killed, six in 1965 and five in 1966,
but in 1967, the total was 44. To this total was added 651 British
military personnel wounded. In all, 382 individuals were killed in
terrorist incidents between 1964 and 1967 and 1,714 wounded.[331]

At the end of June 1967 the British flag was finally hauled down.

> The High Commissioner flew off in a helicopter to the carrier
> *HMS Eagle*. Behind them [sic] the guerrillas fell upon the aban-
> doned stores and barracks, swarmed up the steps to Government
> House, and shot at each other from rooftops.[332]

The SAS lost men in what was seen as a pointless and futile military
situation. The SAS involvement did little to improve the morale of
itself or other military forces. Nobody had had much of a chance to
cover themselves with glory, least of all the politicians.

> I wouldn't say though that the Radfan operation had a major
> impact on the outcome of the political situation out there. I
> think the political situation was actually wending its way –

Radfan operation as a whole was a containment operation I think – a holding operation whilst the British Government worked out how it was going to unwind from Aden although I don't think those who were out there at the time really saw it that way.[333]

The disaster following the initial SAS deployment into the Radfan was a severe blow to such a close-knit organisation. Unfortunately, it reflected the over-confident and unprofessional way in which they had arrived in the theatre and began operations. DLB, who was in charge of the original deployment, recounts in his autobiography that

We finished our tour with the feeling that this had not been an ideal operation.[334]

MWG (second in command of 22 SAS at the time, and the overall commander of SAS troops in the Radfan) remarked in a letter to JW, the CO, written on 11 May 1967, that he thought that paratroops could do what the SAS had been doing:

We are only operating in a super-infantry role of short-range penetration, and tough, well-trained troops could do it equally well. We are only using part of our skills here.[335]

PS, who was an NCO with one of the last SAS patrols in Aden summed up the situation.

For my part, I was happy to leave, and with the benefit of hindsight, I can only wonder why on earth we [the British government] expended so much effort and so many lives on a place that we were abandoning. It makes no sense to me.[336]

The small force of SAS deployed into the Radfan, and the urban warfare of Operation NINA, had no beneficial affect on the campaign. Operation NINA was a clumsy attempt by the SAS to take the war in Aden to the urban assassins. It was brief and ineffectual and merits little analysis other than to see it as an example of local initiative flawed by the lack of strategic management. The SAS felt it had generally been misemployed throughout its involvement, but, as the initial deployment of the first squadron resulted from lobbying by DLB, it cannot blame its involvement on any organisation but itself. Moreover, the affair of RE and NW provided a propaganda coup for the Arab nationalist newspapers.

I think, really, the SAS operations in Radfan and onwards [sic] in Aden, were a reflection of the total chaos that existed in Aden anyway, rather than a failure necessarily by the SAS – whether the SAS would have been better off out of there, I don't know. Whether the SAS had a right to say, whether they choose whether they should be in or out, I don't know because once you start doing that and starting picking and choosing, you cease to be a part of the Army.[337]

What the SAS did learn, from the experiences in Aden and the Radfan, was that even comparative success in counter-insurgency meant little when events were determined by external political pressures. This was a lesson that was to be re-learned in Northern Ireland.

Britain's decision to withdraw from Aden also accelerated the guerrilla war against another of Britain's allies, the Sultan of Oman. During the final year of the Aden campaign, in 1966, Marxist rebels in a remote Aden sultanate bordering Oman's warlike province of Dhofar, were supplying weapons to Dhofari tribesmen, effectively opening up a third front against the British.[338] In only a few years after Aden the SAS would be deployed into Oman.

The SAS had done what was required of them and had sharpened their patrolling skills in a harsh desert environment, which a few years later would stand them in good stead in Oman.[339]

When the British left Aden on 29 November 1967, one of the political beneficiaries of the war was Israel, whose secret aid to the royalist cause in Yemen tied down 60,000 of Egypt's best troops during the 1967 Six Day War. It can be argued that the secret war in Yemen involving JC and DS also helped to prevent an Egyptian or Marxist takeover in Oman and other Gulf states. One certain beneficiary was Soviet Russia, which took over the former British base and comprehensive naval facilities in Aden.

Chapter 7

RETURN TO THE JUNGLE: BORNEO – THE CONFRONTATION

To him the issue was quite clear: 'We had raided into Indonesia regularly and just as regularly been driven off – so they had won.'[340]

Background

Java had been the centre of a great empire where the Dutch, British, French and Americans staked out empires. In 1942 the Japanese seized them all. After the Japanese surrender in Indonesia at the end of the Second World War, the Dutch were met with armed resistance and had left by 1949.

In 1950, Soekarno emerged as president and dictator of Indonesia with the task of governing his nation of 100 million people of many sub-ethnic groups living on 1,000 islands spread over 3,000 miles of ocean. As well as managing his own enormous country, Soekarno also coveted Malaya, Borneo and Singapore.

Borneo, comprising mountains, rivers, swamps and universal forest, is the third largest island in the world. Two-thirds of the island, first Dutch and now Indonesian, is called Kalimantan The rest was acquired in the nineteenth century by the British: Sarawak, to the south west, where the first Rajah Brooke was entreated by the locals to free them from the sultan, and Sabah, to the north west, where there had been virtually no government until it was settled by the British North Borneo Company.

In December 1962 Soekarno supported a rebellion in Brunei by activists seeking to depose the Sultan. Indonesian forces had been secretly involved in the raising and training of an 8,000-strong force of rebels called the TNKU (*Tentera Nasional Kalimantan Utara*: the North Kalimantan National Army). The revolt was crushed by British troops of 17th Gurkha Division and 42 Commando Royal Marines, rapidly despatched from Singapore and Malaya. The Brunei Revolt was merely a prelude to the campaign which followed. Since the SAS was not involved and the issues were mainly domestic, it is not covered in this book.

From 1962 until the overthrow of President Sukarno in March, 1966 Britain had been engaged in limited but substantial warfare with Indonesia, which was attempting to bring down the new Malaysian state by means of armed 'confrontation'. Britain was, in fact, explicitly obliged to come to Malaysia's assistance under the terms of the 1957 Anglo-Malayan Defence Agreement, and some 58,000 British troops were ultimately committed to her defence. The essential value of the defence agreement was that it allowed Britain to keep a strategic reserve in Malaya and Singapore and so make a continuing presence, East of Suez, possible.

'Confrontation'

Denis Healey, Minister of Defence in the crucial period from late 1964 onwards, called the Borneo campaign

> a textbook demonstration of how to apply economy of force, under political guidance for political ends.[341]

In 1962–63, the threat was from small, ill-trained and poorly armed gangs of Indonesian insurgents operating along the lengthy border. The Commonwealth forces' tactics were similar to those of the earlier Malayan emergency: platoons operating independently from company bases. In 1964, the Indonesian government stiffened the border terrorists with regulars. In late 1964, Indonesia stepped up her campaign and trebled the strength of her regular garrisons in the border area, particularly in West Sarawak. In 1965 and 1966, the Commonwealth forces were dealing with the regular Indonesian army in a conventional jungle warfare scenario. It was long-range patrolling, often in company strength, ambushing and attacking relatively large bodies of enemy, often dug in. It had become a company commander's war. The enemy fought with tenacity and skill and used mortars and artillery aggressively and effectively.

In mid-1966, the 'war' ended and the wheel turned full cycle back to 1963: once more battalions were chasing only terrorists, mostly Chinese from Sarawak, trained in Indonesia. Indonesian-sponsored terrorists infiltrating in twos and threes necessitated the re-development of platoon and section patrols and ambushes.

Superficially, this campaign had much in common with the Malayan conflict of the 1950s. In Malaya, the opposition was an irregular, if well-disciplined, guerrilla force with no support provided by external agencies. However, in Borneo, the opposition was well trained, well equipped and well disciplined with many of the officers and SNCOs trained at the Jungle Warfare School (JWS) in Malaya by the British. Others, particularly the special forces, had been trained by American advisors in the past. The forward troops were supported by artillery and medium mortars as well as having a variety of anti-personnel mines at their disposal. The Borneo campaign was the first British campaign since the Second World War which was run without conscripts and employed only regular troops.

On 19 December 1962 Major General Walter Walker[342] was appointed Commander British Forces Borneo – or COMBRITBOR. Walker sat on the State Emergency Executive Committees established for Sarawak and Sabah as well as on the Sultan of Brunei's Advisory Council. He was also a member of the Malaysian National Defence Council and had complete authority in the theatre of actual operations. However, throughout the campaign Walker was to contend that his chief enemies were to be found among the 'top brass' at the Ministry of Defence. He considered that he was simultaneously fighting the Indonesians; the Clandestine Communist Organisation (CCO), who were the internal threat to Sarawak; and the Ministry of Defence, who he believed were pre-occupied with the British Army on the Rhine (BAOR) and were not providing him with the manpower and logistic resources he required.

Since Walker had only five battalions under his command, the only way to police the border was to set up a local surveillance network that could feed back information to him of Indonesian cross-border activity.

Unlike the earlier campaign in Malaya the major threat in Borneo was an external rather than internal one. This problem was compounded by the fact that the border between Indonesia and the territories of British North Borneo and Sarawak stretched for almost a thousand miles over some of the wildest country imaginable, where only the rivers offered some means of communication.

The immensely long border needed watching. On small-scale mapping it was easy to see where the border ran, but on the larger-scale maps there were large areas with nothing marked but what was visible from the air: mountain peaks and ridges, and rivers wide enough to divide the trees. Where it was mountainous the frontier usually followed the watershed between the Kalimantan and British river systems, thus recognising the jungle way of life in which rivers are the arteries of trade and communications with communities living near them. The Indonesians could come across the border almost anywhere, concealed on the ground from but a few yards away by the thick jungle and completely from aerial observation.

Involvement of the SAS

After the success of the Jebel Akhdar campaign, and to a lesser degree the operations in South Arabia, despite being cut back from four to two squadrons, the SAS had not been idle. The importance of language training, which had become apparent in Malaya, had been reinforced by these recent conflicts. Also, the SAS had been fostering closer relationships with the American special forces. This was an initiative driven by the commanding officer – once again the value of the personal lobbying and input by an SAS commanding officer was paying dividends:

> There was a very important visit that the 22 SAS made to American Special Forces at Fort Bragg in the Autumn of 1962 and we had the benefit of major exercises with US Special Forces, against 101 Airborne Division, or parts of it, in the Appalachians, mainly in North Carolina and Tennessee, and the visit was impor-tant because we learnt a great deal from the Americans – I hope they learnt something from us – but we learnt an enormous amount about guerrilla support operations.[343]

As Walker took charge in Borneo, JW, who had played a pivotal role with the early SAS in Malaya, was the SAS commanding officer and waited in Hereford for a call to join what seemed a promising affray. Once again, we see that a driving SAS personality was necessary for the SAS to become involved in a conflict, not as a result of a politi-cal or defence policy decision. This was apparent in Malaya with Calvert and JW; in Oman with Deane-Drummond; and the Radfan with DLB. When the SAS received no communications about events in the Far East, JW took it upon himself to call the War Office to find that, much to his amazement, the SAS had not even been considered, despite its readiness for instant deployment, its outstanding jungle experience, and its knowledge of the local *lingua franca* – Malay.

> The SAS was not written into any plans for war in Borneo and I went to London, at my request, to see the Director of Military Operations and pointed out politely and diffidently to him, that we had a very experienced jungle fighting anti-guerrilla force in 22 SAS.[344]

JW was determined to find a useful role for the SAS to play.

> [a] signal was sent to General Walter Walker, saying that the SAS was available. I took out one squadron and when he saw me and asked me what we could do, I told him, of course.[345]

One objective of Indonesian cross-border raids was the establishment of bases in East Malaysia that could then support and strengthen the CCO. Walker saw that his security forces would be hard pressed to contain a large-scale internal uprising if it occurred, and, if it did, the Indonesian army would be free to dominate the frontier and allow the CCO free rein behind it.

> Unable to deal a knockout blow to Indonesia because of the wider political ramifications and practical difficulties, yet committed to the Malaysians project as the linchpin in Britain's South East policy, the focus of British strategy was to maintain the pressure on Sukarno, denying him victories, in the hope that military failure would exacerbate internal divisions within Indonesia.[346]

Walker needed first-class intelligence which would enable him to achieve one of his objectives – that of 'dominating the jungle'. Dominating 900 miles of frontier with forces equivalent to six infantry battalions plus some local forces would be a daunting task. He could only operate wherever it mattered, and success would depend on knowing where that was. Accurate intelligence about the Indonesian military activities was therefore crucial.

Initially, Walker, who had heard of the SAS tree-jumping operations[347] when he served in Malaya, wanted to use the SAS as a reserve force that could be parachuted into the jungle to secure some of the larger jungle villages and airstrips which were vulnerable to Indonesian airborne assault.

JW diplomatically agreed with Walker in order to get an SAS squadron on the ground in Borneo. He informed Walker that the SAS could do the airstrip job, especially as it seemed that they were the only available unit trained to do so. JW did suggest that, perhaps, General Walker would also like to consider using the SAS on the frontier itself, where they could stay for long periods, get to know the locals and find out what the Indonesians were doing.

In January 1963, the first SAS unit into Borneo, A Squadron, was deployed under the command of Major QS.[348] The squadron flew to Singapore and then to Labuan Island, where they were kept as an emergency parachute force. This delay enabled JW to further advise General Walker on how the SAS might best be employed. This had to be done very tactfully, because JW had already learned that a Gurkha officer does not easily acknowledge that anyone can do anything better than Gurkhas. The Gurkhas provided the majority of soldiers in the campaign and, with Walker also being a Gurkha, there is justification in the frequent criticism that some deployments were based on the perception, by certain staff officers, that only the Gurkhas were good enough to deploy into 'busy' areas. Throughout the Borneo campaign some Gurkha units considered themselves to be more effective than the SAS.

In his autobiography Walker states:

> But their highly professional Commanding Officer, Lieutenant Colonel JW, persuaded me that if I was to dominate the jungle over such a long frontier, he suggested that I should give him the role of deploying the SAS into four-man patrols on the frontier itself, where they could stay for long periods. I had no hesitation in agreeing one hundred per cent with JW's proposal, for it fulfilled four of the six ingredients of success that I had already promulgated, namely: unified operations; timely and accurate information, which meant a first-class intelligence machine; speed, mobility and flexibility; and hearts and minds, namely winning the local people's trust, confidence and respect.[349]

Also, Walker knew that, despite his best effort, his forces might not detect every incursion but, with good intelligence, it would cost the intruders dearly when they returned across the border to their base camps.

Two civilians who knew the borders, and their tribes, better than most were assisting Walker: JWA, a police officer in Sabah, and TH, the world-famous anthropologist. Both had parachuted into Japanese-occupied Borneo[350] in the Second World War and per-suaded the people to resume their ancient, though latterly discour-aged, practice of taking heads.[351] TH's knowledge of the interior was the key to stopping enemy access into Kalimantan. He and his Kelabit tribespeople knew all the trails, for they had used them when fighting the Japanese. A man of strong personality and opin-ions, TH initially had many arguments with Army officers who, he thought, were trying to fight an unconventional campaign with con-ventional tactics.[352]

In Borneo, responsibility had originally been divided between three brigades: West, Central and East. It was decided to break West Brigade into two: West and Mid-West. The brigade fronts then extended 181, 442, 267 and 81 miles. The main battle area, how-ever, continued to be the First and Second Divisions with their correspondingly greater concentration of security forces.

As always, the SAS was thin on the ground and it was important to place them where they could do most good, which was in the First and Second Divisions of Sarawak, where the Indonesian threat and British vulnerability were greatest. Kuching, the capital, was about 25 miles from the border, which was crossed by numerous trade routes with easy access from both sides. Much of the land was cleared for cultivation, making possible the deployment of major military formations. Half the country's entire population was con-centrated there, including many Chinese of whom a substantial pro-portion were, undoubtedly, members of the CCO – a source of dissent within the region.

The First Division, at the western end of Sarawak and strategi-cally the most important of all, was monitored by a troop of 16 SAS men who watched a length of the border equivalent to the English border with Wales. This amounted to six miles per man although in practice the 16 men divided into four patrols about 25 miles apart, with about 25 villages to each.

In April 1963, A Squadron was relieved by the only other SAS sub-unit, D Squadron, and General Walker was complimentary when they left the region.

I should like to congratulate you on your excellent performance.
You have been deployed in your classic role over a 900 mile front
to provide me with my eyes and ears. Above all the work of
your signallers and medical orderlies has been quite outstanding
and they have made a significant contribution both to our intelligence sources and to our efforts to win the support and loyalty
of the tribes.[353]

A number of SAS officers and NCOs were seconded to train the
irregular force, to be called the Border Scouts[354] (also used during
the Malayan Emergency). The importance of such schemes had
been reinforced by the training the SAS had carried out with the US
special forces two years previously. Once trained, the Border Scouts
assisted in border surveillance. Gradually this scheme spread
throughout Sarawak and then Sabah. A few Border Scouts were
added to each SAS patrol, thus enlarging the area they could cover
and greatly improving communications with the local villagers.
Between 17 May and 28 June 1963, some 300 Border Scouts were
recruited, equipped, trained and deployed. In July 1963, the Border
Scouts' training was delegated to the Gurkha Independent Parachute
Company under command of Major John Cross.[355] However, JW
had some concerns about this training:

The one concern I had was that some were trained by the
Gurkhas and some by the SAS, and I said to Walter Walker that
I think there is always a risk when the British Army starts training irregulars that they will start off by training them to slope
arms and form fours and keeping step on the march and this
should not be the approach we have with the Border Scouts.[356]

On 16 September, 1963, the ruler of Malaya, Tunku Abdul Rahman,
created Malaysia, thus preserving the Commonwealth grouping of
Malay and Singapore and the Borneo Territories of Sabah and
Sarawak as a viable political, economic and defensible unit. Only
Brunei chose not to join, preferring to remain a British Protectorate.
It was economically viable with oil revenues, but cooperated whole-
heartedly in resisting Confrontation.[357]

The British saw this union as a stabilising force in Southeast
Asia, but Indonesia denounced it as a neo-imperialist organisation.
Indonesian reaction was immediate and violent: the Indonesian government refused to recognise Malaysia and, in Jakarta, mobs sacked
the British Embassy. Malaysia broke off diplomatic relations with

both Indonesia and the Philippines, who were supporting the Indonesian aspirations. Along the frontier separating Sarawak and Sabah from Kalimantan, Indonesian guerrillas started to increase their border raids.

Walker reviewed the military situation and, with a little prompting by JW, considered the redeployment of the SAS in the changing operational environment. The deployment of the SAS still remained at the tactical level with little or no political involvement in their utilisation.

> When I was in a position to expand and extend the tri-Service operations, the time came when there was less need for the SAS on the British side of the frontier. It was JW who was quick to suggest to me that the correct deployment of his SAS was now on the Indonesian side of the border where, he said, they could harass the enemy and disrupt incursions before they started.[358]

Also, Walker, based on his previous jungle experience, insisted on as many helicopters as there were available. He knew that they would change the form of modern jungle operations. The utility of helicopters for flying patrols, resupply and, later in the campaign, artillery pieces, provided Walker with a force multiplier not available, in any quantity, to the opposition. Ironically, on 4 May, a helicopter crash killed Major Ronald Norman MBE MC, Second-in-Command of the SAS Regiment, and Major Harry Thompson MC, who had won his MC as a squadron commander in the Malayan Emergency. Thompson had been earmarked to take command of the regiment from JW at the end of 1964.

> In Borneo in May 1963 when I had been in command less than a year, the second in command and the O.C. headquarters squadron were both killed in the helicopter crash together with Cpl Murphy, signaller and, [the] head of SIS [Security Intelligence Services] in Singapore, incidentally.[359]

Walker, increasingly conscious of the value of the SAS patrols as a 'screen' in front of the main line of forts and defended posts, sought a third SAS squadron to join the conflict.

> He [Walker] continued to press strongly for a third squadron to be formed, but that would take time. The limitless Borneo

frontier could absorb more SAS or SAS-type men than would ever be available, so it was also decided to train the Guards Independent Parachute Company in the SAS jungle role, with the wild Third Division particularly in mind. Later, the Gurkha Independent Parachute Company too was retrained and added to the strength [of 'SAS-type' forces].[360]

In 1963 it was known that the Indonesians were building up their strength, but, at this stage, the SAS was not allowed to carry out offensive operations. There were, however, contacts with enemy troops. In one of these contacts an SAS soldier was captured by the Indonesians.

It was established later that the Indonesian soldiers had captured Trooper PC, interrogated him and then killed him.[361] The tragedy of PC's death does not explain the poor skills of this patrol. JW had the following observations on these poor skills.

> Overconfidence, the lack of contact for days and weeks on end made all of us, the SAS included, tend to be a little careless of danger.[362] ... but of course they [the SAS] are not infallible and no doubt individuals went and continued to make mistakes on occasions.[363]

This was the major engagement of D Squadron's tour but their tour was extended by two months until June 1964. This length of tour, six months, was considered too long and was not repeated.

> We are now convinced that about 4 months is the longest they should be asked to live under the conditions they meet in BORNEO.[364]

The new Regimental second-in-command, was MWG. He had never served in the SAS before but had an excellent record from the Second World War. He successfully completed the SAS selection aged 42 and joined the Regiment in Borneo. JW was very conscious of the necessity of networking within the Army and within the Services, and he welcomed MWG's urbane skills.

> I was confident that he would be a suitable person to [be] C.O. and he hadn't served in the Special Forces but the fact that he served with me for the best part of a year I think – a year and a

bit. I was never staff trained and therefore I had no, or very few, contacts in the military hierarchy in the War Office or places like that through not having been to Staff College where naturally there 40 or 50 other officers who you came across in the rest of your service, and he had very good contacts and was a big advantage taking over from me.[365]

In early 1964, JW was given permission to establish another squadron. This would be B Squadron, which had been disbanded after Malaya five years earlier. Major JWT was to be the squadron commander.

In August 1964, the Indonesians escalated their campaign, intensifying their incursions and attacks along the Sarawak border and launching sea and airborne attacks on the Malayan mainland. These mainland attacks were unsuccessful, but deprived the Director of Operations of reinforcements which would otherwise have been available to him. By now the Indonesians were deploying units of their regular forces, which were well equipped and highly trained. However, by use of intelligence obtained from the border tribes, the British forces succeeded in remaining one jump ahead of the Indonesians and thus continued to dominate the areas in which they operated. British foreign policy remained an avoidance of escalating the situation.

A combination of military failure and time might open up many ways of encouraging Sukarno to terminate the conflict: a run-down on the Indonesian economy; cuts in the USA aid; pressure from the TNI; strife between the TNI and Indonesian communists; a Chinese-Soviet split that might make one or the other turn against Indonesian; the death of Sukarno; or the fragmentation of Indonesia because of the previous tensions.[366]

At the end of October, No. 1 (Guards) Independent Company completed its second tour of operations and left Borneo. During these tours the SAS had decided to form a Guards squadron from the Company and so they formed the nucleus of what subsequently became G Squadron. The manner in which G Squadron was raised still rankles within the SAS to this day.[367]

On the evening of 5 August 1964, the 1/2 Gurkhas at Long Pa Sia heard gunfire across the border. The nearest SAS patrol was ordered to investigate. Trooper BW, who was the lead scout[368] came across an Indonesian soldier silently cooking his food beside a tree. BW shot him dead and two of the other three members of the patrol, following their training, dropped their packs and ran to the rear of the contact. The Indonesians of about a platoon strength opened fire on the patrol. BW had remained shooting at the enemy and GS, an attached officer from the Australian SAS, stayed with him. BW received a fatal gunshot wound and GS tried to pull him into cover, but BW soon died. GS then withdrew to the RV. Somewhat surprisingly GS did not receive any recognition of his gallantry in attempting to save his British colleague. This may have been because the relationship between British SAS and Australian SAS in Borneo was not particularly congenial.

> I spent a week in Perth with the Australian SAS – I think it was more of a Commando. I remember watching an exercise, and their organisation was different to the British and New Zealand SAS – they seemed to operate differently. I think being Australian, if I may put it like that, they weren't going to be taught by the Poms [British].[369]

This particular contact led to more discussion within the SAS about the somewhat controversial, 'shoot and scoot' standard operational procedure (SOP), which instructed patrol members to drop their packs and immediately withdraw in the event of any contact with the enemy. This meant that, unless individuals could see their comrades, nobody really knew if anyone had been hurt in the contact or not. This policy was to minimise the possible effect of a four-man patrol meeting a much larger enemy force unexpectedly and becoming involved in a protracted and, potentially, unwinnable firefight.

> The whole business of operating in small parties might be suppressed because it was of course peace-time, and casualties would be known about in the national press, and throughout my time in the SAS, and particularly in Borneo. I was concerned that experience in Malaya where we attacked almost always when fired on because the almost certain result was the flight of the terrorists because they – I talked to many deserters in my time there, and their instructions on contacts were to break off and reform – they were not instructed to go into a pitch battle with regular forces because they would have been very silly if they had. But that had a hangover in Borneo in that I produced a controversial policy called 'Shoot and Scoot', and I did this because

I was concerned that when a contact was made we should not automatically go into the attack – whoever is commanding the four man patrol would have to consider scooting, [that is] breaking off and running away.[370]

JW's 'shoot and scoot' policy had been instituted to save life, so that only a few patrol members would be exposed to enemy gunfire. This incident forced JW to rethink his tactics to ensure that SAS dead or wounded were never abandoned.

This was not in the natural spirit of the soldiers of the day, of the time, and it may have contributed to the death of Trooper BW – I don't know that it did but it might have because the patrol broke off when he was shot through the vein and went to the R.V. which would have been (I don't remember) but probably about an hour away, and it meant, that it was never intended to mean, that a wounded soldier should be left and not fought for, so to speak.[371]

The aggressive training and firepower of an SAS patrol should be used to, at least, dominate the initial firefight before withdrawing. Even in an ambush, a vigorous aggressive response will create a sufficient break to enable a small group of men to withdraw quickly, in good order. The author feels that, despite the need for an SAS patrol to remain clandestine, JW's original policy of immediate 'scoot' before any 'shoot' was flawed. A patrol commander's dilemma was whether to leave a possibly wounded man to die or be captured or lose more lives by trying to save him. Later, JW, deeply concerned at the possible back-firing of his principle – wrote to his subordinate commanders:

I believe troops will welcome, and morale that demands, an order that if a man is known to have fallen the patrol will remain in the close vicinity until either they see for certain that he is dead or they recover him alive. I think we should expect to fight to the death for this.[372]

Operation CLARET

While the Indonesians were not finding much support among the local population, however, it was not possible to do more against them unless authority was given to cross the international frontier. This was authorised as a result of Malaysian pressure on the British government in March 1964. The government approved limited cross-border operations up to a depth of five thousand yards inside Kalimantan. There was to be no public announcement; indeed the operations were to be carried out with maximum secrecy.

These operations were to be given the code-name of 'CLARET',[373] and were to be governed by what came to be known as Walker's 'Golden Rules'. Any 'CLARET' operations into Indonesian territory from August 1964 had to be personally sanctioned by Walker. Any temptation to attack Indonesian military bases was resisted by Walker, who believed that major cross-border attacks would defeat their own purpose by forcing the Indonesians to retaliate in like manner, so escalating the war even further. In 1975, Walker stated that:

> Britain could not afford to forget the art of hitting an enemy hard by methods which neither escalate the war nor invite United Nations anti-colonialist intervention.[374]

Walker decided that the first troops to be used to support the SAS in CLARET operations would be Gurkhas; he considered that they were the most experienced in jungle fighting. Walker had been with the Gurkhas throughout his military career and his preference for them on operations was clear throughout the Borneo campaign.

To ensure that the border crossings were clandestine, SAS carried the US Armalite 5.56mm rifles, which were not then issued to the British Army, wore non-regulation boots and carried no personal identification.

> What was a concern was that they [the Indonesians] should capture or kill a soldier with identification on him.[375]

The first CLARET operations were virtually extensions of routine patrolling. It is doubtful whether the Indonesians even realised that they were seeing the beginnings of a new strategy. This was partly because the new series of actions took place so near to the frontier which was, in any case, so loosely defined and partly because their own communications and staff structure were far less able to cope with a flow of reports, and in assessing them, than were the British.

> The role of force was therefore to ensure that the military dimension of confrontation would not succeed. Britain aimed to avoid,

as far as possible, actions that would increase resentment on the part of the Indonesians, and to make it clear that Britain did not seek a war with Indonesia or to inflict a comprehensive military defeat.[376]

During this time, the SAS initiated the abortive Operation VIPER. Operation VIPER was based upon US practice in South Vietnam and involved the deployment of mechanical ambushes using Claymore mines and other explosives along likely infiltration routes. There was one false alarm when some wild pigs were killed by one of the ambushes, involving the deployment of SAS and Gurkha follow-up forces by helicopters. Despite a great deal of time and energy expended over many months, none of these ambushes was successful.

Inevitably, despite Walker's tight control of cross-border operations, there continued to be communication problems.

> Unbeknown to us at the time, the SAS was also ambushing close by and another group had ambushed two boat-loads elsewhere on the Sentimo [River] shortly before we got into ambush. As a result of all this activity the Indonesians were clearly determined to clear the area before trying to use the river again. Whether their clearance operation that led to our engagement was prompted by SAS activity or whether they had seen us the previous day we shall never know. Either way we and the SAS should have been coordinated rather more carefully.[377]

By the end of 1964, there were 54,000 British and Commonwealth troops in Southeast Asia, and 30,000 of these were committed to the Confrontation. This was the largest British military operation since the Second World War. The provision of these numbers of troops, which put a major strain on the provision of Britain's military reserves, led Prime Minister Harold Wilson to comment that if there had been one further call for forces for Borneo the Trooping of the Colour would have to be cancelled.[378]

In December 1964 General Walker had a long-held belief that the Indonesians were planning a major thrust and enhanced the deterrent effect of his troops by mounting CLARET strikes to an increased depth of 10,000 yards. Neither Walker nor the SAS appears to have sought strategic targets to attack, or threaten to attack, in the event of a major escalation of the conflict. SAS operations remained very much at the tactical level.

The SAS command situation, however, was somewhat of an anomaly.

> The SAS was in support of brigades under command of the theatre commander and the same happened in Borneo – 99 Brigade which was 500 miles from headquarters from Borneo and Brunei down in Sarawak, Kuching, the SAS was in support. Sometimes we just had the liaison officer to go to H.Q. with a signalman. In fact, I think we usually had a signaller and LO at brigade H.Q. to co-ordinate. I think they were a bit loose in that, but obviously there was a bit of give and take, and if the brigade wanted the SAS to do something in particular, they could ask.[379]

The infantry was taking care of border surveillance and 'hearts and minds' operations, working from jungle forts close up to the frontier, and constantly patrolling the area with greater numbers and higher frequency than the SAS could ever have managed. Some infantry officers, but particularly those of the Gurkhas, by no means conceded the SAS could achieve any more than their own men.

In January 1965, Lieutenant Colonel JW was replaced by MWG who took over the SAS. JW left the military soon after, but remained in touch with Walker.[380]

In January 1965, the British forces were supplemented by troops from Australia and in February by troops from New Zealand. Australian and New Zealand troops, which included SAS personnel, remained in Borneo until August 1966 and September 1966 respectively.

March 1965, saw the end of General Walker's tour as Director of Borneo Operations. Walker left Borneo under a cloud, not because of this performance during the Confrontation but because of his efforts to save Gurkha battalions that were being disbanded.[381]

The new Director of Borneo Operations was Major General George Lea,[382] who had commanded 22 SAS in Malaya from 1955–57. By the time he took over, the border guerrillas had virtually been destroyed, and he was faced with a war on more conventional lines. It was clear that Confrontation had reached its final stages. The Indonesian commanders had more or less discarded guerrilla tactics and were launching their regulars in conventional attacks on the Security Forces' border positions. It was Lea's task to ensure that the Indonesian Army incursions were broken on the border, and beyond it, and that the conflict did not escalate into a total war. He also had to make certain that a tight grip was still maintained on internal security.

The SAS task was expanding. Three independent parachute companies were watching the border in the less sensitive areas, half a squadron of New Zealand SAS was training in Brunei to take the field in April 1965, and the Australian 1st SAS Squadron would do the same in May. A small SAS headquarters had been set up on Labun Island near the Director of Operations with either MWG or his second-in-command, JS, in charge. MWG asked General Lea and his principal staff officer Anthony Farrar-Hockley whether the SAS might take more offensive action. General Lea agreed, but reconnaissance was still the main task with only the last two days of a patrol permitting offensive action.[383]

In April 1965, an event took place which could have had a strategic impact upon the progress of the conflict and provided a major morale boost for the British and Commonwealth forces. On 9 April a patrol, commanded by Sgt LL,[384] had as its task an ambush on the Koemba River. Several previous attempts had been foiled previously by large swamp areas. LL's patrol eventually reached the river and set up an ambush. The river was very busy and at one stage a luxury motor yacht about 45 foot long came into the area. At the stern was the red and white flag of Indonesia and on a short mast above the bridge another banner which seemed to indicate that senior officers were on board this boat. LL chose not to attack this boat because he saw a woman on board, stating that the British Army does not make war on women.[385] It was later confirmed that on board the boat was Colonel Moerdani,[386] who was commanding the Indonesian Parachute Regiment. Apparently, LL was also concerned that the boat would contain a civil VIP and this could cause some political embarrassment to the British government.[387] Eventually the patrol did later ambush a 44-foot boat and kill a number of Indonesians.

Asked about the incident, JW makes some interesting observations.

> Yes – he [LL] would have hit the ace of spades. We were not afraid of political repercussions because it was considered, at the time, that it was very unlikely that they [the Indonesians] would raise a complaint at the UN, or something like that, that British troops had invaded the Indonesian territory because to do so would have reflected badly on their claims that they were taking over North Borneo.[388]

In May 1965, A Squadron returned to Borneo still under command of Major DLB. Early in this tour, DLB linked up with Lieutenant Colonel NN and his 2/2 Gurkhas. They both wanted the local commander, Brigadier Cheyne, to let them carry out more offensive patrols. The tasking of SAS patrols at this low level, brigade level, demonstrated a lack of awareness of the strategic importance of the SAS, as opposed to tactical-level operations which could, and were, being carried out by conventional infantry.

NN had an aggressive reputation[389] and this may have been why DLB had been drawn to him.

> He commanded a company of 2nd Gurkhas in the vicious fighting against the Japanese in the Arakan campaign in Burma and again throughout the long Malayan Emergency.[390]

NN enjoyed working with the SAS:

> Of all *British soldiers* [sic] I rate them the highest.[391]

This was indeed praise from a Gurkha, even with the qualification 'British'. Gurkhas, to a Gurkha officer, are not comparable with anyone else.[392]

The SAS had fallen into the trap of getting involved in operations at the wrong level and starting to operate as conventional infantry. The next 'combined' operation between NN and DLB, Operation HELLFIRE, did not go particularly well and highlighted some internal SAS command and control issues.[393] As it was, in October 1964, JW found it necessary to chastise DLB.

> I have no objection to you going once on a 'special op' [i.e. a cross-border patrol], but it is quite wrong for you to do it more than once. Not necessary, and would be considered hogging the limelight or far worse gong-hunting [seeking medals], however pure your motives really are.[394]

It should be noted that the 2/2 Gurkhas and 22 SAS were not the only ones aggressively working the length of the Kalimantan border. Many battalions qualified for the honour and had achieved some notable successes: the Australian and New Zealand SAS performed just as effectively as the British, according to impartial observers of whom 22 SAS was not one. The SAS-trained Para companies had been hard at work too, though mostly restricted to border surveillance in wild areas.

In August 1965 Soekarno fell ill and was expected to die. The Indonesian Communists saw their chance and stepped up their preparations for seizing power with a purge of right-wing politicians. At the same time Tunku Abdul Rahman expelled Singapore from the Federation, fearing that the thrusting Chinese would dominate the easy-going Malays in their own country. Southeast Asia wondered anxiously whether Malaysia would fall apart and then be taken over piecemeal. If this happened it would seriously jeopardise Britain's role and position in Southeast Asia.

During 1966, intelligence warned of an imminent incursion from a place called Sentas across the border from Tebedu. Almost a full SAS squadron of 44 men, with numbers made up by New Zealand and Australian SAS, were tasked to carry out a pre-emptive strike.[395] This upset the 2/7 Gurkhas, whose operational area it was. The operation was a disaster and, not surprisingly, the 2/7 Gurkhas were convinced they could have done a better job. It had been an infantry rather than an SAS operation and was an example of the SAS wanting to 'get in on the action' when not the most appropriate troops for the task. This is not an isolated incident and occurs on other operations, such as the Falklands War. The Australian SAS had attached some NCOs to the SAS squadron for the operation but their commander observed:

> Their [the SAS] tasks should have been done by infantry so our chaps did not learn as much as expected ... we did not learn anything from B Squadron that wasn't known before.[396]

Later, Major TH took a squadron[397] and 19 Cross-Border Scouts to ambush the Bembab to Sawah track, which B Squadron had previously discovered. Unfortunately, the ambush was compromised.[398] These two squadron-sized aggressive operations were an embarrassing failure. One failed because of poor personal discipline by an individual, and the other failed due to poor intelligence and poor individual tactics. Towards the end the regiment was allowed to conduct a number of aggressive operations in squadron strength. Not all of these large operations were successfully executed, however, particularly when SAS troops were acting in an infantry role.

> ... was surprised to find that B Squadron [Feb 1966] appeared to have little idea how to operate as a normal infantry company as required during this operation.[399]

These results conflict with Hoe and Morris's flattering comments about large-scale SAS cross-border operations. B Squadron left Borneo in February 1966 and they were not replaced by 22 SAS. The field was left to the Australian and New Zealand SAS.

> By December 1965, two combined plans for the defence of East and West Malaysia and Singapore were drafted in case of a limited war with Indonesia. (Plans DAGGER and FABIAN).[400] If confrontation continued in the longer term then thought would have to be given to increasing military pressure through 'cross-border and other special operations' and to the possible needs to provoke the Indonesians into actions which could be used to justify higher-level military countermeasures.[401]

As time passed, the expansionist aims of the new Indonesian leader, Achmed Suharto, became less and less credible and the cost in casualties rose steadily. On 11 August 1966 the Indonesians signed a peace agreement with Malaysia, ending the war or Confrontation
    On 27 November 1967, Denis Healey, as the Secretary of State for Defence, delivered his oft-repeated statement in the House of Commons:

> When the House thinks of the tragedy that could have fallen on our whole corner of the continent if we had not been able to hold the situation and bring it to a successful termination, it will appreciate that in the history books it will be recorded as one of the most efficient uses of military force in the history the world.[402]

Conclusion

At the time of the first deployment to Borneo in January, 1963, the SAS regiment was down to two-squadron strength. Gradually there was a committal to a more offensive posture as cross-border forays were authorised. At the start, these operations were confined to close reconnaissance on enemy lines of communications and camps, but later they were expanded into a role where the SAS patrols would guide companies of Gurkha and British units into a variety of targets or ambush positions.
    These were deniable operations deliberately managed in such a way so as not to escalate the conflict, thereby forcing it into the

international arena which was, at this time, becoming increasingly occupied by developments in Vietnam.

In Borneo, the SAS was only being used in the tactical reconnaissance role which, although easily within their capabilities, was not entirely appropriate for the level of operational support and effort that an SAS patrol requires. Neither Walker nor Lea wanted to tie up resources by inserting small patrols which could not effectively defend themselves against the type of forces the Indonesians were deploying, but as that was inevitable in the role in which they were being used it was clearly a vicious circle. The only solution would be to insert larger, more aggressively armed patrols, thus losing the advantage of stealth that the SAS clearly possessed.

The deployment of the SAS, despite appearing to please Walker and extend his 'eyes and ears', did not fully utilise the full scope of skills and jungle experience that was available within the organisation. The SAS did assist, in a limited fashion, with the task of finding and fixing the enemy as well as carrying out observation and reconnaissance in the border areas and operating with the indigenous population. However, at no stage were the SAS tasked to carry out operations to attack the enemy's command and control facilities and thereby slow down the tempo of operations and damage their cohesion, nor were any sabotage activities carried out.

In Borneo, the SAS, whilst carrying out meaningful surveillance tasks and participating in occasional, less-than-successful, infantry-type operations, was not fully employed at the appropriate strategic level. This lack of flair and vision in the deployment of SAS is a re-occurring phenomenon and there are few examples of truly strategic utility in their use over the last fifty years.

> The campaign in Borneo was a small war by most standards – by those of Korea and Vietnam, a very small war. At peak strength there were only about 20,000 Commonwealth servicemen in Borneo, with another 10,000 immediately available. The service casualties for the whole period were 114 killed and 181 wounded. The civilians suffered 36 killed, 53 wounded, and 4 captured. The Indonesian forces [allegedly] lost at least 590 killed, 222 wounded, and 771 captured.[403]

The tasks carried out by the SAS in the Borneo campaign were based around short-range and medium-range reconnaissance patrols, and these could hardly be called strategic operations. Early in the campaign, conventional units, albeit paratroopers, were carrying out

the same tasks as the SAS. There seems to have been an unwillingness to provide the SAS with strategic tasks. This reason for this
could be that Walker had neither the vision nor the experience with
special forces to identify suitable military or political targets against
which to utilise the SAS.

When General Lea, who was a former SAS commander, replaced
Walker, the Indonesians, while still prepared to carry out occasional
aggressive cross-border patrols, were not going to carry out any
major military deployments. Lea pushed the Indonesians back from
the border and convinced the Indonesian Army that Confrontation
could not succeed. Since the illusion that there had been no war
had been maintained by both sides, it was easier for the Indonesians
to withdraw without losing too much face.

When SAS patrols combined with infantry units to carry out
attacks on Indonesian positions, particularly when DLB and Cross
worked together, there was a certain amount of success, but the
point remains that the organic reconnaissance elements of the
infantry should have been able to carry out those tasks themselves.
The SAS attack on the camp at Sentas was a failure and the SAS
group was forced to withdraw. The Gurkhas made it known that the
operation should have been carried out by Gurkha infantry troops
and not the SAS.

The Gurkhas played the major part in all aspects of the Borneo
campaign and, when Operation CLARET was approved it was only
the SAS and the Gurkhas who were permitted to carry out the cross-
border excursions. The predominance of Gurkhas, both on the
ground and in the command structures made it inevitable that they
would received the lion's share of the work. However, the extremely
limited media coverage of the campaign certainly meant that Britain
did not have to display to a world audience the operations of the
SAS. It also did not have to expose the fact that the majority of
operations carried out, and the containment of the Indonesian
threat in Borneo, were mainly due to Gurkha 'mercenaries' and not
Britain's own regular soldiers.

The original deployment of the SAS resulted from tenacious lobbying by the SAS commander, JW. Walker, when reminded that he
could have the SAS included on his strength, showed little initiative
in tasking them. He wanted them to be able to parachute into airfields and helicopter landing zones to either deny them to or recover
them from the Indonesians. This was a task that could have been
given to a regular parachute unit. It was only when JW, again lobbying, explained the benefits of having SAS patrols deployed forward

of the main troop positions that Walker started to use them effectively. But it was hardly making the best use of the potential of such a force. In South Vietnam, after Borneo, the Australian and NZ special forces were deployed on similar, medium reconnaissance tasks in the ANZAC task force area.

> Small, precise but deadly pinpricks were required, and the SAS was ideally equipped for such tasks.[404]

Again, these were hardly strategic operations and could have been carried out by infantry or airborne reconnaissance units. At one stage, in 1971, the Australian task force commander, Brigadier SP, became so frustrated with having to use his valuable air assets to deploy and then, almost immediately, have to recover SAS patrols that had bumped into enemy troops that he questioned their value to him at all.[405]

The question that must be asked is whether the SAS was needed in Borneo at all. The short to medium reconnaissance tasks they were given could, not unreasonably, have been given to conventional troops. The SAS could have provided training teams to assist in the preparation of these other units, as they initially did with the Border Scouts, but they did not have to deploy themselves. The SAS are defined as strategic resources in British Army doctrine but there are few examples when they have been provided with strategic tasks. In Borneo, as in most of the conflicts in this book, the SAS deployment was as a result of strong lobbying by the SAS, not because of an identified operational need. A counter-argument could be that if the SAS did not lobby then they may not have been used at all. But, if the SAS, a national strategic asset, relies on its (relatively junior) commanding officer to decide which operations it is to become involved in, then this unique force is surely being misemployed.

Even in 1965, the SAS was still relatively unknown within military circles and this may be the reason for its initial omission from the Borneo order of battle. In Borneo, as in Malaya, once the SAS was used, whether at the correct level or not, there was a requirement for additional troops to do the same job. There were five additional organisations that worked alongside 22 SAS carrying out similar operations in Borneo;[406] only the Australian and New Zealand SAS units remained intact. The others were disbanded or, in the case of the Guards, absorbed to make 'G' Squadron in 22 SAS.

Small numbers of SBS were deployed in Borneo and were tasked to carry out a number of coastal reconnaissance missions and small raids. These had negligible impact on the prosecution of the campaign.

In assessing the effectiveness of the SAS in Borneo, it is again useful to use the simple tool of measuring return on investment. The SAS, at the same time as Borneo, were also involved in pointless operations in South Arabia. They were trying to achieve too much. Again, this may have been a case of ensuring their profile was sufficiently high enough to ensure survival in the next, inevitable, rash of disbandments. The circumstances surrounding the killing of RE and NW in the Radfan negated any psychological benefit gained from the SAS deployment in South Arabia whereas, in Borneo, the covert nature of SAS cross-border operations meant that few in the military and political circles knew what they were doing and the general public were in complete ignorance. If the Indonesians had made serious conventional, or even Special Force, incursions into Borneo or Malaya, then there would have been a definite need for pre-emptive or post-event strategic responses by SAS troops, but Confrontation, as the name implies, was more a case of political posturing and military games of lethal hide and seek. If the SAS had not been available, then conventional forces from specialist units, such as the Paras, would have carried out the necessary short and medium reconnaissance tasks. The SAS could have been retained for deployment against Indonesian high-value strategic assets.

By 1963 Britain's political interest in matters east of Suez had greatly waned. Her military presence failed to deter Indonesia, and the end of the fighting came about principally as a result of internal changes in that country and was only marginally related to the progress of the small war in Borneo. Moreover, since the end of the Borneo campaign was followed in less than two years by a final decision to abandon the east-of-Suez posture, the total effort seemed to have been expended on a fulfilment of an anachronistic obligation rather than on a reinforcement of dispositions for the future.

> Even a well crafted COIN campaign is not a silver bullet if the strategic level policy is flawed.[407]

In a very telling, but less than flattering, comment, Colonel Farrar-Hockley, Chief of Staff on Walker's HQ in Borneo, when asked about SAS operations, said:

> They did a useful job but it was pretty small beer you know![408]

Chapter 8

BACK TO THE DESERT: OMAN – OPERATION STORM – THE DHOFAR WAR

... this campaign may go down in history as the most important and far-reaching ever fought by the SAS. Our [SAS] involvement in Oman, lasting more than four years, rolled back and finally dissipated the tide of Communism which threatened to overwhelm southern Arabia. In shaping this campaign, the SAS should be credited with great military and political foresight.[409]

Background

Following the British withdrawal from Aden and the winding down of the Borneo campaign, 22 SAS was without an operational commitment. JS[410] had replaced MWG as CO, and under his direction and command the unit continued to hone its skills. In 1967, the Guards Independent Parachute Company returned to Britain from Borneo, and after passing selection many of its members were formally incorporated into the SAS as G Squadron.[411] This brought the regiment back up to its full strength of four 'sabre' squadrons and provided valuable extra manpower. The British Empire had practically ceased to exist at this stage, but there were still threats to Britain's vital interests in the South Arabian Peninsula, which would embroil elements of the SAS in some six years of an undeclared war back in Oman, but this time in Dhofar, in the south of the country. Oman, as it had been in 1958 when the SAS was involved in attacking the insurgents on the Jebel Akhdar, remained an absolute monarchy.

Omani Jebalis (jebel – mountain) dancing at the celebration of a wedding in Dhofar, Oman.

> I think it is questionable who was the best organisation to support, whether it was the Sultan [Said bin Taimur] or the terrorist organisation.[412]

The Sultanate, through the detached Musandam Peninsula, commands the southern side of the Straits of Hormuz, through which passes about over 50 per cent of the world's supply of crude oil. Successive British governments, concluding that the protection of these straits is vital to the British economy and matching this to the desire by successive Sultans to rely on British soldiers for their security, formed a delicate synergy. Since the days when Oman owned Zanzibar, Britain has assisted in defending Oman against piracy, then against internal revolt and then, later, against threats from Yemen, Iran and Saudi Arabia.

A similar political interdependence has characterised the involvement of the SAS in Oman. The regiment has fought two successful campaigns there: the first lasting a few months in the winter of 1958/59; the second, a six-year war which ended with the government's victory of 1976. On the first occasion, the regiment, having only served in Malaya since being re-established after the Second World War, was under pressure to prove that it could function, as it claimed, at short notice outside its traditional jungle environment. The second Oman campaign began in 1969, at a time when the SAS had no operational commitments and its usefulness, once again, was being questioned.

In 1969, British Intelligence sources reported that an Iran-trained guerrilla training team had started work among the primitive Shihoo tribesmen of the sensitive Musandam Peninsula. In a brief, inauspicious campaign, a squadron of SAS soldiers was landed on the peninsula by inflatable boats from the Royal Marine Special Boat Service (SBS). Unfortunately, the force landed at the wrong beach, completely confusing the locals and themselves. During the overall operation, one suspect was shot and wounded and one SAS soldier, Trooper 'Rip' Reddy, was killed during a night freefall parachute descent into the area.[413]

Meanwhile, in Dhofar, 1,000 kilometres away, on the border with Marxist South Yemen (PDRY), the Sultan's dictatorial regime had provoked a Communist-led guerrilla war which was seriously threatening his regime. Even within Oman, Dhofar is a far away region of which the majority northern population knows little. It is a hostile mountain area separated from the rest of the Sultanate by 400 miles of desert. It lies between the sand, seas and gravel deserts of the Empty Quarter and the Arabian Sea, sandwiched politically between Saudi Arabia to the west and the PDRY. It has mountains with 4,000-foot peaks on an escarpment that rises steeply from the narrow coastal plains surrounding the capital of Salalah. In June to September, the monsoon, known as the *khareef*, rolls from the sea up onto the hills. This brings a wet mist that lingers for three months at a time turning the hills from a parched brown to a luxurious green. As a result, at that time of the year the Jebel plateau becomes almost a jungle and its deep *wadis* (ravines) are covered by thick undergrowth.

The Dhofaris of the *jebel* (mountain), or Jebalis, are an intolerant, fiercely independent hill people who are nomadic farmers moving with meagre herds of cattle, goats and camels from one scant grazing ground to another. It is a society in which a rifle and a curved dagger, the *kunja*, are carried for status as well as for protection. The Omani villages are normally small, rock-protected areas in the vicinity of a water source.

The isolated and mountainous Dhofar had been even more neglected than the rest of the country by Said bin Taimur, who had little interest in using his growing oil revenues for the well-being of his people. In 1969, some five years after oil had been discovered in

An aerial photograph of the small Dhofar fishing village of Marbat taken before the SAS/Omani pitched battle with the communist *adoo* (enemy) in July 1972.

commercial quantities, there were no hospitals in Dhofar, and only one road out of the coastal plain. Almost all foreign goods were forbidden and Omanis were prohibited from dancing, playing 'foreign' music, smoking, wearing sun-glasses, taking photographs or wearing Western clothes. The penalties for disobedience were either flogging or imprisonment in ancient stone castles. The formerly fertile plains of Salalah, which during the First World War had provided feed for the British and Colonial mounted forces of the army of Mesopotamia, were desolate and dust-blown as a result of wells having been punitively destroyed on the orders of the Sultan.

There were no schools in Dhofar, so Dhofaris who wished to study were obliged to become political exiles. Communist countries were only too willing to host Omani students and so some went to Russia and East Germany while others went to Egypt and elsewhere in the Middle East.

Across the border in Aden and South Yemen, left-wing Arab Nationalists had been engaged in a very successful terrorist campaign against the British since 1963 and it was very likely that the Oman regime would be a fertile ground for insurrection. Fuelled by both Arab nationalism and socialism, Omani exiles founded the

Dhofar Liberation Front (DLF) in the early 1960s. On 9 June 1965, in the mountainous hinterland, Dhofari tribesmen, trained in Yemen, started a sporadic campaign of armed ambush, mine-laying and assassination of government officials.

The Dhofari tribesmen,[414] who regarded themselves as separate from the rest of Oman, were staunch Muslims. They had, however, established the DLF party as a backing for their rebellion. At the same time, over the border in Yemen, another movement was born, the Popular Front for the Liberation of Oman (PFLO),[415] which was essentially Marxist and strongly backed by the Soviet bloc. At first, the tribal leaders were seduced by money and arms promised to them in exchange for an alliance with the PFLO, but soon discovered that they were no match for the highly motivated young revolutionaries who were determined to destroy the ancient feudal tribal structure – prayers were forbidden and detractors were executed.

Not surprisingly, as the despotic regime continued, opposition to Said prospered, and in 1966 he was the target of an assassination attempt by his own bodyguard, several of whom fired at him from a range of a few feet, and missed, while he was inspecting them.[416]

In November 1967, a year after Said's bodyguard had tried to kill him, the British left neighbouring Aden. The hinterland bordering Dhofar then became a battleground for two warring factions within what was South Yemen. It was clear that Said's opponents in the mountains would soon have more room for manoeuvre once the British had departed from Aden. If a guerrilla campaign is to succeed, a sanctuary and a secure source of war materials, preferably near the war zone, must be established. Clearly, the rebels would soon have just this. The war would be lost if something were not done to change Said's disastrous conduct of affairs. This change occurred soon after the election of Edward Heath's Conservative government in June 1970.

The Wilson government of 1970 had announced that there would be a British withdrawal from the Arabian Gulf at the end of 1971, while the Conservative government which followed it was less inhibited about dabbling in the affairs of other states. Both the FO and the Ministry of Defence were worried about an unstable situation in Oman which could prejudice the smooth withdrawal from the Gulf in the following year and affect the security of oil through the Straits of Hormuz. So it was in 1971 that the British government felt impelled to become involved again in Oman, but, as in 1958, only insofar as offering 'discreet help' to Sultan Said bin Taimur. The 1971 Defence White Paper stated that Army personnel

An aerial photo of the fort at Marbat. This fort was successfully defended
against some 250 communist attackers by a small group of Omanis and
SAS in 1972.

on loan to the Sultan of Oman's Armed Forces (SAF) were involved
in operations against the rebels in Dhofar but without any reference
to the SAS.[417]

Lt Col JWT,[418] the new commanding officer of 22 SAS
Regiment, had an interest in Oman from the days of the Jebel
Akhdar campaign and in mid-1971, it appears, obtained clearance
from the DMO in the MoD, and went out to review the situation in
Dhofar.[419] JWT had a great deal of experience in low intensity
counter-insurgency operations and could see the potential for insurgency spilling over into Southern Oman from South Yemen. As well
as on the Jebel Akhdar he had served in Malaya and in Borneo and
knew that any successful counter-insurgency operation needs both a
military and a political strategy. He was adamant that there was a
need for a national aim that would remove the roots of dissatisfac-
tion. He had also identified the need for good intelligence on the
enemy, which at the beginning of the campaign was sadly lacking.
He had also identified that there was enough evidence to show that
many of the original Muslim rebels on the Jebel did not like the
communist indoctrination and repression of their religion. A number
of original rebels wanted to defect. He proposed that these defectors

should be trained and armed to fight against their former colleagues. On the 'hearts and minds' front there was a need for civil action (CAT) and medical teams to improve the health and level of hygiene among the Dhofaris. This strategy became known as the 'War on Five Fronts' strategy. However, Sultan Said had little interest in JWT's strategic philosophy, particularly as it involved providing modern arms to the Jebalis – something he would never accept.

With a very flexible brief from JWT, the ubiquitous Major DLB was sent to the Gulf to see what was happening:

> You can sit in Sharjah for a bit and see if anything's happening, he said. Scratch around, get your feet under the table, *and if something crops up, make sure we're in it.* [emphasis added][420]

On the afternoon of 23 July 1970, less than a month after Heath's election in Britain, Sheik Braik al-Ghafari, an Omani aristocrat and the Wali (Governor) of Dhofar province, entered the Salalah palace to demand the abdication of Sultan Said. It was an act of courage assisted by Sheik Braik's knowledge that the Sultan's son and heir, Qaboos (Sheik Braik's close friend) and key British officers in the administration were part of the plot. Some shots were fired, including some by the Sultan himself, wounding and killing some palace staff, but the Sultan agreed to surrender himself to a British colonel seconded to his armed forces, and abdicate. The RAF flew Said away to London, where he spent the last two years of his life in comfortable exile.

Within 24 hours of his coup, Qaboos began to establish a modern centralised administration, lifting all restrictions on movement within and outside the state, releasing political prisoners and announcing a development plan for the whole of Oman to provide education, housing, communications and medical facilities based on the increasing oil revenues. In the Dhofar itself, a Dhofar Development Committee was to supervise the expenditure of £218 million on roads, schools, clinics, mosques and wells between 1971 and 1975.

Involvement of the SAS

The removal of Sultan Said gave the SAS the chance for which it had been waiting. Within hours of the palace coup, JWT was given authority from the FCO (Foreign and Commonwealth Office), via the DMO's office, to despatch a small SAS team (officially an 'information team') to Salalah. This team provided a bodyguard for the new Sultan commanded by Captain XT.[421] Soon after, JWT also flew out to the capital, Salalah, accompanied by his operations officer. His immediate task was to provide a reliable interim bodyguard for the new Sultan and to make an assessment of the military situation and the needs of the population as a whole.

The change in the control of the country also meant there was a much more receptive political climate in which to expand upon the SAS's assessment of how to defeat the insurgents. 22 SAS planners expanded upon the operational strategy[422] originally prepared by JWT. His strategy was not new and utilised the principles of counter-insurgency warfare as defined by Robert Thompson.[423] Experiences in the Malayan Emergency, Confrontation in Borneo and observing the on-going Vietnam War had shown that a winning strategy involved shaping the perceptions and loyalty of the population at large. The plan for Operation STORM, as the SAS involvement was to be called, involved all the elements of basic counter-insurgency. The plan involved a coherent, discriminate military campaign run by soldiers supported by civilian specialists. As revised by JWT, the basic elements of the strategy were:

A generous and focused civil aid programme including:

the provision of that most scarce commodity, fresh water; a medical campaign to provide aid for the 50,000 or so people living in the Dhofar Mountains, most of whom were regarded by Salalah as enemies; and

a veterinary campaign to improve farm stock, as well as skilled advice about husbandry – the Dhofari society is based on primary produce.

A coherent Intelligence-gathering operation that would gather every scrap of knowledge about the opposition and aimed at identifying them, isolating them and breaking their morale; and to define military operations.

A psychological operation to persuade the rebels to change sides, the basic element of which was an offer of amnesty to tribesmen wishing to surrender and paying additional money for their own weapons as well as others to which they could direct the Government forces.[424]

The SAF, commanded by Brigadier JG, then consisted of a brigade of Arab soldiers led by British officers. The Sultan's officers, with the exception of a few Pakistanis and Arabs in junior grades, were British – serving under contract or seconded from the British Army. The other ranks were made up of Arabs and Baluch[425] in roughly equal numbers; however, as the war progressed, the proportion of Baluch subsequently increased to 70 per cent. The Air Force initially numbered a few transport aircraft and six Strikemaster jets, but gradually increased and soon included numbers of the ubiquitous Bell 'Huey' UH1H helicopter.

As part of the strategy of separating the insurgents from the population physical barriers of barbed wire and landmines were established to cut across PFLOAG (Popular Front for the Liberation of the Arabian Gulf) infiltration routes from the PDRY (People's Democratic Republic of Yemen). The SAF established the unmanned Leopard Line West of Salalah in December 1971 which, because it could not be observed, was not entirely successful. In April 1972, Operation SIMBA, initiated to establish a permanent base at Sarfait close to the Yemeni border at Hauf, ran into difficulties due to the terrain and lack of observation of crucial interdiction routes. Much more successful were the Hornbeam and Damavand lines in 1973–74 and 1975, respectively. Insurgent camel trains were also attacked from the air. Airpower was of great significance in supplying the SAF in the field and enabling the construction of these fortified lines.

At this stage, London would not sanction the use of SAS patrols into rebel territory. Political considerations as well as the need for the soldiers to familiarise themselves with the environment both played a part in this decision, and at this stage, too, a troop of 15 men was just not sufficient. The politics of Oman,[426] as well as those of Britain, made caution necessary.[427] The first SAS casualties occurred late in 1971.[428]

OMAN REBELS KILL BRITISH SOLDIERS IN DESERT WAR
By R H Greenfield – Defence Staff. Two members of Britain's Special Air Service Regt (SAS) have been killed, and four others wounded, by rebel tribesmen during recent 'training exercises' in the Dhofar area of South Oman. Officially a detachment of 22 SAS are in Oman to help train the Sultan's forces for the little publicised but vital war against Communist guerrillas. Despite Britain's military withdrawal from the Persian Gulf, formally completed on Friday, the detachment will remain in Oman. One

member of the detachment Sergeant JMS, 27, of Wembley, was killed in October [1971], and another, Trooper CL, 22, of Ringwood, Hants, in November [1971]. Both died from gunshot wounds. Despite their official role as a training detachment there is a strong suspicion that the SAS are in fact fighting actively against the guerrillas. Local rulers are sensitive to accusations that they are receiving 'colonialist' assistance. Asked why the Sultan's troops should be trained by the SAS rather than men from an ordinary infantry unit, a Ministry of Defence spokesman said it was because of their special knowledge of the desert fighting and of Arabic.

In Britain, it was clear that the premature commitment of the SAS to action, with perhaps the risk of large numbers of casualties, would generate publicity that could have imperilled the whole strategy to maintain Oman's security. Also, because of the SAS's unique constitutional position in Dhofar, reporting not to the Sultan and his military command but to the Ministry of Defence in London, there was a delicate balance to maintain before military operations could begin. This unusual chain of command was implemented because there was no other British Army unit in Oman and therefore was no established reporting system. There were RAF units based on the island of Masirah, off the coast of Oman, but it would not have been appropriate for the SAS troops to be under command of the Masirah RAF base commander. This was despite the fact that the commander of the SAF was a seconded, senior British officer.

Moreover, Britain had agreed an undertaking to maintain the security of Salalah as an operational airfield as a quid pro quo for the continued use of the strategic RAF facilities on Masirah, as it was anticipated that Masirah would be required as part of UK defence policy for at least another five years.[429]

Intelligence coordination was actually one of the poorest aspects of the campaign in the Dhofar, and it was fortunate that PFLOAG did not pose a threat of subversion elsewhere in Oman outside the province of Dhofar, for example in Muscat, the capital. Indeed, there was no police force in Dhofar until November 1971, when it was limited to traffic duties and minor crime investigations in the main town of Salalah itself. Military intelligence was obtained from air and ground reconnaissance as well as direct ground contact, but most was derived from captured insurgents. Initially, the Oman Intelligence Service proved reluctant to share information derived from interrogation of captives until General

Creasey, overall commander of operations in Oman, demanded improvements in 1972.

Meanwhile, the amnesty campaign – much criticised by some British soldiers as a double-edged sword that supplied much war material to the rebels – was reaping a useful harvest of SEPs.[430] The defections were accelerated in September 1970, by a split within the rebel camp between the communists and the Islamic traditionalists, which led to fighting between the two. The attempted counter-revolution was ruthlessly suppressed by the communists and resulted in mass defections to the government. Between September 1970 and March 1971, encouraged by promises of cash, as well as amnesty, a total of 201 rebels surrendered. Some handed over their Kalashnikov AK-47s and were paid an extra bounty of £50. The most useful men were then screened with the aid of Mohammed Suhail,[431] a high-level SEP, and recruited into irregular counter-guerrilla units known as *firqat* (home guard or unit).

Deployed under the name of British Army Training Team (BATT),[432] the training, management and leadership of the *firqat* was one of the most important tasks taken on by the SAS. The *firqat* would have an important political role to play as well as a military one. It was intended that the *firqat*, having defeated the enemy in their own areas, would then police the areas with the *firqat* leaders becoming *walis* or local political leaders.[433] As the operation got under way, SAS soldiers were sent for intensive, ten-week courses in colloquial Arabic at Beaconsfield, before being attached in three- or four-man groups to *firqat* units in their own tribal areas. One such team was to be involved in one of the regiment's most desperate actions since the Second World War.

The SAS remained at the heart of the *firqat*; however, there were always some difficulties in handling the 1,600 members of the 21 different *firqat* that existed by the end of the campaign. Moving to a tribal basis and making each *firqat* responsible for the selection of its own centres, with increased reliability (and although always volatile) they became an effective territorial home guard, driving a real wedge between the insurgents and the tribespeople.[434]

Within the SAS there were concerns about the problems that resulted from paying some of the irregulars better salaries than the Sultan's own regular soldiers, as well as supplying the *firqat* too generously with automatic rifles, ammunition and blankets. There were also chronic problems of command, which depended crucially upon the relationship between the SAS team leader and his 'tribal' second-in-command. According to one British veteran, every *firqat* experienced a mutiny of some sort at some time, and a few *firqat* units were disbanded due to an incompatible tribal mix.[435] Finally, there was a growing tendency among the irregulars to demand more and more supportive firepower from the regular Army and Air Force before they would go into action, a process that cancelled out their natural advantages of stealth and surprise, as well as the guerrilla techniques they understood.

By the end of the summer monsoon, the *firqat* had been built up to a fighting strength of some 600 fighting men and were ready to be committed to the battlefield. On 2 October 1971, Operation JAGUAR was launched, under JWT's command, to get the government forces back on the Jebel and establish a permanent base there. Two squadrons of SAS were committed.[436] The main force consisted of five *firqat* led by teams from 'G' Squadron together with a battalion of the SAF – plus a spearhead of 60 men from B squadron. As a rule, only one SAS squadron at a time operated in Dhofar but a second, B Squadron, was brought in. In the event this reinforcement proved to be crucial, for not only did the strength of the opposition turn out to be far greater than anticipated but G Squadron had also been devastated by hepatitis.[437] It was recommended at the Ministry of Defence that two squadrons should remain until March 1972.[438]

The village of Jibjat, on the top of the Jebel escarpment, was the key to JWT's strategy; stores, ammunition and water were airlifted in during the following two days, 2–3 October, to consolidate his hold on the position. Jibjat was to act as the base for a two-pronged attack outwards into enemy-held territory on either side of the Wadi Dharbat. All groups were involved in heavy fighting over the following five days as they slowly consolidated their hold on the area above the wadi that the *adoo* had reluctantly ceded, withdrawing into the ravine itself. A new base was secured at a place nicknamed White City and was put in a state of all-round defence, covered by solidly constructed sangars, from which aggressive patrolling by small groups of SAS and *firqat* was conducted. SAS headquarters moved up to White City; from there JWT could organise the building up of a fortified position known as the Leopard Line using patrols, mines and barbed wire to cut off *adoo* supply routes into Oman from the Yemen. The line itself consisted of three strongpoints garrisoned by SAF, from which BATT and *firqat* patrols could operate. It was not totally impenetrable but it did succeed in sharply reducing the supplies reaching the *adoo*; and this idea of linear defence was replicated with other similar defence positions.

The immediate priority was to establish a civil aid and official government presence up on the Jebel to prove to the Jebalis that government forces meant to stay there and would not leave the villagers to the mercy of the *adoo* when the next *khareef* arrived. The government centres began successfully with the establishment of the first permanent presence of the government on the jebel, in October 1971, at 'White City' later named Medinat Al Haq (City of the Truth) above the Wadi Darbat. It was quickly followed by the organisation of the first cattle drive in November 1971 to bring livestock to a market. A Civil Aid Department (CAD) was established in 1973 headed by a former member of the SAS and, as areas of the Jebel were cleared, the CAD would fly in pre-fabricated schools, clinics and shops. By June 1975 a total of 35 wells had been dug and 150 miles of vehicle tracks prepared. An efficient propaganda campaign was also waged through leaflets, which highlighted the Marxist threat to Islam. Radio Dhofar was also significant, with transistor radios being first given and later sold cheaply to Jebalis. Information specialists devised a highly effective campaign around the slogan, 'Islam is our Way, Freedom is our Aim', which thoroughly discredited the appeal of the insurgents' Radio Aden.[439]

The deployment of the squadrons was not without internal tensions among the SAS commanders and between them and JWT.[440]

In the spring of 1972 the SAF mounted a major operation along the coast and established a base hard up on the Yemen border at a place named Simba. That marked the start of a far more aggressive attitude on the part of the Sultan's forces which gradually took on more and more responsibility for running the campaign. In March, an advance party of a special forces battalion arrived to man the Hornbeam Line and was the forerunner of what was to become the Imperial Iranian Battle Group (IIBG), later joined by a Jordanian special forces' detachment. One of the greatest operational difficulties for commanders was coordinating operations with the IIBG, since virtually all decisions had to be personally approved by the Shah himself.

One grave problem caused by the monsoon in the summer of 1972 was that the positions along the Leopard Line could no longer be supplied and it had to be abandoned. The loss of the line enabled *adoo* patrols to sneak up close to Salalah and fire rockets into the town and the airfield to prove that they were still there. The essential difficulty remained that of cutting off the enemy supply routes running over the border from Yemen. The Simba position that the SAF had established down the coast at Sarfait on the border had only limited success in achieving this. The *adoo* hated it and regularly shelled it, but it was overlooked by a series of hills behind which supply convoys could move in dead ground. To hinder shelling of the capital itself, the SAF established blocks across the wadi mouths down which the *adoo* moved from the mountains; these were known as the Diana positions. The success of the Leopard Line, however, led to the construction of the Hornbeam Line, which ran 40 miles inland from the coast at Mugsayl. This consisted of a continuous stretch of wire backed by defensive positions every 2,000 metres. It was not totally *adoo*-proof but only small determined groups on foot and without heavy weapons could get through it at night.

During 1973, the SAS squadrons continued to rotate into Oman, training the *firqat* and manning positions on the Jebel, and gradually extending their hold over the surrounding areas by establishing new posts, each with a resident BATT and *firqat* team. The Iranians also built up their forces and by the end of that year the SAF had doubled in size, with the Dhofar area becoming a command for a brigadier.

The Omanis themselves could then begin to see the battle turning in their favour, as well as the tangible results of the modernisation programme instituted by Sultan Qaboos. This does not mean, however, that Oman had become a sideshow for the SAS, and one-quarter of the regimental strength remained committed to the Oman.

It had been the intention of the British government to withdraw the SAS in late 1972,[441] but defeating the rebels had become an extended operation due to the nature of the environment and the climatic changes created by the Khareef. This constant mist and fog provided cover for the insurgents to re-equip and reinforce without interference from the Oman Air Force. The operations being carried out had become more conventional and less appropriate for SAS troops, and it was at this stage in the campaign that consideration was given to replacing the SAS with specialist infantry soldiers, such as the Parachute Regiment.

In August 1975, I was briefed by Major Roger Miller, [the] officer commanding Patrol Company 3 PARA, that the SAS had requested support from Parachute Regiment Patrol companies to assist them in Oman. He said all the soldiers would have to be volunteers. However, the deployment did not take place and I heard nothing further about it.[442]

B Squadron returned in the spring of 1973 for what should have been a quiet time during the monsoon period. A troop commander, Captain MK, was sent with seven men to take charge of the base at Mirbat, a small town on the beach to the east of Salalah. Just outside the town and separated from it by a shallow wadi stood an old stone fort which was garrisoned by a group of Dhofar Gendarmerie, together with the BATT house and the house of the *wali*, the local governor. The whole area was surrounded by a wire fence and at the fort there was a 25-pounder artillery piece. The SAS team was equipped with an 81 mm mortar, .5 Browning heavy machine gun and several GPMGs.[443] This was the scene for the battle of Mirbat – often described as an Omani version of Rorke's Drift.

The successful defence of Mirbat has been frequently defined as the high point of the SAS campaign in Oman. The battle is covered in great detail in a number of publications[444] and resulted in the guerrillas losing many of their best men; more importantly, they had been defeated when the odds were in their favour.

Towards the end of 1974, Brigadier John Akehurst[445] took over command of the Dhofar area and was the architect of the final victorious campaign. His strategy was to press the enemy slowly but surely back towards the Yemen border. He re-established the old Leopard Line, renamed the Hammer Line, and moved the bulk of the Iranians into an old desert airstrip known as Manston. The Iranian units were keen to fight but tended to operate as a mass, backed up by massive firepower, which was not really suitable for operations against small groups of guerrillas.

In December 1974, the SAF started a large offensive south from Manston towards Rakyut on the coast, aiming to seize a large *adoo* stores complex in the caves at Shershitti. An operation originally intended to last 24 hours continued for three weeks, though without occupation of the caves by government forces. What did happen, however, was that the approaches to the caves were denied to the rebels by constant fire from 76 mm guns mounted on armoured cars and were never again used as stores caves. According to one officer involved in the campaign, it was from that point on that the guerrillas began to lose to the SAF in straight military battles. Like Mirbat, it was a body-blow to the guerrillas' credibility.

The final assault of the war was to be launched by helicopter at dawn on a day in October 1975. Its object was to seize high ground above a 2,000-foot-deep wadi in the mountains near the border with South Yemen, while a column of armoured cars and bulldozers would advance, simultaneously, from the plain to control the foothills. But, at the last moment, what was to have been a simple diversion became the main pivot of the attack. The diversion was from an isolated, air-supplied mountain-top position held by government troops at Sarfait. Such an attack was, predictably, an extremely risky manoeuvre and both sides knew it. The descent was by steps down a series of cliffs, the first of which was an almost sheer 600 feet. Government troops had tried to break out once in 1972 and they had failed. On the night of 14 October the Muscat Regiment probed its way down these cliffs to take the first plateau. There was no opposition.

The main attack then went in from Sarfait the same night and by morning the government forces held a three-mile corridor to the sea, cutting the guerrillas' last supply line. From then on, the guerrillas' chief priority was to reach the safety of South Yemen. For many of them it was a long, pitiless march along waterless tracks north of the mountains they had controlled for five years. The war ended formally a few months later with a ceasefire between South Yemen and Oman.

It was over money that the SAS almost suffered a mortal blow to its image, and possibly its military survival. The autonomous, and largely unsupervised, SAS teams of three to four men, often commanded by a junior NCO such as a corporal or sergeant, were responsible for paying their *firqat* in cash. The money was provided from government sources based upon the number of men in the *firqat*. The team would submit details of their *firqat* members and would receive, in turn, money to pay them. Unfortunately, greed overcame a large number of the SAS and a culture of claiming money for non-existent 'ghost *firqat*' became entrenched and went on for a number of years encompassing all the squadrons in turn.[446] This fraud only stopped when an SAS officer reported the matter to the CO. Interestingly, this officer was ostracised by the soldiers for publicising and curtailing what was, obviously, a lucrative income supplement. Disbandment was certainly a possible option if this political time bomb had exploded. The SAS, however, survived this unsavoury episode for two reasons; the first was the total lack of media coverage of the campaign and, second, was the Omani government's lack of concern about losing the money.

> I found myself threatened by a scandal which could have destroyed not only my own reputation, but that of the SAS as well. We discovered that in Oman members of the Regiment had been drawn into practices which involved misappropriation of firqat funds. I was left feeling deeply disturbed. The affair came

as a reminder that the SAS are prone to the same weaknesses as people in any other sector of society, and need careful handling if they are not to cross the narrow gap between, on the one hand, doing a brilliant job at the cutting-edge of an operation, and, on the other, allowing themselves to be sucked down into actions which at first seem no more than a slight stretching of the rules.[447]

The matter did reinforce the fact, if it needed reinforcing, that SAS soldiers are a cross-section of the community and affected by temptation just like everyone else.[448]

An almost universally observed characteristic of elite units is their lack of formal discipline – and sometimes a lack of substantive discipline as well. A prolonged disregard for formal discipline can lead to disaster ... Also, a prolonged decline of formal discipline within an elite unit seems conducive, at least, to an erosion of obedience to political authorities.[449]

The insurgency was brought to an end with Qaboos's formal declaration that the war was over on 11 December 1975.

Conclusion

A classic 'hearts and minds' operation – winnable because it was about communism and not Islam![450]

The fortunes of this war, which had swung from the near collapse of government forces in 1970 to their outright victory by 1976, followed the gradual penetration of Dhofari society, in which the *firqat*, trained and advised by the SAS, reoccupied the mountains using water wells as the ultimate currency of persuasion. Increasingly ambitious, orthodox military operations were carried out, which required thousands of Iranian and Jordanian, as well as Omani, soldiers to cut the guerrilla supplies coming from South Yemen. This was accomplished by building a series of communication barriers, which employed barbed wire, booby-traps, mines and electronic ground sensors. Air and naval bombardment was used to soften up hostile areas before such operations took place, and everything that might aid the guerrillas, including cattle, was removed. The first of the barriers, the Hornbeam Line, covered 35 miles and took 12 months to build.

The closer government forces came to the border with South Yemen, the more they came under attack from 130 mm artillery fired from within that territory by regular forces. Government helicopters and strike planes were constantly menaced by some of Russia's latest anti-aircraft missiles supplied to the guerrillas. Contrary to some opinion in Britain, the war was not a totally one-sided affair. If it had been, it would not have lasted as long as it did. In the light of subsequent events in Iran and Afghanistan and their impact on Western oil supplies, the strategic importance to British economic interests of winning the war can hardly be overstated.

Dhofar was only a small-scale conflict, although one in which failure would have had enormous repercussions for the West's strategic interests. Oman overlooked the strategically vital oil route of the Strait of Hormuz, through which oil tankers carried 30 per cent of the United States' oil requirements, 70 per cent of Europe's and 90 per cent of Japan's.[451]

By the time the war ended in 1976, the combined anti-guerrilla forces numbered about 15,000 men. The SAS commitment most of the time was a single squadron averaging about 80, and even this figure could vary by as many as 30 more or, more frequently, less. The SAS stayed on in Oman until September 1976, carrying on their work with the *firqat* and running civil aid programmes. The SAS paid a price and during the six years of the conflict the regiment lost 12 men killed in action and several more permanently disabled. The impact of the small groups of SAS men had been out of proportion to their numbers. But the decisive effect of the Regiment on the war was more diffuse and more subtle than its skill at arms.

Putting the SAS involvement into relevant statistical comparisons is a clarifying exercise. At peak, the British had perhaps 500 men in Oman in one capacity or another, of which only 80, on average, would be from the SAS. There were two squadrons of approximately 120 SAS involved in Operation JAGUAR, which was the major excursion to establish a presence on the Jebel. This pales in comparison with the Sultan's Armed Forces (SAF), who deployed about 10,000 troops in Dhofar by 1974. PFLOAG probably had about 2,000 active fighters and 3,000 part-time militia, at its peak, in 1968–69.

> Whilst in the early stages, it was an SAS task, in the latter stages the Regiment was used as glorified infantry and the task should have been handed over to a Para battalion.[452]

The SAS are credited with the success of the campaign, but this must be balanced against the political and military environment at the time of their involvement.

> Dhofar was a classic example of the Regiment being used effectively. You could argue that we should have sorted the place out sooner.[453]

The despotic Sultan bin Tamour had been deposed and replaced by his benevolent son, who immediately after the coup made it plain that he was committed to bringing Oman into the twentieth century. He was also publicly committed to major investment into the Dhofar province. This immediately removed the major cornerstone of the communist-dominated DLF policy. Moreover, the anti-Islamic philosophy of the revolutionaries was totally at variance with the religious Dhofaris, and the torture and murder of dissident tribal elders was an anathema to the Jebali culture of respect for tribal elders. Indeed, it led directly to the defection from PFLOAG of 24 of the most experienced of the former DLF guerrillas in September 1970, who became the nucleus of the first unit or *firqat*. The communists were unlikely to achieve success under these circumstances. The insurgents certainly had a safe haven in South Yemen, one of the key fundamentals of a successful insurgency, and from this safe haven they were able to obtain sufficient quantities of weapons and explosives for their campaign. However, in order to move themselves and their equipment and supplies to the Jebel and make effective use of them they had to cross some extremely difficult terrain. The terrain could also help the rebels as well as hindering them, as it could to the Sultan's forces but, in this case, the Oman forces had total air superiority with ground-attack aircraft as well as transport aircraft to overcome some of the disadvantages of the terrain. This air superiority was negated, to a certain degree, during the three month-long *khareef*, when visibility on the coast was limited and on the Jebel, minimal.

Added to this was the overwhelming superiority of the Oman armed forces, with major manpower and logistic support from Iran as well as Jordan. The series of operations that concluded the war were conventional with artillery and air support vital to success.

The soldiers of the SAF were mainly Northern Omanis or Baluchis and had little time or respect for the rebellious hill people. The Jebali-speaking Dhofaris used Arabic as a lingua franca as it was not their first language, whereas it was for the northerners. Also, the

Baluch soldiers had gained a reputation for heavy-handedness when operating near or around Jebali villages and, before a permanent government presence was established on the Jebel, their punitive raids after attacks or mining by the *adoo* created great animosity among the tribesmen.

The SAS brought an interface with the Jebalis which was invaluable in the integration of surrendered *adoo* into the government forces. The wisdom of carrying out language[454] training had its success in the ability of the linguists in SAS patrols to be able to communicate directly with the *firqat* and their leaders. The *firqat* were an invaluable public-relations tool who were able to spread the word, through tribal and family connections, to those still fighting against the government that surrendered *adoo* would not be mistreated.

The work of the SAS with the *firqat* can be considered as an important factor in infiltrating representatives of the government into the lives of the isolationist Jebalis. In this respect, there was a similarity with the involvement the SAS had with indigenous peoples in previous campaigns of Malaya, Borneo and, to a limited degree on the Jebel Akhdar and in the Radfan. In those campaigns the SAS also worked with the local aborigines or hill peoples. The key to the success of the SAS was based upon the type of individual soldier in the SAS who was normally older and more independent than his counterpart in the rest of the armed forces. Moreover, because of the deployments of the SAS, most of the soldiers had operational experience, giving them the confidence to operate in small groups isolated from their colleagues, working with the somewhat temperamental *firqat*.

The actual operational effectiveness and efficiency of the *firqat* is subject to scrutiny. The courage of individual Jebalis, either fighting for the government or against it, has not been disputed, but the actual combat record of the *firqat* is not overly impressive. The SAS 'minders' frequently had to change or even postpone or cancel military operations because of problems with the *firqat*. These problems could vary from total uninterest in the planned operation, and lack of 'sufficient' artillery and/or air support, to the fact that they wanted more food for that particular week.

Also, as the British had found in Malaya, money was a strong incentive to the rebels to surrender and to bring in their weapons. Once in a *firqat*, the former *adoo* were paid, fed and clothed.

Before the conclusion of the war, as the *firqat* forces increased and became part of the formal Oman forces, some of the SAS teams working with them were supplemented by British contract officers.

These officers had often been former seconded officers and so knew the language and, to a certain degree, knew the Jebalis.

Inevitably, in this assessment of the SAS impact upon the insurgency in Oman there is a high degree of operations-oriented analysis. This analysis establishes that the tactical importance and effectiveness of the SAS has been overemphasised, particularly when compared with the overall numbers of forces fighting for the government. However, there was a strategic utility in the use of the SAS for it provided the UK government with an 'anonymous' military force which could be deployed without the knowledge of the general public but which, despite the small numbers of SAS soldiers involved, provided the UK with an inordinate amount of prestige within Oman. The maintenance of this prestige, coupled with a continuing demonstration of the UK's commitment to the stability of Oman, aided the British government's foreign policy in the Middle East in general, and in Oman in particular.

The war was also the least publicised of any war in which British forces have been involved. British involvement was not advertised in any way outside the services. The British Government did not want to draw attention to its involvement for fear that they might be starting a campaign, which they would be unable to pursue[455] – as they had recently experienced in Aden. The Sultan of Oman had total control over entry into his country; he simply did not allow the world's press in. They could speculate as much as they liked outside but they had very little hard fact to go on.[456]

Once again, starting with JWT's informal visit to Salalah in 1969, and DLB's visit to Sharjah in 1970, there was no formal, strategic direction to the deployment of the SAS into Dhofar. JWT's instructions to DLB, to ensure that if anything was happening to make sure the SAS 'were in on it', typifies the ad hoc and almost cavalier process of involving SAS in areas of perceived national importance. Furthermore, once the SAS was deployed into Dhofar, albeit in small numbers, there were no examples of strategic vision in the tasks they carried out. Most of their involvement followed a similar pattern to Malaya, Radfan and Borneo. These were low-key, tactical operations working with the indigenous population. There are no examples of surgical strikes or decapitation operations to neutralise DLF or PFLOAG leadership or seriously negate the effectiveness of the support provided to the rebels by South Yemen. For example, PFLOAG leaders would often visit the town of Hauf just across the Oman border into South Yemen. Also, the South Yemeni 130 mm artillery was a major source of difficulty in the maintenance of such exposed SAF locations as Sarfait and could have been disrupted by an SAS offensive direct-action deployment, as could the camel caravans bringing *adoo* weapons and ammunition through the Negd desert region. Such traditional Special Force operations could have had a significant impact on the insurgents' capability and upon the conflict.

The operations of the SAS during Operation STORM were very low key, debatably strategic, and followed a low-risk, low-publicity precedence set in previous campaigns in Asia and elsewhere in the Middle East. The SAS casualties were few but made a significant impact on a small unit.[457]

In conclusion, the environment for success in defeating the insurgency was established by replacement of the despotic Sultan Said by his son, Qaboos and the introduction of Qaboos's benevolent regime. The involvement of the SAS in Oman had a certain strategic utility with regards to UK Middle East foreign-policy objectives, such as the retention of the RAF facilities on the island of Masirah, but it was not a war-winning contribution and had a negligible impact upon the final outcome.[458]

PART THREE

CONVENTIONAL WARS

Chapter 9

The Falklands War: Operation Corporate (19 May–14 June 1982)

Background

Ever since the end of the Second World War, Argentina had claimed sovereignty over the Falklands islands and South Georgia. The political situation had fluctuated over the years but the islands remained a British colony inhabited by people of entirely British stock, as they had been without a break since 1833, and intermittently for decades before that. In November 1981, a new Argentinean junta headed by General Galtieri gave orders to prepare plans to seize the islands and South Georgia.

The Argentinean invasion was preceded by the arrival in South Georgia in mid-March 1982 of Argentinean scrap metal workers and a party of marines, landed from a naval transport ship. They raised the Argentinean flag.

On 2 April 1982, an Argentinean marine battalion group in armoured tracked amphibious vehicles landed at Port Stanley. The British Royal Marines group of some 70 marines surrendered. Photographs of surrendering Royal Marines with their hands held above their heads were, to their mortification, quickly distributed worldwide.

For some days before the invasion, intelligence had been building up in Whitehall that the Argentineans were up to something, but nothing was done to deter them. However, the Royal Navy had quietly been making some preliminary moves. On 30 March, Rear Admiral Woodward, off Gibraltar with a flotilla on exercise, was briefed on the deteriorating situation by Admiral Sir John Fieldhouse, the CinC Fleet, who was visiting the exercise. On 31

March, the First Sea Lord, Admiral Sir Henry Leach, persuaded the prime minister, Margaret Thatcher, to give approval for a task force to be ready to retake the Falklands.

There have been those who went as far as to describe Britain's battle to recover the Falkland Islands as 'A damned close run thing', as the Duke of Wellington was moved to do after Waterloo. It should also be recalled that there were several entirely competent organisations which initially suspected the whole operation was doomed. In no particular order they were:

> the United States Navy, which considered the re-capture of the Falkland Islands to be a military impossibility; the Ministry of Defence in Whitehall, which generally regarded the whole idea as far, far too risky; the Army, which considered it to be ill-advised, for lack of a 'proper' advantage ratio in land force numbers; the Royal Air Force, which, seeing little role for themselves on account of the vast distances, and no chance of a navy surviving in the face of an air force, was inclined to agree; the Secretary of State for Defence, Mr (now Sir) John Nott, since success in it would probably overturn the 1981 Defence Review.[459]

Operation CORPORATE, the war fought by Britain to regain the Falkland Islands from their Argentine occupiers, was in many ways a modern version of old-style colonial conflicts – an attempt at high-tech gunboat diplomacy. A large contingent of special forces was involved in the war – two squadrons from the SAS, the Royal Marines and Special Boat Squadron – and there were also the specialist troops of the Royal Marine Mountain and Arctic Warfare Team (MAWT), Patrol Companies from 2 and 3 Para and support from the Royal Artillery teams of Naval Gunfire Support[460] observers.

Involvement of the SAS

> 22 SAS wasn't invited down to the Falklands, they just turned up on the quayside.[461]

The commanding officer of 22 SAS Regiment at the time was Lieutenant Colonel NX, who heard about the invasion from the BBC news and, following in the well-trodden 'marketing' footsteps of numerous of his predecessors, promptly set out to get his men involved. While his operations and intelligence cell in the Regimental HQ at Hereford scoured around for maps and any available information about the distant islands, D Squadron commanded by Major *RP* was put on immediate alert for a move south. This meant pulling men back from leave, from courses and even from foreign assignments. *NX* offered the squadron's services to Brigadier Julian Thompson of 3 Commando Brigade, whom he flew to see on 3 April. Two days after the invasion, an SAS advance party flew out to the British staging post on the Ascension Island off the west coast of Africa. The following day, the rest of the squadron, together with their kit, left for Ascension.

> ... I had to convince both John Nott, the Defence Minister, and the Admiral of the Fleet, Sir Terence Lewin, Chief of the Defence Staff – and through them the Inner Cabinet and the Prime Minister that the risk was acceptable, and that the SAS could make a significant contribution to the plan for recovering the islands. To maintain the closest possible liaison, we established an SAS cell in Fleet Headquarters at Northwood, and there our people[462] took part in the central planning of operations. We also maintained a cell in the Central Staff at the MOD – and of course, just because a war was brewing up in the South Atlantic, our other commitments did not come to a sudden end. The counter-terrorist team, for instance, remained on standby, as usual, and the Regiment continued operations in many more distant theatres.[463]

In line with SAS tradition, DLB went on a marketing expedition to ensure that 'his' regiment was involved in any forthcoming conflict:

> Realizing that any attempt to recapture the Falklands would be first and foremost a naval operation, I, myself, went to Fleet Headquarters at Northwood to see Admiral Sir John Fieldhouse, Commander-in-Chief of the Fleet. He received me most civilly, and seemed enthusiastic about the possibilities for action by the SAS which I suggested – principally that we should infiltrate reconnaissance patrols ahead of any invasion force, so that they could give our people an accurate idea of how the Argentines had deployed their occupying forces.[464]

NX joined D Squadron the next day, bringing with him an SAS headquarters element, and soon linked up with Thompson's HQ at 3

Commando Brigade (which was then the task force's principal land element). As a member of Thompson's planning staff, NX developed a special forces strategy, which envisaged using D Squadron in a raiding or OA (offensive action) role, together with G Squadron in the information-reporting role. In addition to the two SAS squadrons, the special forces' effort was bolstered by the presence of the SBS.[465] However, the SBS remained under naval control. On 6 April, Colonel NX, a small staff from Regimental Headquarters, and G Squadron commanded by Major OG embarked on HMS Fearless, a commando landing ship which was Brigadier Thompson's floating command post. NX and his HQ worked in a Portacabin lashed on to the deck.

A former SAS officer serving with the Parachute Regiment describes the situation:

> Like much of the Falklands Campaign in the early stages there was a scrabble to get in on the act and deploying two [SAS] squadrons, plus the SBS and MAWT[466] was probably overkill. The result was that they made tasks for themselves. The result was that strategic troops were used in a tactical mode. At the bottom end it meant that company and battalion [infantry elements] patrolling was heavily restricted. At the same time the information they were gathering was so classified it never got down to the units it should have.[467]

Although it is a principle of special forces' operations that they should be commanded at the strategic level — that is, by the overall commander in any particular 'theatre' — Operation CORPORATE was a naval-led operation being controlled by the Headquarters of the Commander-in-Chief of the Fleet (HQ CinC Fleet) at Northwood in Middlesex. The Navy had little experience of deploying and operating special forces, and the first difficulty to be overcome stemmed from the unfamiliarity of the naval hierarchy with the potential scope and the degree of support required for SAS operations. This was solved comparatively easily in the UK by establishing an SAS liaison cell within HQ CinCFleet and by the personal intervention of DLB who ensured that the CinC, Admiral Fieldhouse, was fully briefed on SAS capabilities. Down in the South Atlantic, the difficulty was considerably more problematic — the chain of command and the reporting chain was to Major General JME.[468] The full extent of the confusion over who was responsible for tasking special forces patrols at each stage in the campaign, and how the intelligence they acquired should be disseminated within the force, never seems to have been completely resolved. The whole picture has also been crowded by inter-unit rivalries and jealousy which have tended to obscure facts in relation to some aspects of SAS operations.

> For once [sic] our own command structure was not altogether satisfactory. I remained in charge of strategic planning and decisions made in the United Kingdom, and NX, who established his headquarters on board *HMS Fearless*, controlled tactical operations at the other end. When we were both on Ascension, he, being the determined, strong character he is, had insisted on going south with 'D' Squadron and taking a small Regimental headquarters with him. My view was that, with the bulk of the Regiment still in the UK, and plenty of able junior commanders forward, he should have stayed behind to direct affairs at, and from, Hereford. Against my better judgment, I let his enthusiasm sway me, and allowed him to go. On reflection, I believe I was wrong to do so – but to this day he and I cannot agree on the issue.[469]

In the period immediately after the landings, the contribution of the SAS – and other special forces – was less obviously useful than before the arrival of main force troops of 3 Commando Brigade. As a result, the no man's land between the main Argentinean position around Stanley and the British beach-head became very crowded with various special forces operatives.

> After the war criticisms were made that the intelligence which the SAS patrols produced was never passed on far enough down the chain to be of practical use; I think this was true, but the fault lay with the system, not with the men on the ground.[470]

Initially the two SAS squadrons were deployed separately and were controlled directly by their own squadron officers, while the CO remained on board Fearless at Ascension. D Squadron, after only a short pause on Ascension, embarked on board the Royal Fleet Auxiliary (RFA) *Fort Austin*, to form part of a force detached to recapture the island of South Georgia. This was a political decision as the government was under pressure to instigate some form of action. G Squadron's mission was reconnaissance, and on arrival at Ascension it was re-embarked on the *RFA Resource*, which sailed south with the main carrier battle group.

At the sharp end, the deployment worked very well; our communications allowed NX to talk to Hereford and London with
the greatest clarity – and it was extraordinary to be able to discuss things in detail with someone 8000 miles away. But
at home, the arrangement led to problems. In NX's absence, the
Second-in-Command of 22nd SAS assumed control, and
although in himself he was admirable, he did not have the same
authority as the Commanding Officer. Whenever he was faced
with a difficult decision, he had to refer it to NX, which
inevitably wasted time; also, I found that I myself was having to
spend longer in Hereford than I should have.[471]

The South Georgia mission was known as Operation PARAQUET.[472]
The original plan called for one troop of D Squadron to join this
force, but RP, the OC, decided to take the whole squadron 'as they
all wanted to have a slice of the action'.[473] In addition to D
Squadron, 2 Section of the SBS and M Company of 42 Royal
Marine Commando were to be deployed. Initially there was some
confusion over the command structure. Major GS of M Company
was extremely surprised, as was the Navy, when instead of the
expected SAS troop, a whole squadron commanded by another
major trans-shipped from the Fort Austin. Surprisingly, considering
the principle of command at the highest level, GS was given command and the plans were approved by Brigade HQ. This was much
to the chagrin of RP and may explain his decision to ignore advice
on local weather conditions. The whole process had been complicated by an almost total lack of intelligence about the island and the
size of the Argentine presence.

On 21 April, contrary to advice given by those with more knowledge of the local area, RP deployed 19 Troop, a specialist mountain
troop, on to the Fortuna glacier by helicopter with the mission of
gathering intelligence on the whereabouts of the Argentine troops.
Once there, they found that the combination of the weather and
the difficult terrain made movement impossible. All three Wessex
helicopters managed to land on the glacier to embark the men, but
two of them crashed in the process. Thirteen men were stranded
out on the glacier with two wrecked helicopters and in no condition
to spend a further night in the open. The remaining helicopter,
dangerously overloaded, managed to bring the soldiers back to the
ship, where it had to crash-land on the heaving deck as it was
unable to hover.

> At the outset of the campaign we narrowly escaped a catastrophe in South Georgia, where we launched Operation Paraquet, an attempt to recover the island, but hopelessly underestimated the severity of the weather on the Fortuna Glacier.[474]

Catastrophe had been averted, but only just, as the task force's airlift capability had been reduced by two-thirds.[475] Two days later, on 23 April, *RP* deployed 17 Troop, a boat troop, in five Gemini inflatables. Two suffered engine failure with their notoriously unreliable engines and started drifting towards the Antarctic. They were rescued once again by the remaining helicopter. Three patrols did manage to get ashore and establish themselves in a position to observe the enemy. In a desire to use his specialist troops, his mountain troop and boat troop, against local advice, *RP* put the individuals in those troops at unnecessary risk and two valuable helicopters were lost in the process of recovering some of them. This was an inauspicious start to the campaign by the SAS but was an indication of the type of issues that would reflect poorly on the deployment of the regiment and overshadow other successes.

> It was unfortunate that the County class destroyer HMS Antrim took fright at the appearance of a World War Two vintage Argentinean submarine, which resulted in the South Georgia task force dispersing at a critical moment. Consequently all that GS had was a small element of M Company, elements of D and G Squadrons, the Special Air Service, whose performance so far had cost two valuable helicopters, and a Special Boat Service section. There were suspicions that the Special Air Service was taking its operational orders direct from London anyway.[476]

Despite having to take precautionary evasive action against the Argentine submarine, the *Santa Fe*, GS's force laid down a barrage from the warships' guns against the Argentinean settlement. A mixed force was then flown in by helicopter to a point about two miles away from the settlement; as they moved over the ridge they saw that the buildings were displaying white sheets. GS moved forward to take the official surrender of the demoralised garrison.

On 28 April, D Squadron transferred to the destroyer *HMS Brilliant* and set off to rejoin the main task force as it prepared to insert the first reconnaissance patrols from G Squadron. Starting on 1 May, over a period of three days, eight four-man patrols were inserted by Sea King helicopters from the aircraft carrier *HMS*

Hermes. The earlier intention to parachute into position was abandoned as being too risky. Each team was landed up to twenty miles from its ultimate lying-up position and had to carry everything needed for an indefinite stay.[477]

The positioning of such observation posts was a somewhat random process as the maps available were inadequate and there was little knowledge of the Argentinean dispositions. Once a covert OP had been established, a grim routine set in with the men not permitted to engage the enemy unless under attack themselves. Each OP position was different, but common to all was the cold and unforgiving terrain. Most of the Falklands is rock covered by peat bog, and when digging one soon encounters either granite or water.[478] The construction and manning of long-term OPs had been the mandate of 21 SAS and 23 SAS, the territorial army units of the SAS, for use in Central Europe, but the skills and equipment for the maintenance of long-term OPs had not been maintained by 22 SAS who, on the whole, looked down upon their part-time colleagues carrying out this role.

The Argentines were equipped with radio direction-finding equipment, and transmission times had to be kept to a bare minimum. Surprisingly, in the Falklands the individual patrols were not equipped with radios capable of sending burst transmissions – lengthy messages encoded into a special machine and then sent out in a matter of seconds. These radios were commonly used by the TA SAS in OPs. However, the squadron's HQs, as well as Regimental Headquarters, had the latest satellite telephones which enabled them to communicate easily with each other and back to Hereford. Also, close Special Force relationships had led the Americans to send over several of their newest radio sets and the system enabled men on shipboard or on shore in the South Atlantic to talk to Hereford or London in perfectly clear speech and with total security. The availability of these communications to the SAS did cause a certain amount of irritation to the Task Force command who felt, with a certain amount of justification, that one of their subordinate organisations, whenever it felt it was necessary, was circumventing the established and formalised chain of command.

Simultaneously with the G Squadron observation patrols, small SBS teams were also paddling ashore to check out all possible landing sites for the task force. Using the same techniques as the SAS, they established themselves in hides to observe their assigned area as well as scouting suitable beaches for amphibious landings with deep water and easy beach exits.

The SBS had allegedly carried out a beach profile recce [reconnaissance] and had confirmed that the beach slope was such that the landing craft would have no trouble in landing troops directly onto the beach. This information was quite incorrect and the heavily laden troops had to wade ashore in 3–4 feet of freezing water.[479]

D Squadron rejoined the main carrier force and was transferred on board *HMS Hermes* to plan their next mission. *RP* suggested mounting a raid on Pebble Island, off the coast to the north of West Falkland, where a small enemy garrison was thought to be.[480] Initially, the overall task force commander, Admiral Woodward, was not enthusiastic about the idea as he would have to risk his ships by moving them in close enough for helicopters to insert the raiding force. The sinking of *HMS Sheffield* on 4 May had made everyone painfully aware of the threat from Exocet missiles and the loss of one of the carriers might well have caused the government to call off the attempt to recapture the islands. Moreover, on 8 May, the decision had been taken to send the landing force south from Ascension and nothing was to be allowed to interfere with this operation.

The Navy remained lukewarm about the planned raid until indications were received that there might be a radar transmitter on the island which could have detected the movement of the ships of the landing force. RAF over-flights failed to detect it, and it was reluctantly agreed to put D Squadron ashore. After a 24-hour postponement, two patrols were inserted on to West Falkland opposite Pebble Island on 11 May with orders to set up an OP and, if there was no sign of opposition, they were to paddle across the island and carry out a reconnaissance of the airstrip at the settlement. They observed 11 assorted enemy aircraft on the airstrip and that information was radioed back to *Hermes*. Immediate plans were made to insert a full raiding party to destroy the aircraft and eliminate the garrison. The only problem was the continued chronic lack of helicopters, but on the night of 14 May three Sea Kings flew in the squadron and a naval gunfire support team.

Lifted in by helicopter, they [D Squadron] destroyed six Pucara and four Turbo-Mentor aircraft, and one Skyvan transport. Still more important, they denied the Argentines further use of the airfield. The defenders, taken completely by surprise, managed to inflict only one minor injury.[481]

However, in this case, as the garrison and airfield were well within range of the warships' main armament, and observed and controlled naval gunfire was actually used in the raid, it may well have been more prudent, and without risk to the sparse remaining helicopter assets, to have destroyed the aircraft and completely demoralised the garrison with the use of naval guns alone.

On 13 May, Brigadier Julian Thompson, Commander of 3 Commando Brigade RM, issued his orders for the forthcoming landings. Codenamed Operation SUTTON, they would take place at night at San Carlos Water on the north-eastern side of East Falkland, with the purpose of establishing a beachhead before dawn on the following morning.

Three days later, however, the plan for the landings had to be changed when it became known that the Argentineans had deployed a company-sized force on Fanning Head, which over-looked San Carlos Water. In addition, it was reported that a force of airmobile troops, comprising an infantry regiment and a company of special forces, supported by some artillery and helicopters, which had previously been thought to be in the area of Fitzroy, was located north of Darwin. Worried that this force could be lifted rapidly to Sussex Mountain in the event of the enemy detecting the landings at San Carlos, Brigadier Thompson decided to alter his plans. 2 Para would land before first light and move to secure Sussex Mountain as quickly as possible, and 40 Commando would land shortly afterwards and occupy San Carlos Settlement. 3 Para and 45 Commando would land at dawn to secure the settlement at Port San Carlos and Ajax Bay, respectively. Before the landings, at 0100 hours, a diversionary raid would be mounted by the SBS at Fanning Head, to the north of San Carlos Water. Supported by naval gunfire, the SBS would keep the Argentineans occupied while the landings were in progress. Meanwhile, D Squadron 22 SAS, supported by *HMS Ardent*, would carry out an attack on Darwin to divert enemy attention from the landings and to pin down any reserve force there.

No date for the landings had been announced, although they were believed to be imminent. However, on the afternoon of 20 May *HMS Broadsword* came alongside the *MV Norland* and a signal was fired on to the *Norland's* deck. It contained the news that Operation SUTTON would start in the early hours of the following morning.

On 18 May, the assault force arrived from Ascension to rendezvous with the carrier group, and NX was reunited with his two squadron commanders. Most of G Squadron was still in OPs in the field and the landing was planned to take place on 21 May. It was intended to insert D Squadron to tie down the enemy garrison which the SAS had located around Darwin and Goose Green. For this mission, they had to transfer with all their gear from HMS *Hermes* to the commando landing ship HMS *Intrepid*, sister to HMS *Fearless*. The move took place on 19 May and was a purely routine five-minute flight between the two ships. Several trips were necessary and the final load was a mixture of senior NCOs, men from D Squadron and G Squadron and several attached specialists including an RAF flight lieutenant. Nobody on board bothered with immersion suits as the Sea King took off. The helicopter had to make a second pass as another one was still on the flight deck of *Intrepid*. As the helicopter circled it appears a large bird impacted with the air intake and the pilot had insufficient height to recover control. Twenty men from the regiment and its support formations died, including two squadron sergeant-majors and six sergeants. It was a terrible blow for such a small unit to lose so many irreplaceable senior NCOs at one stroke. Unfortunately, the SAS had chosen to ignore operating procedures which directed that senior staff were not to travel in the same aircraft for exactly this reason.

> Not all, but the majority, were badged SAS, and the tragedy was one of the most severe ever suffered by the Regiment.[482]

The following night, D Squadron had to get back into action as the Darwin/Goose Green raid was to go ahead, as planned. There was a G Squadron OP in the area, which had been in place for nearly three weeks, so there was sufficient intelligence available about the position of the Argentine troops on the ground. At the same time, the SBS mounted a similar raid on Fanning Head where they had to eliminate an Argentine outpost which could fire on ships approaching the site of the main landings the following morning.

Both raids achieved their aim and the landings on the morning of 21 May were not interrupted by enemy ground forces. However, this appears to have been more by luck than good organisation, as described by a Parachute Regiment SNCO involved in the landings:

> 2 Para was the first conventional unit ashore and they landed at San Carlos on 21 May 1982. The night beach landing was a complete shambles. We were advised that there was an SBS patrol observing the landing area and as we approached they would indicate the status of the beach by torch Morse signals –

'A' meant the beach was completely clear; 'B' meant there were possibly some Argentineans in the vicinity; [and] 'C' meant that it could be an opposed landing. In the event we received no signals at all. When the complete battalion was ashore a soldier was observed approaching the beach-head. He was challenged and [he] turned out to be a member of the SBS who did not know the battalion had landed and then said that they [the SBS] were expecting the battalion the following day. Our experience of Special Forces was very unimpressive.[483]

The majority of the brigade was successfully established ashore before the first of the devastating Argentine air raids on the ships of the task force in the exposed San Carlos anchorage.

Early that same morning, two Hercules lifted off from Ascension carrying 6 Troop and 8 Troop of B Squadron, who parachuted into the sea off the Falklands as replacements for the men lost in the helicopter crash and were picked up by the frigate *HMS Andromeda*.[484]

On 25 May, the various commanding officers from the task force were summoned to an Orders Group by Brigadier Thompson at his floating command post, on *HMS Fearless*. The successful landing had been inhibited by frustrating delays in getting sufficient stores ashore to break out from the bridgehead, the main problem being the chronic lack of helicopters – which was exacerbated when the *Atlantic Conveyor* was sunk by Exocet missile with the loss of three Chinooks.

A member of the SBS was shot and killed by an SAS patrol from G Squadron when, allegedly, the SBS were in the wrong area. The SAS reaction to this incident was that the SBS had strayed into 'their' area and got what they deserved. Not surprisingly, this incident soured relationships between the two organisations even more.[485]

> A problem which soon manifested itself was the poor passage of information both within and between units. In some instances this resulted in what were termed 'blue on blue' contacts.[486]

Covert observation patrols were still out in force at various locations, concentrated around the hills overlooking Port Stanley, and on the island of West Falkland on which there was still a considerable enemy garrison at the settlements of Fox Bay and Port Howard. Those forces had been masked by SBS patrols who had called down regular naval gunfire missions. One of the SAS OPs was compromised and the commander killed.

On the night of 9–10 June a naval gunfire support team was flown on to Beagle Ridge, six miles north of Port Stanley, with orders to observe activity in the town and to call down fire from warships as required. This four-man party was flown in to a reception committee from D Squadron which had been patrolling in the area for some time, while gradually the main force assembled along the line of hills to the west of the town, ready for the final attack.

What remains surprising is that the SAS was not tasked with carrying out offensive operations against the battery of 155mm howitzers located on the outskirts of Stanley and which were able to bring down effective fire upon the advancing British troops right up until the Argentine surrender. Nor were they tasked to engage and destroy the Argentine C130 transport aircraft which made nightly runs into Stanley bringing in supplies, troops and certainly adding to the morale of the beleaguered troops in Stanley. The C130 visits also continued right up until the end of the war. Both these tasks were well within the capability of NX's troops.

On the night of 11–12 June, D Squadron arrived in the area and RP decided to mount a raid in support of the main action. D Squadron plus a troop from G moved off at last light, in rigid raiders,[487] which embarked them together with the necessary weaponry. As they neared their landing point, however, they were heavily fired upon from shore positions,[488] and, as they attempted to withdraw, the Argentine hospital ship anchored there illuminated the scene with its searchlights in order to identify and illuminate itself appropriately under the accepted rules of war. In this somewhat ill-planned and unnecessary operation with all the boats damaged and with two men injured, the raiding group made its way back safely into Blanco Bay. Thompson, who was heavily involved in the main operation against Port Stanley had become somewhat exasperated by the activities of the SAS clouding the battlefield as it got smaller and smaller. When he was asked for assistance by the SAS raiding party, he allegedly replied that, as the SAS had got themselves into such a situation, they could get themselves out.

> They had been illuminated by a searchlight from the Argentine hospital ship in Port William and well and truly brassed up [shot up] by air defence guns firing in the anti-boat role. They needed casevac [casualty evacuation] urgently. Somebody in the Command Post was heard to mutter, 'Bloody Special Forces; the whole world has to stop for them, I suppose.' Fortunately for them they landed up with 2 PARA who took care of them until they could be evacuated.[489]

It had become apparent that the enemy no longer had the will to fight. NX and a Spanish-speaking Royal Marine officer had been conducting freelance psychological warfare on the enemy via the local medical radio network for several days. On Monday 14 June, NX was informed that General Menendez was ready to discuss surrender terms. In the early afternoon, he flew in a Gazelle helicopter, with a large white flag underneath the helicopter weighed down with a lump of rock, into Port Stanley. Later that evening the Argentine commander formally surrendered to Major General JME.

Operation Mikado

Certain aspects of the Falklands campaign, as waged by the SAS on the Argentine mainland, remain opaque. Thatcher made her initial stance on possible attacks against the Argentine mainland clear, although this did change as the threat of Exocets against British ships became more severe.

> There was some concern (entirely misplaced) that we were preparing an attack on the Argentine mainland [early May]: whether or not such attacks would have been made any military sense, we saw from the beginning that they would cause too much political damage to our position to be anything but counter-productive.[490]

Britain went to war to regain control of the Falklands and was not, officially at least, at war with Argentina. Operations within that country, had they become compromised, of which there was always a risk, could well have hampered diplomatic efforts internationally. The greatest single threat to the survival of the task force as a whole came from the air-launched Exocet missiles of the type that sank HMS Sheffield. It was known that Argentina could deliver them from their Super Etendard aircraft, but at the time there was uncertainty over the actual number of missiles available. In fact there were only four and the last one was fired on 30 May, missing its intended target.

> What I think the SAS could have been involved in more was the strategic things on mainland Argentina, and they never worked – well it came in too late but I just wonder really whether if they

[had] worked better earlier they wouldn't have perhaps had some effect on the episode.[491]

The prospect of escalating the war to involve the mainland was a potentially thorny one, but contingency plans were drawn up on the not entirely confident assumption that the War Cabinet would sanction the extension of hostilities beyond the Total Exclusion Zone if there was a reasonable chance of destroying the Exocets. Clearly the insertion of a covert team to monitor air activity at, say, Rio Gallegos was not without risk, but it was a task well suited to the special forces, and DLB was keen on the idea of eliminating the Exocet threat at source.

> The critical thing was these bloody Exocets – if they had gone on they were going to sink our ships – and the ships went on sinking. The strategic plan was 25% casualties among ships, which is quite a lot actually, and then what was going to happen? Were we going to pack up, or we would have lost the war, or what? The whole thing was a fine run thing![492]

Militarily there would have been a strong case for eliminating the Exocet capability and there is no reason why an experienced SAS team could not have done so by destroying the aircraft on the ground. As a precaution, an SAS officer was flown – under temporary diplomatic cover as an assistant military attaché – to the British Embassy in Santiago, in anticipation of the need to establish local caches of food and clothing for evading SAS patrols from over the frontier. His mission was to reconnoitre the border, recommend routes across, and prepare replenishment dumps and a reception system to sustain the 30 or so men who might be expected to trek into neutral Chile. The British ambassador, John Heath, was not informed of this individual's true role.

The flight of the Sea King helicopter to deposit the initial SAS recce patrol into Argentina swiftly developed into a farce as the aircraft made its landing and the SAS occupants squabbled among themselves as to their location.[493] On 20 May, the day before the main amphibious landing at San Carlos, a burnt-out Sea King was abandoned on the mainland and its crew of three turned up several days later at the British Embassy. The official version was that they had experienced difficulties while on patrol and had sought refuge in the nearest neutral country.

> ... what happened was that an officer was sent [to carry out a recce in Chile]. There were two attempts to get people onto the mainland to intercept these [Exocet missiles] and the first attempt was these helicopters which were going to go in ...[494]

Once landed on the mainland,[495] either by a diesel submarine, by helicopter or by parachute, the teams could establish a covert observation post and communicate directly to Hereford via the SAS's encrypted satellite channels, which were difficult to detect or intercept. In these circumstances, the SAS teams could provide the Task Force with early warning of Super Etendard sorties in sufficient time for the Sea Harriers to scramble and arrange an appropriate reception committee. Having completed their mission, at the conclusion of hostilities the patrols could be exfiltrated by submarine, or perhaps could trek overland to neutral Chile.

A discounted, alternative option was an air raid to destroy the Super Etendards and the Exocets on the ground. Another was an assault on the mainland airbase by special forces, delivered either by parachute or in an Entebbe-style[496] raid with troops rapidly disembarking from Hercules transports, locating and destroying the target aircraft and missiles, re-embarking and flying off into the night. This concept had the entrepreneurial flair of the 'old' SAS and it boasted more of a chance to identify and sabotage critical equipment.

However, any comparison with the Israeli raid on Entebbe was not entirely realistic, not least because of the difference in the intelligence data available. The British intelligence information available on Argentine military resources was appallingly negligible. The Israelis had enjoyed the benefit of up-to-date eye-witness reports of the local situation and knew the precise locations of their objectives. In contrast, the SAS had no such advantage, and were handicapped by a total lack of knowledge regarding the exact whereabouts of the crews, aircraft and the missiles.

22 SAS HQ, but without their commanding officer who, as we have noted, was in the Falklands, began setting out the options for B Squadron, the only sabre [operational] squadron not already operationally committed. The very first issue under consideration was not the delivery of the troops to the target, but the target itself. According to DLB's plan, codenamed Operation MIKADO, the entire squadron would be loaded on to two C130 Hercules transports which would crash-land on Rio Grande's runway. The squadron's objective was to seek out and destroy the five Super

Etendards parked on the tarmac, and disable the three remaining air-launched Exocets known to be in the Argentine arsenal before disappearing into the night. While superficially attractive, MIKADO demanded high-quality information of the kind that was not available from SIS.

Led by their OC, Major SFG,[497] B Squadron gathered in the regimental briefing room early in the morning for a final pep-talk before they departed, and SFG explained the crucial importance of destroying the Exocets. Sergeant Major XH – one of the regiment's most highly respected, longest-serving NCOs – sought out SFG and voiced his concerns. In his judgement the operation amounted to needless and deliberate sacrifice and he 'resigned' from the Squadron. SFG accepted his reasons for withdrawing.[498] A few moments later, with only minutes to go before the coaches were due to arrive, SFG expressed the view to DLB that the raid was not viable. DLB was infuriated to learn of SFG's doubts at the eleventh hour, especially as he had fought so hard in London to obtain the War Cabinet's approval for a scheme which B Squadron previously had assured him was feasible. DLB immediately replaced SFG[499] with Major AP.[500]

Some 22 years later, one of the most senior SAS officers still has strong feelings about the matter: 'He [Major SFG] behaved disgracefully.'[501]

Surprisingly, XH was not returned to his unit (RTU'd) nor punished; instead he was allowed to serve out the remaining eighteen months of his service still in the regiment and retired on a full pension. Most members of the regiment consider this dissension as close to a mutiny as it could be and there has been a stigma attached to B Squadron ever since.[502]

> I think, that if NX had been here [at the SAS HQ in Hereford] – you might have had a different outcome – you might have had the Squadron Commander perhaps court-martialled or got rid of, or he might have done it because NX was there, and he was the CO with a different relationship.[503]

As elements of B Squadron,[504] under the command of Major AP, arrived in Ascension, they received a signal from Hereford advising them that Operation MIKADO had been postponed. This was apparently because an Argentine radar picket had been discovered off the mainland coast, thereby extending the radar cover and making the approach of a pair of Hercules more susceptible to detection.

The B Squadron experience [Op MIKADO] left the Squadron, to a man, disillusioned with the hierarchy after the Falklands. I told the CO that we needed a proper wash-up on the whole thing to see that in future to see that [sic] we did not see the same things go wrong again. There was also a lot of strong feeling from the members of both G and D [Squadrons] who felt they had had a bad deal. There was no proper debrief with the Regiment or the Squadrons.[505]

The Franks Report, formally entitled the Falkland Islands Review, which was handed to Mrs Thatcher on 31 December 1982 and released to the public on 18 January 1983, came to the conclusion that the Argentine decision to invade the Falklands had been taken so late that it would have been impossible to foresee or prevent, and accordingly 'we would not be justified in attaching any criticism or blame to the present Government'.[506]

While Thatcher may have failed to read the danger signals and been slow to tackle Whitehall inertia, she responded with ruthless alacrity once the Falklands crisis was upon her, as can be seen by her creation of the War Cabinet, her selection of its membership – from which she excluded the Chancellor of the Exchequer, Sir Geoffrey Howe – and her determination to circumvent John Nott's team of ministers at the Ministry of Defence. In these decisions her consultation was minimal, but her instinct for political survival prevailed.

The question of whether the raid on Rio Grande could have succeeded without massive loss of life is still a subject for much debate. Although the defenders were not equipped with a single portable missile system, their light flak units remained effective, despite their age. The Argentineans admit they had not anticipated such a bold stroke by the SAS, but insist, as they would, that their troops were kept at a high state of readiness.

Conclusion

After the Iranian Embassy [siege], when the Falklands started, the writing was on the wall. A lot of things went wrong but were not addressed. The SAS was starting to believe what the tabloids said about itself. The mindset was ... If you wear the beret[507] you are capable – Wrong![508]

Operation CORPORATE had cost the lives of 255 members of the British forces and of the Falklands civilian community. Of the deaths, 217 were the result of action with Argentinean forces, 28 of helicopter or aircraft crashes, and 10 of the accidental fire of British forces. Comparing these deaths with other conflicts in which Britain has been involved since the Second World War, they are not as high as in Korea (537 deaths), Malaya (525 deaths) and Northern Ireland (352 deaths up to the end of the Falklands War) but the Falklands deaths are more than were suffered in any of the Palestine, Cyprus, Indonesia, Aden or Oman conflicts. Connor makes some telling observations on the special force casualties of the campaign:

> ... he [Lt Col NX, the CO] also exposed his men to needless risk in operations that were not strategic and therefore not the proper province of the SAS.[509]

Once the Argentineans had invaded, the British government handled the Falklands situation with some skill, securing the vital support of the USA and the EEC and having Argentina condemned in the Security Council of the UN. The naval task force of 44 ships and 28,000 men was despatched with an efficiency which compared well with Suez, 26 years earlier. It involved frightful risks in view of the lack of adequate air cover and air warning. Six ships were sunk and ten damaged. Many more would have been lost had the timing fuses in Argentinean bombs been correctly adjusted. A successful Exocet strike on one of the carriers would have put paid to the expedition and the government. Britain's national honour and international law had been upheld. Whether these were vital British interests must be the subject of continuing debate.

Apart from the Falkland Islands Review, the Ministry of Defence commissioned an after-action report, written by Colonel David Parker of the Parachute Regiment, to document the lessons learned during the campaign. Although still classified, it is believed to be the most candid account of just how close to failure the entire campaign had been, amounting to a catalogue of wrong decisions at every critical moment. It is quite chilling to learn that some units on the front line outside Stanley were down to their last six rounds of ammunition on the day of the surrender, with no prospect of new supplies. Its conclusion was, quite simply, that the task force was lucky not to have been confronted by opponents meeting Warsaw Pact standards, a damning indictment of both staff and hardware.

The new Conservative government of Margaret Thatcher seemed to heighten Britain's world role and prestige in the 1980s. An Anglo-American rapport was established that had not existed since the days of Macmillan. Thatcher appeared to enjoy popularity in the USA unmatched by any British leader since Churchill. This served Britain well during the Falklands War when US aid was invaluable. The government was able to repay their favour in 1986 when alone among America's European allies Britain permitted US jets to operate from British territory against Libya.

The SAS received patronage from Margaret Thatcher, who was a frequent visitor to the SAS base in Hereford, just as the growth of American special forces during Vietnam[510] was due to significant patronage from Kennedy. The political impact of the regiment was matched by the political access enjoyed by its senior members. Both DLB and NX, as a result of the storming of the Iranian Embassy, were personally known to Margaret Thatcher and had direct access to her.

> Working at or near the hub of events, I quickly appreciated the colossal contribution to the campaign made by the Prime Minister.[511]

The subject of special forces having direct access to the highest political level, even when working 'under command' of a local commander, often leads to ill-feeling and animosity. This is especially when a decision made by the task commander is not acceptable to the SAS, who then use the alternative chain of command to put pressure on changing the particular decision. Cohen indicates the inherent problems with such a situation:

> The existence of a unified chain of command for each service fulfils certain fundamental military needs – the coordination of operations for example. More important, it preserves the essence of a good military organisation – hierarchy and obedience. These are virtues not merely for the conduct of war, but for the conduct of sound civil-military relations. The regular transmission of orders and assignment of responsibility should make the military a responsive tool of policy. A divided, circumvented, or unclear chain of command causes resentment and confusion among the military and deprives civil authorities of the chance to control military action. If permitted to do so, elite units may seek – and achieve – independence from the chain of command to the detriment of military planning and civil-military relations.[512]

The strategic and tactical value of some of the regiment's activities during the conflict were later to be severely criticised.[513] Two key operational targets on the Falklands were the 155 mm guns at Port Stanley, which had caused a number of casualties to the British forces during the campaign and the regular C130 flights which came into Stanley airfield on a nightly basis. It is surprising that no Special Force operations were targeted against either the artillery battery or the airfield.

> The weather did not stop an Argentinean C130 landing at Stanley airfield that night [14 June], as on most previous nights. [This was a] reflection of the frustration felt by the whole brigade that the air blockade was not effective.[514]

Few recent British campaigns have been fought with less military information and intelligence about the enemy. In difficult weather conditions, the SAS and SBS teams became the eyes and ears of the task force commanders, as well as providing a reliable raiding force. As a result, the information provided by special forces teams on land was vital to those whose task it was to plan operations. However, the SAS was criticised by 2 Para for its failure to correctly estimate the size of the enemy garrison at Goose Green[515] and Mount Darwin.[516]

> [In the Falklands War] we received 'duff information' from the SAS observing at Goose Green.[517]

In the Falklands, three out of four SAS squadrons had been deployed, the largest concentration of the regiment at any one time and place since the Malayan campaign. The unit's operational experiences, both good and bad, should have been examined. Post-operational 'cleansing sessions' were aired at regimental briefings, a system which had been carried out since the days of the Jebel Akhdar campaign.

> The SAS is great at suppressing these things – is it right? Perhaps they ought to come out in the open a bit more than they have.[518]

But, there was no regimental de-briefing after the Falklands War nor, interestingly enough, after the Gulf War in 1990.

What was unforgivable was that there was not a proper 'internal' wash-up [debrief] of the operation, leaving many members of the Regiment disgruntled and disillusioned with the system.[519]

The distinction between 'strategic' and 'tactical' deployment of the SAS frequently depends upon the operational requirements at the time. The senior SAS commander at the time makes observations about these aspects of the SAS involvement in Operation CORPORATE.

Well, by definition – the SAS, as you say, were trying to get in on the action and that is what they are all about, and if they weren't they wouldn't probably be as successful as they are, overall. I don't have very strong views about this – I think that the SAS, and the Falklands, were being sucked into a tactical battle at the end, and there is nothing unusual in that – I mean Lassen [Major Anders Lassen VC wartime SAS] he got killed in a tactical battle where the SAS was, essentially, being misemployed at the end of the war – well they were there and the job had to be done – what do you do – do you sit around in barracks and get somebody else to do it or what? You go and do it don't you, and I think in the Falklands, in the end, I think probably the concept was right – there were strategic groups that went in ahead and so on. I think then, the battle over ran really, and they wanted something to do – so they grabbed whatever was going and I don't think that is altogether wrong, it might even be wrong not to do that at that stage.[520]

Outwardly, as far as the SAS was concerned, the Falklands War was highly successful.[521] However, in reality the regiment did not perform effectively in the majority of the tasks it carried out. The main area of effectiveness and success was in the establishment and maintenance of long-term observation posts and hides from which the movement of Argentinean troops was observed and reported. Not all the information received was accurate, as in the case of Goose Green, and the author has been advised of a number of incidents of patrols deliberately positioning themselves in less dangerous, protected positions and sending 'false' location reports. The majority of the information did not ever get to the units involved in the actual fighting. The success of one or two observation posts was outweighed by a number of matters: the actions of RP at South Georgia in rashly disregarding the advice of arctic 'experts' and jeopardising men and valuable helicopters; the unnecessary raid on Pebble Island, once again by *RP*;[522] the inaccurate information provided by the SAS about the enemy forces at Goose Green prior to the 2 Para attack; the unnecessary and almost disastrous 'diversionary' raid on the fuel tanks at Stanley, led by *RP*; the lack of strategic vision in allowing the Argentinean 155 mm artillery and the nightly C130 flight to remain unmolested throughout the campaign; and finally the 'lack of enthusiasm' for Operation MIKADO by *SFG*, the officer commanding B Squadron, despite the fact that the destruction of the Argentinean Exocet missile capability had become critical to the continued successful prosecution of the war.[523]

The SAS patently had a role in this war but their performance and effectiveness was flawed by a lack of strategic vision combined with poor operational skills and less than committed personnel. Furthermore, they remained in the conflict past the stage where their contribution was assisting the main war-fighting effort and thus become a considerable distraction on the battlefield.

The Falklands campaign was not an unqualified success for the SAS. Expectations were high and, in combination with a command hierarchy that was largely naval-led – and thus unfamiliar with special operations – there was a degree of over-emphasis on offensive action tasks coupled with an unrealistic expectation of what might be achieved by them.

Unfortunately, these errors were repeated in the next conflict in which they participated – the Gulf War of 1991.

Chapter 10

THE GULF WAR: OPERATION GRANBY (1990–1991)

Background

> War, after all, is not Nintendo. War is not about technology or
> toys. War is about killing.[524]

Saddam Hussein of Iraq had long-standing ambitions on the oil-rich
sheikdom of Kuwait and its oilfields which he had always intended
to fulfil. On 2 August 1990, he ordered his troops to invade Kuwait
precipitating an international crisis which culminated in the Gulf
War of 1991. The attack was a near complete surprise and the
Kuwait forces were rapidly overrun.

Operation GRANBY, as it was called by the British (the
Americans' name was Operation DESERT SHIELD), had as its first
aim to deter Saddam Hussein from further aggression. Then, gradually, as the weeks went by, the Coalition posture changed from one
of defence to one of offense: from seeking to contain the Iraqis, to
driving them out of Kuwait, first by threats and finally by force. On
29 November, the United Nations passed Resolution 678, which
authorised the use of force to expel Iraq from Kuwait if it did not
withdraw by 15 January 1991.

By the end of 1990, Coalition intelligence reports suggested that
Saddam Hussein had an army of half a million men established in
positions of strength, with armour and artillery, in Kuwait and along
the Saudi frontier. It was also expected, further, that he might well
use the chemical and biological weapons which, it was believed,
were included in his arsenal. The Coalition strategy was to build up

their own land forces to a level that was considered adequate before commencing an all-out air attack and then not to engage the Iraqi troops on the ground until Allied air power had reduced their effectiveness by at least 50 per cent.

The air war started on 17 January 1991, after nearly four months of stand-off and preparation; it continued unabated, night and day, for the next five weeks. Saddam's Air Force was grounded or dispersed, his communications severely disrupted, his command centres destroyed, his biological and chemical factories put out of action, his Navy eliminated, and his soldiers in the desert completely demoralised by continuous bombing[525] carried out by ranks of B52[526] bombers dropping thousands of conventional iron bombs. When the ground war started, the Coalition forces drove through the weakened enemy with minimal opposition, and, in barely a hundred hours, the war was at an end, with very few Coalition casualties.

When Saddam Hussein's troops invaded Kuwait on 2 August 1990, few imagined that the outcome would be the deployment of some 45,000 British service personnel as part of a huge coalition army. During the build-up of that force there were predictions about casualties running into thousands from poison gas and there was consideration of a possible nuclear option by Iraq. In the event, the expulsion of the Iraqi dictator from Kuwait was achieved with remarkably few coalition casualties but enormous numbers of Iraqi casualties. This was a war of high-technology air-power against a conventional low-technology, mainly conscript, army.

DLB, shortly before his retirement, was appointed, personally, by Margaret Thatcher[527] to command the British forces in the Gulf.

I also wanted the commander of our forces to be someone in whom I – and they – would have complete confidence. The MoD came up with several names but only one man seemed to be right for the job – Sir DLB. Tom King [Defence Secretary 1989–92] was reluctant to see him appointed: DLB was within a week of retiring and the other candidates clearly had much to be said for them. But I wanted a fighting general. I knew the qualities of DLB from his command of the SAS operation at the time of the 1980 Iranian Embassy siege and from the Falklands. I also knew that he spoke Arabic – of some importance when part of a large multi-national force with a crucial Arab element. So I told Tom King that DLB was not retiring now if I had anything to do with it: and if he did not go to command our forces in the Gulf, he would be coming as personal adviser on the conduct of the war to Downing Street. He went to the Gulf.[528]

Involvement of the SAS

Despite the number of books written about the SAS involvement in the Gulf War of 1990–91 there is a scarcity of detail about what tasks were to be carried out to justify their involvement. Their utilisation was somewhat strained, and despite attempts by some of those involved at the tactical level to justify their usage there is no evidence of political or strategic direction in their employment. What we do observe, once again, is SAS involvement based upon aggressive lobbying by the senior SAS individuals and the SAS headquarters and not as a result of the need for their specific skills and talents. Like the Falklands War it was a costly venture for such a small organisation.

.... the Coalition had no tasks for the SF [special forces] and did not want them cluttering up the battlefield as they did in the Falklands.[529]

DLB arrived in Saudi Arabia in early October, where he was confronted by a number of immediate problems. One was the lack of intelligence about the enemy, just as in the Falklands War, and another was the presence of large numbers of Western civilian hostages in Iraqi hands. Saddam Hussein was threatening to imprison them at strategic sites around the country to deter attack by Coalition forces.

The SAS, as always, sniffing the potential for involvement in a conflict had a sub-unit in the United Arab Emirates, D Squadron, officially on a training exercise. This squadron was earmarked for an optimistic operation to free those hostages.

A proposal that an SAS squadron should parachute into Iraqi occupied Kuwait City, jumping from a Hercules at between 400 and 600 feet, was never put into effect. This would have been a suicide mission, but would certainly have got the Regiment plenty of publicity![530]

However, the operation was never mounted, and the captives were released by Saddam Hussein in late December 1990. As late as 11 November there seemed to be no other useful mission that special forces could perform.

The Commander-in-Chief of Allied Forces, Norman Schwarzkopf, was notoriously sceptical of the utility of special forces, having witnessed at first hand the comparatively poor performance of the Green Berets in Vietnam and in Grenada where, as a major general, he had been sent in on the second day of the invasion to attempt to restore order to the chaotic situation that prevailed.[531] He was not convinced that special forces had any useful role to play and that Iraqi targets could be eliminated by use of air power or armour.

Moreover, DLB who, as always, was keen to deploy the SAS, the unit which had been so much a part of his military career, also had difficulty in defining a strategic role for them to play. The traditional SAS tasks in conventional desert warfare, harking back to the Second World War, encompassed raiding, harassment and information reporting, but DLB also knew that these tasks could, and were, being achieved through the Allies' completely overwhelming air superiority.

As has happened in almost every conflict the SAS has been involved in, the role that was ultimately given to the SAS was one that they had developed, and promoted, for themselves –

> Their task would be to cut roads and create diversions which would draw Iraqi forces away from the main front and sow fears in the mind of the enemy that some major operation was brewing on his right flank. At the back of my own mind was the idea that the SAS might also be able to take out mobile SCUD missile launchers.[532]

In December, with the hostages freed, the SAS was ordered to plan deep-penetration missions into both Iraq and Kuwait. However, DLB had two criteria with which special forces operations must comply:

> I myself was not prepared to recommend special operations unless two conditions were fulfilled: one was that there must be a real, worthwhile role for the SAS to perform, and the other that we must have some means of extricating our men in an emergency.[533]

It was agreed that the SAS would cross the border on the day the air war started and a second squadron, B Squadron was flown out from England, straight from a spell as the counter-terrorist response standby team.

There was, at that stage, a level of controversy about the methods of insertion, with some patrols wishing to be dropped by helicopter to operate on foot, while others preferred to drive in by Land Rover and motorcycle. Taking vehicles meant that heavier weaponry could be carried and that the patrol would have a high degree of mobility; but opposed to that was the risk of detection in terrain which offered little cover. The action radius of foot patrols was limited and they would have no means of escape if detected, but they could conceal themselves far more easily. This was not a new problem, and was one that had been encountered by David Stirling during desert operations in the Second World War, where he had emphatically chosen the motorised option of deployment.

The objectives of the patrols were not clearly defined and, in general, the patrols were to carry out offensive actions against Iraqi installations and units. As an additional task, they were to provide observation posts to keep watch on the Iraqi supply routes. In a somewhat overly democratic fashion, especially considering the lack of desert expertise by most of the current SAS personnel, it was left to individual patrols to decide for themselves their method of insertion. Some opted to work on foot; others drove in. In terms of communications they were vastly better served than they had been in the Falklands and most patrols carried a portable satellite navigation aid (GPS) which could pinpoint their position to within a few metres in often featureless desert. Once over the border, however, and settling into position, the mission was significantly altered when the first Scud missile was launched against Israel.[534] While the diplomats exerted the strongest pressure to keep that country out of the war, the mobile Scud missile launchers became priority number one for the SAS, as they proved difficult to locate from the air.

> It was only after a hard sell that it was agreed they [the SAS] should operate against the Scuds.[535]

The area in which the men were operating was a high rocky plateau in the west of Iraq, which at night became bitterly cold, the effects of which had been underestimated.

The SBS were also carrying out clandestine operations,[536] and once again rivalries erupted between SAS and SBS, with Falconer stating:

The SAS was acting like a bunch of soccer hooligans leaping all over the desert looking for someone to bash and getting lost in the process.[537]

And Camsell:

Once again Hereford were the masters of putting their noses in where it [sic] was not wanted.[538]

These comments differ from the view taken by DLB in *Storm Command*:

It became apparent that the SAS had done the Coalition proud, as I had always felt they would, *provided* they were given a definite task [emphasis added].[539]

On 23 October an SBS patrol destroyed a considerable stretch of the main communication cable running from Baghdad to the front-line units. They were flown in by two Chinook helicopters, did the job and were all safely extricated.

This was a high-risk operation, separate from the SAS deployment, carried out by the Special Boat Service with great skill, determination and courage in a most hostile environment.[540]

The 'success' of the SBS in this task led them to being given a mobility role in the Second Gulf War with embarrassing consequences.[541]

One of the B Squadron foot patrols, B20 (Bravo Two Zero)[542] was discovered shortly after having been inserted by a Chinook helicopter, on a mission to hunt for Scud launchers and to cut communications cables along the main supply route running west from Baghdad. The other patrols meanwhile continued their aggressive patrolling work behind the lines and a column of vehicles even drove into Iraq on a resupply mission.[543]

Closer consideration of the SAS's role in the Gulf War reveals many shortcomings that were not evident during the euphoria apparent at the time of the 'victory'.

The Regiment paid the price for mistakes made over the previous six or seven years. Old lessons went out the window.[544]

What does emerge is that three squadrons were deployed with little or no notion as to how to employ them and it was only when the

Scud menace became apparent that the mobile patrols inside Iraq were employed to search out and destroy the launchers. As to how many were eliminated, exaggerated claims were made but it seems that the successes, if any, were slight. Many of the difficulties encountered by SAS patrols behind the lines were caused by inadequate maps, faulty communications and poor intelligence of the targets they were to attack. We have seen the problems that Bravo Two Zero's commander had to face with regard to communications and these were the same in the other patrols. It is noteworthy that the two other B Squadron patrols, one on foot and one vehicle mounted, were both aborted by their commanders shortly after arrival inside enemy territory.

> As for the Falklands but worse. I encouraged Andy McNab to write Bravo Two Zero and when I read it I was surprised, nay amazed, at the naivety and the lack of understanding of the Arabs and the desert within the squadron [B Squadron]. Sometime between Oman [Operation STORM] and Iraq, humility had slipped away from the SAS.[546]

Even more serious was the question of command and control. Contrary to well-established procedures, Squadron OCs went into the field instead of directing and managing their patrols from the forward operating base. In their absence, the management task was left to staff and intelligence officers, who had not had the benefit of SAS training. Lack of relatively inexpensive kit such as sufficient numbers of GPS satellite navigation systems meant that the available men had to travel together in sizeable groups instead of breaking down into the classic four-man patrols.

> There was a serious lack of appropriate equipment.[546]

Vehicle convoys also had difficulty in communicating with Allied aircraft, as was the case with Bravo Two Zero.

The other major Gulf War patrol that has been extensively recounted was the A Squadron operation that attacked a large Iraqi communications centre known as Victor Two. Both A and D Squadrons were split up into two half-squadrons for the run into Iraq, but unlike Bravo Two Zero they were motorised.[547]

> Some good ops [operations] using classic 'hit and run' tactics from the Second World War but not learning from the experience.

Bravo Two Zero should have taken some form of transport with them just like they did in the Second World War.[548]

In a somewhat bizarre incident, a squadron commander was relieved of his command during the course of a patrol, to be replaced by the Regimental Sergeant Major.[549] The officer concerned was from SBS and was the first SBS officer to command an SAS squadron, and his being in command in the first place was a result of a new policy of cross-postings within the Special Forces Group. Whatever the facts of the case, the place to weed out unsuitable officers is at base and not when committed to an operation.

The SAS patrols went into Iraq when the air war started, and although they were originally tasked to take on targets of opportunity the mission soon changed to that of Scud hunting. However, there is doubt that the patrols of A and D Squadrons – and of the American Delta Force, who joined the Scud hunt shortly after the SAS deployment – actually achieved their aim to disrupt launches of Scud missiles aimed at targets in Israel and Saudi Arabia.

Between 17 and 26 January 21 Scuds were fired at Israel and 22 at Saudi Arabia, whereas from 27 January to the end of the war, nearly a month later, 19 Scuds were fired at Israel and 23 at Saudi; in other words, there was a reduction in the number of firings but not a huge one, and it would be difficult to claim that it was the result of SAS action specifically rather than, for example, air attacks.

A second question mark has been raised over the number of Scuds that were actually destroyed. A United States Congressional Investigation, as well as the United Nations team investigating and destroying Iraqi weapons of mass destruction, both concluded independently that there was no solid evidence that any Scuds had been destroyed, either by air power or special forces. Intelligence information collected after the war indicated that the Iraqis had possessed 19 mobile Scud launchers and the UN were able to account for all of them.

Special forces attacks on communications centres and infrastructure targets probably had little ultimate effect on an enemy who were shown, after the launch of the main ground offensive on 24 February, to have neither the will nor the means to resist.

Conclusion

The conflict was so one-sided, the American technological advantage so great, that when the land battle actually came, it was little more than a massacre, more reminiscent of Omdurman than El Alamein.[550]

Looking at the Gulf War operations, several issues about the SAS deployment are apparent. Three quarters of the regiment were deployed, it was a major engagement for the unit, yet the men were used as a form of shock infantry instead of being reserved for targets of strategic importance. Moreover, they were deployed into the desert with inadequate intelligence, maps and even, in some cases, defective equipment.

The significance of SAS operations is open to debate. The SAS was used hundreds of kilometres west of Kuwait, well away from where allied ground forces were to advance, so its attacks on Iraqi units had little impact except psychologically. The only SAS role of real importance was its attempts to locate Scud launchers for destruction by Allied aircraft.

The SAS reached a compromise about their tactics in characteristic fashion. As is traditional in the regiment, the decision about how to deploy was largely left to the patrol commanders and reached by democratic discussion. Two of the observation patrols decided to go in on foot. The leader of one of these groups took a quick look round the area in which the helicopter landed him, saw that it was lethally flat and insisted, with no mean courage, on immediately being flown out again.

> *RB*[551] was the patrol commander who decided not to deploy his patrol when he arrived at the patrol location and returned to the main base. Apparently, he actually received white feathers when in fact he was the only patrol commander with the moral courage, and confidence, not to deploy into a poor area.[552]

One other patrol was lifted in to operate on foot and others drove in aboard specially equipped Land Rovers and motorcycles.

In his book about the Gulf War, DLB states that Norman Schwarzkopf declared:

> The performance of the 22nd Special Air Service Regiment during Operation Desert Storm was in the highest traditions of the

professional military service, and in keeping with the proud history and tradition that has been established by that Regiment.[553]

However, in his autobiography,[554] Schwarzkopf makes no mention at all of the SAS or their activities.

As long as Mrs Thatcher remained Prime Minister the SAS had sponsorship at the highest level. But in the Gulf War – when Mrs Thatcher and her patronage had gone – the SAS was starved of intelligence, equipment, access and influence, and largely denied a strategic role in the conflict.

During the war, A, B and D Squadrons of 22 SAS[555] struck dozens of targets. Numerous isolated Iraqi outposts were dealt with by the groups, but in many other cases they called in air power. SAS soldiers claim their use of air strikes allowed them to destroy several of the Scud missile launchers Saddam Hussein was using to hit Israel.

> The battlefield and in the air seemed to be so overwhelming as to leave no gap which Special Forces could usefully fill. (In this, it turned out, I was wrong, for the SAS did later perform an absolutely vital role, that of destroying mobile Scud launchers, which proved to be beyond the powers of the air force, even with the overwhelming supremacy which it established.)[556]

Contrary to DLB's supposition, little evidence was provided then, nor has any been provided since, to confirm that any Scuds at all were located or destroyed by SAS forces.[557]

> The actual effectiveness of this Scud hunt is hotly disputed.[558]

These events re-emphasised the special relationship of Britain and the USA even though British forces were only 10 per cent of those provided by the USA. During the build-up the Prime Minister was ousted and replaced by John Major. This war, like the Falklands, was perhaps good for British self-esteem, but in reality it illustrated comparative national decline. Kuwait had been a British Protectorate since 1899 and there remained vital economic links with the tiny state despite the ending of its Protectorate status. In 1917 and 1941 British forces had occupied the whole of Iraq, and in 1961 single-handedly deterred Iraq from attacking Kuwait. But by 1990 Britain was clearly incapable of defending Kuwait: only as a cog in the much greater American machine could Britain assert her presence in the Middle East.

The war against Iraq in 1991 was the largest commitment of British forces to a military operation since the Falklands War of 1982, and while the USA clearly led the Coalition forces in defeating Iraq, Britain's military played a significant role as junior partner. Furthermore, Britain's diplomatic stance during the crisis that led up to the war was virtually indistinguishable from that of the USA, tending to give the impression of a united coalition while the position of many other European states was decidedly less supportive.

The principles by which the SAS should operate were set out by Stirling, and perhaps the most important element of Stirling's thinking had been his tactical approach, which relied upon the use of small groups of soldiers deep behind enemy lines. The need to use small numbers delivering 'disproportionate violence' is still central to SAS tactics.

The deduction to be made from this is that 'successful' offensive special forces operations are characteristic of armies on the defensive, and one might well speculate that the benefits they bring are, to a great extent, psychological: they comfort commanders that they retain the ability to take the initiative, at least in a small way. This is equally the case in counter-insurgency as it is in conventional operations.

For all the 'hype' that has surrounded the activities of the SAS in the Gulf War the reality is that their impact was marginal at best.

> ... the planning and implementation of operations was amateurish.[559]

Their attempt to repeat the role of the SAS in the Second World War was completely marginalised by the massive Allied material and technological superiority. In the Gulf War the SAS repeated some of the faults of proliferation and self-generation of roles that bedevilled desert operations carried out by their predecessors during the Second World War.

> It grieves me to say it, because they [the SAS] lost several men, but their actual impact on the war was negligible.[560]

PART FOUR

COUNTERING TERRORISM, AND INTERNATIONAL HUMANITARIAN OPERATIONS

Chapter 11

Northern Ireland

The IRA are the core of the terrorist problem; their counterparts on the Protestant side would probably disappear if the IRA could be beaten. But the best chance of beating them is if three conditions are met. First, the IRA have to be rejected by the nationalist minority on whom they depend for shelter and support. This requires that the minority should be allowed to support, or at least acquiesce, in the constitutional framework of the state in which they live. Second, the IRA have to be deprived of international support, whether from well-meaning but naïve Irish-Americans, or from Arab revolutionary regimes like that of Colonel Gaddafi. This requires constant attention to foreign policy aimed at explaining the facts to the misinformed and cutting off the weapons from the mischief-makers. Third, and linked to the other two, relations between Britain and the Republic of Ireland have to be carefully managed. Although the IRA have plenty of support in areas like West Belfast within Northern Ireland, very often it is to the South that they go to be trained, to receive money and arms and to escape capture after crimes committed within the United Kingdom.[561]

Background

The subject of the 'troubles' in Northern Ireland is extremely complex, and a detailed introduction is necessary to set the scene for the involvement of the SAS.

In Northern Ireland, British troops were committed to the streets following the formal request of the Northern Ireland government

A member of the SAS carrying out a reconnaissance patrol near Crossmaglen in South Armagh, Northern Ireland.

for military assistance on 14 August 1969 amid increasing communal and sectarian violence. Deployment was intended to safeguard Catholic areas in the light of the virtual collapse of the Royal Ulster Constabulary (RUC) under the pressures arising from the escalating civil rights campaign by the Northern Ireland Civil Rights Association over the previous two years. Living standards had improved in the 1950s and had stimulated the growth of a Catholic middle class, Catholics forming 38 per cent of the population by 1969.

The prime minister of Northern Ireland, Captain Terence O'Neill, had hoped to draw these Catholics into public life, but merely raised greater expectations than could be satisfied by the limited concessions on offer amid continuing discrimination against Catholics in housing and employment. In the event, it was to be the Catholic working-class community who were to be drawn into confrontation with the RUC. The RUC rapidly became exhausted and demoralised in the disturbances that ensued and troops were ordered in as an 'aid to the civil power'.

The troops were initially welcomed by the Catholics. However, the Army did not, deliberately, establish a permanently strong presence in the Catholic areas, which had became effective 'no-go' areas shielded not only from Protestants but also from normal policing. The Army was increasingly seen to be acting in the interests of an institution discredited in the eyes of the nationalists, namely the Stormont government.

The old-style Marxist IRA, which had continued to exist since the division of Ireland in 1921 and had conducted unsuccessful campaigns in Britain and Northern Ireland both in 1939 and between 1956 and 1962, was caught by surprise by the course of events. Its hesitancy resulted in a breakaway by mostly northern militants, who formed the Provisional IRA (PIRA) in December 1969, determined to provoke and exploit confrontations between troops and the Catholics. Street violence increased throughout the spring of 1970 and reached its peak in 1971–72. The first soldier was killed on 6 February 1971.

Internment had worked well during the limited IRA campaign of 1956–62 and, against the Army's advice, was again introduced on 9 August 1971.[562] Internment was marked by poor and defective police intelligence while the fact that only Catholics were arrested exacerbated the situation on the streets. Direct rule of the province was assumed by Westminster on 24 March 1972. It was welcomed by the Army mainly because it was likely to lead to clear political direction. However, the Army was directed not to enter the IRA designated 'no-go' areas, and to scale down overt patrolling and surveillance. The error of the Heath government to negotiating a 'pause' with PIRA enabled them to regroup within these 'no-go' areas and led to the so-called 'Bloody Friday' on 21 July, when a series of 22 bombs were detonated in Belfast city centre. On 31 July 1972, Operation MOTORMAN was mounted with 27 battalions to repossess the 'no-go' areas. Internment ceased in December 1975, but direct rule has continued, although an assembly and power-sharing executive was restored to the province in 1998.

With the ceasefire of PIRA in July 1997 and the entry of its political representatives, Sinn Fein, into all-party talks in September 1997, there were further splits in the Republican movement. Continuity IRA and its political wing, Republican Sinn Fein, had already emerged in 1986 after Sinn Fein recognised the parliament in the Irish Republic. The Real IRA and its political wing, the 32 County Sovereignty Movement, emerged in late 1997 with an estimated 400 members and was responsible for the Omagh bomb attack in August 1998. It, too, then issued a ceasefire statement, although incidents have continued, not least in London with bombs on railway lines and a rocket attack on the headquarters of MI6 on the Thames Embankment.

On the other side of the sectarian divide, various Protestant para-militaries have emerged, including the Ulster Defence Association (UDA), which has links with the Ulster Freedom Fighters (UFF) and has perhaps between 1,500 and 2,000 members, and the Ulster Volunteer Force (UVF), which has perhaps between 750 and 1,000 members.

The Provisionals, Irish National Liberation Army (INLA) and the other Republican groups have enjoyed sanctuary across the international frontier with the Irish Republic. This has been described as a 'leaking sieve', although the Republic has stronger anti-terrorist legislation than Britain and much of the problem relates to the 123-mile length of the border.

The Provisionals provided a challenging threat and the six accepted elements of a successful counter-insurgency strategy, as identified by the likes of Robert Thompson[563] and used successfully by the SAS in Malaya and Oman, were applied with varying levels of success. Namely, the recognition of the need for a political rather than a purely military solution; the necessity for complete civil–military cooperation; the equal necessity for a coordinated intelligence effort; the need to split active insurgents from their supporters; the use of appropriate military measures; and the need for long-term political reforms to prevent a resurgence of trouble.

A peace forum was elected in May 1996 and negotiations eventually led to an agreement in April 1998, allowing for recognition of the principle of consent, by which Ulster would remain part of the United Kingdom so long as the majority willed it so, an assembly and a power-sharing executive, a North–South ministerial council, a so-called Council of the Isles, and a commitment to paramilitary disarmament. The new executive began work in 1999, but the peace process remains a tentative one, not least from the failure of PIRA and the Real IRA to commit themselves to decommissioning their weapons.

In Northern Ireland, a separation of population from insurgent has not proved possible given the intransigent nature of the respective communities. Indeed, symptomatic of the problem was the Ulster version of the Berlin Wall, constructed in 1969 to separate Catholic and Protestant areas.

Much rests on the current, but interminable, 'peace process', which may or may not prove successful in the long term. Clearly, however, for reasons largely beyond the control of the security forces, the campaign against terrorism in Northern Ireland has not fulfilled a number of those requirements identified as keys to successful counter-insurgency.

Intelligence Gathering and Covert Operations

In the 1970s there was a migration of intelligence experts to the province, which inevitably resulted in overlapping competencies and rivalries. The Army naturally needed its own sources of information, so set up an extensive intelligence-gathering operation, while at the same time MI5 arrived on the scene. Affairs in the Irish Republic were monitored by the Secret Intelligence Service (SIS)/MI6 which, generally speaking, did not communicate easily with anyone else. Not to be outdone, the RUC greatly expanded its own Special Branch. They had the advantage of years of experience on the ground, but the web of family and religious ties in Ulster led to mistrust on the part of the Army – which has never fully understood the tribal structure of the local society.

A variety of methods were used to fill the manifold intelligence gaps, including local censuses, confidential telephone numbers, constant patrolling, P (Person) checks, snap searches and vehicle checks. Possibly four million vehicles were stopped between 1 April 1973 and 1 April 1974 alone. Deep interrogation, based on sensory deprivation, was also used on some suspects following internment. These interrogations were highly successful and placed the IRA under major threat.[564]

Earlier covert operations were problematic. The first military plain-clothes organisation was the Mobile Reconnaissance Force (MRF),[565] which was initiated by General FK. After the MRF was compromised by the IRA, covert surveillance operations were carried out by 14 Intelligence Company[566] [abbreviated to 14 Int or 'The Det'[567]]. This was later named 4 Intelligence and Security Company and made part of the Intelligence and Security Group. This group had a troop of SAS attached. However, there was clearly a lack of coordination between the Army and Special Branch of the RUC, which also maintained its own surveillance units. Rivalries between MI5 and MI6 also exacerbated these coordination problems.

The Police Field Research Unit (FRU), established in 1980 to deal with informers, has also been a subject of controversy in recent years. In 1989, in investigating allegations of collusion between the UDR and Protestant paramilitaries, the Stevens Inquiry exposed

An urban observation post (OP) in a derelict building in Belfast, Northern Ireland watching a known IRA meeting place.

the use of informers by the FRU, one of whom was to be convicted of a number of terrorist offences. Subsequently, there have been other allegations that some murders had been permitted to occur in order to preserve the cover of an agent placed in the UDA. The 'super-grass' informer system was employed very successfully between 1982 and 1986, but 50 of the 120 individuals convicted on such evidence later had their verdicts overturned and further trials were suspended.

Involvement of the SAS

Despite their high media profile the SAS physical involvement in Ireland has been quite small and, in relation to the numbers of conventional troops operating there, its impact has been minimal.

In August 1969, some uniformed elements of 22 SAS was first deployed to Ulster at the request of MI5 and they operated quite openly in uniform and used SAS open-top Land Rovers. This was Operation CUFF. It does not appear to have been a success and there was a certain amount of indiscipline within the unit leading to complaints from the RUC.[568] There had also been a later attempt by the SAS to become involved in operations in Ireland:

> The SAS was *persona non-grata* in Northern Ireland for political reasons, and I wanted them to go there rather along the Radfan lines. I was forbidden and I wasn't allowed to talk about it or do anything about it, and actually, in retrospect, I am very glad because it is a mess, Northern Ireland.[569]

At the time, the SAS was also involved in the war in Oman and was unable to commit large numbers of troops to Northern Ireland. It was only when that conflict in Oman ended that SAS troops returned there at the behest of the Wilson government.

On 7 January 1976 a statement from 10 Downing Street announced that elements of the SAS Regiment were to be based in South Armagh for 'patrolling and surveillance tasks', and it was emphasised that they would wear uniform and carry normal-issue weapons. They were to be based with an Army battalion at a former mill, Bessbrook, in South Armagh. In Ulster itself the Army was ambivalent about the new initiative but the RUC certainly did not welcome it: they felt it was both a slight on their own efficiency and a further attempt by the mainland to take control of the war against the terrorists. The initial SAS detachment was sent to Bessbrook[570] to form the advance party for the rest of the squadron some weeks later. The numbers finally involved were about 60 operatives plus support – nowhere near the 150 claimed by the IRA. At Bessbrook Mill the SAS detachment was co-located with the resident infantry battalion based there. When the SAS arrived, there was a Scottish infantry battalion working from the mill; however, by the time the first SAS detachment had changed over this resident battalion was replaced by 3 Para. The Paras were not impressed with the SAS.

> When we were stationed in Bessbrook Mill in South Armagh with the SAS in 1976 we were very unimpressed with the poor tactical procedures of the SAS patrols. It was if they thought they were either invisible or bullet-proof. This may have been because most of the NCOs had never served in Northern Ireland before and gained their operational experience in the jungles of Borneo or the deserts of Oman.[571]

The decision to send in the SAS was essentially a political one, which dictated the publicity surrounding the deployment. Public opinion had gained the impression that the IRA could kill British soldiers with impunity in the border area of South Armagh, and there had also been a spate of sectarian murders during the latter part of 1975. The government of Harold Wilson was under pressure to be seen to be doing something.

Many of those involved in the conflict, both RUC and military, felt that their job was to win over the hearts and minds of the local population rather than let loose, as they thought, a 'bunch of trigger-happy hoodlums'.

> The catalyst for me came when 22 SAS was first deployed in Northern Ireland and as Commanding Officer I had to dissuade the then Commander Land Forces from posting a platoon of RMP to the SAS detachment's base to control it. Even so, his distrust was such that he insisted that the detachment would have no access to any other intelligence than that of the reconnaissance platoon of the battalion with whom it was based, and would serve merely under the command of that battalion. It took a great deal of work at very high level to unravel that one. I was also present when a three star general advised the Commander in Chief of UKLF not to send the Regiment on an overseas operation because its soldiers could not be trusted to behave.[572]

This perception was reinforced by the fact that all SAS personnel had their personal weapons forensically tested[573] *before* they deployed to the Province.

> All SAS weapons, including spare barrels, replacement weapons or repaired weapons (where the repair is likely to affect the ballistic signature of the weapon) are to be forensically tested before being deployed in the Province. Results of the tests are to be forwarded to the RUC.[574]

Moreover, once in the Province they were not permitted to contact any Special Branch except through non-SAS liaison officers.[575] The initial utilisation of the SAS was plagued by a lack of understanding about their capabilities on the part of senior Army commanders, who wanted them to operate in patrols of eight to ten men. These misunderstandings and concerns were not restricted to military commanders but also to politicians.

> Ministers attached some importance to this safeguard [the forensic
> testing of weapons] when the Unit [22 SAS] was originally
> deployed.[576]

When properly established the unit reverted to its normal pattern of
four-man teams and instituted a programme of covert observation
throughout the South Armagh area. Even the chain of command
was unclear in those early days as the squadron was at first placed
under the command of a lieutenant-colonel commanding the local
battalion, who had little knowledge of their abilities.

> The SAS [merely] formed part of the reinforcement which was
> sent to the general area in the wake of the very high levels of
> killing suffered during the first week of the year [1976].[577]

The initial deployment of the SAS to Bessbrook Mill in South
Armagh was a classic example of how not to use special forces and
contradicted almost every accepted principle for their successful
usage. There was no strategic role; they were deployed at battalion
level; they were unable to utilise their specialist weapons; and they
did not have access to good, high-level intelligence.

> In the early stages the operation was amateurish and lacked any
> proper direction – sending in a squadron straight off the Jebel
> being an example. As it progressed, the Regiment became more
> sophisticated and it [Northern Ireland] provided useful training
> and experience in counter-terrorist operations, which has stood
> the Regiment in good stead in recent years.[578]

The first SAS success was on 12 March 1976 when one SMcK, who
had already been interned for three years and was known to Army
intelligence as a leading IRA operative, was arrested by an SAS
patrol. A month later, PC who, it was admitted by the IRA, was a
staff officer in the First Battalion [sic] of their South Armagh
Brigade was shot when he attempted to attack a member of the SAS
patrol that had arrested him.

The next major incident involving the SAS was a major embarrassment to the government and reinforced the view prevalent
among many senior officers in Northern Ireland that the prime
minister had saddled them with a gang of amateur cowboys. Late in
the evening of 5/6 May 1976 two armed SAS men in civilian
clothes, driving a locally registered car, were arrested at a police

The author in a rural observation post (OP) watching a suspected IRA bomb-making factory 'somewhere' in South Armagh, Northern Ireland.

checkpoint some 600 yards inside the border of the Republic. They claimed that they had made a map-reading error and assumed that they would be released, since in many places the border is not clearly defined. They were arrested by the Gardai (Southern Irish Police). Meanwhile, two other cars containing more armed members of the SAS, who had set out to find their colleagues, ran into the same checkpoint. The Gardai arrested them also. The Gardai had in custody eight members of the SAS with three vehicles and an impressive collection of weapons.[579]

The soldiers were given bail of £40,000, which was provided by the British Embassy. The British Embassy was not convinced that the soldiers would return to the Republic to answer bail and sought confirmation from the MoD that they, the MoD, would accept financial liability if the money was forfeited.[580]

> You spoke to me on Friday about the cheque for £40,000 which the British Embassy, Dublin had lodged with the Special Criminal Court when release on bail was granted to the eight SAS soldiers. This letter is to confirm that should the £40,000

become forfeit the Ministry of Defence accepts financial liability and will reimburse your Department.[581]

In an attempt to maintain morale the commander of the SAS Group, Brigadier JWT allegedly stated that if the soldiers had to appear again in court in Southern Ireland he would resign. Interestingly, the soldiers did have to appear again in Southern Ireland but JWT chose not to resign.

> [The SAS] had been sent in by the Prime Minister, Harold Wilson, who committed them without warning in a deliberate blaze of publicity. There had been a few minor problems – as when some men strayed over the border into the Republic – and every time something went wrong, the IRA sought to make capital out of the incident, working up a campaign of black propaganda against the Regiment.[582]

This SAS 'incursion' into Southern Ireland caused major political friction between the UK and the Republic. Several factors made the situation more complex and, from the Republic's point of view, possibly more sinister. At the beginning of the same month, May, the body of a Seamus Ludlow had been found close to the border near where the SAS patrols were apprehended. Also, on 1 February 1976, Private Meehan of the UDR [Ulster Defence Regiment] was arrested several miles inside the Republic with a sub-machine gun, 35 rounds of ammunition, and his uniform in the boot of his car. He was remanded in custody for three months by the Irish authorities and then received a six-month custodial sentence. The Irish Judge at Meehan's trial made the point that he was making an example of him. This meant that there was a very real chance that similar, or longer, sentences could be given to the SAS soldiers. The matter was considered of such seriousness that the British government considered a number of measures to be taken if the soldiers were given prison sentences.

> If [the SAS soldiers are] imprisoned there are a considerable range of more or less drastic sanctions which could be taken against the Republic. They include an embargo on trade, a ban on remittances, withdrawal of social security benefit for Irish citizens, prohibition or limitation of Irish immigration and the ending of voting rights of Irish citizens in this country.[583]

There were also questions in the House of Commons as to whether 'SAS successes were worth the damage that has been done by this incident'.[584]

The soldiers were acquitted of the serious offence of possession of firearms with intent to endanger life, but each was fined £100 for having unlicensed weapons.[585]

During 1977, the SAS squadron was no longer concentrated in South Armagh, but was divided up into its component troops and spread throughout the province; one troop was left at Bessbrook in 3 Brigade area; one was based in Londonderry with 8 Brigade; and a third went to 39 Brigade at Belfast. The fourth troop was held as a reserve under the direct command of the Commander Land Forces. It is quite clear that at the time the SAS was seen as a possible answer to the IRA and it was official policy to use them offensively whenever there was a possibility of confrontation. The fact that terrorist shootings had diminished in South Armagh 'bandit country' was cited as evidence of their success. But, there were to be two incidents in 1978 that caused the politicians and the military to reconsider SAS deployment and tactics.

In the first, in June 1978, the SAS shot dead three IRA.[586] In the second, on 16 July, a 16-year-old was shot dead by the SAS ambushing a weapon cache.[587] The result was a public relations disaster for the Army and led to the first, and so far, only trial of SAS personnel for murder in a Northern Ireland court. The two men were acquitted, as the prosecution was unable to prove that the men had gone there with the intention of killing whoever entered the cemetery. Once again, the SAS felt completely let down by their commanders and the thought of being found guilty of murder and being imprisoned for 'doing their duty' was of great concern to everyone in the regiment. Needless to say the IRA scored a propaganda triumph, which they exploited with their normal effectiveness.

By the end of 1978, after the first two years of a regular SAS presence in the province, ten people had been killed, three of whom had had nothing whatsoever to do with a terrorist organisation. A stop was placed on offensive ambushing and for five years the SAS regiment killed nobody in Northern Ireland. Instead, the RUC expanded its own Special Branch undercover squads and assumed a far greater responsibility for the clandestine conflict in town and countryside. The SAS was not removed from the province, but its tasks became more and more directed towards purely covert observation and intelligence-gathering tasks. Their aim continued to be to collect evidence upon which successful prosecutions could be based and to arrest terrorists caught in the act of carrying out illegal activities.

On 2 May 1980, Captain RW became the first member of the SAS to be killed in action in Northern Ireland. He was tasked to search a house for a cache of weapons. His patrol entered the wrong building and RW, waiting outside, was killed by a burst of automatic fire (US M60 belt-fed machine gun) from an IRA group in the adjoining building.

At the end of 1980 a new group structure was evolved with the creation of the Intelligence and Security Group (Northern Ireland) which combined 14 Int and the SAS elements under one commanding officer. At the same time, the SAS element was reduced to an enlarged troop of some 20 men who went to Ulster on a one-year posting, establishing an element of continuity. In case of need, reinforcements could be flown in from Hereford at short notice.

During the early 1980s a number of former SAS officers held senior appointments in the Province – NX, who been the CO during the Falklands War, took command of 39 Brigade in November 1983, and in 1985 Major General ZZ was appointed Commander Land Forces.

The next few years were a relatively quiet period for the SAS, although their covert observation activities did not diminish. In the spring of 1987, indications from an informer led the security forces to believe that a big operation was planned by the IRA in North Armagh.

In May, several IRA active service units joined forces for an attack on a small police station in the village of Loughgall in North Armagh. The IRA plan was to place a massive bomb in the bucket of a stolen JCB digger and drive it into the police station before detonating it. The SAS set up an operation which killed the eight members of the IRA as they attacked the police station. A civilian who inadvertently drove into the operation area was also killed.[588]

As far as the authorities were concerned, Loughgall had been a satisfactory operation and 1987 had been a disastrous year for the IRA. Electoral support for Sinn Fein, the political wing of the movement, had decreased, Loughgall had considerably reduced IRA operatives available for offensive operations, and, at the end of October, French customs seized a shipment of arms from Libya destined for the IRA armoury. But, almost certainly in retaliation, the IRA detonated a bomb at a Remembrance Day ceremony in the town of Enniskillen killing 11 civilians and parading servicemen, and injuring more than 60 others.

The following March, the IRA set out to plant a bomb in Gibraltar and three terrorists involved were shot dead by the SAS.[589] The families of the three terrorists killed in Gibraltar were awarded damages against the British government in the European Court.[590]

> On Saturday 6 March [1988] three Irish terrorists were shot dead by our security forces in Gibraltar. There was not the slightest doubt about the terrorists' identity or intentions.[591]

This operation ended with the British government, and SAS, in the international dock. The matter was extensively aired at the time and much has since been written about it.[592] An active service unit consisting of three IRA terrorists, planning to plant a bomb, which could have killed and injured servicemen as well as hundreds of innocent bystanders, had been eliminated. The tone of the newspaper headlines on the following Monday was one of jubilation, but that afternoon in the House of Commons the then Foreign Secretary, Sir Geoffrey Howe, made a statement concerning the affair on behalf of the government. He laid out the facts as known but said that the IRA vehicle concerned did not actually contain a bomb,[593] and that the three dead IRA members were unarmed when they were shot and killed.

The fact that the terrorists were unarmed handed the IRA a propaganda victory and forced the government to reopen the whole question of an alleged 'shoot to kill' policy. The relatives of the deceased have successfully claimed compensation through the European Court from the British government. Again, the government found itself on the defensive, forced to explain the apparent cold-blooded killing of the terrorists, and once again the SAS was accused of being Thatcher's assassins with a 'licence to kill'. What had originally been a disaster for the IRA was turned into a triumph; they had three new martyrs to mourn.

Conclusion

They [the IRA] should be wiped off the civilised world![594]

Between 1983 and 1987, the 10,000 or so members of the uniformed regular Army in Northern Ireland killed three members of the Provisional IRA. During the same five-year period, the SAS troop was involved in the fatal shooting of 20.

> While government might appear impotent, the SAS, unrestrained
> by legal restraints or liberal inhibitions, could deal out justice.[595]

It was this aggressiveness that obtained results, not necessarily particular 'specialist' tradecraft. Tactical intelligence provided may have been of a better order than that available to conventional units, but the method of carrying out further information gathering or, indeed, carrying out executive operations, was conventional infantry work. The initial utilisation of the SAS in Northern Ireland was fraught with internal military politics, police politics, and interference from a variety of agencies. Troops were billeted with conventional units where every patrol or vehicle leaving from, and returning to, a location was recorded; senior officers who had once been junior officers and who harboured resentment from some bygone snub by an SAS trooper or officer in Malaya, Aden, Borneo or Oman were in a position to maliciously interfere in the day-to-day operations of SAS groups. Battle-experienced SAS troopers had to queue to eat in canteens with 19-year-old REME artificers. Moreover, SAS specialist weapons, such as those used by the Hereford-based counter-terrorist team, were not permitted to be used on Northern Ireland operations until some years into the SAS presence there.

The SAS, during their initial years of deployment, were not permitted to communicate directly with members of the RUC Special Branch and had to liaise through Special Branch Liaison Officers. The reason for this 'arm's-length' communication was never convincingly explained to SAS operators in Northern Ireland and it could only have been due to fears by senior police and military officers that the SAS might set up a parallel 'third force' and carry out their own operations without the involvement of the large police and military hierarchy in the Province. This fear was extended to the requirement for SAS personal weapons to be forensically tested *prior* to SAS deployments.

There is a school of thought that the SAS had to be involved in Northern Ireland because almost every member of the rest of the army had served there:

> Of course, there is that argument, that if you've got a major operation eating up masses of military resources and you are not involved – after a while, people say what are all these red hot guys doing down in Hereford. Here we are running all these operations and they haven't got a role – do we really need them – should they be there or should they be somewhere else and

this has always been a concern, certainly in my day – maybe not
so much now.[596]

However, this is not a valid reason for the deployment of a Special
Force. There was some degree of success with the utilisation of the
SAS to supplement 14 Int in carrying out executive actions against
identified terrorists, but this 'hunter-killer' system could have been
provided by a specifically trained force. The SAS had been involved
in similar operations with Operation NINA in Aden but these were
not successful.

The initial reason for the introduction of the SAS into South
Armagh was a political ploy by Harold Wilson to try and change the
growing perception by the British public that the armed forces, and
so, by implication, the government, was impotent against the terrorist activities of the republican terrorists and, to a more limited
degree, the loyalist terrorists, in the border areas of Northern
Ireland. The introduction of the SAS and its early successes did provide the results the government wanted; however, inevitably, the use
of a force with such clandestine capability was going to attract the
full weight of the IRA propaganda machine. In the Republican
media, the SAS has been held responsible for just about every crime
committed, and blamed for all sorts of unaccounted-for bodies that
have been found.

The successes of the SAS have been contradicted by the perception by some sections of the public and the media that, in a number
of cases, the SAS may have fired without challenging their targets.
Regardless of the fact that the time available to challenge is directly
related to the level of threat in these close-range, face-to-face situations, it remains a fact that the uninformed believe that the security
forces – that is, the 'good guys' – must always issue a challenge, and
be heard to challenge. Moreover, there is also a belief that there is
an ability by the military to 'shoot to wound' only. This is an expectation that the SAS should be able to shoot armed terrorists in the
arms and legs, incapacitating them, allowing for the option of an
arrest. The decision of the European Court on the killings in
Gibraltar by the SAS merely confirms this view. Not surprisingly,
SAS operatives continue to be amazed at the naivety of the public
about the implications of counter-terrorist operations, especially
regarding those split-second decisions made in totally adverse tactical and environmental conditions.

The introduction of the SAS into Northern Ireland provided the
Wilson government with some political breathing space at a time

when attempted control of the paramilitary terrorists in the Province, particularly in South Armagh, by the security forces seemed to have failed. In the short term, this was a strategic success but the beneficial impact upon public morale on the British mainland, and among those in the Province who wanted peace, was eroded by a series of mistakes and questionable shootings by the SAS. The majority of the SAS deployed into Northern Ireland had been involved in Operation STORM in Oman for several years and were quite used to using their weapons – firing and being fired at. Their approach to an 'internal security operation' was, not surprisingly, very robust compared to the rest of the Army, who had been working under limitations since 1969. This robust, no-nonsense approach achieved its aim over the first two years of the SAS deployment, but thereafter the tactical successes of the SAS in killing terrorists was overshadowed by the impact of these killings upon British foreign relations with the Republic, the USA and elsewhere. The SAS was learning that aggression does not always bring long-term success particularly in an internal security situation.

The involvement of the SAS in Northern Ireland can be succinctly described as a highly visible start then fading away. Two main events were at Loughgall, which was a tactically effective operation with a limited military impact but which created adverse publicity, and Operation FLAVIUS in Gibraltar, which created a major international political problem for the Thatcher government.

The main successes against the paramilitaries in Northern Ireland were primarily as a result of the completely covert operations of 14 Int. The initial involvement by the SAS in managing the selection and training of personnel for 14 Int in the UK was necessary and highly effective, but when both organisations were deployed operationally there was a certain degree of 'conflict' between the two. The SAS considered the 14 Int specialists to be 'Walter Mittys', and the 14 Int believed the SAS were clumsy hooligans who, because of their need to 'get in on the act', negated the results of their long-term, dangerous covert surveillance operations.

The SAS only began to operate successfully and effectively when they replaced the 'sabre' squadrons with a dedicated troop which deployed for 12 months. This refinement in using SAS resources has demonstrated there is a role for them in Northern Ireland as a very real defence policy option.

Chapter 12

INTERNATIONAL TERRORISM

Terrorism – the calculated use of unlawful violence or threat of unlawful violence to inculcate fear; intended to coerce or to intimidate governments or societies in their pursuit of goals that are generally political, religious or ideological.[597]

Terror cannot be overcome by the weapons of the mind but only by counter terror.[598]

Introduction

Terrorism in the early 1970s came in a bewildering variety of forms, often characterised by names from local conflicts or personalities. Much of the problem stemmed from the internal struggles in the Middle East, which spawned a variety of Palestinian groups opposed to Israel. These groups saw any Western government which supported Israel as a legitimate target. They were also prepared to attack Israeli installations overseas and were not above carrying out operations in Europe. After the fall of the Shah, Iran played a prominent role in the terrorist stakes by exporting militant Islam. In addition to the Middle Eastern groupings, there was home-grown terrorism of the European variety, from Maoist urban guerrillas to Italian neo-Fascists and ethnic freedom campaigners.

A hostage situation involving head of state or a family member, or the violent occupation of a strategic or highly symbolic facility is the most threatening event (excluding the release of chemical or biological agents into the atmosphere) that could impact upon a

An SAS training team working with an East African presidential guard and teaching them bodyguard and VIP protection skills. The coloured bibs are used in training to remind each individual of his duties and his place in the escort group or presidential vehicle column.

nation and is one that requires the immediate deployment and intervention of a specialist force. Every other situation can be managed by conventional military forces, suitably trained. It could be argued, therefore, that there is no requirement for the maintenance of expensive, highly trained forces, which could be politically dangerous if under-utilised. The smaller the specialist force established, the fewer controls against excesses are required and the lower numbers of highly trained specialists being deposited in the marketplace once their active service is completed. There still remains a need, however, to maintain an unconventional warfare 'think-tank' that retains the ability to consider likely targets of national importance in an international context and, in the event of hostilities, consider methods of destroying or neutralising them by decapitation strikes.

Involvement of the SAS

The SAS man of the late 1960s was still a specialist infantry soldier with no real training in counter-revolutionary warfare (CRW) techniques, although some experience of such work had been gained by those involved in the under-cover squads in the back-streets of Aden. After Borneo, the SAS was seeking a new role in the world of postcolonial warfare and began developing its close-quarter battle (CQB) training to provide a pool of close protection experts to act as bodyguards. There was a great demand for their services, both as guards and as trainers, for the forces of friendly powers. Individuals and small teams travelled all over the world for a number of years.

> ... during 1972 and 1973 we [the SAS] had officers and men in twenty-three different countries, ranging from the Far East to South America, many engaged on highly sensitive projects.[599]

However, the SAS's involvement in Operation STORM in Oman reduced the manpower available for such missions. A training cadre at Hereford was maintained and a CRW wing was established to monitor developments worldwide. This was later complemented by the even more secretive Revolutionary Warfare Wing (RWW), which carried out training for national resistance groups on behalf of the British government in Cambodia and Afghanistan.

In the spring of 1972, DLB, CO of 22 SAS, directed a troop commander, Captain LO,[600] to write a paper outlining a role for the SAS in countering terrorism. LO proposed a special team, on short-notice standby, trained in techniques of CQB and hostage rescue, which could be deployed in support of the police to help end any terrorist incidents on British soil. DLB forwarded the paper to SAS Group HQ and it went from there to the MoD, where it came to rest.

> At that time it was clear Government policy that the military should have no part in dealing with unrest in the United Kingdom. Police primacy was absolute – and this was hardly surprising, as the Government was more concerned about industrial unrest than terrorism.[601]

The government of the day, in the continuing light of the troubles in Northern Ireland, was most unwilling to be seen to be developing a role for the military in policing mainland Britain, and it no doubt hoped that the problem of major international terrorist incidents would not affect Britain. The hostage crisis at the 1972 Olympic Games in Munich concentrated political and military minds on the new threat of international terrorism.

A member of the SAS training team being escorted on foot by the presidential guard trainees as they arrive at a stadium.

Within three days of the Munich massacre the Prime Minister, Edward Heath, had asked the DMO what measures the Army could take to respond to a similar incident.

> The massacre occurred on Tuesday, 5 September [1972]. That Friday evening, as I was about to leave for home, I got a call from the Director of Military Operations, Major General Bill Scotter, who said he had been asked by the Prime Minister what the Army could do in response to terrorism. Our paper on the subject had quickly been dragged out, and Scotter wanted to know how long it would take to create the force which LO had proposed.[602]

LO's concept was revived and brought to life in the form of Operation PAGODA, the SAS counter-terrorist team: a permanent squad on 24-hour standby to deal with any major terrorist situation in Britain.[603]

> When we set up the whole of this counter-insurgency set up, the great problem was being allowed to talk to the police. I mean, when I was CO, I was forbidden to talk to the police at all, not even to talk to them – couldn't discuss these matters with them and really the only thing that opened that door was the shooting at the Olympic Games and the need to form a counter-terrorist force and the fact that the only people that ever thought about having a counter-terrorist force happened to be the SAS.[604]

The SAS Special Projects Teams[605] were the subject of much scrutiny and imitation by Britain's allies: both the Australian and New Zealand SAS have added a very similar capability to their armoury of operational techniques, while the USA created Delta Force.[606]

The SAS was not exactly unprepared[607] to take on the role of developing techniques to counter terrorism as they already had a vast amount of experience in training marksmen for close protection work, which mainly involved highly accurate pistol shooting.[608] Inter-police cooperation was vastly expanded to coordinate intelligence-gathering, and that information became available to the SAS, which was also briefed by the SIS and MI5.

Initially, the SP or Pagoda Team numbered 20 men drawn from all four squadrons, who were trained by the SAS's CRW wing. Their first deployment was in January 1975 when a civilian airliner was hijacked at Manchester Airport by an Iranian student armed with a pistol.[609]

In December of the same year, during an incident in London, the fact that there was an SAS anti-siege unit was broadcast by the BBC at the instigation of the government. The incident, known as the Balcombe Street siege, was the first time that the British public were made aware of the developments in anti-terrorism in mainland Britain.[610]

During those early years, when squadrons were being rotated to the Oman and training had to be maintained for the European war threat, the small CRW capability had little real opportunity to practise its skills, other than to relentlessly rehearse for any eventuality. Contacts, both formal and informal, were maintained with overseas anti-terrorist units, new weapons were tried out and intelligence about potential enemies was collected.

In the Netherlands the authorities were grappling with the problem of terrorist outrages committed by South Moluccan exiles, and the SAS was called upon for advice and technical assistance. In Germany, the so-called Red Army Faction was waging a bitter guerrilla war against the authorities although many of the leaders, including Andreas Baader, had been arrested in 1973. It was this group that indirectly led to the involvement of SAS CRW specialists in a successful German operation against a hijacked Lufthansa aircraft in Mogadishu, Somalia.[611]

As a direct result of the Mogadishu operation, the government ordered an expansion of the UK's counter-terrorist (CT) role, and a full squadron was deployed at Hereford in rotation. New equipment was obtained especially in the field of communications and weaponry. Continuous training is necessary to keep a CT response team at full readiness and by 1980 the original one-roomed 'killing house' had grown to include six rooms, with terrorists and hostages being represented by paper targets. There was also a mock-up of the interior of an airliner. Also, several aircraft fuselages and railway carriages had been assembled at the SAS training area in a former Second World War ammunition storage complex near Hereford.

On 30 April 1980 B Squadron, the in-role counter-terrorist team was carrying out routine training in Hereford. At 11.48 their pagers went – the reason for the alert was that a telephone call had been received[612] informing the SAS duty officer that a group of terrorists had taken over the Iranian Embassy in Princes Gate, London. The 'Embassy Siege' has been covered in numerous books and articles and several TV programmes. Most accounts state that the SAS team left Hereford and travelled to London on their own initiative, before clearance had been given by the Ministry of Defence.

> NX, the Commanding Officer was on to me at SAS Group Headquarters in London, asking us to obtain confirmation from the Ministry of Defence that a major incident was brewing. When Whitehall failed to produce any definite reaction, NX did not wait, but despatched his team immediately.[613]

The background to the siege, the deployment of the SAS as part of Operation NIMROD, and the ultimate resolution, is well known, mainly because it was acted out in the full glare of the television cameras. In spite of the distaste felt by the SAS for publicity, one could conjecture that the government was not exactly displeased. The success had demonstrated that Britain was not tolerant towards political hostage-taking on her soil.[614] In the years following the siege the size of the counter-terrorist team increased, with larger numbers of 'attached' personnel.

> The support elements with the SAS have grown over the years and I feel that this is not always been a good thing – just look at the Int Corps – 'The Green Slime' [sic].[615] Selection should always be the route to an active role within the SAS. At one stage, going back onto the SP team, I found that the 'Doc', medics and the ATO [Ammunition Technical Officer – bomb disposal specialist], all had 'black kit' [counter-terrorist team specialist items – black fireproof overalls, respirators, body-armour and pistols] and were ready to join on the end of the 'snake' [single file of assault group] going into the stronghold [terrorist location]. I upset a few souls by stopping this practice, saying, 'Let us do our job first and secure the stronghold. Then you can do yours!'[616]

As far as the regiment was concerned, it wished to sink back into obscurity and get on with the round of tours in Northern Ireland and with training for the next 'incident', but speculation about the role of the regiment refused to die away.

The Princes Gate affair combined with operational cuts in the Security Services directly led to the formation of the RWW; a secret department within a secret regiment. Essentially, with tasks directly opposed to those of the CRW – that is, to teach revolutionary warfare – the first task of the RWW was covert training of indigenous forces. The RWW was a hand-picked group from within SAS; the so-called cream of the specialised crop.[617] The first forces trained by the RWW were groups of moderate Taliban united with 'elements of the resistance' in the Northern Alliance. The second operation was to bolster a coalition led by the Khmer Rouge, in exile, which Washington wanted to run Cambodia.[618] This was to keep Vietnam out and to minimise the influence of the Soviet Union, Vietnam's ally, in the area.[619] Disregarding any question of the ethics of working with the Taliban, Northern Alliance and the Khmer Rouge, the deployment of these RRW-trained teams was entirely consistent with strategic utilisation of the SAS as part of British foreign policy and a task for which the regiment was entirely suited.

In late July 1981, at the request of the Gambian government,[620] a small SAS team of three men was deployed to Gambia and was instrumental in countering a coup by Marxist-oriented rebels.[621] The mission was a classic example of a few men, inserted into the right place and with initiative and determination, being able to master a fluid situation.[622]

An SAS instructor supervising a range practice by the presidential guard trainees using Soviet automatic weapons.

On 3 October 1987, in a completely unpublicised operation, the SAS stormed cells in the top-security Victorian Peterhead prison in Aberdeen, releasing a prison officer who had been taken hostage by prisoners. This was a radically different deployment and one which demonstrated the growing government dependence upon the SAS to resolve 'difficult' situations.

Operations in Civilian Clothes

> ... the SAS has always been a strictly military unit, has always operated in uniform (except occasionally when seeking special information ...)[623]

The subject of 22 SAS operating against terrorists while wearing civilian clothes, as opposed to wearing military uniform, is somewhat controversial. Counter-terrorist operations may be required to be carried out within the United Kingdom or internationally. The SAS has frequently operated in civilian clothes, while armed, in the United Kingdom, and particularly in Northern Ireland. Working on its own or in close cooperation with 14 Int or Special Branch, the

SAS has carried out a number of offensive operations in Northern Ireland which have resulted in the death of or injury to IRA operatives. The wearing of civilian clothes in these operations was not a matter of concern. However, the operation in Gibraltar, in which three IRA operatives were killed by SAS soldiers in civilian clothes, caused a certain amount of unease among politicians and discomfort among military commanders.

The actual status of SAS personnel wearing civilian clothes on military operations with regard to international law and the Geneva Convention has become blurred. SAS operations are generally grouped into two areas: conventional SAS operations in uniform are classed as 'green role' operations; counter-terrorist operations are classed as 'black role' operations. The black role alludes to the black fireproof suits and respirators worn by SAS operatives such as those seen during the Iranian Embassy siege in London in 1980. However, black-role tasking can certainly involve operations in civilian clothes, either to get close to subjects in order to obtain information or on offensive operations, as in Gibraltar. To confuse matters even further, they could also be a requirement during green-role operations to wear civilian clothes in order to carry out certain reconnaissance tasks. Members of the SAS have a somewhat cavalier attitude towards the matter of wearing civilian clothes on operations.

> The Geneva Convention will not figure highly in the soldiers' horizons if the operation is deemed worthwhile. If the political will is present the thirst for action will be the over-riding factor.[624]

If the SAS personnel captured during Operation DESERT STORM had been captured in civilian clothes, then there would have been a strong likelihood of them being treated as spies and not legitimate combatants.

> If you start putting soldiers into civilian clothes in order to deceive the enemy, ... you are in danger of contravening the Geneva Convention and then you ask yourself, if the SAS are contravening the Geneva Convention they have set themselves outside it and if that is the case they can be treated differently so far as the enemy is concerned because they are no longer a part of the armed forces. [S]o you are on the threshold here of some very grey areas and sensitive divisions between what might be and what is.[625]

An SAS instructor supervising a range practice by the presidential guard trainees. The trainees are practising instinctive shooting using their personal handguns.

These matters have been raised prior to SAS operations, and the following advice was provided by a commander:

> Use your own judgement [about the wearing of civilian clothes on operations] but be prepared to answer for your actions.[626]

On a number of occasions non-attributable overseas operations have been carried out by SAS operators in civilian clothes, but these men were required to 'resign' from the regiment while they were involved in their particular operations.[627]

In counter-terrorist operations one of the main problems is obtaining accurate intelligence on which to base future operations. Without that intelligence counter-terrorist forces will be forced to remain reactive to terrorist activities. There is a temptation for governments and individuals to operate outside the law, either national or international, in order to obtain intelligence which may assist in disrupting terrorist activities that could have resulted in numerous civilian casualties. This particular issue has achieved particular prominence following the terrorist attack of '9/11'.

> I'm afraid sometimes when fighting terrorism you have to break the rules, you have to go into the backstreets and gutters and enter the dirty world of paid informers to get a result.[628]

There are real concerns among SAS operatives that if an SAS operation, civilian-clothes or uniformed, is compromised then they will
be 'hung out to dry' by the politicians and their own military hierarchy. As a concerning precedent, members of the SAS refer to events
that occurred in NI where, on two separate occasions, SAS soldiers
were prosecuted for incidents that, although they were carried out
while the soldiers were on duty, could have led to lengthy custodial
sentences.

> Anyone undertaking such operations should be given guaranteed
> support and assurances that they and their families will be
> looked after.[629]

Conclusion

Despite the plethora of specially armed and trained UK police units
who have been carrying out 'operations' in the UK, with limited success it must be said, the SAS will remain the nation's primary
counter-terrorist resource working closely with national intelligence-
gaining agencies. The SAS is a military organisation with international capability, but it must always work closely with civilian

A fully trained presidential bodyguard escorting President Nyrere of
Tanzania to an official function in Dar Es Salaam.

An SAS trained Middle East counter-terrorist team carrying out a practice assault on a wide-bodied passenger aircraft. The specialist ladders are designed to enable the team to reach and open the doors of the aircraft.

agencies in order to have access to the highest level of intelligence if it is going to be able to effectively target the main threats to the nation. A number of SAS personnel continue to train and work closely with MI6 so that there is a pool of trained SAS personnel available for MI6 operations. The SAS, however, would be very reluctant to form a joint organisation with MI5 and MI6.

> The SAS should work closely with MI5 and MI6 purely for the availability of intel [intelligence]. Other than that you can't trust them. History is littered with double agents.[630]

> I think we should keep our military structure but, as in the past, allow SAS personnel to be borrowed and returned. I think it is the military discipline, and SAS ethos and culture, that have saved the SAS from going down some disastrous road.[631]

Although outside the scope of this book, the events of 11 September 2001 have dramatically increased the stakes involved in what has become a battle against global terrorism. The political and military scope for the utilisation of special and elite forces has been increased. International boundaries and borders are no longer as sacrosanct as they once were, and public interest in the military detail of counter-terrorist operations is less concentrated. The British government's foreign policy regarding the battle against this 'new' terrorism is firmly and publicly entrenched with that of the USA. SAS forces have been deployed in Afghanistan and Iraq working alongside similar American forces. Inevitably, defence policy and the utilisation of scarce resources such as the SAS will ensure that the organisation will, more and more, be the 'point of the blade' in the asymmetric battle against terrorism.

West German GSG9 counter-terrorist team members and members of the FBI training together at the FBI Academy, Quantico during a workshop involving 22 SAS planning for a winter Olympics in the USA.

Chapter 13

SUPPORT FOR INTERNATIONAL HUMANITARIAN OPERATIONS/PEACEKEEPING OPERATIONS

Introduction

Tony Blair, during his time as the British prime minister, dramatically increased the military profile of the UK, particularly in respect of NATO peace-enforcing and peacekeeping operations. Moreover, Blair's government made its bilateral association with the USA a cornerstone of its foreign and defence policy – where the USA went, so Britain followed. In 1995, Britain made the biggest single contribution to the UN/NATO peacekeeping force in Bosnia. How far this rose from a genuine humanitarianism and how far from a desire to maintain the importance of NATO and Britain's profile at the UN is an open question. Once again in Kosovo in 1999, Britain took a leading role in securing the eviction of the Serb Army from the province. However, what was very clear was the dependence of Europe on American air power. France in particular resented this dependence and pressed for the development of a more independent European military force. Although Britain was prepared to contribute to a European military force, she insisted, much to the irritation of the French government, on its integration into a NATO planning structure.

Most conflicts where international operations have been undertaken can, in one way or another, be defined as intra-state and low intensity, with primarily regional consequences. These conflicts are characterised by a high degree of civil strife and a lack of clearly defined actors. Instead, there is often a multitude of actors who are undisciplined and difficult to control even within the factions that are in conflict. More often than not, various agreements painstakingly negotiated by one or more 'external parties' are soon broken. There is frequently a breakdown of law and order because the national infrastructure has imploded or there is a governmental inability, or unwillingness, to maintain even the rudiments of a state structure. Frequent human rights' transgressions occur and the lines between guerrilla warfare, terrorism and pure criminal activity are constantly blurred.

This picture is very often complicated even more by the presence of non-government organisations (NGOs) and government organisations, who all have their own agendas, often detrimental to other similar organisations. In order to function effectively these organisations have to seek support from one or several of the warring parties, adding to the confusion on the ground and exacerbating the difficulties of peacekeeping forces. In addition, a larger influx of NGOs will demand a higher level of cooperative efforts on the part of the peace forces, both to work with various NGOs and to act according to military needs, as well as simultaneously keeping a political focus on the perceived long-time solution.

The breakdown of a central and civil infrastructure frequently leads to the creation of large numbers of refugees, both internally displaced people and refugees having to flee the country altogether. Since conflicts tend to follow the refugees, this is a factor that often severely undermines any efforts to solve conflicts on a more long-term basis.

As a consequence, the 'traditional' scene for a (UN) peace operation, with clear and well-defined actors giving their consent for the international community to intervene, has gone. This is also underlined by the fact that future wars, or armed conflicts, might be fought over issues such as drugs and illegal immigration, as well as over more 'traditional' issues such as territory or political influence. In addition, various combinations of the above are also likely to appear. To deal with such conflict situations, Britain needs a multifaceted 'toolbox', including a combination of military, social, economic and political tools. It is obvious that Britain must retain a full range of military capabilities and that it must not lose the capacity to wage asymmetric high-intensity warfare.

Involvement of the SAS

During the 1990s, the SAS became involved on the fringes of military and humanitarian intervention missions carried out by the UN, NATO and the European Union. This was part of the rapid growth of peace-support, peace-enforcement and peacekeeping duties that were increasingly being undertaken by the British government. SAS operators were deployed in Macedonia, Serbia, Chechnya, Columbia, Ecuador, the Democratic Republic of Congo, the Philippines and Uzbekistan. The SAS found itself operating with conventional British units in complex deployments where the main participants were not just the military but NGOs.

In Bosnia, by the time the Dayton Peace Accords were signed in 1995 it has been estimated that between 200,000 and 250,000 people – Croats, Bosnians and Serbs – had died.

Bosnia

In early 1994, a ten-man SAS team was sent into the Serb-controlled town of Maglai, at the request of General Sir NX – the head of UN Protection Force (UNPROFOR). In the spring of 1994, the Croats and Moslems in Bosnia were prepared to recognise each other's borders on condition that their respective lines could be mapped and agreed to by 12 April. For NX, a former SAS officer, the sensitivity of the matter and the short time-frame made it natural to turn to the SAS. As noted on earlier occasions, NX has frequently marketed his 'old' organisation – from Princes Gate to the Falklands and now the Balkans.

The force was sent down under cover as part of a signals regiment and they operated under the banner of the UN. The official name for members of the SAS group was United Kingdom Liaison Officers (UKLO). In reality, the SAS teams in Bosnia were used for a number of tasks other than map-making along the Croat–Moslem lines. In essence, the SAS in Bosnia worked as the eyes and ears of General NX. In short, they performed classic special forces tasks in Bosnia with the emphasis on intelligence gathering.

NX also established small teams of 'Joint Commission Observers' (JCOs) composed of SAS personnel. These JCOs provided NX with an alternative source of information and intelligence. On 15 March the JCOs were sent in to assess the situation on the ground and to locate drop zones for Air Force food drops. When, a few days later, a British relief force drove through Serb lines, SAS forward controllers directed NATO aircraft fire to provide cover. In April, at Gorazade, an SAS team directed air strikes against Serb positions. During the JCOs' withdrawal from Gorazade, through the Serb lines, one of the observers, Corporal Rennie, was

shot and killed and his companion injured. In August of 1995, the
SAS infiltrated the Serb lines that ringed Sarajevo to report to
NX the location of Serb armour, artillery, and anti-aircraft units.
When the UN, eventually, took offensive action, the intelligence
supplied by the SAS teams on the ground ensured the accuracy
of the NATO aircraft air strikes which took place.[632] At the time
of writing, 2009, I believe the SAS still, on accasion, operates in
Bosnia.[633]

Kosovo

The aggressive bombing campaign and subsequent military occupation of Kosovo by NATO and the UN in 1999 was a deliberate result
of the failures that occurred in Bosnia. In 1999, NATO's forces,
without a UN Security Council mandate, attacked the Serbs in
Kosovo. It is very debatable whether this military intervention plan
worked. It may have initially protected the Albanian ethnic minority
population of Kosovo from the Serbs, but they then turned on the
Serbs once the Yugoslav military forces had been withdrawn, and the
region remains completely unstable. Britain's subsequent decision to
join with the Americans to operate on a unilateral basis in
Afghanistan and Iraq could be seen as a direct result of the 'lessons'
it had learned in Kosovo.

SAS operations in Kosovo involved reconnaissance, identifying
targets for air strikes, and training members of the Kosovo
Liberation Army (KLA). The KLA was given training in order to
utilise their local knowledge in the event of a NATO ground assault
but also to enable the SAS to identify the key personnel within the
KLA organisation. SAS patrols, once again, working with other
NATO special forces, provided the 'eyes and ears' inside the province
for NATO's planners. Consequently, by the time the bombing cam-
paign was drawing to a close in June 1999, there were special forces
teams from Britain, France, America, Canada and Germany inside
Kosovo. Both the UK and the USA set up clandestine camps inside
Albania to teach the KLA effective guerrilla tactics against Slobodan
Milosevic's forces as they began the ethnic cleansing of Kosovo's
Albanian population.

The KLA, officially disbanded after NATO occupied Kosovo in
June 1999, simply went underground, resurfacing in the Presevo
Valley in southern Serbia and in neighbouring Macedonia as

guerrillas, staking a claim for territory. The ethnic Albanians in the area have always ignored borders and their loyalty is to their individual clans and possibly to the wider idea of a Greater Albania. The only way to inhibit the flow of men and munitions into Macedonia was to deploy small teams of special forces who matched the KLA in the mountains.

In March 2001, SAS teams were deployed to the Kosovo–Macedonian border to help seal infiltration routes used by Albanian guerrillas to smuggle reinforcements and munitions to rebels threatening the stability of the southern Balkans. The SAS was drafted in to try to end the confrontation between ethnic Albanian insurgents operating in the rugged Sar Mountains and Macedonia's 11,000-strong government army. The SAS faced former KLA soldiers it helped to train during NATO's 78-day conflict with Yugoslavia in 1999.

> The emerging possibility of Kfor soldiers fighting the rebel army that NATO helped to 'liberate' Kosovo less than two years ago has caused alarm in the alliance's headquarters in Brussels and in western capitals. Embarrassingly for Kfor, it emerged that two of the Kosovo-based commanders leading the Albanian push were trained by former British SAS and Parachute Regiment officers in the days when NATO was more comfortable with the fledgling Kosovo Liberation Army (KLA). A former member of a European special forces unit who accompanied the KLA during the Kosovo conflict said that a commander with the nom de guerre of Bilal was organising the flow of arms and men into Macedonia, and that the veteran KLA commander Adem Bajrami was helping to co-ordinate the assault on Tetovo. Both were taught by British soldiers in the secretive training camps that operated above Bajram Curri in northern Albania during 1998 and 1999.[634]

During the period from 1997 to 2000, SAS operatives employed surveillance operations to identify and arrest 12 of the 18 suspected 'war criminals' apprehended by NATO peacekeepers. There were three unsuccessful attempts to capture Karadzic, the former Bosnian Serb president, The Hague's most wanted fugitive. All failed due to a lack of political consensus.[635] SAS operatives have complained that this campaign to bring Bosnian war criminals to justice at the international tribunal in The Hague is made more difficult by French intransigence and the 'body bag' obsession of the American special forces.

Sierra Leone: Operation BARRAS –
10 September 2000

In late 2000, 200 British soldiers were in Sierra Leone as part of a force training the government army in the country. Initially, 1,000 British troops were sent to Sierra Leone to help with evacuation of foreign nationals. They then went on to provide logistical support to the UN operation and training for government forces. In May, the troops secured the capital, Freetown, and the airport, and were involved in clashes with the Revolutionary United Front, the main rebel faction.

Eleven officers and SNCOs of the British training contingent, from the Royal Irish Regiment, had been travelling in three Land Rovers on what they lightheartedly called a 'Rambo patrol'. This was an unauthorised and highly unprofessional drive around the local area. This vehicle patrol inadvertently entered a roadblock manned by the 'West Side Boys',[636] an armed rebel gang, and the soldiers were disarmed and taken hostage.

The SAS operators had been on the ground several days before the assault, conducting reconnaissance among the swamps of Occra hills where the hostages were held. On the morning of 10 September 2000, the hostage situation was successfully resolved when a company of 150 paratroopers, from 1 Para, working with D Squadron[637] 22 SAS assaulted the rebel camp and rescued the hostages.

In the rescue operation, the British forces suffered one death,[638] one serious injury, and 11 minor injuries. The West Side Boys lost 25 fighters killed and 18 were captured.

> What was interesting about SL [Sierra Leone] was that this was probably the first time that the SAS and PARAs had carried out a simultaneous assault on an objective. The PARAs, I believe, took out the perimeter defences and provided the fire support with 81s [81 mm mortars] and the SAS took out the stronghold [enemy main camp]. For the SAS to have carried out this task they would have required nearly two squadrons. In this case it was a hostage rescue task [not the conventional camp assault] where the SAS have[sic] more experience and training.[639]

The operation to rescue the six British soldiers and their Sierra Leone Army liaison officer was completed in nine hours and the participants were rewarded with an unusually large number of gallantry awards and decorations.

Conclusion

Unlike the USA, the British government does not have an aversion to diluting what it sees as the military's combat-warrior ethos by planning for peace-support operations. Many years of operations in Northern Ireland have demonstrated that the British soldier can be multi-skilled. British foreign policy is comfortable with the fact that planning for operations such as Bosnia or Kosovo does not necessarily mean a soft option. It means having the troops, equipment and all the associated skills necessary to conduct complex operations, over a sustained period, in often hostile environments.

The involvement of the SAS in the Balkans was, and is, extremely small. It really began due to the personal involvement of General NX, who, following a familiar theme, wanted his 'boys' involved in the hostilities. The use of the SAS in this environment did expose their unsuitability for tasks which are operationally attractive but which can quite effectively be carried out by other conventional troops. As an indirect result of events in the Balkans and elsewhere a new military organisation, the Special Reconnaissance Regiment has been formed.

Similarly, Operation Barras in Sierra Leone was a very brief hostage-release operation involving members of the SAS and the Parachute Regiment. It received a great deal of media attention in the British press but it had limited political and strategic relevance. What it did do, however, was to reinforce the manpower limitations of the SAS, and as a result a Parachute Regiment battalion, the Special Forces Support Group, has been relocated to South Wales to provide direct support for future SAS operations.[640]

PART FIVE

CONCLUSION

Chapter 14

Conclusion

Whether there was ever really a 'guiding hand' I sometimes doubt – in my experience we rather made it up as we went along.[641]

Imperial Policing

From 1950 until 2000 the SAS was involved in a number of campaigns in several of parts of the world. During these 50 years it gained an enviable reputation for professionalism. But a lot of this reputation is actually based on myth and not substantiated by actual reality.

The building blocks for the new post-war SAS was established in the jungles of Malaya as a result of the determination, foresight and aggressiveness of Mike Calvert. In Malaya, the SAS was established at a time when 'the situation was bad and getting worse'.[642]

In Malaya, the results of the SAS operations, in terms of enemy kills, are very small compared with other regiments. However, the SAS brought a different type of operation into the theatre. Colonel JW is one of the key personnel who was involved in the development of the SAS at that stage, and agrees that, on balance, the results seem small, and this has been substantiated by Chin Peng, the CT commander. In his autobiography, Chin Peng indicates that the SAS, although he does not use their name, were fundamentally successful in interrupting his couriers from working together. Without information passing between its units, the CTs became ineffectual and so the deep-penetration patrolling of the SAS disrupted the communication network of the CTs. Moreover, the SAS were regular soldiers and not, like the majority of servicemen in Malaya, conscripts. SAS soldiers made several tours of Malaya becoming proficient in the Malay language, which is also the *lingua franca* of the aborigines. This language ability allowed the SAS to mix with the aborigines, who, it is suggested, provided assistance to the terrorists.

The successful use of SAS troops in quelling the rebellion on the Jebel Akhdar in Oman was very fortuitous. The commander of the Oman forces, Colonel DS, had requested a battalion of paratroopers or marines to assist his troops storm the mountain redoubt of the rebels. However, the British government was not prepared to allow large-scale British forces to be involved in the conflict. The SAS was leaving Malaya after six years fighting in the jungle. It was also provident that the DMO in London was aware of the SAS, as was FK who worked for him. It is not intended to decry the efforts of the SAS in forcing the rebels from the top of the Jebel Akhdar, but it is frequently forgotten that their efforts were supported by a large number of troops from the Oman army, other British troops, as well as by a substantial number of fighters and bombers from the Royal Air Force. This huge air-support programme caused major damage to the irrigation systems and crops of the rebels on the plateau with major morale problems for the unsophisticated tribesmen, and their families, living in their caves.

The Jebel Akhdar campaign can be considered one of the few post-war examples of effective use of British special forces politically, strategically and tactically. It was also unique in the fact that it is one of the few campaigns in which senior officers of the SAS did not have to market the capabilities of their own unit.

The SAS involvement in Aden and the Radfan was a pointless exercise and contributed nothing to either the expertise of the unit or the success of military operations in the area. A sub-unit of the SAS was carrying out desert warfare training in the Yemen and it became operationally involved when a squadron commander offered his forces to take part in an operation. The events that followed show that the utilisation of the SAS in this campaign was badly thought out with, in one particular instance, tragic consequences. This was the disastrous operation in which two SAS personnel were killed and their bodies, which were left behind, were mutilated. This operation was a public relations disaster because the families of the soldiers involved did not know that they were overseas. The irony of the event was that the task that was to be carried out by the SAS, marking a parachute dropping zone, was a task that was in the normal remit of the paratroopers taking part in the operation.

All the operational tasks carried out by the SAS in Aden and the Radfan could have been carried out more effectively by infantry units. The deployment of the SAS was more to do with personal adventurism than being based upon a military or political need.

The use of the SAS in Borneo was pedestrian and lacking in flair and imagination. There was no attempt to identify and eliminate key facilities and individuals in Indonesian territory. The deployment of the SAS was typified by the fact that the commanding officer actually had travelled to the War Office in London to 'hawk his wares'. He reminded the staff officers there that the SAS existed, and that it probably had the greatest knowledge of jungle operations of the entire Armed Forces.

> I went to London at my request to see the Director of Military Operations and pointed out politely and definitively to him, that we had a very experienced jungle fighting anti-guerrilla force in 22 SAS.[643]

The achievement of the SAS in Borneo was interesting but, again, of little strategic import in itself. The tasks they carried out could have been undertaken as effectively by well-trained infantry.

The SAS operations in Borneo were primarily concerned with intelligence gathering. However, as the campaign progressed, British troops were permitted across the border into Indonesian territory. Initially, only the SAS and Gurkha units were permitted across the border. This was Operation CLARET. Once again, the operations of the SAS could have been, and were eventually, carried out by infantry units such as Paras and Gurkhas. The deployment of SAS showed little imagination or flair. In one particular wasted opportunity, an SAS patrol was in a position to ambush the commander of all the Indonesian elite airborne units opposing the British forces in Borneo but the patrol commander chose not to give the order to fire because there was a woman accompanying the Indonesian commander's party. According to JW, the patrol commander had the 'ace of spades' in his hands. It was on specific high-value, high-impact tasks like these that the SAS should have been employed. There were certain political limitations to the use of British troops along the Borneo border but the strategic use of the SAS was very limited indeed. In fact, the British SAS left Borneo before the end of the Confrontation leaving New Zealand and Australia and SAS troops working along the border with other small groups.[644]

In Oman, Colonel JWT, the SAS commanding officer, had sent Major DLB, a squadron commander, to the Gulf to 'sniff out' opportunities for the regiment. Once again, deployment of SAS troops was reliant upon the opportunism of its commanding officers. The SAS identified a role for themselves in Oman that they could competently carry out and made a case for their involvement. There is no evidence to show that there were any overarching political policies that were dependent upon the involvement of the SAS. The MoD, probably at the level of Director of Military Operations, identified the need for a small self-contained military group to provide a close protection team for the new Sultan. This initial involvement, if not prompted by JWT, was certainly used by him to involve larger numbers of SAS troops in the campaign. The SAS was the ideal organisation to become involved in Oman. They were discreet, not involved in Northern Ireland, and their soldiers were familiar with the terrain and the peoples. These were all 'selling points' that JWT utilised.

Following the successful coup against the father of the present Sultan of Oman, the SAS deployed to the southern state of Dhofar and stayed here for some six years working closely with the Jebalis, the mountain people. Only one squadron was deployed at a time, except for Operation JAGUAR, when two full squadrons were deployed.

The SAS are often credited as being responsible for the Omani successful struggle against communism in Dhofar, but what is frequently overlooked is the large numbers of Omani, Baluchi and Iranian troops who carried out most of the fighting. It was frequently said by members of the SAS itself that specialist troops, such as the Parachute Regiment, should have been doing most of the operations they were doing.

With some foresight, the regiment had realised that language training[645] would be important in its work. The many years it spent in Malaya, where many of the regiment members learned Malay, had its uses when SAS units were deployed to Borneo, where Malay was also spoken. Following the Jebel Akhdar campaign, Arabic language training was also carried out. The deployment of the SAS in Dhofar was a long-running, covert operation which it could be argued was, once again, a case of – 'we have 'em, let's use 'em'. The SAS have an aggressive reputation – or, more precisely, a reputation for offensive action – and there was a need for a hard-hitting autonomous unit to work in Oman alongside the SAF, and latterly with the *firqat*. The SAS already had experience in Oman from the Jebel Akhdar campaign, and they were involved in the immediate aftermath of the palace coup against the old Sultan, so there was a certain inevitability in their involvement. Their involvement was heavily promoted by JWT and DLB. A Five Point Plan, which was used as the 'success template' for the campaign, has been credited to both JWT and Colonel ZZ.

After Oman there was a brief period of quietness with SAS deployed worldwide on training teams as well as internal training. However, in 1976 Harold Wilson publicly ordered the SAS to Northern Ireland. The role given to the SAS was purely political and not one that utilised its skills. What it did bring to the 'conflict' were mature, aggressive soldiers who were quite prepared to use their weapons. This was in sharp contrast to the rest of the British Army, who had been regularly travelling back and forward to the Province on numerous tours of duty where they were pilloried by all and where soldiers were more worried about having an accidental discharge with resultant disciplinary and financial penalties than they were about shooting terrorists.

> The SAS are much more likely ... to shoot first and ask questions later. They have a restless violence ... Violence is the SAS trade-mark.[646]

After Oman, the SAS was also involved in two brief conventional conflicts – the Falklands War and the Gulf War. In neither conflict did the regiment perform particularly well – strategically, tactically or politically. The Falklands War was costly in reputation because of a number of poorly planned and executed operations which were carried out for reasons of personal aggrandisement rather than operational necessity.

Conventional Wars

There is a suggestion that the SAS believes that the 'blooding' of troops untried under fire is sufficiently important that it can become an operational imperative in itself. The need for the regiment to undertake operations is paramount: the only way that soldiers who have never been in combat can be tested. However, its involvement in the Falklands War started poorly and was dogged with controversy. Its first operation nearly cost lives and did lose precious assets through the foolhardy actions of an SAS commander.

The Falklands campaign became a competitive arena for SAS, SBS and Parachute Regiment patrol companies with at least one fatal consequence. The SAS philosophy of aggression did result in a ground raid on Pebble Island, but it was a raid that was neither special nor innovative and it could have been carried out as effectively, but with less risk to troops and vulnerable ships, by the naval gunfire that in fact supported the raid. A potential *coup de main* operation by the SAS, along the lines of the Israeli Entebbe raid, was reluctantly planned by a squadron commander, who was replaced at the eleventh hour and fortunate to be only relieved of his command and not court-martialled: an event that would have caused much adverse publicity to the SAS. A SNCO of the squadron also refused to participate in the planned operation. This proposed strategic operation onto the South American mainland became a comedy of errors with claims and counter-claims of cowardice, and with the initial reconnaissance patrol involved retiring, having achieved nothing, to a neutral country after a squabble among themselves on arrival by covert helicopter in Argentina.

The last operation carried out by the SAS in the Falklands War was aborted when a planned boat landing near Port Stanley was engaged by an Argentinean anti-aircraft battery and then illuminated, legitimately, by the lights of an Argentinean hospital ship as it withdrew. Some members of the raiding party were injured. The raid, successful or otherwise, would have had absolutely no impact on the advance into Port Stanley and was a reckless misuse of SAS assets. The closing days of the campaign resulted in unseemly jostling between the SAS and SBS for final honours despite the fact that both groups should have left the conflict some time earlier, their job done, instead of remaining to clutter up the battlefield. There has also been post-conflict squabbling about the quality of information provided by SAS patrols and OPs – particularly prior to the battle at Goose Green. The campaign provided limited combat experience to the SAS but at a high cost in manpower and credibility.

The first Gulf War demonstrated quite clearly that the role of special forces in a highly technical conflict can be extremely limited if they are deployed in the conventional battlefield arena. This was a highly sophisticated war (on one side only) in which there was little place for the relatively unsophisticated skills of four-man SAS patrols, particularly those on foot. Again, the involvement of the SAS in the Gulf War was more a result of a desire to be involved than as a result of a strategic requirement. In that particular environment there was little that special forces could do that was not already being done, or capable of being done, by air resources. The geographic environment was such that distances and lack of cover virtually nullified the effectiveness of foot-borne or Land Rover-borne SAS. Poor equipment and individual over-confidence led to losses, which were avoidable, especially as the majority were related to the weather and not the enemy. These were areas that had been extensively operated over during the Second World War and it is inexcusable that archival historiography material was not available to inform SAS operators about the severe variants of temperature and ground.

Internal special forces squabbling demonstrated a lack of maturity. This is surprising as the SAS like to think, with a certain historical precedence, that they are the architects of special forces operations. The attempt to replicate, in this operational arena, the role of the SAS in the Second World War was elbowed into irrelevancy by the massive Allied material and technological superiority.

In an incident without precedence, a squadron commander of major rank (who was also the first SBS officer to command an SAS squadron) was publicly removed, on the orders of the commanding officer, by the Regimental sergeant major (RSM) from an operational area where he was deployed with his troops.[647] Also, a SNCO mess meeting was held by the same RSM in the middle of a hostile area, an exercise that can only be described as a childish attempt at gaining personal publicity and which demonstrated a dangerous and foolhardy lack of professionalism. Moreover, public and literary disagreement between authors of various post-war 'I was there' publications have greatly discredited the organisation. When the SAS goes to war, both in regular conflict and in the fight against terrorism, it does so with a broad spectrum of public approval, and it is only a small minority who see the regiment as some sort of governmental Praetorian guard. However much it may shun publicity, the regiment is often thrust into the limelight by the activities of its members once they have left the Army.

There is no evidence available to date that confirms that any of the SAS operations impacted upon the successful prosecution of the war – particularly the highly publicised 'scud-hunting'. This war did not demonstrate any particularly unique Special Force skills or tradecraft other than the introduction of some unique terrain-crossing vehicles and the continuing use of motorcycles. It was obvious from the beginning of the conflict that due to the size of the operational terrain, the speed of the conflict, and the technical, equipment and air dominance of the Coalition Forces there were few, if any, strategic tasks for the SAS. The operations that were carried out were predictably and tactically ineffective and caused the SAS a number of casualties, killed and captured carrying out missions of spurious importance.

Post-war Developments

During the 1960s and early 1970s, 22 SAS and the two territorial SAS units, having evaded the clutches of the Parachute Regiment and occasional threats of disbandment, became firmly established and took on, more or less, the form in which they exist today, The SAS also developed its own identity, ethos and set of tribal customs during that period. It was the rise in international terrorism and the campaign of violence in Ulster that was to change the role of the regular regiment, and ultimately to propel it into the public limelight for the first time. Although the SAS was not a secret organisation, it naturally shunned publicity and it was in the government's interest to play down the regiment's activities, such as in Oman.

The post-war SAS faced difficulty in becoming accepted by the military establishment.

> The military bureaucracy remains instinctively hostile to the elite
> units which take their best men, garner excessive publicity, and
> resist a bureaucratic control.[648]

In the early 1960s a permanent headquarters entity was established as a directorate to oversee all three regiments. Based in London this was initially an appointment for a full colonel – later changed to a brigadier – with the title Director SAS Group. One of the earlier incumbents was Colonel YT, whose original mind contributed a great deal in developing new roles for the SAS at the end of the era of colonial wars. The prime role of all three regiments in the 1960s, however, was to prepare for the Third World War scenario in Europe so, much of the training was concentrated in Germany, Denmark and Norway, with occasional exercises elsewhere.

After its brief sojourn in Malvern, 22 SAS moved to Bradbury Lines in Hereford in 1960, which was then a wartime hutted camp without any particular security precautions. It was not until 1979 that work started on the construction of permanent buildings. In those early days the selection centre was based at Dering Lines in Brecon, run by a captain and three NCOs. We have seen how the remaining two squadrons became three with the reforming of B during the Borneo confrontation and the addition of G in 1967. C Squadron, although still considered part of the SAS 'family', ceased official relations with Hereford when Rhodesia declared independence in November 1965.[649] On 31 December 1980, the Rhodesian SAS disbanded. A telegram from 22 SAS in Britain paid tribute to them:

> Farewell to a much admired sister unit. Your professionalism and fighting expertise has always been second to none throughout the history of the Rhodesian SAS. C Squadron still remains vacant in 22 SAS orbat [order of battle].[650]

A succession of effective commanding officers built up the regiment during the 1960s, starting with Calvert and JW, sometimes called the 'founders' of the post-war SAS, which no longer had to look outside for its leaders. The officer problem was essentially at junior level, as it was difficult to find sufficient subalterns prepared to take time out from the promotion chains of their parent regiments to accept the inherent risk to regimental careers on passing selection. The high failure rate, on average 70 per cent, deterred many from applying. For those who passed there was a three-year tour as a troop commander which for many young officers was a difficult transition to make. The newly badged captain would find himself in charge of a group of men, many of whom were older than he and often far more experienced. Among the 'other ranks' in the SAS there has always been a traditional suspicion of the officer class, who tend to be referred to as 'clowns' or 'Ruperts' – until they have proved themselves. Rank does not confer status either way in the regiment; only ability.

Many of those who made the grade as troop commanders and left after their three-year tours were bitten by the SAS 'bug' with the ambition to return as a major commanding a squadron – and perhaps even aspiring to command an SAS regiment. It has been said that an SAS career can be a bar to promotion for an officer, yet in the last decade of the twentieth century a large number have reached General rank. Particularly notable is DLB, who commanded successively a troop, a squadron, the regular regiment and SAS Group, before his command of British ground forces in the Gulf War which made him a full general, and a household name. This greater representation of the SAS at the highest military level can only be advantageous for it with a greater understanding of the regiment's capability being promulgated at both senior military and political levels. It also demonstrates quite clearly that service in the unit is now acceptable to the military hierarchy and the days of SAS officers 'bumping into a glass ceiling'[651] have passed.

The system of officers doing finite tours of service with the SAS ensures a constant influx of new ideas and prevents the sort of mental stagnation that can sometimes infect organisations that retain the same cadre of personnel. This tried-and-tested system is constantly at risk in times of officer shortages. Shortage of officer and other-rank recruits together with the high wastage rate during selection has, from time to time, led to accusations of a lowering of the entry standards, which the SAS has stoutly refuted. It was regarded as preferable to have a patrol commanded by a junior NCO rather than an unsuitable senior NCO and similar application to the command of troops with officers and SNCOs.

During the early 1960s, a basic pattern of selection was established. Volunteers came from within the ranks of the Army and were normally in their mid-twenties. If accepted for service in the regiment they had to drop down to trooper, regardless of rank in their 'parent' unit. Initially they served a three-year tour and, if still acceptable, could stay on as permanent cadre, thus ensuring an element of continuity.

The territorial regiments benefited from the formation of an SAS Group Directorate: they grew more professional in their approach, and their selection and training systems became integrated. During the 1960s and 1970s, however, there was a certain amount of friction between them and the regular regiment, the members of which tended to look down on the territorials as amateur soldiers. Men from 22 SAS disliked being attached to them as instructors, and were regarded by the TA as overbearing and condescending. Yet TA soldiers consistently did extremely well in NATO competitions, beating the regulars on many occasions. Some of the more hide-bound regulars even resented the fact that TA men wore the same insignia, badge, beret and wings as they did; they viewed the part-timers as a form of second-class SAS.

An essential change of emphasis for 22 SAS occurred during the 1960s in the quiet period between the campaigns in Aden and Oman. The commanding officers of that period were faced with the need to 'sell' their services, just as David Stirling had done in the Middle East in 1941, and their thoughts turned to the world situation in general. The late 1960s had witnessed the start of international terrorism on a large scale and the spectre of governments giving in to terrorists' demands, powerless in the face of threats. In Britain, the police were neither trained nor even entitled to undertake paramilitary style operations on the mainland, and the various intelligence-gathering organisations had no comparable military arm. A hesitant start was made when a CQB training facility was initiated at Hereford, the syllabus of which owed much to experience gained in Aden with the 'keeni-meeni' patrols. The purpose was to train bodyguards, mainly for foreign potentates, although from time to time the regiment did provide marksmen for duty in British embassies in particularly threatened locations. In a rare glimpse of politically driven strategic utility, CQB-trained teams from Hereford imparted their skills to friendly foreign countries on the behest of the FCO.[652]

Political Utility

Political minds became even more concentrated as a result of the murder of Israeli athletes at Munich during the Olympic Games in 1972.

> If it means teaching underhand tactics such as assassination and spying – let us teach them. The next war need not be fought in accordance with agreed rules.[653]

Perceiving the need for a trained team to deal with such a situation in future in Britain, the government authorised the establishment at Hereford of the CRW wing. Initially consisting of one officer and four instructors, it was tasked to train a team of 20 men drawn on a rota basis from all four squadrons. At the same time, an intelligence database was compiled of all available information on terrorist organisations, and an intense study was made of new weapons for the embryo unit. The CRW's role was later supplemented by the establishment of the RWW.

The late 1960s and early 1970s may have been a period of transition for the SAS, but the new interest in counter-terrorist activity did not mean that general military standards were allowed to drop. It is a fact, nevertheless, that the end of the disengagement from overseas territories meant that British forces were no longer required to fight a series of brush-fire wars in Third World countries. An exception was the Falklands War – but that was a one-off affair that nobody expected to happen; the fall of the Soviet bloc was equally unexpected. Inevitably, public perceptions of the SAS were to change, reflecting to a large extent the polarisation of views within British society. Previously, very few people had even heard of the SAS, and to those who had it was a small elite army unit. But as a result of 'coming to the aid of the civil power' in the British Isles, members of the regiment became far more subject to the scrutiny of journalists, many of whom were distinctly unsympathetic. Epithets in the left-wing press, such as 'Maggie's Butchers', were one side of the coin, counterbalanced by jingoistic headlines in some of the tabloids every time the SAS allegedly went into action. In previous years nobody had worried if a few terrorists, freedom fighters, insurgents or guerrillas had been shot in some distant land. The shooting of people in Belfast or Gibraltar became somehow different, depending upon which side of the political divide one stood. The more anonymous the regiment tried to be, the more the public appetite for information was whetted.

Many of the operational missions being carried out by the unit could just as easily be assigned to infantry units, or to the Parachute Regiment or Royal Marines. The success of combining the two types of organisations was demonstrated successfully on Operation BARRAS in Sierra Leone. A battalion of paratroopers, the Special Forces Support Group, has now been earmarked to provide support to SAS operations.

The perceived 'success' of the SAS has come about more by accident than design and certainly not by the involvement of military visionaries and freethinkers like the initiators of the original SAS. Maybe such visionaries are neither required nor effective in times of less than national peril?

With the end of the Cold War and its ideological competition, it is clear that the pattern of military activity has been changed. Moreover, increasing globalisation and the economic and political links that bind major states have made inter-state conflict much more difficult to sustain unilaterally. In Western societies, too, the growing unwillingness to risk large-scale casualties in warfare has coincided with the so-called 'revolution in military affairs' resulting from technological development to produce the kind of 'virtual war' practised in the Gulf and in Kosovo. However, 'cyber-war' and the supposed 'New World Order' ushered in by the collapse of communism have not prevented inter-state nor intra-state conflict. Indeed, insurgency remains as prevalent, especially where the state system has remained under-developed in many parts of Africa, Asia and Latin America. Moreover, new, particularly mineral-based, imperatives have also encouraged insurgencies, which in some cases have increasingly blurred the distinctions between war and organised crime. Insurgency, therefore, remains a crucial challenge in the contemporary world.

> So fashionable has SOF (Special Operations Forces) become of late that, as was to be expected, exaggerated ambitions for their future role have been mooted.[654]

By their mere availability and past successes, elite units may subtly distort policy-makers' perspectives on politico-military problems. This does not imply that policies are undertaken just because the tools to execute them exist. Rather, elite units sometimes seem to offer an easy way out of a serious problem, and in so doing mislead political decision-makers. The dangers and costs that elite units impose on democratic regimes are, then, by and large subtle ones. By their very existence elite units affect the choices of policy-makers. They may seem to offer a quick fix, a deceptively easy way of handling a problem, and so encourage decision-makers to make inappropriate policy decisions. It is, however, important to point out the flip-side of this coin; in most of the operations that the SAS has conducted, the impact on the general scene was at best marginal. Despite the 'hype' that often surrounded SAS operations, the actual 'force multiplier' effects that were strived for seldom appeared. Furthermore, in the cases where the SAS have been used as counter-terrorist forces, opponents have claimed that a 'shoot-to-kill' policy has been in force. In addition to potentially criminalising soldiers, this is a policy that could undermine the government's claim to be upholder of law and order, something that, in the long run, can adversely affect society.

The SAS is an institutionalised specialist force – although politicians still make use of its symbolic value. The British government has kept its activities secret, hoping to use the unit as a discreet, non-publicised intervention force. Ironically, the curtain of secrecy surrounding the SAS made it an intriguing topic for speculation. Its reputation grew in inverse proportion to what was known about it, to the point that the government could use it effectively as a symbol *because* of the mystery surrounding it.

> The thing about the SAS is that they have an image which has nothing whatsoever to do with their reality. To the public they are perceived as a team of daredevils made up entirely of chaps who look and behave like a magnificent mixture of Errol Flynn, 007 and Batman. Everything about them contains a substantial

amount of rumour and hidden threat, coupled with sudden, fast, decisive action – their attack on the Iranian Embassy in London, their reputation as the scourge of the IRA in Belfast, their apparently simple removal of terrorists in Gibraltar.[655]

Aside from their ability to perform such conventional light infantry tasks as raiding and reconnaissance, they are useful in an age increasingly characterised by terrorist attacks, hijacking and kidnapping. Moreover, elite units can set high standards for other units, particularly if they are used as 'leader nurseries'. However, elite units can pose severe problems for a democracy's army. From a purely military point of view they may drain off high-quality manpower from the rest of the army, foster inappropriate tactics, and demoralise remaining forces. Elite units create other, less obvious difficulties for sound civil–military relations: they may weaken or subvert the chain of command, erode discipline, and convey misleading impressions to a variety of audiences.

The SAS has shown in Afghanistan and other places that it is well suited to perform special missions, including peacekeeping and peace enforcement, on a *limited level*. SAS troops are better trained, better equipped and better informed, and therefore well prepared to handle sensitive missions.

> The SAS soldier is much more capable of working on his own or in small groups. He is much more confident and able in difficult situations. This is partly due to the age difference. I have found this true in civilian life in places such as Iraq.[656]

It is also an important point, too often neglected, that *limited and smaller* but well-prepared groups can achieve more in terms of conflict management, and even humanitarian help, than a larger force that too often 'overstays' its welcome. This is mainly due to the fact that a smaller force comprised of highly trained and skilled individuals will have to work more closely with the very people it is there to help. A more sensitive approach towards the local population, and their needs, can build a long-term solidity that makes a renewal of fighting less likely. One can also avoid some of the possible traps that can come with a prolonged military mission where the end result too often turns out to be making the receiving population dependent on aid instead of building up a more long-term, self-sustained political and economic structure. It should also be pointed out that this in no way means that the SAS ought to take the place of conventional British forces: it remains best suited to complementary political and military actions. Furthermore, the smallness of an SAS deployment does not necessarily mean a weaker 'deterrent factor'. On the contrary, the knowledge that one is facing highly skilled and trained troops can be a powerful deterrent in itself. Also, if armed violence is unavoidable the chances of limiting the fighting – and, thereby, the casualties – are better with a well-trained force that can perform the mission swiftly and with minimum, but highly focused, levels of violence.

The kind of mission that the SAS was involved with in Bosnia, with an emphasis on peacekeeping and humanitarian tasks, is likely to be the kind of mission the international community will encounter in the twenty-first century. What these examples have in common is that, in countering such conflict and human misery, small and specially trained forces might be a far more useful, and cheaper, way of dealing with at least some of these problems than the deployment of large conventional forces. The role of larger forces will remain for the foreseeable future, but their role might diminish as the focus of international operations shifts towards a more regional approach and as conflicts turn from 'inter-state' to 'intra-state'.

From a psychological point of view it is argued that an international operation might gain far more strength and credibility if the warring parties know that the SAS is deployed. If deadly force has to be used in an international operation, as a last resort, it should be used with determination and as swiftly as possible. Some observers believe that Britain must retain a full range of military capabilities and that it must not lose the capacity to wage high-intensity warfare. The USA, in particular, has an aversion to diluting what it sees as a warrior ethos through the involvement of its forces in peace-support operations. Planning for such operations means having the troops, and the equipment, to conduct lengthy and complex operations far from a home base. These tasks may not involve the use of massed firepower and the destruction of an obvious enemy, but the intervention is generally designed to assist people and improve their lot – not kill them.

If one considers the existence, purposes, nature and structure of armed forces as being primarily influenced by a state's defence policy, the recent evolution in the formulation of British Special Forces policy can be seen as very welcome. Since 2000 there has been a slow but gradual progression from an emphasis on the pursuit of single service concerns and objectives towards a more integrated holistic approach to responding to the demands of a rapidly and radically changing world.

> To survive against global terrorism long-standing concepts of fair play may have to be reconsidered – we must learn to subvert, sabotage and destroy our enemies by cleverer, more sophisticated and more effective methods than those used against us.[657]

In one sense the age of the elite light infantry unit has passed. Many of the specialist units of the Second World War served temporary needs and flourished only in the confusion of that huge conflict. More important from our point of view, however, is the fact that elite units can no longer be expected to fight anti-colonial guerrilla wars as in the 1950s and 1960s. Western Europe no longer holds significant colonial possessions – and seems unlikely to fight a major anti-communist, counter-guerrilla war – but now has a greater concern about fighting a war against Muslim fundamentalists. Also, the age will continue to be one of terrorism: kidnappings, hijackings and hostage-taking. Unfortunately, the smaller elite units will find frequent demands for their talents in the future. From the point of view of civil–military relations, though, these units present fewer problems than their elder cousins of the 1940s, 1950s and 1960s. The nature of their training may require secrecy rather than intensive press coverage: the nature of their tasks (e.g., storming a hijacked airplane) requires few soldiers. The possibility must not be ruled out, unfortunately, that such units may tempt politicians to order military operations which, unlike Entebbe or Mogadishu, may fail – such as the tragedy at Lanarca, Cyprus in 1978 and Malta in 1985[658] – or lead to unanticipated military commitments.

Elite units of the guerrilla, counter-guerrilla, and commando type offer politicians in democracies both a tool of policy and a source of fantasy. When elite units are used for purposes that are not really defensible in military terms, a number of effects harmful to military efficiency occur. Democratic politicians should resist the temptations offered by elite units. Without such restraint the defence of a modern democracy can only suffer.

> Given the contemporary and widely anticipated future dominance of irregular over regular warfare, it is not surprising that SOF around the world are entering a golden era.[659]

During the 1960s it was government policy to disengage from commitments outside Europe and to rely on a nuclear deterrent capability supplied by the Americans. Yet, paradoxically, on both occasions that this country has officially gone to war since then, we have been obliged to project considerable forces over large distances into theatres over which we possessed little intelligence in advance. In both cases, the Falklands and the Gulf, special forces provided a considerable amount of vital intelligence for a relatively small cost in terms of equipment and manpower. As Britain withdraws from Germany and reduces its armed forces, there are many who state that it may end up with insufficient manpower to meet its international commitments. In the future these will involve the defence of British interests overseas and taking part in United Nations or European 'peace-making' operations. It may well be that the SAS and other such units will find a ready-made field of employment within multinational forces, especially as other European countries tend to look to their police to provide counter-insurgency expertise.

Finale

From a shaky re-start in 1952, the SAS has refined itself, learnt from its mistakes and, above all, been able to adapt to changing circumstances in a democratic society that is traditionally wary of military elitism. Yet the lessons of history demonstrate that such societies, once they lose the will to defend themselves, often on ethical grounds, are easy prey for the terrorist or the dictator.

Shortly after the commitment in the Gulf War, the SAS also became embroiled in the conflict that marked (and still marks) the demise of Yugoslavia as an entity. Like Northern Ireland, the fighting in Bosnia and Kosovo has been notably a tribal conflict with religious undertones, unleashing bitter ethnic tensions, the origins of which are centuries old. When British troops first became involved as part of the UN peacekeeping force in the autumn in 1992, it was inevitable that elements from 22 SAS would become involved.[660]

It is evident from an examination of the major campaigns and operations involving special forces in the twentieth century that the case in favour of them is perhaps not as watertight as might be imagined. The fairest way of judging the effectiveness of any Special Force is assessing its value in the form of 'return' set against the 'investment'. The 'return' is the strategic, operational or tactical effect on the battle, campaign or even war. The 'investment' is made up of a multitude of components.

> ... two comparisons: first, that of strategic return with the scale
> of investment and second, that of the scale of investment in spe-
> cial operations forces with the scale of effort necessary if regular
> forces attempted the missions.[661]

Most invariably, two of special forces' tasks, offensive action and
intelligence gathering, produce the best 'return' when carried out as
adjuncts of the campaign, or battle, being fought or about to be
fought by the main body of the army. There are a few examples of
offensive action far removed from main force activity producing
a good 'return', but these must be judged from a strategic point
of view.

Arguably, the same criteria can be applied to the third special
forces function: actions with resistance movements. The effectiveness or otherwise of resistance movements is a contentious subject.
But there is a perfectly respectable point of view which argues that
few, if any, resistance movements conduct successful overt military
operations (as opposed to clandestine activity), unless operating in
concert with a main, conventional force; even if that force was some
distance away.

The idea of a guerrilla or resistance movement possibly supported
by a 'private army' from a sponsor nation has often been seized upon,
usually by politicians, in an effort to win cheaply, without the
expense, in terms of blood and treasure, the main battle.
Unfortunately such expenditure is unavoidable if one wishes to defeat
an equally strong and determined opponent. The point is that wars
are won by main force navies, armies and air forces; especially armies.

There is a wealth of talent, skills, intellect and entrepreneurial
spirit in the large pool of manpower in the armed forces of a nation
in arms, including all manner of free-thinking spirits and individualists. But it is a totally different situation in the United Kingdom; all
special forces soldiers come from within the tiny professional armed
forces. This is not intended as a criticism of what are highly dedicated and accomplished people, rather to point out that in wartime
there are types with much to offer, who would not sit comfortably in
a peacetime army. But it would be grossly unfair to label all members of special forces 'anti-social irresponsible individualists'. It is
also an exaggeration to say that men join the special forces to avoid
danger and death. Some might have done, but the vast majority,
young and brimming with energy, joined for action, not to avoid it.
One of the problems, as alluded to earlier, was satisfying the urge,
one might almost say lust, for action of these people, when time

after time operations were cancelled, or opportunities for fighting simply did not present themselves – sometimes for years.

The contribution of special forces to a victory is often hard to measure, because it cannot be calculated solely in terms of enemy hardware destroyed, but in other ways: morale, both of one's own side and the enemy's; the enemy's reactions in terms of withdrawing troops from one area to reinforce another; and assistance to an ally who might otherwise withdraw from the contest. One has to seek answers to questions such as what will be the effect of not mounting special forces operations against the enemy in a particular theatre or campaign? Will this mean that the enemy's rear areas are safe, so he does not have to provide guards at regular intervals along his line of communication, on his airfields and key points, and escorts on trains and road convoys? It is very difficult to quantify or provide subjective evidence which categorically proves that X thousand troops were removed from the main front as a result of special forces operations in the enemy rear. Even in the intelligence field, the instances when a particular piece of information is the one factor that sways the battle are rare. More usually several intelligence-gathering sources, each providing a piece, build the jigsaw puzzle to the stage where it can be used as one of the tools to stage-manage the operation. It is the synergy of all the intelligence-gathering means working together that produces the whole.

The current role of 22 SAS covers the entire spectrum of conflict from peace to general war. The most obvious role is that originally envisaged by David Stirling, which is offensive operations, such as raids, special attacks and harassing operations in time of war. These raids might be conducted against strategic targets deep in the enemy's rear or indeed in his homeland, as well as against targets in support of conventional operations. A further role is that of intelligence-gathering both in wartime operations and in operations other than war (OOTW). These operations include surveillance of enemy activities, and reconnaissance before conventional land operations, including inserting small parties of SAS into a country threatening British interests.

International terrorism has given greater importance to hostage-release operations. In addition, in OOTW there might be a need to rescue British diplomats, tourists or hostages from a foreign territory. The Russo-Georgian War of August 2008 has demonstrated that requirements develop at short notice. In war, hostage-release operations could include liberating prisoners of war or political prisoners as well as recovering or extracting personnel or sensitive items from enemy-controlled areas.

The potential of de-stabilising operations should not be ignored. These tasks could include the provision of military advice and assistance to guerrilla forces in areas that might be occupied by enemy forces. Consideration should be given to obtaining the capability to conduct these operations in an enemy's homeland or in other territories that he might have occupied.

The SAS also has a continuing role to play in promoting UK interests in time of peace and, in this respect, the SAS will continue to be used to provide specialist training assistance to overseas forces. While this task is not confined to special forces, they are uniquely trained for this activity. They are highly trained in the use of small arms and are used to working independently and in small groups in sensitive situations. SAS teams could be deployed in support of a legitimate government to train irregulars combating revolutionary forces, just as the SAS operated in the Oman in the early 1970s.

While it is widely recognised that the SAS is a strategic asset, that recognition has come only slowly. The operational experience of the post-war SAS has been at the operational or tactical levels of war, rather than at the strategic level. In Borneo the SAS provided operational intelligence to the Director of Operations, assisting him in deploying or redeploying his conventional infantry units to meet changing Indonesian concentrations. The ambushing of Indonesian parties and the guiding of larger infantry groups to attack the Indonesians was part of an overall operational concept but was essentially tactical in nature. The danger of the SAS success in Borneo and Oman was that senior officers might believe that in future conflicts the SAS might again be used only in limited roles.

This is not to say the SAS should not be used at the operational level. The priority must be given to its use at the strategic level. The SAS must retain a high degree of flexibility and should not be limited to a set role. SAS commanders and staff need to predict change and be ready to react quickly to any changes in the international strategic environment. The challenge for the future is for the SAS to maintain this flexibility and to continue to explore the possibilities for its use as a strategic asset.

The lessons that are being learned during the first decade of the twenty-first century from the British, and American, military's inability to quickly quell Iraqi and Afghan insurgents will be studied by both governments as well as guerrilla movements the world over. This will force a re-evaluation of battle strategies, and other than war with a strong military power, such as China or Russia, British forces can expect their main military threat to come from Iraqi-style insurgencies rather than from Islamist militant attacks.

Although more than six years have passed since US-led forces toppled the Saddam Hussein regime in Iraq in 2003, at the time of writing in 2009 the insurgency continues to disrupt efforts to stabilise the country. Iraqi nationalist guerrillas – rather than foreign-led jihadists – have had the largest impact on the allied forces in Iraq, and have caused most of the casualties.

Given the relative success of the guerrillas in Iraq, insurgent, rebel and militia movements, as well as governments worldwide that fear a potential US attack (and an attack also from the UK, given that it has demonstrated its allegiance to US foreign policy) will adapt the lessons learned from the insurgency to fight their own battles. General David Petraeus, Commander of US Forces in Iraq stated in August 2008 that 'British Special Forces had played an "immense" role in taking out terrorist bomb-making cells and insurgent leaders over the last five years'.[662] This is not surprising, as tactics perfected in one conflict usually are adapted for another. Not since Vietnam has a guerrilla movement successfully tested the full weight of the most advanced force in the world. Its survival has reaffirmed the merits of adding guerrilla warfare to tactical arsenals, especially for an outmatched military. As a result of the Iraqis' successful experiment, it appears that British forces in key regions, such as the Middle East, will face deadlier threats over the next decade of the twenty-first century from Iraqi-style guerrilla campaigns than from militants.

A main reason for this, perhaps, is that an incessant guerrilla war that constantly chips away is proving to be more effective than major attacks that briefly create a result, but do little to change the situation on the ground. Iraq, of course, is not writing the manual, but simply adding to lessons learned from other guerrilla campaigns. Ideally, by engaging in a guerrilla war, an outmatched country would at least be able to draw out the conflict long enough to settle on more advantageous terms.

Non-state actors also will take cues from the Iraqi insurgency, trying in particular to replicate the diffuse nature of the insurgency's command and control structure, which has contributed to the Iraq occupying forces' inability to disrupt its operations. Despite the difficulties they are likely to encounter in their own campaigns, governments and non-state forces in the Middle East and perhaps elsewhere will apply Iraq's guerrilla war lessons to better prepare to battle British troops and their allies.

My task here is to give a British perspective on the future of land warfare. At the outset it's worth saying that whatever those operations may be like, two things are going to be almost certain. I say 'almost' because never say never. But it is increasingly unlikely from a British perspective that operations will be exclusively national and it's unlikely that they'll be exclusively land-based. Those two aspects, therefore, of coalition/multi-nationality, and the joint dimension I think are two markers that need to be laid down right at the beginning.[663]

This suggests the main threat British forces, and the UK's positions in key regions where military intervention is launched in the coming decades, will probably come not from isolated jihadist attacks, but from Iraq-style insurgencies conducted by state and non-state actors.

Although the Middle East is likely to see the first wave of Iraq-adapted guerrilla warfare, countries far beyond the Middle East are learning, too. Like North Korea, many nations have been preparing guerrilla campaigns for decades. However, without a real war to fight, it is difficult to know what works and what does not against state-of-the art tactics employed by the most highly trained and best-equipped military forces in the world. The Iraq war is providing some of the answers.

In these situations the SAS provides the government with a capability for a graduated response short of employing more conventional forces, thereby minimising the chance for over-reaction and escalation beyond that which is required. The SAS is a relatively economical asset in training and equipping as well as on deployment. For a small commitment it can achieve a disproportionate effect.

Special forces would not be committed without direct government approval, and their employment must be to achieve national objectives. Moreover, the government would be unlikely to authorise special forces' operations unless they had confidence in the ability of the special forces and the capability of its commanders. Therefore, there continues to be a critical need for the politicians, as well as the Service Heads, to have a close understanding of special forces and special operations. This requirement has been recognised with CT operations for which the DSF is the advisor to the Cabinet Office Briefing Room. However, in times of low-level conflict the SAS might be employed outside UK. In delicate diplomatic or strategic situations when the government may be faced with a number of options, including the use of force, a special operations option should always be considered, and the requisite forces should be readily available. The British command system, under which DSF headquarters has operational control of all special forces, provides an effective mechanism which recognises the strategic and unique nature of special force operations and places special force units under a dedicated headquarters that has the expertise and staff to coordinate and manage these resources. DSF also helps to identify and refine the asset requirements and support capabilities of the RAF and Royal Navy. Both of these services have a high regard for the SAS but are not always aware of SAS requirements, nor are they necessarily trained and equipped for special forces operations.

> The SAS does provide individuals who can operate and think under pressure. Tasks will continue to come up which require their specific skills. However, I do believe that the SAS should try and integrate more into the main stream so that they can have a reality check and the rest can see their benefits. I think where the SAS went wrong in the past is that it became too insular and held on to some heavy dross! It does need to maintain high standards of professionalism whether it is on ops or not.[664]

In this book I have considered two main questions:

> 1. Does my analysis of historical experience indicate that the SAS had a strategic impact upon events during 1950–2000?

> 2. From the British government's point of view has the deployment of the SAS had a strategic utility?

The SAS may have had significant tactical input but in most cases (with the possible exception of operations in Oman), the answer to the first question is no.

With regard to the second question, the British government had little or no knowledge or understanding of the SAS. There has been no one close to government to promote the SAS and to offer guidance in its usage. It has become obvious that government knowledge has been lacking because of a number of factors:

> a rigid military hierarchy in which the SAS was an insignificant part;

> an antipathy towards elite forces that was prevalent at the end of the Second World War and which continues today;

a general lack of understanding of special forces;

a smallness in size (of the SAS) which is manifested in negligible
or even limited political power and impact; and

no body of established strategic theory within government on
which to operate.

The history of the post-war SAS demonstrates that there has been
little clear thinking about the whole issue of special forces and special operations. The history of the SAS is one of a continuing search
for an acceptable role within the armed forces which generally have
little idea of how to use the unique skills of the unit. There is no
doubt that Stirling's[665] original conception of the SAS and the role
he envisaged for it have grown somewhat with the telling.[666] The
paradox is that at the time the SAS has been accepted as a
respected and relevant part of the Army's order of battle, it probably
needs to move away from the operational control of the military to
ensure that the nation is best able to use its expertise.

And it is true that they are Britain's deadliest and most effective
armed force.[667]

In summarising SAS involvement in conflicts since 1950, there is
little evidence of any macro-strategy in their deployment. The fact
that 22 SAS has been able to survive, and indeed prosper, in a generally unfavourable environment for more than 50 years is a tribute
to the entrepreneurial skills of a number of commanding officers
and the dedication of the men in the regiment. The strength of the
unit – and, indeed, the future value of the SAS as a strategic asset
– rests squarely on the character, skill and resolve of the individuals
in it and those politicians controlling it.

As far as success or failure [are concerned] there will always be
a lucky element in any operation and it is the ability of the men
on the ground to take opportunities which count.[668]

Encouragingly, events that have taken place after this research was
completed seem to indicate that instead of accepting current
mythology, the SAS has taken a step back and reviewed its perform-
ances in recent years. It has re-evaluated its structure and management, along with those of other specialist agencies, such as the SBS

and 14 Int. A new support unit has been formed to combine intelligence-gathering resources. This new regiment is called the Special Reconnaissance Regiment (SRR). Also, the 1st Battalion the Parachute Regiment has been moved to barracks in Wales to be a complementary force working alongside the SAS. These elements, until recently, were working together operationally in Iraq.

> The SAS, working alongside MI6, The Special Reconnaissance
> Regiment and the Special Forces Support Group, are based in
> The Station, a high security area in Baghdad's Green Zone.[669]

The SAS is finally evolving a coherent philosophy with appropriate policies to establish itself as the organisation it needs to be, not as the organisation it used to be in another war and another time. The SAS is, at last, extracting itself from a self-imposed time-warp.

It should not be forgotten, however, that elite unit prominence occurs only during a politico-military crisis, for it is then that politicians look for easy, safe solutions and the public searches for heroes.

> The sum of these experiences and operations has made the Regi-
> ment a very sought after capability – often referred to as the 'magic
> dust of SF' that will get successive governments out of a pickle![670]

APPENDICES

Farewell Speech on the Disbandment of the Special Raiding Squadron (SRS) November 1943 By Lieutenant General Miles Dempsey, Commander 13 Corps

'It is just three months since we landed in Sicily, and during that time you have carried out four successful operations.

'You were originally lent to me for the first operation-that of Capo Murro di Porco. That was a brilliant operation, brilliantly planned and brilliantly carried out. Your orders were to capture and destroy a coastal battery, but you did more.

'I left it entirely to you what you did after that, and you went on to capture two more batteries and a very large number of prisoners. An excellent piece of work.

'No one then could have foretold that things would have turned out as they have. You were to have returned to the Middle East after that operation, but you then went on to take Augusta. You had no time for careful planning; still, you were highly successful.

'Then came Bagnara and finally Termoli. The landing at Termoli completely upset the Germans' schedule and the balance of their forces by introducing a threat to the north of Rome. They were obliged to bring to the east coast the 16th Panzer Division which was in reserve in the Naples area. They had orders, which have since come into our hands, to recapture Termoli at all costs and drive the British into the sea. These orders, thanks to you, they were unable to carry out. It had another effect, though. It eased the pressure on the American Fifth Army and, as you have probably heard, they are now advancing.

'When I first saw you at Az-zib and told you that you were going to work with 13 Corps, I was very impressed by you and by everything

I saw. When I told you that you had a coastal battery to destroy, I was convinced that it was the right sort of job for you.

'In all my military career, and in my time I have commanded many units, I have never yet met a unit in which I had such confidence as I have in yours. And I mean that!

'Let me give you six reasons why I think you are as successful as you are – six reasons which I think you will perhaps bear in mind when training newcomers to your ranks to your own high standards.

'First of all, you take your training seriously. That is one thing that has always impressed me about you.

'Secondly, you are well-disciplined. Unlike some who undertake this specialised and highly dangerous job, you maintain a standard of discipline and cleanliness which is good to see.

'Thirdly, you are physically fit, and I think I know you well enough to know you will always keep that up.

'Fourthly, you are completely confident in your abilities-yet not to the point of over-confidence.

'Fifthly, despite that confidence, you plan carefully.

Last of all you have the right spirit, which I hope you will pass on to those who may join you in the future'

General Dempsey paused before explaining that he had a further six points, which he always tried to bear in mind when handling the unit.

'These principles,' he continued, 'if I may call them such, are:

'First, never to use you unless the job is worthwhile. That is to say, unless the effect to be gained more than compensates for the risk taken in putting you in; and there is always considerable risk in using troops like yourselves.

'Secondly, never to put you in too far ahead of the army. Always I must be able to reach you in twelve to twenty-four hours: if you are a small party, in twelve hours; if a large party, at the most in twenty-four hours.

'Thirdly, I must be prepared to use the whole of my force, including artillery and tanks if need be, to reach you within that time. One reason is that YOU always seem to stir up trouble wherever you go.

'Fourthly, I always try to give you as much time as possible for careful planning.

'On the other hand, I bear in mind that I must not hesitate to use you quickly if the opportunity suddenly arises. Such a case was Augusta, and you succeeded as only a well-trained unit could succeed.'

'Finally, once you have carried out your job, I must get you out as quickly as possible to enable you to refit and to reorganise.'

Lieutenant General Miles Dempsey
Commander 13 Corps
November 1943

These Men are Dangerous. D. Harrison. Cassell and Company, London. 1957. pp. 98–100

Letter From Brigadier Mike Calvert to his SAS Officers on the Future Employment of SAS Troops – October 1945

FUTURE OF SAS. TROOPS

To:

Lt-Col W. Stirling

Lt-Col D. Stirling, D S O

Lt-Col R. B. Mayne, D S O

Lt-Col B. M. F. Franks, D S O, M C

Lt-Col I. G. Collins

Lt-Col E. C. Baring

Lt-Col The Earl Jellicoe

Lt-Col D. Sutherland

Lt-Col D. Lloyd Owen, M C

Major J. Verney, M C

Major R. Farran, D S O, M C

The Director of Tactical Investigation, Maj-Gen Rowell, has been ordered by the Chief of Imperial General Staff, that his directorate should investigate all the operations of the Special Air Service with a view to giving recommendations for the future of S. A. S. in the next war and its composition in the peace-time army. The actual terms of reference were:

An investigation of S. A. S. technique, tactics and organisation without prejudice to a later examination of all organisations of a similar nature which were formed and operated in various theatres of this last war.

Brigadier Churchill is Deputy Director of Tactical Investigation and lives at Flat 110, 4 Whitehall Court, London, S W 1 (Whitehall

9400 Ext 1632), just behind the War Office. The Officer immediately concerned is Lt-Col C. A. Wigham. Lt-Col Wigham has in his possession all the reports on S. A. S. operations in W. EUROPE The reports on SAS operations in ITALY and in the MEDITERRANEAN Theatre are also being obtained and forwarded.

I have given Lt-Col Wigham your names so that he may either have a talk with you to obtain your views and to find out about incidents which are not clear in the reports, or to ask you to write your views to him.

We all have the future of the SAS. at heart, not merely because we wish to see its particular survival as a unit, but because we have believed in the principles of its method of operations. Many of the above-named officers have had command of forces which have had a similar role to that of the SAS, as well as being in the SAS at one time.

The object of this investigation is to decide whether the principles of operating in the SAS manner are correct. If they are correct, what types of units should undertake operations of this nature, and how best to train and maintain such units in peace, ready for war. I will not start now by writing about the principles of SAS, which have been an intrinsic part of your life for the past few years, but I will mention what I think are some of the most important points which needed bringing out. The best way to do this is to consider the usual criticisms of the SAS type of force.

1. 'The Private Army'
From what I have seen in different parts of the world, forces of this nature tend to be so-called 'Private Armies' because there have been no normal formations in existence to fulfil this function - a role which has been found by all commanders to be a most vital adjunct to their plans. It has only been due to the drive and initiative of certain individuals backed up by senior commanders that these forces have been formed and have carried out their role.

2. 'The taking up of Commanders' valuable time'
This has often been necessary because it has very often only been the commanders of armies who have realised the importance of operations of this nature, and to what an extent they can help their plans. The difficulty has been that more junior staff officers have not understood the object or principles of such forces. They have either given us every help as they have thought us something wonderful, or they have thought we were 'a bloody nuisance'. I feel

that the best way to overcome this is, that once the principle of the importance of Special Raiding Forces operating behind the vital points of the enemy's lines is agreed to it should become an integral part of the training of the army at the Staff College, military colleges, and during manoeuvres, etc. Students should be asked not only what orders or directives or requests they have to give to the artillery, engineers, air, etc. but also what directives they would give to their raiding forces. There should be a recognised staff officer on the staffs of senior formations whose job it is to deal with these forces, i.e. the equivalent of a C.R.E. (Commander Royal Engineers) or C.R.A. (Commander Royal Artillery) This should also be included in the text books, F S R (Field Service Regulations), etc.

3. 'These forces, like airborne forces, are only required when we pass to the offensive, which - judging by all previous wars - is when the regular army has been nearly wiped out in rearguard actions whilst the citizen army forms, i.e. about 3 years after the beginning of the war'

The answer here, I feel, is that it is just when we are weak everywhere that forces of this nature are the most useful, and can play a most vital part, in keeping the enemy all over the world occupied. Also there is little difference between the roles of SAS and 'Auxiliary Forces' who duck when the enemy's offensive rolls over them and then operate against the enemy's L of C [Lines of communication] from previously constructed bases. An SAS formation, by its organisation and training, is ideally suited to operate in this defensive role.

4. 'Overlapping with S.O.E. [Special Operations Executive] and other clandestine organisations'

My experience is that S.O.E. and SAS are complementary to each other. SAS cannot successfully operate without good intelligence, guides, etc. S.O.E. can only do a certain amount before requiring, when their operations became overt, highly trained, armed bodies in uniform to operate and set an example to the local resistance. S.O.E. are the 'white hunters' and produce the ground organisation on which SAS operates. All senior officers of S.O.E. with whom I have discussed this point agree to this principle.

5. 'SAS is not adaptable to all countries'

This has already been proved wrong. SAS is probably more adaptable to changes of theatres than any regular formation. Also, as I have said in 4 above, SAS work on the ground organisation of

S.O.E. It is for S.O.E. to be a world-wide organisation with an organisation in every likely country. Then when necessary, SAS can operate on this organisation using their guides and intelligence, knowledge, etc.

6. 'Volunteer units skim the regular units of their best officers and men'

Volunteer units such as SAS attract officers and men who have initiative, resourcefulness, independence of spirit, and confidence in themselves. In a regular unit there are far less opportunities of making use of these assets and, in fact, in many formations they are a liability, as this individualistic attitude upsets the smooth working of a team. This is especially true in European warfare where the individual must subordinate his natural initiative so that he fits into a part of the machine. Volunteer units such as the Commandos and Chindits (only a small proportion of the Chindits were volunteers although the spirit was there) have shown the rest of the army how to fight at a time when it was in low morale due to constant defeat. A few 'gladiators' raises the standard of all. Analogies are racing (car, aeroplane, horse, etc), and Test teams.

7. 'Expense per man is greater than any other formation and is not worthwhile'

Men in units of this nature probably fight 3 or 4 times more often than regular units. They are always eager for a fight and therefore usually get it. If expense per man days actually in contact with the enemy was taken into account, there would be no doubt which was the more expensive type of formation. I have found, as you will have done, the 'old familiar faces' on every front where we have seen trouble. I consider the expense is definitely worth it without even taking into account the extra results. One SAS raid in North Africa destroyed more aeroplanes in one day than the balloon barrage did during 6 years of war.

8. 'Any normal battalion could do the same job'

My experience shows that they definitely cannot. In NORWAY in 1940, a platoon of marines under a Sgt ran away when left on its own, although they had orders to stay, when a few German lorries appeared. Mainly owing to the bad leadership of this parade ground Sgt, they were all jittery and useless because they were 'out of touch'. A force consisting of two Gurkha companys and a few British troops of which I was one was left behind in 1942 in Burma to attack the enemy in the rear if they appeared. The Commander, a good Gurkha officer with a good record, when confronted with a perfect opportunity (Japs landing in boats onto a wide sandy beach completely unaware of our presence), avoided action in order to get back to his Brigade because he was 'out of touch', and could not receive orders. By avoiding action, the unit went into a waterless area and more perished this way and later by drowning than if he had attacked.

My experience with regular battalions under my command in Burma was that there were only 3 or 4 officers in any battalion who could be relied on to take positive action if they were on their own, and had no detailed orders. This 'I'll 'ave to ask me Dad' attitude of the British Army is its worse feature in my opinion. I found the R A F and Dominion officers far better in this respect. I have not had experience with the cavalry. They should also be better. Perhaps cavalry could take on the SAS role successfully? I admit that with training both in Burma and North Africa there were definite improvements amongst the infantry, but in my opinion, no normal battalion I have seen could carry out an SAS role without 80% reorganisation.

I have written frankly and have laid myself open to obvious criticism, but I consider this such a vital point I do not mind how strongly I express myself. I have repeated this for 5 years and I have nowhere seen anything to change my views, least of all in Europe.

I have mentioned some points above. You may not agree with my ideas but I write them down as these criticisms are the most normal ones I know.

Other points on which the DT1 wants to obtain information are:

1. Obtaining of recruits. Has anybody got the original brochure setting out the terms and standards required?
2. Obtaining of stores and equipment. Here again, I imagine S.O.E. has been the main source of special stores. My own H Q is producing a paper on this when in England.
3. Signal communication. This is of course one of the most important parts of such an organisation and it has, as in other formations, limited the scope of our operations.
4. Foreign recruits and attached civilians.
5. Liaison with R A F. and Navy.
6. Command. How is an organisation of this sort best commanded and under whom should they be?
7. Suggestions re survival in peacetime including auxiliary formation, command, technical development, etc.

You may expect a communication from Lt-Col Wigham. Please give your views quite candidly. They certainly need not agree with those I have written down. I am sending Lt-Col Wigham a copy of this letter so that it may give you something to refer to if necessary. I hope, from the army point of view, and for all that you have worked for and believed in during the last few years, that you will do everything you can to help Lt-Col Wigham to obtain all the information that he requires. We can no longer say that people do not understand if we do not take this chance to get our views put before an impartial tribunal whose task it is to review them in the light of general policy, and then make recommendations to the C. I. G. S. Send along any reports or documents you have got. Lt-Col Wigham is thirsting for information.

J. M. CALVERT
Brigadier,
Commander,
Sloe House,
Halstead, Essex.
12 Oct 45.
J M C/L G M.

Colonel JW –
Malayan Scouts SAS

The Secretary, S. A. S. Regimental Association.
9th December 1981

Dear Sir,

In view of the extreme pro and anti views on the Malayan Scouts S.A.S. I feel obliged to express an opinion. My qualification is that I was the only officer to serve from the formation of the Malayan Scouts in 1950, who also served on subsequent tours until December, 1964.

The first Squadron to form, and there was only one in 1950, contained many good soldiers. Three of the first four troop Commanders in my opinion would have done well in that capacity at any time subsequently when I was serving. There was also a minority of all ranks who were unsuitable. It is true that operational standards in the early years were poor compared to those gradually attained over the next decade. This is neither surprising, nor should the junior officers and soldiers be blamed. Apart from the not entirely relevant experience of veterans of the Burma war we had no skilled instructors and very largely taught ourselves.

Before excessive criticism is made of the CO, Mike Calvert and other senior officers, it should be remembered that the situation in Malaya was bad and getting worse. Calvert was under pressure to get results and get them quickly. The training of A Squadron was not extensive; subsequent squadrons almost literally were trained on operations. I commanded in quick succession all three British squadrons and was never in my life faced with so hard, even impossible, a task.

The Rhodesian Squadron in 1951 had a three weeks' training exercise before operations, advised by me and one NCO, with perhaps nine months' jungle experience between us. A case of the blind leading the blind! This Squadron with a high percentage of potentially outstanding S.A.S. soldiers never realised its full potential in Malaya because it was never properly trained. The same mistake was not made with the New Zealand S.A.S. Squadron when it joined us in 1955.

Perhaps the strongest and most justified criticism of the Malayan Scouts was poor discipline, in and out of the jungle ... Numerous widely publicised, sensational and mainly true stories circulated for years and very nearly led to the disbandment of the unit. Calvert's comparison was that a building site can be a rough and mucky place until construction is finished. But if Calvert must accept much of the blame, he deserves credit too for his far-sighted perception of the broad strategy and tactics of counter-insurgency, which I learned mainly from him, with subsequent additions from the splendid Z Reserve of the wartime S.A.S. whom I met at Otley in Yorkshire in 1952 for two weeks T. A. camp. It was their example which inspired me to spend as much as possible of the rest of my military career in the service of the S.A.S.

Yours truly
JW

LETTER FROM GHQ FARELF TO THE WAR OFFICE ABOUT THE MALAYAN SCOUTS (SAS)

GHQ, FARELF 22 December 1951

To:
The Under Secretary of State,
The War Office, Whitehall,
London, SW 1

Subject: MALAYAN SCOUTS – SPECIAL AIR SERVICE REGT.

1. The employment of the Malayan Scouts (Special Air Service Regiment) has been under consideration at this HQ and the following conclusions have been reached.

ROLE
2. The role of the Malayan Scouts (Special Air Service Regiment) is to operate in the deep jungle areas not already covered by other Security Forces, with the object of destroying bandit forces, their camps and their sources of supply. No other units in Malaya are so suitably organised or equipped for this task which is vital in bringing the bandits to battle. The result is that the unit is becoming a 'Corps d'Elite' in deep jungle operations and is a most valuable component of our armed forces in Malaya.

ORGANISATION
3. In order to increase the efficiency of the Special Air Service Regiment, certain changes are now considered necessary in the establishment, but these changes are largely on the administrative

side, which has been the weak link in the past. The Regiment is now to be organised on a four squadron basis as shown on the outline War Establishment, at Appendix 'A' attached. This reorganisation shows a decrease of two British officers, but an increase of 52 British other ranks. However, certain of the administrative appointments can be suitably filled by National Servicemen, thereby economising in the use of the more experienced volunteers.

TACTICAL OPERATIONS

4. The Regiment is having increasing successes in their operations all the time. Their initial operations involved many weeks of patrolling deep in the jungle, which had the effect of disturbing bandits in their camps and providing a great feeling of insecurity among them. The next main operations the Regiment took part in were deep jungle penetrations in connection with other operations by Infantry battalions. These were very effective and provided many bandit kills. The Regiment is at present taking part in a most difficult operation in North Malaya, from which valuable results are expected.

TERMS OF SERVICE

5. This paragraph is covered by Reference 'B', (Author's addition: this reference is omitted) which in short recommends a two year tour, with the option of extending for a period of one year.

TRAINING

6. The unit is authorised to recruit a percentage of parachutists, as there is a role for them during the emergency in Malaya and in wartime in the Far East. With the longer tour it may be possible to retrain a number of volunteers as parachutists by arranging local refresher courses for them. This is now under investigation, but there is no intention of carrying out basic parachute training in this theatre.

TITLE

7. It is felt that the present title of the Regiment indicates that the unit will only operate in Malaya and that volunteers would be more attracted if the words 'Malayan Scouts' were deleted from the title and that the Regiment should be known as a Special Air Service Regiment, with a suitable number to be selected by the War Office. It is believed that '22nd Special Air Service Regiment' would fit in with the present order of battle. It is presumed that the Rhodesian Government should be consulted before the change of title is approved.

RECOMMENDATIONS

8. (a) That the Regiment, reorganised as on the attached outline
       War Establishment remains in this theatre during the emer-
       gency (Note: the revised complete War Establishment will be
       forwarded to the War Office in the normal way with the
       Minutes of the War Establishment Committee).

   (b) That the Regiment includes a proportion of National
       Servicemen in certain selected administrative appointments.

   (c) That the initial tour be increased from 18 months to 2 years.

   (d) That the title of the Regiment should be a 'Special Air Service
       Regiment', with a number selected by the War Office, and if
       this is approved, that action should be taken to inform the
       Rhodesian Government of its wider implications.

(Sgd)
for General, Commander-in-Chief,

Appendix 5

Letter Written By Lt Colonel John Sloane to Maj Leot Hart on Taking Over Malayan Scouts (Sas)

Special Air Service Regiment (The Malayan Scouts)
c/o GPO,
Kuala Lumpur Malaya

From: Lt. Col. J. B. M. Sloane

20 August 1951

Dear Hart,

I have recently taken over this Regiment, arriving after Mike Calvert had left, and amongst many other things, I am trying to make my number with everyone who has shown an interest and helped us in the past and, I hope, will assist us in the future. Hence my writing to you.

The past history of events I find most confusing and in many ways unfortunate but I have no intention of dwelling on them; rather do I regard them as lessons for the future. I think the best thing I can do is to tell you briefly what we are doing at present; this is, of course, confidential.

The main task is to endeavour to get the Regiment on a sound and lasting basis. To this end the whole of the administration is being overhauled and reorganised; this is a major task since for a large part of the unit's life it has been regarded as unnecessary; how wrong and how expensive this conception has proved to be.

Secondly, the whole of the Regiment's future is up for consideration. Later in September a committee of 'distinguished' soldiers is meeting to consider our future; we, of course, are the main 'witnesses'. My approach to this is that we must have stability and permanence; we must be given a much wider role, not tied to Malaya.

A new War Office Establishment is also being submitted to rectify some of the more obvious errors in the present one. What success we shall have remains to be seen.

I must say I find myself in rather a peculiar position here, since I have had nothing whatsoever to do with SAS, or anything approaching it, during my service. I was also whisked into this job shortly after my battalion left Korea and am still in something of a daze.

We shall be concentrating in Singapore shortly for six weeks' rest and retraining, and I hope that this will do the Regiment a lot of good.

I would be most grateful if I knew we could count on your support and perhaps you could let me know how you feel about things.

Yours aye,
John Sloane

Major L. E. O. T. Hart, MBE.,
The SAS Regiment,
HQ 21 SAS Regt (Artists) TA.

'122 Days In The Jungle' – An Article About the SAS in Soldier Magazine – April 1954

Men of the 22nd Special Air Service Regiment set out to win the goodwill of a primitive people – and set up a new endurance record for Malaya.

Forty men marched out of the jungle, and a Punjabi barber threw up his hands in despair. He had good reason, for each of them carried more than four months unhindered growth of hair. They had been operating for 122 days on the Perak-Pahang mountain range of Malaya, among aborigines so primitive that they cannot count more than 5. In the six years of the Malaya 'emergency' no other soldiers had spent so long a stretch in the jungle. They had set out from a jungle road-head in central Malaya, a specially-picked squadron of the 22nd Special Air Service Regiment, 80 strong. Two were killed in action, 13 were evacuated by helicopter owing to injuries of sickness, and 25 were tactically detached.

Operation ASP
December 1954 – March 1955
SAS Regimental War Diary Entry

The Regiment is currently engaged in 'Operation ASP', the details for which cannot be released. All Squadrons have operated in the area and are continuing to do so.

The 'bag' to date is:

8 DEC 54. Three CTs killed, one male and one female CT escaped from an assault on a CT camp. This attack was personally directed by Major J L A Painter, RA.

21 DEC 54. On this occasion an 'incident' developed when 15 CTs ambushed 4 Troop and wounded Sgt Waters who has now recovered.

21 JAN 55. A small patrol comprising Lt P Jewson RA, and Tprs Vincent and Maginnis (2 Troop) contacted 3 CTs, killing one and wounding another.

25 FEB 55. CTs fired on 19 Troop base and lost one of their number, killed by Tpr Archer.

1 MAR 55. 3 CTs fled from 4 Troop, bumped into 18 Troop and suffered one wounded.

10 MAR 55. Sgt Levett leading a five man patrol from 19 Troop contacted 3 CTs all of whom were killed.

16 MAR 55. 4 CTs attacked a four man patrol consisting of Lt G H Gordon RTR, and Tprs Bache, Mayer and Hannam, who suffered no casualties and 2 CTs were positively killed, 1 CT probably died of wounds, 1 escaped.

17 MAR 55. 6 Troop, commanded by Lt J J King, ambushed a cultivation, and Tprs Mundell, Dench and Longstaff share the lone CT who was killed.

After a good start this operation has been less productive of late. However a vast number of camps and cultivations have been and are being found and destroyed. The security of the deep jungle continues to be denied to the CTs and we have reason to believe that this lack of security, and the fact that the CTs are unable to cultivate in this part of the deep jungle, is being a major contribution to operations in this part of Malaya.

Operation CLARET – Borneo Cross-Border Operations 'Golden Rules'

1. Every operation to be authorised by DOBOPS – himself authorised by the Commander-in-Chief, Far East.

2. Only trained and tested troops to be used. No soldiers were to go across during their first tour of duty in Borneo.

3. Depth of penetration must be limited and attacks must only be made to thwart offensive action by the enemy and must never be in retribution or solely to inflict casualties. Civilian lives must not be risked.

4. No operation which required close air support – except in an extreme emergency – must be undertaken.

5. Every operation must be planned with the aid of a sand-table and thoroughly rehearsed for at least two weeks.

6. Each operation to be planned and executed with maximum security. Every man taking part must be sworn to secrecy, full cover plans must be made and the operations to be given code-names and never discussed in detail on telephone or radio.

7. Identity discs must be left behind before departure and no traces – such as cartridge cases, paper, ration packs, etc. – must be left in Kalimantan.

8. On no account must any soldier taking part be captured by the enemy – alive or dead.

These rules for cross-border operations were decreed by General Sir Walter Walker. Director of Borneo Operations (DOBOPS) 1963–65. Pocock, Tom. *Fighting General*, p.197

TENETS OF THE SPECIAL AIR SERVICE REGIMENT

1. The unrelenting pursuit of excellence;
2. maintaining the highest standards of discipline and all aspects of the daily life of the SAS soldier, from the occasional precision drilling on the parade ground even to his personal turnout on leave. We have always reckoned the high standard of discipline in each soldier was the only effective foundation for Regimental discipline. Commitment to the SAS pursuit of excellence becomes a sham if any single one of the disciplinary standards is allowed to slip;
3. the SAS brooks no sense of class and, particularly, not among the wives. This may sound a bit portentous but it epitomises the SAS philosophy. The traditional idea of a crack Regiment was one officered by the aristocracy and, indeed, these regiments deservedly won great renown for their dependability and their gallantry in wartime and for their parade ground panache in peacetime. In the SAS we share with the Brigade of Guards the deep respect for quality, but we have an entirely different outlook. We believe, as did the ancient Greeks who originated the word 'aristocracy', that every man with the right attitude and talents, regardless of birth and riches, has a capacity in his own lifetime of reaching that status in its true sense; in fact in our SAS context an individual soldier may prefer to go on serving as an NCO rather than have to leave the Regiment in order to obtain an officer's commission. All ranks in the SAS are 'one company' in which a sense of class is both alien and ludicrous. A to visit the Sergeants mess SAS HQ in Hereford vividly conveys what I mean; and
4. humility and humour: both these virtues are indispensable in the everyday life of officers and men – particularly so in the case of

the SAS which is often regarded as an elite Regiment. Without frequent recourse to humour and humility, our special status could cause resentment in other units of the British Army and an unbecoming conceit and big-headedness in our own soldiers.

Colonel Sir David Stirling OBE DSO
15 November 1915 – 6 November 1990

'WE ARE THE PILGRIMS, MASTER...'

The following lines are inscribed on a clock tower that is located inside the camp of 22 Special Air Service Regiment, in Hereford. On brass plates around the sides of the clock tower are the names of members of the Special Air Service Regiment, including those from Rhodesia (the original C Squadron), who have been killed in the line of duty.

> We are the Pilgrims, master; we shall go
> Always a little further; it may be
> Beyond that last blue mountain barred with snow
> Across that angry or that glimmering sea.

These evocative lines have become synonymous with the Special Air Service but they originated in the words of a play by James Elroy Flecker 1884–1915:

HASSAN
The Story of Hassan of Bagdad
and how he Came to Make the Golden Journey to Samarkand
(A play in five acts):

MASTER OF THE CARAVAN
But who are ye in rags and rotten shoes,
You dirty-bearded, blocking up the way?

ISHAK
We are the Pilgrims, master; we shall go
Always a little further; it may be

Beyond that last blue mountain barred with snow
Across that angry or that glimmering sea,
White on a throne or guarded in a cave
There lies a prophet who can understand
Why men were born: but surely we are brave,
Who take the Golden Road to Samarkand.

HASSAN
Sweet to ride forth at evening from the wells
When shadows pass gigantic on the sand,
And softly through the silence beat the bells
Along the Golden Road to Samarkand.

ISHAK
We travel not for trafficking alone;
By hotter winds our fiery hearts are fanned:
For lust of knowing what should not be known,
We take the Golden Road to Samarkand.

NOTES

Chapter 1

1   The SBS continued to exist after the end of the Second World War in various iterations, but it has a primary skills base of water-borne techniques. After almost continued, service-based, competitiveness the two organisations have formed a joint headquarters under the direction of the Director of Special Forces, an Army Brigadier. They now have an uneasy synergetic existence.

2   The British Army regimental system, as it evolved during the nineteenth century was a response to the need to police the Empire. Infantry battalions were paired, with one of the battalions serving in the dominions or colonies, and the other sending replacements from home. This was a system set up by the Cardwell reforms of 1873.

3   Gray, C.S., *Explorations in Strategy*, Greenwood Press, CT, 1996, p. 290.

4   Gray: *Explorations in Strategy*, p. 149.

5   See Bartlett, C.J. *The Long Retreat. A Short History of British Defence Policy 1945–1970.* Macmillan Press, London, 1972; Chichester, Michael and Wilkinson, John. *The Uncertain Ally – British Defence Policy 1960–1990.* Gower Publishing Company, Aldershot, 1982; and Hopkinson, William. *The Making of British Defence Policy.* The Stationery Office Ltd, Norwich, 2000.

6   Thatcher, Margaret. *The Downing Street Years.* Harper Collins Publishers, London, 1993, p. 8.

7   Williams, Paul. 'Who's making UK foreign policy?' *International Affairs.* Number 5, 2004, pp. 911–29.

8   See Beaumont, Roger. *Military Elites.* Robert Hale and Company, London, 1974; Cohen, Elliot A. *Commandoes and Politicians – Elite Military Units in Modern Democracies.* Harvard University, USA, 1978; Gray, C.S. *Special Operations – What Succeeds and Why?* National Institute for Public Policy, Washington, 1991; Gray, *Explorations in Strategy*; Hamish, Ian. A and Neilson, K. *Elite Military Formations in War and Peace.* Praeger Publishing, Westport, CT, 1996; McRaven, W.H. *Spec Ops.* Presidio Press CA. 1996, Novato Press, 1995; Thompson, J. and Imperial War Museum. *War Behind Enemy Lines.*

Macmillan, London, 1998; Tugwell, Maurice and Charters, David. *Special Operations and the Threats to United States Interests in the 1980s.* National Defense University Press, Washington, DC, 1984; Kiras, James. *Rendering the Mortal Blow Easier: Special Operations and the Nature of Strategy.* Book. July 2004. (Unpublished) The Graduate Institute of Political and International Studies, University of Reading.

9   Kiras: *Rendering the Mortal Blow Easier*, p. 8.

10   'Special – of a particular kind, for a particular purpose'. *The Concise Oxford Dictionary* 7th Ed., Oxford University Press, Oxford, 1984.

11   'Elite – the choice part; the best (of a group)'. *The Concise Oxford Dictionary* 7th Ed., Oxford University Press, Oxford, 1984.

12   Gray: *Explorations in Strategy*, pp. 144–9.

13   *Ibid.*, p. 144.

14   *Ibid.*, p. 144.

15   Luttwak, Edward. *A Dictionary of Modern War*. The Penguin Press, London. 1971.

16   *Ibid.*, p. 199.

17   22 *Special Air Service Regiment – Rules for War – 1970*. 5th Ed., 1972. Author's collection.

18   A dropping zone is a specified area for the dropping of paratroops.

19   Calvert, Michael. *Fighting Mad*. Airlife Publishing Ltd, Shrewsbury, 1996 (2nd Ed.), pp. 45–52.

20   McNab, Andy. *Bravo Two Zero*. Bantam Press, London, 1993; and Ryan, Chris. *The One That Got Away*. Brassey, Inc., London, 1997.

21   Thompson and Imperial War Museum: *War Behind Enemy Lines*, p. 7.

22   Churchill, Winston S. *Their Finest Hour* (3rd Ed.). Bantam Books, New York, 1962.

23   Gray: *Explorations in Strategy*, p. 148.

24   The speech was delivered by the commanding officer of 22 SAS at the unit's jubilee celebrations held at Stirling Lines, Hereford on 27 July 2002.

25   Seven Palestinian terrorists of the 'Black September' group stormed the Israeli athletes' compound at the Olympic Games stadium and took nine Israeli athletes hostage. The terrorists demanded an escape aircraft and were flown by two German helicopters to an airfield at Furstenfeld-bruck. In an amateurish and unsuccessful rescue operation by the German police the hostages were killed by the terrorists. Four of the terrorists were killed in the rescue attempt and three captured. The Munich Olympics Massacre was the catalyst for the formation of hostage-rescue units by most major countries.

26   Cohen, Elliot. *Commandoes and Politicians – Elite Military Units in Modern Democracies*. Harvard University Press, Cambridge MA, 1978, p. 74.

27   Thompson and Imperial War Museum: *War Behind Enemy Lines*, p. 8.

28   Foot, M.R.D. *The 4th Dimension of War, Volume I. Intelligence, Subversion, Resistance*. Manchester University Press, Manchester, 1970, p. 19.

29   See Chapter 5, Army Doctrine Publications (ADP), Volume 1. *Operations*. 1994; and Joint Service Publication (JSP) 439. *Special Forces Operations*. 1994.

30   Operation BARRAS was a combined operation with the D Squadron 22 SAS and a rifle company from the Parachute Regiment in which British Army personnel who had been kidnapped by a rebel gang in Sierra Leone were rescued. The operation was carried out on 10–11 September 2000.

31   90,000 copies of the magazine *SOLDIER* – which reported the action and referred to the SAS, using publicly available information – were recalled and pulped. This was the first time the magazine, which has been produced for over 60 years, had ever been recalled and so, not surprisingly, media and public interest was heightened as a result. See Hall, M. 'Army magazine gagged over SAS jungle raid', *Sunday Telegraph*, 29 October 2000, p. 6.

32   DLB. P. *Storm Command*. Harper Collins, London, 1992 and *Looking For Trouble*. Harper Collins, London, 1994.

33   Cohen: *Commandoes*, p. 95.

34   It used to be the case that once or twice a year two or three members of the SAS members went for two weeks training with MI6. If suitable jobs came up they could be called in by MI6 to do them. The case used to support this was that of Navy frogman Commander Lionel 'Buster' Crabb RNVR GM OBE, who was the subject of a major Cold War incident when he disappeared while, allegedly, spying on equipment fitted to Russian warships making a goodwill visit to Britain in 1956. A measure of how sensitive the government still finds the matter is the fact that the cabinet papers concerning the Crabb affair, which should have become open to the public under the 30-year rule in 1986, are now to remain sealed until 2057!

35   PRO/WO296/95. Northern Ireland: operational matters; legal aspects; SAS incursions into the Republic of Ireland. 1 Jan–31 December 1976.

36   PRO/DEFE5/195/23 – SAS in Europe 1973; and PRO/DEFE5/197/5 – Higher Direction and Employment of Special Forces (SF) 1973. Apparently, asbestos contamination is affecting a number of MoD files which have been stored in the 'old' MoD Building in London. A cynic might consider this obfuscation on behalf of the Government.

37   A squadron composed of Rhodesian volunteers, C Squadron, served with the SAS in Malaya from 1951 to 1953. The title C Squadron remains vacant in the 22 SAS order of battle.

38   A squadron of New Zealand volunteers served with the SAS in Malaya from 1955 to 1957.

39   A squadron of volunteers from the Parachute Regiment served with the SAS from 1955 to 1957.

40   As a comparison, although statistics are not always helpful, The Suffolk Regiment deployed to Malaya in May 1949 and left in January 1953, and during that time they killed 198 terrorists, against 21 of their own, of whom 12 were killed in action.

41   Cohen: *Commandoes*, p. 101.

Chapter 2

42   Churchill, Winston, S. *The Second World War*. Vol. 2. Their Finest Hour. Bantam Books, New York, 1962, p. 211.

43   Clarke, Dudley. *Seven Assignments*. Alden Press, Oxford, 1949.

44   In 1938, Captain Orde Wingate, a professed Zionist, while serving in Palestine established small bodies of well-trained and well-armed men composed of Jewish settlers reinforced by small numbers of British soldiers and led by British officers to protect Jewish settlements from Arab efforts to

resist their territorial encroachments. These were the Special Night Squads (SNS).

45   Wavell, Archibald Percival. Field Marshal. 1883–1950.
46   See Royle, Trevor. *Orde Wingate, Irregular Soldier*. Weidenfeld and Nicolson, London, 1995.
47   'When I commanded in Palestine in 1937–38, I had on my staff two officers in whom I recognised an original, unorthodox outlook on soldiering; and I pigeon-holed their names in my mind should I ever command an army in war. One was Orde Wingate, the second was Dudley Clarke. I was fortunate enough to be able to use them both.' Clarke: *Seven Assignments*, p. 7, Introduction.
48   Dudley Clarke is credited with the name Special Air Service: Clarke: *Seven Assignments*, p. 219.
49   Warner, P. *The SAS: The Official History*. Sphere Books Ltd, London, 1983 (1971), p. 76.
50   Arthur, Max. *Men of the Red Beret. Airborne Forces. 1940–1990*. Hutchinson, London, 1990, pp. 15–18.
51   Herclerode, Peter. *PARA!* Arms and Armour Press, London, 1992, p. 23.
52   *Ibid.*, p. 146.
53   Layforce was disbanded at the end of 1941. Of its units, 22 Commando had lost 25 per cent of its force through death and injury in Syria in June 1941; rearguard actions in Crete had cost 7, 50 and 52 Commando as well as elements of 8 Commando, dearly. On the disbandment some soldiers were shipped back to UK and some were retained as 'Middle East Commando'.
54   Laycock, who was almost rejected by Dudley Clarke at an interview for the Commandos, became the youngest Major General in the British Army at 36. As Sir Robert Laycock KCMG CB DSO he became the first Colonel Commandant of the SAS.
55   Composed of 2 officers and 15 other ranks.
56   Churchill, Winston, S. *The Second World War*. Vol. 3. The Grand Alliance. Bantam Books, New York, 1962. Appendix A. Book 2. 23 July 1941. pp. 688–9.
57   The unsuccessful raid against Rommel by 59 men of 11 Commando under Lieutenant Colonel Geoffrey Keyes on 17–18 November 1941 was the last example of Dudley Clarke's original commando concept, and in the future commando would be used as special assault troops preceding general offensives.
58   Often spelled Lewes. He was the inventor of the 'Lewes Bomb' designed to destroy and then ignite fuel tanks and fuel containers.
59   Some 50 parachutes destined for the parachute battalions in India 'accidentally came into the hands' of Lewis in Alexandria.
60   Newsinger, J., *Dangerous Men*. Pluto Press, London, 1997, p.b.
61   Newsinger: *Dangerous Men*, p. 7.
62   MCLEOD. 1/10. 1948. Memorandum on the origins of the Special Air Service (SAS) by Col David Stirling. 8 November 1948.
63   Newsinger: *Dangerous Men*, p. 7.
64   The LRDG established under Ralph Bagnold, in June 1940, primarily as an intelligence-gathering organisation. The success the patrols established by Bagnold (a most unrecognised individual) helped to break down official opposition to the plethora of commando-type formations, specialised units and

'private armies' that were fulfilling novel and essential roles at the time, roles for which conventional forces were neither trained nor equipped.

65 Newsinger: *Dangerous Men*, p. 45.

66 Lloyd Owen, D. *Providence Their Guide*. George C. Harrap and Co. Ltd, London, 1980, p. 15.

67 The majority of the original members of the unit had been recruited from the New Zealand division and Rhodesians from the South African units because it was believed, and proven correct, that these colonial personnel with their pioneer backgrounds would be ideally suited for such an organisation.

68 Wynter, H.W. *Special Forces in the Desert War 1940–1943*. Public Record Office, Kew, 2004, p. 122.

69 Originally, the variety of mixed head-dress was consolidated on a white beret modelled on that of 1CCP (Compagnie de Chasseurs Parachutistes), who had joined L Detachment from Britain. However, the colour of the white beret was not conducive to good relations with other units and it was changed to a beige beret and remained so until the SAS Brigade was formed under 1st Airborne Division in January 1944. The PARAs directed the SAS to wear the maroon beret of the airborne.

70 Warner: *SAS*, p. 322.

71 *Ibid.*, pp. 83–4.

72 Wynter: *Special Forces*, p. 307.

73 *Ibid.*, p. 366.

74 Cowles, Virginia. *The Phantom Major*. Oldhams Press Ltd, Hertfordshire, 1958, p. 286.

75 Warner: *SAS*, p. 20.

76 Farran, Roy. *Winged Dagger*. Collins, London, 1948, p. 157.

77 Formed in 1941, the SSRF had operated under joint control of the Chief of Combined Operations and the Special Operations Executive, seeing action off the coasts of France and Africa – it had become part of 62 Commando in January 1943.

78 Strawson, J. *A History of the SAS Regiment*. Guild Publishing, London, 1985, pp. 90–1.

79 General Dempsey became the Colonel Commandant of the SAS in 1952.

80 The new Brigade composed of 1 SAS and 2 SAS (British and Commonwealth); 3 SAS (French – 2 RCP); 4 SAS (French – 3 RCP); 5 SAS (Independent Belgian Squadron until April 1945); and F Squadron, GHQ Regt (Signals and communications). F Squadron came from a unit known variously as the GHQ Liaison Regiment or 'Phantom'. Founded by Lt Col G.F. Hopkinson, Phantom was an intelligence, reconnaissance and signals unit with the task of gathering intelligence in forward areas, and behind enemy lines, and radioing the information back to GHQ.

81 SAS troops were directed to replace their beige berets with the maroon berets of the airborne. This was the beginning of friction between airborne forces and the SAS which continues to this day.

82 The Papers of General Sir Roderick McLeod GBE KCB (1905–80) are held in the Liddell Hart Centre for Military Archives, King's College London.

83 William Stirling was very concerned by the fact that the SAS which had been used as commando assault troops in Sicily and Italy were now to be used as conventional paratroops not as small sabotage groups.

84 Warner: *SAS*, p. 145.
85 MCLEOD 1/1 1944–. Typescript memorandum entitled 'Summary of casualties inflicted on the enemy by Special Air Service (SAS) troops during operations in 1944' [containing statistics compiled from official reports on Axis forces personnel killed, wounded or taken prisoner; transports captured or destroyed; railways, bridges, communications and military installations destroyed; equipment captured; SAS casualties].
86 Strawson: *History of the SAS*, p. 121.
87 Farran: *Winged Dagger*, pp. 261–8.
88 See Calvert, Michael. *Prisoners of Hope*. Leo Cooper, London, 1952.
89 See Kemp, Anthony. *The Secret Hunters*. Michael O'Mara Books, London, 1986.
90 MCLEOD 2/2 1945 – *Notes on the future of SAS* [containing proposals for an SAS role in China, Indo-China and Siam under South East Asia Command (SEAC)]. 7 May 1945.
91 Sykes, Christopher. *Orde Wingate*. Collins, London, 1959, p. 327.
92 Churchill: *Second World War* Vol. III, p. 399.
93 Verney, John. *Going to the Wars*. Collins, London, 1955, p. 147.
94 Lloyd Owen: *Providence*, p. 229.
95 ULTRA was the code name given to the process by which the cipher experts at Bletchley Park in the UK had managed to solve some of the German Army's Enigma cipher machine's many keys. This source of information was not admitted by the British Government until 1974 and those who had been privy to the secret in the Second World War were under an obligation to keep silent about it.
96 See Hoe, A. *David Stirling, Authorised Biography*. Little, Brown and Company, London, 1992.
97 Slim, F.M. *Retreat into Victory*. Cassell and Co, London, 1956, p. 549.
98 Weale, Adrian. *Secret Warfare*. Hodder and Stoughton, London, 1997, p. 137.
99 Calvert makes a convincing argument but the nation had become tired of war, the pool of personnel from whom to select special forces personnel was dramatically diminished, and there was no obvious and urgent operational and strategic requirement to continue maintaining a regular special forces unit.
100 See Appendix 2.
101 Strawson: *History of the SAS*, p. 278.
102 See MCLEOD 2/3 1945. Memorandum on the formation of the proposed SAS Territorial Army unit.
103 Churchill, Winston, S. The Second World War. Vol. 5. Closing the Ring. Bantam Books, New York, 1962. Appendix B. Book 2. 25 January 1944, p. 601.
104 Jones, Tim. *Post War Insurgency and the SAS. 1945–1952. A Special Type of Warfare*. Frank Cass Publishers, London, 2001, *passim*.

Chapter 3

105 Briefing to SAS troop commanders by the commanding officer on 11 November 1975.
106 For a selection of information about the SAS and its organisation and training see the following books: Connor, K. *Ghost Force*, Weidenfeld and Nicolson,

London, 1998; Dickens, P. *SAS, The Jungle Frontier*. Arms and Armour Press, London, 1983; Dickens, P. *SAS, Secret War in South East Asia*. Ballantine Books, London, 1992 (reprint of 1983 *SAS, The Jungle Frontier*); Geraghty, Tony. *Who Dares Wins. The Story of the Special Air Service 1950–1980*. Arms and Armour Press, London, 1980; Kemp, Anthony. *The SAS – Savage Wars of Peace. 1947 – Present*. Penguin Books Ltd, London, 1994; Ramsay, Jack. *SAS. The Soldiers' Story*. Macmillan Publishing Ltd, London, 1996; PR. *Eye of the Storm*. Michael O'Mara Books Ltd, London, 2001; PS. *The Joker. 20 Years Inside the SAS*. Andre Deutsch Ltd, London, 1999; Strawson, J. *A History of the SAS Regiment*. Guild Publishing, London, 1985; and Warner, P. *The SAS The Official History*. Sphere Books Ltd, London, 1983 (1971).

107 A 'badged' SAS operative is one who has successfully completed the SAS selection course and continuation training which takes place over nine months.

108 Kennedy, Harold. 'Forces under stress', *National Defense*. October 2004, pp. 34–5.

109 Based upon their experiences in the Vietnam War, the New Zealand SAS and the Australian SAS increased their patrols to five men so that patrols could carry a wounded man, which they did not believe was possible with a patrol of only four members.

110 This involves preparing and electronically condensing a message before transmitting it in a brief 'squirt' or series of brief 'squirts' designed to foil sophisticated radio-direction finding equipment, which scans frequencies for activity and then triangulates to give accurate information on the location of the transmitting station.

111 During the Falklands War, the observation post of Captain Gavin Hamilton was compromised by Argentinean radio-direction finding equipment and attacked. Hamilton was killed and he was awarded a posthumous Military Cross.

112 Interview CCC 2 November 2004.

113 '... outdated entry skills that have [been] transformed into hobbies and sports'. Interview FFF 5 January 2005.

114 Interview DDD 11 November 2004.

115 Interview CCC 2 November 2004.

116 *Ibid.*

117 SAS recruits are all volunteers and a commanding officer must forward to the SAS any application from a soldier, sailor or airman to attend a selection course.

118 The selection course is over a three-week period, culminating in Test Week. Officers have an additional week. Two selection courses are held each year, one in winter and one in summer. There are advantages and disadvantages in attending a selection course in either of the climatic periods.

119 A covert military surveillance organisation operating in Northern Ireland.

120 Interview HHH 21 January 2005.

121 The parent unit rank, or 'shadow rank' as it is known, continues to gain promotion. For example, a corporal in the Royal Engineers would become a trooper on passing selection, but the rank of corporal would be retained on his regimental records and his promotion would be considered along with other similar-ranked soldiers in the Royal Engineers. There have been cases of an SAS trooper holding the shadow rank of a Warrant Officer First Class (WO1) – the highest non-commissioned rank in the Army.

122 Since its reformation the SAS has almost prided itself in the fact that service in 22 SAS meant financial sacrifice. It was seen as an indication that soldiers had altruistic reasons for serving in the SAS. However, in the late 1970s, former SAS soldiers started earning enormous salaries as bodyguards and security consultants to sheikhs and wealthy businessmen in the Middle East. This started an exodus from the regiment and special forces pay was introduced in 1979 to try and retain this skilled manpower – it was relatively successful. The pay increase occurred just before the siege at Princes Gate, and older serving members of the regiment believed that recruits now came into the SAS for the wrong reasons – money and glamour.

123 Interview DDD 10 November 2004.

124 Successful recruits are presented with their berets by the commanding officer in a low-key ceremony. Interestingly, in a professed egalitarian organisation, the SAS winged dagger cap-badge for soldiers is made of cloth on a beret with a leather head-band, whereas the badge for officers is made of woven metallic wire and the beret has a silk head-band.

125 Interview HHH 21 January 2005.

126 Interview BBB 20 October 2004.

127 British soldiers thought that, on the whole, British officers dressed like the storybook character, 'Rupert Bear' because they tended towards check-pattern trousers, yellow pullovers and brown shoes. Sometimes portrayed as a term of affection, it is actually used by NCOs in the SAS as a term of derision towards officers.

128 Interview GGG 6 January 2005.

129 Briefing to 22 SAS troop commanders by their commanding officer on 11 November 1975.

130 The concept of 'too early' is interesting because, in the military system, the officer is in charge and, in the event of a problem, it would not be an acceptable excuse for an officer to state that it was 'too early' for him to have taken charge from his NCOs.

131 Interview CCC 10 November 2004.

132 Briefing to SAS troop commanders by the commanding officer on 11 November 1975. Written briefing to SAS Troop Commanders by the Commanding Officer dated 11 November 1975 (Author's collection)

133 Interview BBB 20 October 2004.

134 Interview BBB 20 October 2004.

135 Interview DDD 10 November 2004.

136 Interview CCC 10 November 2004.

137 See McNab: *Bravo Two Zero*; Ryan: *The One That Got Away*; and Asher, Michael. *The Real Bravo Two Zero*. Cassell, London, 2002.

138 Interview DDD 4 November 2004.

139 The SAS term for 14 Int operatives was 'Walts', as in Walter Mittys.

140 Rennie, James. *The Operators – The Army's Top Secret Elite*. Century Publishing, London, 1996, p. 202.

141 Falconer, Duncan. *First into Action*, Little Brown and Company, London, 1998, p. 246.

142 Camsell, Don. *Black Water, By Strength and by Guile*. Virgin Publishing Ltd, London, 2000, p. 172.

143 *Ibid*, p. 227.

144 Connor: *Ghost Force*, p. 258.

Chapter 4

145 Morris, James. *Farewell the Trumpets*. Faber and Faber Ltd, London, 1978, p. 517.

146 FSC remained in the Malayan jungle for over three years being withdrawn by submarine from Pankor Island in 1945. After the war, in which he received a DSO for his service, he became a warden at Reading University. He committed suicide, shooting himself in the summer of 1971. The Malays have established a permanent memorial to him at Emerald Bay on Pankor Laut, Pankor from where the British submarine extracted him and took him to Force 136 HQ in Ceylon (Sri Lanka). The author visited FSC's Emerald Bay in 1971 and 2004.

147 FSC, F. *The Jungle is Neutral*. Times Books International, Singapore, 1997, p. 13.

148 Short, Anthony. *In Pursuit of Mountain Rats. The Communist Insurrection in Malaya*. Cultured Lotus, Singapore, 2000, p. 21.

149 Sometimes referred to as Lai Te.

150 See Peng, Chin. *My Side of History*. Media Masters Pte Ltd, Singapore, 2003.

151 In his autobiography, Chin Peng states that he unmasked Lai Tek as a long-term British agent in March 1947, and later that year Lai Tek was murdered in Bangkok by members of the Thai Communist Party. See Peng: *My Side of History*, pp. 179 and 190.

152 FSC refers to him as 'Chen Ping'. See FSC: *The Jungle is Neutral, passim*.

153 Barber, N. *The War of the Running Dogs*. Williams Collins Sons and Co Ltd, London, 1971. As explained in Barber's preface notes.

154 This is the same officer who was involved with David Stirling in 1941.

155 James, Harold and Sheil-Small, Denis. *A Pride of Gurkhas*. Leo Cooper Ltd, London, 1975, p. 8.

156 *Ibid.*, p. 9.

157 In 1952 a memorandum from the Secretary of Defence stipulated that the insurgents/bandits would be officially known as 'communist terrorists' or 'CTs'. – undated (1952) 'Official Designation of the Communist Forces' PRO, CO 1022/48SEA 10/172/01.

158 Short: *In Pursuit of Mountain Rats*, p. 132.

159 Lieutenant Colonel Walker was an important operational innovator during the whole of the Emergency and during the later Borneo campaign, where he was appointed the Commander of British Forces.

160 See PRO WO279/241 The Conduct of Anti-terrorist Operations in Malaya.

161 Short: *In Pursuit of Mountain Rats*, p. 133.

162 A former Force 136 officer who had remained in the jungle during the Japanese occupation of Malaya.

163 Short: *In Pursuit of Mountain Rats*, p. 133.

164 Barber: *The War of the Running Dogs*, p. 62.

165 *Ibid.*, p. 62.

166 *Ibid.*, p. 95.

167 Barber: *The War of the Running Dogs*, p. 131.

168 Thompson, Robert. *Make for the Hills*. Leo Cooper Ltd., London, 1989, p. 97.

169 Barber: *The War of the Running Dogs*, p. 148

170 Interview AAA 25 August 2004.

171 See Calvert: *Fighting Mad.*

172 During one of his reconnaissance trips Calvert was ambushed: 'my driver and
I were moving at a fair pace along a jungle road when a burst of machine-gun
fire came from the thick bush, slightly ahead of us. We jerked to a halt and
flung ourselves into a ditch by the side of the road. For the first time in more
than five years I was under enemy fire and when a grenade landed neatly
beside me in the ditch I thought it was for the last time. I snatched up the
grenade, hoping to be able to throw it out before it went off, and then I
noticed that the pin was still in position. A piece of paper was attached to it
and a scrawled message said; 'How do you do, Mr Calvert?' It could mean only
one thing. Somebody I had known, and probably trained, in the old days in
Hong Kong or in Burma, was now on the other side, fighting for the
Communists'. Calvert: *Fighting Mad*, p. 202.

173 *Ibid.*, p. 202.

174 *Ibid.*, pp. 202–4.

175 *Ibid.*, pp. 202–3.

176 *Ibid.*, pp. 202–4.

177 *Ibid.*, p. 205.

178 Interview AAA 25 August 2004.

179 Interview AAA 25 August 2004.

180 It should be noted that the involvement in, and contribution to, the Briggs
Plan by Briggs's senior administrator, Robert Thompson, is at variance with
the version of events provided by Calvert. Thompson worked in Calvert's
headquarters in 77th Chindit Brigade during the second Chindit campaign
and they knew each other well. However, Thompson makes no reference
whatsoever to Calvert's involvement in Malaya and, more importantly,
Calvert's contribution to the key components of the Briggs Plan. More surprisingly, Thompson's autobiography makes no reference to Calvert's, nor the
SAS's, involvement in the Malaya campaign. This is odd because Thompson
was at the heart of the Malayan administration and would be aware of all the
various military operations and forces being employed, particularly those
operations of a special force nature. After all, Thompson had been in the
Chindits and was also a founder member of Ferret Force. Support from
Thompson, who was in such a key position in the civilian administration, as
well as being close to Briggs, might have made Calvert's life a little easier in
the early days of the SAS formation. But, for whatever reason, Thompson
chose to ignore the role of Calvert and the SAS throughout the Malayan
Emergency.

181 The Malayan Scouts wore shoulder titles on their olive-green jungle uniforms,
and under the titles were the green patch and yellow kris (S-bladed Malay dagger) of the Malaya military command.

182 At one point, Roy Farran, former wartime SAS, was offered command of a
squadron in the newly formed unit, but the War Office blocked the appointment in October 1950. This block was because Farran, when he was working
in covert operations in Palestine, had been court-martialled and found not
guilty of murdering Alexander Rubovitz, a member of a Jewish terrorist organisation, LEHI (more commonly known as the Stern Gang after its leader
Avraham Stern, who had disappeared in May 1947). Some years later Farran's
brother was murdered in England by a parcel bomb meant for Farran himself.

Farran, who lived in Canada, used to receive a Christmas card each year from the terrorists in the Stern Gang. He died in June 2006.

183 Calvert: *Fighting Mad*, p. 206.

184 *Mars and Minerva*. December 2002, p. 19.

185 'Men were allowed to grow beards in the jungle, which was a sensible idea in that they hid their white faces, but when the men came out they were allowed to keep them on, contrary to all the traditions of the Army. The sight of smelly, scruffy, bearded soldiers was one which caused almost apoplexy in the Staff and derision among all the other units in the Army. It was a very bad mistake.' Interview AAA 25 August 2004. Calvert's own views on beards were based upon his experiences in the jungles of Burma, but the attitude of other units in Malaya towards the wearing of beards out of the jungle was quite different to those days of the Second World War. 'Opinions differ on beards. Some people would not be without one while others can't stand them at any price. I can take them or leave them. I grew a big, black bushy one on the first Chindit campaign; this time I stayed clean-shaven. But in wartime beards definitely have their uses. If a man thinks he looks tough he will often be tough and, more important, act tough.' Calvert: *Fighting Mad*, p. 166.

186 Interview AAA 25 August 2004.

187 Interview AAA 25 August 2004.

188 Calvert: *Fighting Mad*, p. 205.

189 See Appendix 3. Letter written to the SAS Regimental Association on 9 December 1981.

190 Interview AAA 25 August 2004.

191 Cole, Barbara. *The Elite – The Story of the Rhodesian Special Air Service.* Three Knights Publishing, Transkei, 1984, p. 10.

192 Interview AAA 25 August 2004.

193 Calvert: *Fighting Mad*, p. 208.

194 PRO – WO216/494 – Report on the Malayan Scouts – Special Air Service Regiment. See Appendix 6.

195 Interview AAA 25 August 2004.

196 See Appendix 4 – The letter was written on 20 August 1951.

197 Hoe, A. and Morris, E. *Re-enter the SAS*, Leo Cooper, London, 1994, p. 100.

198 Interview AAA 25 August 2004.

199 'The first selection course was for 7 days, I took it to Snowdon by train and then walking with the intention of sorting them out with map reading and endurance test – it was chiefly notable that I contracted Malaria in the middle of this, and my endurance was far more severely tested than the recruits.' Interview AAA 25 August 2004.

200 Interview AAA 25 August 2004.

201 Major Harry Thompson was DLB's first squadron commander and was unimpressed with DLB and had every intention of having him returned to his unit. However, this was countermanded by the commanding officer at the time, Deane-Drummond, and DLB was moved to a job in the headquarters. Thompson, it has been stated, was destined to become the commanding officer of the regiment, but he died in a helicopter crash early in the Borneo campaign. It is worth considering whether DLB's career fortunes would have been the same if Thompson had not died. DLB: *Looking For Trouble*, p.126

202 DLB: *Looking For Trouble*, p. 89.

203 The author was advised by an impeccable source that DLB was described by an SAS officer, who served with him for many years in the SAS and became his commanding officer, as a 'serial opportunist'. It is not apparent whether this description was meant to be pejorative or a compliment.

204 DLB: *Looking For Trouble*, p. 116.

205 *Ibid.*, p. 124.

206 Oliver Brooke, George Lea's predecessor as commanding officer, broke his back in a tree-jumping operation and was crippled for life.

207 Cole: *The Elite*, p. 12.

208 Hoe and Morris: *Re-enter*, p. 187.

209 Cole: *The Elite*, p. 11.

210 Connor: *Ghost Force,* p. 116.

211 Kemp states that D Squadron was raised locally. See Kemp: *The SAS*, p. 27.

212 Kemp believes that D Squadron was first commanded by JC, one of the wartime SAS 'Originals'. See Kemp: *The SAS*, p. 27.

213 Allen, Charles. *Savage Wars of Peace, Soldiers' Voices. 1945–1989.* Michael Joseph Ltd, London, 1990, p. 55.

214 DLB: *Looking For Trouble*, p. 102.

215 Interview AAA 25 August 2004.

216 The Parachute Regiment squadron did not have any CT kills during its tour in Malaya from 1955 to 1957. There are some contradictory comments about the ability of the Parachute Regiment soldiers in 22 SAS operations in Malaya. During the Borneo campaign Parachute Regiment soldiers, particularly from Patrol Companies, were also deployed with 22 SAS on operations.

217 Interview AAA 25 August 2004.

218 Interview AAA 25 August 2004.

219 Strawson, J. *A History of the SAS Regiment.* Guild Publishing, London, 1985, p. 165.

220 In July 1954, Captain P. Head of the Royal Artillery was observing the SAS deployment into Op TERMITE in central Malaya, and stated: 'It should be borne in mind that the SAS at that time was far from the elite body of today, and it was the dumping ground for every battalion CO's misfits.' This was obviously still the general view of the rest of the Army over three years *after* the SAS had been reformed! Head, P. '"O" Field Troop – 1st Singapore Regiment Royal Artillery Malaya 1953–1955. Part 2'. *Journal of the Royal Artillery.* Spring 2002, p. 62.

221 See FK. *Gangs and Counter Gangs.* Barrie and Rockcliff, London, 1960.

222 See Reid-Daly, R.F. and Stiff, Peter. *Selous Scouts – Top Secret War.* Galago Publishing (Pty), Alberton, 1982; and Reid-Daly, R.F. *Pamwe Chete.* Kovos Day Books, Johannesburg, 1999.

223 Interview AAA 22 October 2004.

224 'I remember Ip [Ip Kwang Lau], he was the first SAS guy I saw in Bradbury Lines [SAS camp in Hereford] when I came for Selection in 1964. I staggered through the gates and there was this Chinaman doing one-handed press-ups in front of the Guard-room. I recall a story that 'Mush' Morrison [SAS soldier in Malaya] shot a CT in the head while Ip was shaking hands and talking with him on a jungle track'. Interview DDD 22 December 2004.

225 He was based with the SAS in Hereford and retired there. He died on 19 February 1996.

226 PRO – WO216/494 – Report No: 1/57.

227 See Hoe and Morris: *Re-enter the SAS*.

228 Interview AAA 25 August 2004.

229 Peng: *My Side of History*, pp. 406 and 410.

230 Interview AAA 25 August 2004.

231 The Australians did not have special forces operating during the Emergency but they did have infantry units deployed. Chin Peng may have been confusing the Australians with the NZ SAS patrols.

232 Peng: *My Side of History*, p. 395.

233 Interview AAA 25 August 2004.

234 See Appendix 5 – O'Leary's remains were located by an SAS patrol behind an ambush position they were about to use and recovered by Allan Glass, an officer of the Malayan Police who had been attached to the SAS. O'Leary was identified by a gold earring he wore.

235 Peng: *My Side of History*, p. 403.

236 Thompson, Robert. *Defeating Communist Insurgency. Experiences from Malaya and Borneo*. Chatto and Windus Ltd, London, 1966, p. 155.

237 Interview AAA 25 August 2004.

238 Peng: *My Side of History*, p. 395.

239 Geraghty: *Who Dares Wins*, pp. 39–40.

240 Hoe and Morris: *Re-enter*, p. 205.

241 Interview AAA 25 August 2004.

242 Interview AAA 25 August 2004.

Chapter 5

243 On 20 August 1968 the 'Voyska Spezialnoye Naznachenia' (special purpose troops) abbreviated to 'Spetsnaz', a force which had grown to some 14,000 troops, launched its first major operation spearheading the Soviet invasion of Czechoslovakia, a Soviet satellite which was no longer considered reliable by Moscow. Spetsnaz troops took over control of Prague airport as well as capturing Alexander Dubek, the Czech Prime Minister, and his cabinet and taking them to Moscow.

244 Bartlett: *The Long Retreat*; Curtis, Mark. *The Ambiguities of Power – British Foreign Policy Since 1945*, Zed Books Ltd, London, 1995; Hopkinson: *The Making of British Defence Policy*; Mockaitis, Thomas R. *British Counterinsurgency in the Post-imperial Era*, Manchester University Press, Manchester, 1995; Neillands, Robin. *A Fighting Retreat. The British Empire. 1947–1997*, Hodder and Stoughton, London, 1996; Pocock, Tom. *East and West of Suez. The Retreat from Empire*, Bodley Head, London, 1986; Vital, David. *The Making of British Foreign Policy*, George Allen and Unwin Ltd, London, 1968; and White, Nicholas. J. *Decolonisation – The British Empire Since 1945*, Addison, Wesley Longman Ltd, Essex, 1945.

245 Additional information on the political arena of this period is available in authoritative works by Kyle, Keith. *Suez*. Weidenfeld and Nicolson, London, 1991; Balfour-Paul, Glen. *The End of the Empire in the Middle East: Britain's Relinquishment of Power in her Last Three Arab Dependencies*. Cambridge

University Press, Cambridge, 1994; and Lapping, Brian. *End of an Empire*. Granada Publishing, London, 1985.

246 Deane-Drummond, A.J. 'Operations in Oman'. *The British Army Review*. September 1959, p. 7.

247 See DS. *Arabian Assignment*. Leo Cooper, London, 1975, pp. 3–12.

248 *Ibid*. p. 11.

249 A village north east of the capital, Muscat.

250 Nizwa, sometimes spelled as Nazwa, the former capital of Oman.

251 DS: *Arabian Assignment*, p. 12.

252 See FO1016/656 – SAF operations against Jebel Akhdar in 1958.

253 DS: *Arabian Assignment*, p. 41.

254 *Ibid*., p. 60.

255 Armoured scout cars armed with a 30 mm Browning machine gun.

256 DS: *Arabian Assignment*, p. 68.

257 See PRO – FO1016/656 – correspondence dated 20 February 1958 from HE Sir Bernard Burrows KCMG – Political Resident in the Persian Gulf – Bahrain.

258 DS: *Arabian Assignment*, p. 68.

259 See WO337/8 Jebel Akhdar reconnaissance report February 1959

260 General Sir FK had served with distinction against the Mau Mau in Kenya, and against the communists in Malaya in 1957. He was Commander-in-Chief, UK Land Forces from 1982 to 1985. He was knighted in 1980.

261 FK. *Bunch of Five*. Faber and Faber Ltd, London, 1977, p. 167.

262 FK: *Bunch of Five*, p. 167.

263 'In outline my suggestion was that four or five specially selected officers should be established in suitable posts around the foot of the Jebel Akhdar. Each one would be provided with a substantial sum of money and a few strong and resourceful soldiers to act as guards, drivers and escorts. Each officer would also need a reliable English-speaking Arab to act as an interpreter and some trackers. Once on the plateau, they would discard their disguise and start operating against Talib's irregulars with a view to engaging Talib, Ghalib and Sulaiman in due course.' FK: *Bunch of Five*, p. 168.

264 *Ibid*., p. 170.

265 See PRO – WO305/976

266 There is a discrepancy of dates between DLB and the PRO records.

267 DLB: *Looking For Trouble*, p. 127.

268 DLB was due to finish his tour with the SAS and, reluctantly, return to conventional soldiering with his parent regiment, the Durham Light Infantry.

269 DLB: *Looking For Trouble*, p. 128.

270 Deane-Drummond, A.J. *Arrows of Fortune*. Leo Cooper Ltd, London, 1997, p. 164.

271 DLB: *Looking For Trouble*, p. 127.

272 Connor: *Ghost Force*, p. 48.

273 Ironically, Deane-Drummond reviews Connor's book and comments acidly on Connor's version of the SAS involvment. 'The Jebel Akhdar description is fanciful nonsense – he [Connor] only joined the SAS three years later. Somebody must have told him bar stories which were not backed up by facts.' *Mars and Minerva*. September 2001, p. 44.

274 FK: *Bunch of Five*, p. 173.

275 Deane-Drummond: *Arrows of Fortune*, pp. 164–5 (author's emphasis).
276 JWT later commanded 22 SAS, the SAS Group and the Sultan's Armed Forces.
277 Hart's platoon of the Muscat Regiment had gone up to the top of Jebel on the Hijar track but, at night, had withdrawn because of their relatively small numbers.
278 See PRO – WO305/976 – 22SAS Official History – operations in Oman 18 November 1958 – 28 February 1959.
279 DS: *Arabian Assignment*, p. 78.
280 See JC. *One of the Originals. The Story of a Founder member of the SAS*. Pan Books Ltd, London, 1991, *passim*.
281 DS: *Arabian Assignment*, p. 76.
282 *Ibid.*, pp. 79–80.
283 ZZ. *SAS Operation, Oman*. William Kimber and Co Ltd, London, 1980, p. 16.
284 'To the undisguised fury of men who had just completed a hard campaign in some of the most demanding terrain on earth, they were then forced to spend the next few weeks doing "flag marches" back on the plateau – a pointless show of strength to villagers who were already well aware of where power now lay on the jebel and a task that could easily have been performed by the Sultan's own infantry'. Connor: *Ghost Force*, p. 56.
285 DLB: *Looking For Trouble,* p. 150.
286 DS: *Arabian Assignment*, pp. 89–90.
287 See WO337/9 – Operations in Muscat and Oman – 1952–1959.
288 Deane-Drummond, A.J. 'Operations in Oman'. *The British Army Review*. September 1959, p. 14.
289 FK: *Bunch of Five*, p. 201.
290 The article, entitled 'Brilliant but little known British Desert Action', was published in *The Times*, 9 April 1959.
291 DLB: *Looking For Trouble,* p. 151.
292 This sort of article, in either publication, would certainly not be countenanced today.
293 *ff*. Deane-Drummond. 'Operations in Oman', pp. 7–14.
294 Newsinger: *Dangerous Men*, p. 18.
295 *Ibid.*, p. 19.
296 See Lees, David. *Flight from the Middle East*. HMSO, London, 1980.
297 Weale, Adrian. *The Real SAS*. Sedgwick and Jackson, London, 1998, p. 93.
298 Lees: *Flight from the Middle East*, pp. 131–3.
299 DS: *Arabian Assignment*, p. 69.
300 See PRO – FO1016/656 – correspondence dated 20 February 1958 from HE Sir Bernard Burrows KCMG – Political Resident in the Persian Gulf – Bahrain.
301 Operation Order No. 1 dated 5 January, 1959, signed by the 'Deputy Field Commander all troops Oman' – Deane-Drummond.
302 Deane-Drummond: *Arrows of Fortune*, p. 191.
303 FK: *Bunch of Five*, p. 167 (author's emphasis).

Chapter 6

304 Morris: *Farewell the Trumpets*, p. 517.
305 See DEFE 13/68 – Aden – Threat to the security of the Protectorate.

306 JC: *One of the Originals*, pp. 158–86.

307 See DS: *Arabian Assignment*; and DS. *Irregular Regular*. Michael Russell (Publishing) Ltd, Norwich, 1994.

308 One of the directors of this PMC was Colonel Jim Johnson, a former CO of 21 SAS. Johnson and Major David Walker, another former SAS officer, became directors of the London-based PMC, KMS Ltd. KMS received a certain amount of notoriety from the company's association with Lt Col Ollie North and the US 'Contra scandal'.

309 DLB: *Looking For Trouble*, p. 202.

310 Paget, J. *Last Post – Aden 1964–67*. Faber and Faber Ltd, London, 1965, p. 46.

311 De Butts, F.M. 'The Aden Protectorate Levies'. *The British Army Review*. April 1961, pp. 16–24.

312 Paget: *Last Post – Aden*, p. 54.

313 DLB: *Looking For Trouble*, p. 213.

314 *Ibid.*, p. 213.

315 *Ibid.*, p. 214.

316 Interview AAA 25 August 2004.

317 22 SAS Association *Newsletter*. March 2002, p. 10.

318 A small protective shelter made from rocks. It was not possible to dig deep protective trenches due to the rocky surface.

319 When asked about this in October 2004, 'The GOC [Major General JH Cubbons] made a bit of a balls [sic] handling that. The family didn't know where they were which was common practice then – I don't know whether it is now, and then he went and blew it to the press without the families being told it was happening – it was possibly just a reflection of his personality as much as anything – I don't think he thought it through, the implication of what was happening'. Interview BBB 20 October 2004.

320 Thompson, J. *The Imperial War Museum Book of Modern Warfare*. Pan Macmillan Ltd, London, 2003, p. 233.

321 22 SAS Association *Newsletter*. March 2002, p. 7 (author's emphasis).

322 LL. *Soldier Against the Odds*. Mainstream Publishing Company, Edinburgh, 1999, p. 265.

323 Kemp: *The SAS*, p. 80 and see also LL: *Soldier*, p. 286.

324 See WO32/18518 – Aden – Half-Yearly Security Reports.

325 See WO386/22 – Report on Operations 14 April–30 June 1964.

326 See Kemp: *The SAS*, p. 79.

327 Interview BBB 20 October 2004.

328 'Q' operations were of a covert nature and involved disguised personnel or vehicles which, at first, appear innocent but conceal weapons or armed personnel who quickly adopt an aggressive role. In the Second World War, Q ships were disguised merchant vessels armed with concealed four-inch guns and automatic weapons to destroy any U-boats which approached them on the surface. The author used 'Q cars' in South West Africa against SWAPO terrorists who liked to ambush 'soft skin' civilian vehicles.

329 See PRO WO276/431 General Headquarters East Africa – Special Forces.

330 Beckett, Ian F. *Modern Insurgencies and Counter-insurgencies – Guerrillas and their Opponents since 1750*. Routledge, London, 2001, p. 157; and Paget: *Last Post – Aden*, p. 149.

331 Beckett: *Modern Insurgencies*, p. 157.

332 Morris: *Farewell the Trumpets*, p. 517.
333 Interview BBB 20 October 2004.
334 DLB: *Looking For Trouble*, p. 224.
335 DLB: *Looking For Trouble*, p. 224.
336 PS. *The Joker. 20 Years Inside the SAS*. Andre Deutsch Ltd, London, 1999, p. 160.
337 Interview BBB 20 October 2004.
338 Connor: *Ghost Force*, p. 131.
339 Kemp: *The SAS*, p. 80.

Chapter 7

340 A comment made to Christopher Bullock by an Indonesian Army officer 12 months after the end of Confrontation. Bullock, Christopher. *Journeys Hazardous*. Square One Publications. Worcester, 1994, p. 170.
341 Healey, D. *The Time of My Life*. Penguin Ltd, London, 1990, p. 289.
342 During Walker's service in Malaya, where he served with his Gurkha battalion, he briefly commanded Ferret Force and established the Jungle Warfare School at Kota Tinggi. He had not previously operated directly with the SAS.
343 Interview AAA 25 August 2004.
344 *Ibid.*
345 *Ibid.*
346 Tuck, C. 'Borneo 1963–66: Counter-insurgency Operations and War Termination'. *Small Wars and Insurgencies*. Volume 15, Number 3 (Winter 2004), p. 94.
347 This was a 'skill' that was neither tactical nor effective and which killed or critically injured a large number of SAS personnel in Malaya, including a commanding officer.
348 QS had won a George Medal, as a policeman, in London tackling a stolen vehicle by hanging onto the radio aerial. He was known affectionately in the SAS as 'Crazy Horse'. His son also became a troop commander and squadron commander in 22 SAS.
349 Walker, W. *Fighting On*. Morgan Technical Books, Gloucester, 1997, pp. 198–9.
350 Interestingly, TH's biography makes no mention whatsoever of JWA during wartime operations in Borneo or later during the Confrontation.
351 Heimann, J.M. *The Most Offending Soul Alive – Tom Harrisson and his Remarkable Life*. Aurum Press Ltd, London, 2002, *passim*
352 Harrisson accused the British Army officers commanding the infantry companies and battalions of trying to sweep a jungle area as if it were a forest in Germany, instead of realising that the enemy, and they themselves, could only penetrate it where there were trails, and only he and his tribesmen knew where these trails ran.
353 Walker: *Fighting On*, p. 199.
354 Shapter, I.R.D. 'The Border Scouts'. *The British Army Review*. August 1967, pp. 36–42.
355 See Cross, J.P. *A Face like a Chicken's Backside*. Arms and Armour Press, London, 1996.

356 Interview AAA 25 August 2004.

357 The Sultan of Brunei's keen co-operation extended to lending a house to General Walker and also one to the SAS. The SAS house, which had been used by the Japanese Kempetei (secret police) during the Second World War, was called the Haunted House. The Haunted House provided space for an operations room, communications centre and accommodation for patrols returning from the jungle. It was shunned by the local population because of its history, which was good for the security of the SAS.

358 Walker: *Fighting On*, pp. 200–1.

359 Interview AAA 25 August 2004.

360 Dickens: *The Jungle Frontier*, p. 76.

361 A patrol was tasked to accurately establish the true position of the border as well as searching for signs of the enemy. Sergeant Richardson was to walk the supposed border from Ba Kelalan in the South and eventually meet Sergeant Creighton's patrol on the River Plandok. As Richardson's patrol was following a river they saw a man fishing. One of the patrol, Corporal Tony 'Lofty' Allen, spoke to him in Malay but the man shouted and ran away. Somewhat surprisingly, Allen was wearing a yellow sweatband and a civilian shirt. As a result of searching the area the patrol located an unoccupied camp with slit trenches, protected by logs and earth, and jungle huts made of leaves. About 300 metres away from this camp was another camp. This one had housed a unit of the irregular force, TNKU, which had launched the Brunei revolt. The patrol went into cover for the night but returned to check the camps the following day. The camps remained unoccupied so the patrol continued eastward to find a suitable place for the next night stop. This is where their patrol skills seem to have fallen down. Allen removed his shirt and *without his weapon*, [author's emphasis] just his 'parang' [machete] went to 'cut poles for a bed' and, while doing so he came across four armed men. Allen ran back to the patrol's position and there was a brief firefight and the patrol 'bugged out' as per their operational procedures and made their way separately back to the RV [previously designated patrol rendezvous]. At the RV, the remainder of the patrol was unable to find the fourth member of the patrol, Trooper PC. Dickens, P. SAS. *Secret War in South-East Asia*. Ballantine Books, London, 1992.

362 LL provides candid details of a disregard for tactical operating procedures when he was commanding an ambush inside Indonesian territory. LL: *Soldier*, p. 245.

363 Interview AAA 25 August 2004.

364 See PRO – WO32/19269 – correspondence from FARELF dated 20 September 1963.

365 Interview AAA 25 August 2004.

366 Tuck. 'Counter-insurgency Operations', p. 94.

367 According to Connor, 'roughly 90 per cent of SAS men at the time were, like me, former Paras. The fear that the SAS would be even more vulnerable to absorption by the Parachute Regiment if more men were recruited from it undoubtedly influenced the decision to look to the Brigade of Guards for the new SAS squadron, but it was only part of the reason. All of us felt that the senior officers were simply taking their revenge for the irreverence and insubordination they had had to put up with from men who knew the job better than they. Guardsmen in G Squadron would be more malleable, less likely to

question their decisions. It has led to a continuing imbalance and the disproportionately large number of Guardsmen among the senior NCOs and senior
officers in the Regiment as a whole remains a source of friction.' Connor:
Ghost Force, p. 138.

368 It is surprising that a platoon of Indonesians, some 30 soldiers, was able to
remain undetected, even when cooking, by an alert SAS patrol.

369 Interview AAA 25 August 2004.

370 *Ibid.*

371 *Ibid.*

372 Dickens: *The Jungle Frontier*, p. 132.

373 See Appendix 3.

374 Smith, E.D. *East of Katmandu. The Story of the 7th Duke of Edinburgh's
Gurkha Rifles. Volume II, 1948–1973.* Leo Cooper, London, 1976, p. xvi.

375 Interview AAA 25 August 2004.

376 PRO. DEFE. 13/475. Annex A to COS 176/65. *Measures to Counter
Indonesian Confrontation.* 21 October 1965.

377 Bullock: *Journeys Hazardous*, p. 117.

378 Wilson, H. *The Labour Government 1964–70: A Personal Record.* Penguin Ltd,
London, 1974, p. 71.

379 Interview AAA 25 August 2004.

380 'I got on very well with Walter Walker and I kept in touch with him. He was a
well known public figure and very much a soldier's general. He got involved
with David Stirling and a thing called GB77, in 1977, I think it was. I told
David Stirling that I thought it was very ill-advised for a Colonel and a
General to start a political party which could be pictured as a military involvement in political affairs. They would be very ill-advised to do it – they didn't
pay any attention to me, of course. It died a natural death.' Interview AAA 25
August 2004.

381 Walker: *Fighting On, passim.*

382 When he became Director of Borneo Operations in 1965, Major-General
George Lea was 53 years old; he had started his military career in 1933 when
he was commissioned into the Lancashire Fusiliers. By the time he took over
in Borneo the Indonesian sponsored guerrillas had virtually been destroyed,
and he was faced with a war on more conventional lines. It is always difficult
to take over towards the end of a campaign; to do so from someone like
Walker must have been particularly difficult. But if Lea was not as flamboyant
as Walker, he had a quiet charm and determination of his own which was soon
apparent in the months of fierce, company-size actions which followed.

383 On 15 August 1965 an SAS patrol moved across the border in order to watch
traffic on the River Sembakung, south east of Labang and which supplied
a considerable number of Indonesian troop locations and bases. Ambush
positions would be selected by SAS patrols and the 1/7 Gurkhas would follow
with an attack. However, following a reconnaissance this area was not consid-
‚ered appropriate for an infantry ambush. The SAS patrol had Gurkha
Lieutenant Manbahadur attached to them as the patrol's fourth member. I find
it extraordinary that a non-SAS-trained soldier was permitted to operate with
one of their patrols. Conversely, it demonstrates that non-SAS-trained soldiers
can carry out 'SAS' tasks. During the Borneo campaign Gurkhas, guardsmen,
and paratroopers carried out similar tasks to the SAS.

384 LL: *Soldier*, p. 150.

385 This was a surprising comment for LL to make, because the SAS, and others, had no such reservations against killing women CTs nor cutting off heads for recognition purposes in the Malayan Emergency.

386 General Moerdani visited the SAS base in Hereford some 12 years later and met members of the SAS ambush party.

387 This level of political awareness is unusual among SAS SNCOs, who are not known for their combat reticence. The killing of the Indonesian Colonel would have had a major detrimental effect upon the morale of the Indonesian troops in the area.

388 Interview AAA 25 August 2004.

389 The names given to the operations commanded by NN give some indication of his aspirations – BLOOD ALLEY; KINGDOM COME; HELL FIRE; and GUITAR BOOGIE.

390 Bullock: *Journeys Hazardous*, p. 173.

391 Dickens: *The Jungle Frontier*, p. 230.

392 *Ibid.*, p. 231.

393 The operation involved 65 Gurkhas and 1 Troop and 4 Troop SAS; DLB went with 4 Troop. The SAS went in three days before the Gurkhas and established themselves in ambush upstream from Babang Baba. DLB was at the rear of 4 Troop's ambush, with the signaller, coding and encoding messages. The ambush was sprung, killing some 16 Indonesians. The ambush party, as rehearsed, then raced back to the RV, catching DLB and the signaller somewhat unawares, and they had to very hurriedly pack the radio and codes. The British withdrew at speed and the Indonesians, in normal fashion, reacted very aggressively including firing mortars at them. The Gurkhas, meanwhile, had arrived at their ambush position, and with them they had a New Zealand gunner officer, Captain JMS. Twenty-five Indonesians walked into the ambush and some 12 were killed. The ambush then turned into a major battle and the Gurkhas had to withdraw under a lot of pressure, leaving three men behind in the process. These were the company sergeant major, the signaller and Captain JMS. One of the SAS attached to the Gurkhas called in artillery fire. This landed very close to Captain OM and 1 Troop, who were also operating nearby. OM withdrew some distance and tried to find out what was going on from the A Squadron commander, DLB, who was of course on patrol, miles away, and out of touch. The three missing men eventually returned to the border after dramatic events. It had been a close-run thing and it was fortunate that DLB's absence from his command post did not adversely influence events too drastically.

394 DLB: *Looking For Trouble*, p. 234.

395 As the lead groups entered Sentas, which they were not sure was actually occupied by the Indonesians, they were engaged by heavy fire, including a heavy anti-aircraft machine gun. One of the British SAS soldiers threw a phosphorus grenade, which bounced off an *attap* (grass-roofed) hut and exploded among his colleagues. Now illuminated by both burning huts and burning people, the SAS had to withdraw. The enemy did not press forward immediately and, at the RV, four men were missing. Three of these men rejoined the squadron, reaching the border before the remainder did. However, the missing patrol member was blown up at the RV by a SAS defensive claymore mine because he had not been recognised by his colleagues. Remarkably, he was not seriously injured and also eventually made it back to the border.

396 Horner, D.M. *Phantoms of War – A History of the Australian Special Air Service.* Allen and Unwin, Sydney, 2002, p. 153.

397 In the operation was Trooper JWE (brother of BW, who had been killed on a previous operation) and *XH*. XH was later to resign as the B Squadron sergeant major when he was required to go on Operation MIKADO during the Falklands War.

398 The ambush had an unimpressive start. While in the ambush position someone 'passed wind' as two locals passed in front of the ambush. The locals carried on, but blazed a tree, to mark the area. This action was seen by one of the soldiers in the ambush and TH was informed. TH chose to remain because, even though he knew the Indonesians would probably react aggressively, they would be expecting a small SAS patrol not a complete squadron. The ambush was initiated when an Indonesian patrol entered the area but other Indonesians immediately charged the ambush position most aggressively as well as firing mortars into the immediate area. The ambush had already killed some 11 Indonesians and TH decided to withdraw.

399 Horner: *Phantoms of War*, p. 153.

400 PRO. DEFE. 13/475. Annex A to COS 203/65. *Command and Control Measures in the Event of Limited War with Indonesia.* 9 December 1965.

401 Tuck: 'Counter-insurgency Operations', p. 107.

402 Walker, Walter. 'Borneo'. *The British Army Review.* August 1969, p. 15.

403 James, Harold and Sheil-Small, Denis. *The Undeclared War.* Leo Cooper Ltd, London, 1971, p. 192.

404 Horner: *Phantoms of War*, p. 122.

405 In spite of the tactical successes of the Australian SAS in Vietnam (together with the NZSAS – the New Zealanders provided an SAS Troop from December 1968 to February 1971) their operations were the subject of criticism. Brigadier SP commanded the Australian Task Force from October 1968 until September 1969, and later wrote: 'In Vietnam, some of their [the SAS] operations appeared to be successful. That is, they provided information and greatly contributed to harassment and attrition. But we were never successful in contacting enemy – based on that information – by normal infantry. What happened, too, was that the time spent on the ground between insertion and extraction of SAS patrols got progressively shorter. In fact, they were requesting almost immediate extraction – in some cases minutes only – which made the whole operation farcical and expensive in helicopter hours.' Weale: *The Real SAS*, p. 148.

406 These included the Gurkha Independent Parachute Company; Parachute Regiment Squadron; Guards Independent Parachute Squadron, a demi-squadron of New Zealand SAS; and a squadron of Australian SAS.

407 Tuck: 'Counter-insurgency Operations', p. 108.

408 Kemp: *The SAS*, p. 71.

Chapter 8

409 DLB: *Looking For Trouble*, p. 263.

410 'He [JS] is a great personality but I never thought he would reach higher command. I thought he would command 22 SAS satisfactorily but I did not rate him as a high flyer in the military ... Most enjoyable socially'. Interview AAA 25 August 2004.

411 On passing the arduous SAS selection course and continuation training, SAS soldiers revert to the rank of trooper whatever their previous rank. They retain their permanent unit rank for 12 months for pay purposes. Units, however, retain those soldiers attached to the SAS on promotion lists and they continue to be promoted within their parent units even though they may be on a lower 'shadow' rank in the SAS. When the soldiers from the Guards Independent Parachute Squadron passed the selection course they were formed into G Squadron but, contrary to accepted practice, they were permitted to keep their original ranks. This caused great resentment throughout the SAS and was seen as a blatant example of the 'Guards Regiments' Old Boy System' in action.

412 Interview BBB 20 October 2004.

413 This was probably the first operational fatality of its kind in the British Army. The drop, by a freefall troop, was peculiarly hazardous – a 'HALO' (high-altitude, low-opening) from 10,000 feet with equipment into a depression surrounded by 4,000-foot mountain peaks. Among the regiment it has been said that Reddy's altimeter was incorrectly set, but the reason given in various publications is that the heavy Bergen pack he carried shifted its position causing him to become unstable, resulting in a fatal, tangled canopy deployment.

414 There are two sayings about Dhofaris – the first is 'Me against my brother, my brother and me against the family, the family against the tribe and the tribe against the world.' This explains the almost continuous blood feuds on the Jebel. The second is 'If you find a Dhofari and a snake in your bed – throw out the Dhofari first!' The Dhofaris were extremely hostile to outsiders, including other Omanis.

415 Later changed to the grander title of the People's Front for the Liberation of the Arabian Gulf (PFLOAG).

416 It is part of the legend of Sultan Said that he then drove himself to his principal Army garrison (leaving behind a wounded Pakistani palace guard commander) to tell its British commander: 'We seem to be having a little trouble down at the palace. I wonder if you would be so good as to come down?'

417 See 1971 Defence White Paper Chapter II, paragraph VI.

418 'He was a driver and an enthuser and was very good with troops in the Parachute Regiment style rather, a bit flamboyant and tough talking.' Interview AAA 25 August 2004.

419 None of those interviewed had any knowledge of JWT's visit being strategically directed from a senior military or political level. It was part of the SAS way of 'looking for business' or, as encapsulated in the title of DLB's autobiography, *Looking For Trouble*.

420 DLB: *Looking For Trouble*, p. 262 (author's emphasis).

421 In 1984, Col *XT*, as a contract officer, commanded the Sultan of Oman's Special Force Regiment based on the Jebel and composed of Jebalis, a number of whom had fought against Sultan Qaboos in the war.

422 There is some disagreement among the SAS about the originator of the 'Five Fronts Strategy'. Connor, in his book *Ghost Force* believes it was Lt Col ZZ: 'The boss of D Squadron, Major ZZ, had developed his own blueprint for success in Operation Storm, involving what was known as the "Five Fronts"' – whereas others give the credit to JWT. Connor: *Ghost Force*, p. 157

423 Thompson: *Defeating Communist Insurgency, passim.*

424 See Akehurst, John. *We Won a War*. Michael Russell Publishing Ltd, Wiltshire, 1982; Connor: *Ghost Force*; DLB: *Looking For Trouble*; and ZZ: *SAS Operation Oman*.

425 The Baluchis came partly from the large colony in the Sultanate, but mostly from Gwadur, an enclave on the Baluchistan coast which belonged to the Sultan, who maintained a resident there of British nationality until 1958. In 1958 Gwadur was sold to the Pakistani government, but the old Sultan retained, by agreement, his right to recruit in the territory. There were always plenty of volunteers to serve in Oman. The Baluch had a reputation for brutality against the Jebalis.

426 Sultan Qaboos clearly would not want it to be thought his own British-officered armed forces were incapable of dealing with Dhofar's communist-trained guerrillas.

427 See PRO DEF 25/187 SAS Operations in Oman. Publicity. 25 October 1971.

428 22 SAS Association *Newsletter* March 2001, pp. 2–3.

429 See PRO DEF 25/187 Oman 14 December 1971.

430 The term SEP had connections with and connotations of previous British Army counter-insurgency campaigns in Malaya and Kenya, and was not generally used to describe surrendered former *adoo* [enemy] in Oman.

431 One of the SAS team's first operations was to organise a leaflet drop over rebel territory. Despite some concerns about the leaflets' Arabic syntax, and that only a tiny percentage of the intended audience was literate anyway, the operation produced an unexpected prize. The best military brains among the guerrillas at the time included Mohammed Suhail, a former soldier in the Sultan's British-officered Trucial Oman Scouts. Suhail had been sent to Mons Officer Training School at Aldershot, sponsored by the Foreign and Commonwealth Office (FCO). He was a good soldier, a very good rifle and machine-gun shot on his course, and top of the FCO sponsorship list. On his return to Oman, however, he was disillusioned with the Sultan Said regime and joined the rebel opposition in the mountains. This first leaflet, with its offer of amnesty from the new ruler, Sultan Qaboos (himself a British-trained officer), brought Suhail back again to the side of the new Sultan to work with the Sultan's Intelligence staff and the SAS.

432 As part of the subterfuge covering the SAS deployment, the SAS teams were called British Army Training Teams (BATT) and the SAS units were normally known as 'Bat Teams'.

433 PRO DEF 25/187 The Dhofar. Letter by the Chief of the General Staff (CGS) dated 13 December 1971.

434 After the successful conclusion of the war, a large number of *firqat* were incorporated in the Sultan's Special Forces (SSF), which initially had been recruited purely from Jebalis and contract British (former 22 SAS) officers and SNCOs. The SSF camp was based on the top of the Jebel at the site of a former SAS/*firqat* base called 'Raven's Roost'. The establishment of the SSF regiment in the middle of the Jebel was an effective method of ensuring the continuing loyalty of the Dhofaris. The SSF insignia was based upon that of 22 SAS, although their beret was purple – an imperial colour personally chosen by Sultan Qaboos.

435 Interview EEE 17 December 2004.

436 PRO DEF 25/187 Minute to the Prime Minister from the Chief of the Defence Staff (CDS) dated 30 July 1971 Assistance to the Sultanate of Oman – proposing the deployment of two squadrons of SAS. PRO DEF 25/187 The Dhofar. Letter by the Chief of the General Staff (CGS) dated 13 December 1971.

437 It was at this stage that JWT had a confrontation with one of his squadron commanders, Major 'Duke' Pirie, who believed his soldiers had been asked to do more than enough. Pirie was held in high regard by the members of B Squadron, and his reluctance to carry out JWT's instructions stemmed from his desire to give his troops time to recover from an extremely exhausting period of operations and his concern was that the soldiers would be more vulnerable to enemy action in their current condition. JWT over-ruled him and several SAS men were killed or wounded in the engagement that followed. This was not the first time that JWT was at odds with his own officers.

438 PRO DEF 25/187 *Dhofar*. Letter by the Chief of the General Staff (CGS) dated 13 December 1971. This letter recommended the retention of two SAS squadrons until March 1972.

439 Connor was unimpressed with the intentions of the SAS commanders: 'ZZ had lost much of his remaining credibility within the Regiment after saying that if there were to be casualties he would rather lose an SAS man than a member of a firqat. He later denied making the remark, but I was there when he said it. His rationale was that we could stand a loss, whereas the firqat might just melt back into the mountains, but it was an inappropriate and unfortunate message to give to his own troops.' Connor: *Ghost Force*, p. 172.

440 'The friction between the two men [ZZ and JWT] reached a climax over the disciplinary action ZZ tried to impose on one troop officer (From ZZ's own Regiment, the Devon and Dorset Regiment) in Dhofar. Having lost confidence in the officer's ability to run his troop, ZZ relieved him of command and sent him back to the HQ in Salalah, ready to be returned to England and RTU'd [returned to unit]. ZZ's commanding officer, Lt Col JWT, arrived at the HQ on a tour of inspection and immediately countermanded the order. The unfortunate officer unpacked and repacked his bags several times as each man stuck to his guns, but, in the end, a face-saving compromise was reached. The officer was moved sideways to another squadron (B Squadron), allowing both ZZ and JWT to claim that they had achieved their objective.' Connor: *Ghost Force*, p. 158.

441 See PRO DEF 25/187 The Dhofar. Letter by the Chief of the General Staff (CGS) dated 13 December 1971.

442 Interview HHH 21 January 2005.

443 General Purpose Machine Gun – a Belgium FN designed, British-made, 7.62 mm, belt-fed, medium machine gun – normally used by the SAS mounted on a tripod.

444 This battle has been exhaustively covered in numerous publications. Some examples are: Allen: *Savage Wars of Peace*; Connor: *Ghost Force*; Geraghty: *Who Dares Wins*; ZZ: *SAS Operation Oman*; Kemp: *The SAS*; Strawson: *History of the SAS Regiment*; Cole and Belfield: *SAS Operation STORM*.

445 See Akehurst: *We Won a War*.

446 The fraud was widespread and was perpetuated by SAS NCOs as each squadron was replaced in Oman. 'When I first arrived in the SAS base camp at Salalah [Oman] I was shown three or four AK47 [enemy assault rifles]

under my bed by one of the sergeants. He told that these were for my "Ghosts".' Interview FFF 7 January 2005.

447 DLB: *Looking For Trouble*, p. 288.

448 '[The fraud] was the political problem [sic] that if the Omanis and the Sultan saw that British troops had been supporting them and behaving like this, what was this going to do to our diplomatic relationships between the two countries. It has got political connotations and you start drawing attention to yourself [SAS] which isn't acceptable, and this is very much the case then – it was quite a sensitive time and Lord Head [Viscount Head, formerly Secretary of State for Defence and High Commissioner for Malaysia] was the Colonel Commandant at the time – was very much in an advisory role over this and he liaised with the Omanis over it. Why did it happen? Well, if money is around, temptation is around – there is always somebody who is going to take advantage of it. I think what is regrettable is that, if I remember rightly, it had been going on for some time passing from hand to hand.' Interview BBB 20 October 2004.

449 Cohen: *Commandoes*, p. 74.

450 Interview EEE 17 December 2004.

451 Lt Col ZZ, a squadron commander and then the commanding officer of the SAS, who had also served in the Jebel Akhdar campaign, described the Oman operation as 'a classic of its type in which every principle of counter-insurgency operations built up over the last fifty years in campaigns around the world by the British and other armies was employed.' ZZ: *SAS Operation Oman*, p. 14.

452 Interview GGG 8 January 2005.

453 Interview CCC 2 November 2004.

454 After Malaya, and following a major exchange visit to the American Special Forces in Fort Bragg in summer 1962, the SAS realised the importance of language training, and a case was put to the MoD for increased funding to provide language training for at least one man in each four-man patrol. The initial languages were Malay and Arabic based on the SAS experiences to date but also Thai because Thailand was seen as a potential area of conflict spilling over from Vietnam. Interview AAA 25 August 2004.

455 See PRO DEF 25/187 *SAS Operations in Oman – Publicity*. Dated 25 October 1971.

456 In 1980, only some four years after the war in Oman had finished, the first book about the war was written by a senior SAS participant, Lt Col ZZ. In the furore following the publications of books after the second Gulf War he defends his writing in the SAS House Journal: 'My own book on the Regiment's activities in the Dhofar War was written with the full encouragement of HQ D SAS & SAS Group, and incidentally the then Colonel Commandant. So much rubbish was being written about the Regiment at that time, the mid 1970s, that it was decided to tell some of the truth about the Regiment to restore the balance. Hard as it may now be to believe with the Regiment's standing being so high, it was not always so. *During my time in command of 22 SAS, a large number of people in positions of authority and who controlled directly or indirectly the deployment of the Regiment did not understand it at all* (emphasis added), and had a confused idea of the type of people it recruited. This was, in my opinion, because of the unnecessary

overall blanket of security imposed by the Regiment itself at that time on everything about it. A great deal of what the Regiment currently does is secret, but not all of it; and most of what the Regiment did some years ago has merely become history.' *Mars and Minerva*. December 1994, p. 2. (Plus ça change, plus c'est la même chose!)

457 'We took heavy casualties in Oman, in purely human terms; the politicians regarded them as entirely acceptable. Twelve SAS men were killed and many others were wounded. The numbers were small, but they represented almost 10 per cent of the actual fighting strength of the Regiment's Sabre Squadrons.' Connor: *Ghost Force*, p. 172.

458 The war in Oman also had some additional benefits for members of the SAS. As a result of Oman, a large number of irreplaceable soldiers were leaving the regiment for highly paid employment in the commercial sector, particularly in the Middle East where their language skills and local knowledge were sought after. The regiment lobbied hard within the MoD, which finally bore fruit in 1980 with the introduction of Special Forces Pay.

Chapter 9

459 Woodward, Sandy. *One Hundred Days. The Memoirs of the Falklands Battle Group Commander*. Harper Collins Publishers, London, 1992, p. xvii.

460 'Naval bombardment was devastating and caused severe morale loss to the enemy.' UK 5th Infantry Brigade Post-Operations Report July 1982.

461 Camsell: *Black Water*, p. 171.

462 Major OCV. Parachute Regiment/SAS.

463 DLB: *Looking For Trouble*, p. 346.

464 *Ibid.*, p. 342.

465 This campaign was the first since the end of the Second World War in which the SAS and the SBS worked together operationally. Some individuals from the SBS had previously operated with the SAS in Northern Ireland, to gain experience, but there was not a history of combined operations. The two organisations did not operate successfully together in the Falklands nor were they any more successful working together in the 1990 Gulf War.

466 The Royal Marine Mountain and Arctic Warfare Team – specialists in winter warfare and who were tasked with training all arctic warfare for the defence of NATO's northern flank.

467 Interview GGG 8 January 05.

468 Fifty-three years old at the time of the Falkland's War, JME had served thirty-five years in the Royal Marines, winning a Military Cross as a troop commander in Malaya and a bar as a company commander in Sarawak; he had commanded 42 Commando in Northern Ireland. Ironically, it was the actions of the IRA which brought JME to this new appointment; he should have retired before the Argentineans invaded the Falklands but a serious IRA bomb injury to JME's superior, Lieutenant General Pringle, extended JME's service by the few months necessary to give him this Falklands command.

469 DLB: *Looking For Trouble*, p. 346.

470 *Ibid.*, p. 345.

471 *Ibid.*, p. 346.

472 This soon became corrupted to 'Paraquat' after a well-known brand of weed killer.

473 Geraghty, Tony. *Who Dares Wins. The Story of the SAS 1950–1992.* Little Brown, London, 1992, p. 333.

474 DLB: *Looking For Trouble*, p. 344.

475 'Our Special Forces had landed on the Fortuna glacier in South Georgia to carry out a reconnaissance. The first attempt to get them in had had to be abandoned because of high wind and heavy snow. During a temporary and slight improvement in conditions our men were successfully landed. But the weather then rapidly worsened with a South West wind gusting over 70 knots. Their exposed position on the glacier became intolerable and they sent a message to HMS Antrim asking for helicopters to take them off. The first helicopter came in and, blinded by the snow, crashed. A second suffered the same fate. MOD did not know whether any lives had been lost. It was a terrible and disturbing start to the campaign.' Thatcher: *Downing Street Years*, p. 205.

476 Van der Bijl, Nicholas and Aldea, David. *5th Infantry Brigade in the Falklands.* Leo Cooper, South Yorkshire, 2003, p. 38.

477 Despite the fact that 22 SAS had a specific research and development cadre a lot of their equipment proved unsatisfactory, especially the boots, and trench foot became a problem. Poor footwear had also been a major problem when the SAS was manning long-term OPs, in very adverse conditions in winter in the countryside of Northern Ireland, and the 'official' solution was to give the soldiers money so that they could buy boots from the local outdoor equipment shop. Poor equipment has frequently been a concern of SAS soldiers, and equipment problems occurred again during the Gulf Wars and more recently in Afghanistan.

478 One patrol, commanded by Captain NY, endured 26 days on Beagle Ridge above Port Stanley. (Awarded an MC, NY later became commanding officer of 22 SAS and then commanded the Sultan of Oman's Special Forces (SSF) on contract.)

479 Interview HHH 21 January 2005.

480 'An Air Force detachment of six Pucaras, a number of Aeromacchi MB.339As and 326s, STOL light transport aircraft and two Puma helicopters was based on Pebble Island. In addition, the Argentinians had sited radar there to cover the approaches to San Carlos. Somewhat surprisingly, no Argentinian Army units were deployed on the island to provide local protection.' Herclerode: *PARA!*, p. 307.

481 DLB: *Looking For Trouble*, p. 345.

482 *Ibid.*, p. 345.

483 Interview HHH 21 January 2005.

484 The aircraft carrying 8 Troop, B Squadron had to turn back in mid-flight for technical reasons, so only one troop actually dropped on the first mission. Each man wore a diver's dry suit, carried swim fins and had a flare strapped to his wrist so that he could be located once in the water. It was classed as an operational drop, one of very few to have been carried out by the Regiment since the campaign in Malaya.

485 See McManners, Hugh. *Scars of War.* Harper Collins Publishers, London, 1993, p. 231.

486 Herclerode: *PARA!*, p. 312.

487 Inflatable high-speed boats normally manned by Royal Marine coxswains.

488 The Argentine 3rd Battalion (Marine Infantry Battalion) sent H Company to guard its naval facilities. Lieutenant Ricardo Marega's 1st Platoon garrisoned Naval Air Base Calderon on Pebble Island from 26 April until the Argentinian surrender. It put up limited resistance to the SAS raid on 14/15 May largely because a fire was thought to have damaged the aircraft and not explosive charges. 2nd Platoon remained in Stanley on internal security duties and had a quiet war. 3rd Platoon defeated the SAS raid on the Cortley Ridge fuel dump during the last night of the war. Van der Bijl and Aldea: *5th Infantry Brigade in the Falklands, passim.*

489 Thompson, Julian. *No Picnic.* Cassell and Co., London, 1995 (2nd Ed.), p. 153.

490 Thatcher: *Downing Street Years*, p. 221.

491 Interview BBB 20 October 2004.

492 *Ibid.*

493 Interview CCC 10 November 2004.

494 Interview BBB 20 October 2004.

495 The disadvantage of the insertion programme was the lack of a guarantee that the Sea Harriers, equipped only with the Blue Fox radar that performed so poorly over land, would be able to successfully intercept aircraft leaving mainland bases in the very limited time available. While the SAS observation posts might give an hour's warning of the Super Etendards being airborne, they would be unable to indicate either the rendezvous point for in-flight refuelling or their chosen target. In addition, there was considerable risk in leaving SAS teams in such a heavily guarded environment for a period likely to exceed two weeks. In addition, there was a logistical problem regarding a submarine insertion. There were three British submarines operating in the South Atlantic as part of underwater component designated CTF 324: *HMS Conqueror*, which had shadowed and sank the *General Belgrano*; and the two despatched from the Royal Navy base at Faslane, *HMS Splendid* and *HMS Spartan*. All were nuclear hunter-killers, entirely inappropriate for operations in shallow water. Unfortunately the nearest diesel boat, ideally suited for clandestine missions, was an 'O' class patrol submarine, but she would not arrive in the Total Exclusion Zone for a further three weeks.

496 On 3 July 1976 the Israelis had achieved almost complete success in rescuing terrorist hostages. They flew three Hercules aircraft, undetected, 2,250 miles from Tel Aviv to Uganda. Operation JONATHAN achieved a total surprise, and the entire operation was completed in just 99 minutes, without the 20 per cent losses anticipated by the planners. The Israeli tactical commander was killed in the raid.

497 Major *SFG* was an officer from the parachute-trained 9 Squadron, Royal Engineers, who had previously served one tour as a troop commander in Dhofar and Northern Ireland before returning to the Regiment as a squadron commander in 1981. After retiring from the Army, he served in the Sultan of Oman's Special Forces (SSF) as a contract officer for several years before joining a UK commercial company.

498 This was a very magnanimous response by the SAS when the moral implications of an NCO refusing to participate in a legitimate operation are considered.

499 After six months, a period he spent on leave and undertaking odd jobs around the SAS base, *SFG* was returned to his parent regiment, the Royal Engineers.

500 DLB: *Looking For Trouble*, p. 347.

501 Interview BBB 20 October 2004.

502 B Squadron was also involved in the very public failures of the 'Bravo Two Zero' patrol in the later Gulf War.

503 Interview BBB 20 October 2004.

504 'The Paymaster arriving at Ascension Island with his briefcase full of Wills forms and ADAT [military life insurance] forms gave all [B Squadron] a clear indication of what some people thought the outcome of the Rio Grande Op [Op MIKADO] would be.' Interview CCC 9 November 2004.

505 Interview CCC 9 November 2004.

506 See *The Falklands Island Review (The Franks Report)*. Pimlico Publishing, London. Crown Copyright 1983.

507 The SAS beret is awarded after the successful completion of an arduous selection course and a nine-month specialist training course.

508 Interview DDD 4 November 2004.

509 Connor: *Ghost Force*, p. 263.

510 'In the US, senior Green Beret leaders were keen to be linked with Kennedy and his "Wars of National Liberation" policy. However, in doing so without having continued representation the Green Berets won the tactical fight (recognition, resources, mission) only to lose the strategic battle (tactical misuse as tripwire "tethered goats" to provide indications and warning of major VC movement).' See Kiras: *Rendering the Mortal Blow Easier*.

511 DLB: *Looking For Trouble*, p. 344.

512 Cohen: *Commandoes*, p. 73.

513 'Throughout the campaign, intelligence dissemination was particularly poor. The problem appeared to be a fundamental lack of resource co-ordination. Consequently at battalion level very little *accurate* intelligence was received. There was little direction of the Battalion's patrolling programme and the activities of the SAS was particularly frustrating. SAS operations before both DARWIN and WIRELESS RIDGE inhibited the battalion's own patrolling activities but no proper debrief of the SAS was ever made available to the battalion.' 2 PARA Post-Operations Report, 24 November 1982.

514 Thompson: *No Picnic*, p. 154.

515 2 PARA was informed by the SAS that there was only a company of Argentinians at Goose Green. In the event, when 2 PARA attacked on 28 May 1982, there was more than a battalion located there. The general feeling among the PARAs was that the SAS had not got in close enough to assess the strength of enemy forces at Goose Green.

516 A four-man SAS patrol, commanded by Corporal *WKL*, had been in the Goose Green area for two weeks, attempting to assess the Argentine strength.

517 Interview HHH 21 January 2005.

518 Interview BBB 22 October 2004.

519 Interview CCC 9 November 2004.

520 Interview BBB 20 October 2004.

521 'Even if the performance of the Special Air Service during the campaign was open to improvement, their psychological value as "super soldiers" was helpful.' Van der Bijl and Aldea: *5th Infantry Brigade in the Falklands*, p. 213.

522 It appears that *RP* was intent on trying to re-establish his personal reputation after his tour as a troop commander during Operation STORM in Oman

(Connor: *Ghost Force*, p. 158). Despite some often questionable tactical activities during the Falklands War he was awarded a DSO.

523 Woodward, *One Hundred Days*, *passim*.

Chapter 10

524 See Marcinko, R. and Weisman, J. *Rogue Warrior*. Pocket Books, New York, 1992.
525 'Until the first Gulf War – air support has always been strategically of questionable value.' Interview BBB 20 October 2004.
526 The author observed B52 bombing raids in South Vietnam, and their destructive power is awesome. The effect of the B52 raids on Iraq troops in open desert, sheltering in unsophisticated bunkers, would have been totally destructive and utterly demoralising.
527 Thatcher's admiration for DLB was wholeheartedly reciprocated by him, and her downfall came as a great shock to him.
528 Thatcher: *Downing Street Years*, p. 825.
529 Interview GGG 7 January 2005.
530 Newsinger: *Dangerous Men*, p. 37.
531 Schwarzkopf, Norman. *It Doesn't Take a Hero*. Bantam, London, 1992, *passim*.
532 DLB: *Storm Command*, p. 156.
533 *Ibid.*, p. 156.
534 The claim that, by undertaking the Scud hunt in western Iraq, special forces kept Israel out of the war is based on a somewhat optimistic and naive view of the pragmatic Israeli stance in Middle Eastern affairs.
535 Interview GGG 7 January 2005.
536 This was the first time that the post-war SBS were deployed on a special forces operation that had no maritime connection. The success of this task compared with the 'failure' of a number of SAS tasks did nothing to help the inter-organisational jealousy.
537 Falconer: *First into Action*, 1998.
538 Camsell: *Black Water,* p. 226.
539 DLB: *Storm Command*, p. 224 (author's emphasis).
540 *Ibid.*, p. 223.
541 Knowsley, Jo. 'Day of Reckoning for Special Forces who Ran Away', *Courier Mail* (Australia). 5 May 2003. This article details the compromise of an SBS lying-up place by Iraqi forces forcing the SBS personnel to disperse in some great disorder. The SBS left behind numerous vehicles as well as weapons, communications systems and, most disturbingly, ground-to-air missiles, which it is believed had been used to shoot down American and/or British aircraft. The incident has been confirmed by other sources but the details were never publicised in British newspapers, and there is a view that the British government issued a direction to the British media not to reveal the details of the incident.
542 DLB gave an outline account of what happened to that patrol in his books but its commander, Sergeant 'Andy McNab', has told another story, which contradicts DLB's version in a number of ways. These stories have again been contradicted by another member of the patrol, Chris Ryan, who has also written a version of the events surrounding the particular patrol. Ironically, events

recorded by McNab and Ryan have both been debunked by Michael Asher, a TA SAS officer who walked the route of the patrols and interviewed local participants after the war. He writes about his findings in his book *The Real Bravo Two Zero.*

543 In a display of bravado the Regimental Sergeant Major (RSM), PR, held a 'formal' Warrant Officers' and Sergeants' Mess meeting in the open desert, at which routine Mess matters were discussed, decisions were reached and minutes taken. This was generally to be considered such folly that, after the war, a painting of the event which had been presented to the Special Forces Club in London was removed from the lobby after complaints from members.

544 Interview CCC 2 November 2004.

545 Interview DDD 4 November 2004.

546 Interview CCC 21 December 2004.

547 The half-squadrons travelled in the standard 110 Land Rovers and had several motorcycles to act as scouts with the bulk of their stores carried on a Unimog truck. Each convoy consisted of roughly 30 men selected from each of the specialist troops of the squadron concerned. The activities of the A Squadron A20 (Alpha Two Zero) patrol have been written up extensively by several SAS participants in the war, notably 'Cameron Spence' and 'Yorky Crosland'.

548 Interview EEE 11 November 2004.

549 PR: *Eye of the Storm*, p. 284.

550 Newsinger: *Dangerous Men*, p. 37.

551 When the SAS deployed in Afghanistan Helmand Province in November 2001 with the US special forces, *RB* was involved in a major action in the caves in the area, as a result of which he was recommended for one of the UK's highest bravery awards – which he declined. The units chosen for the assault were 'A' and 'G' Squadrons. Once again, the SAS was misused and deployed, effectively, as a company of light infantry. There was a desire to give the SAS an operational role independent of the Americans. It is interesting to note that the British liaison officer with the US Special Operations Command at MacDill, in Tampa, Florida, and involved with this example of the misuse of the SAS, was Lieutenant General *RP* of South Georgia 'fame' during the Falklands War.

552 Interview CCC 21 December 2004.

553 DLB: *Storm Command*, p. 268.

554 Schwarzkopf: *It Doesn't Take a Hero*, pp. 385–465.

555 G Squadron, the Regiment's other regular sub-unit, remained in UK responsible for the national counter-terrorist response.

556 DLB: *Storm Command*, p. 102.

557 Urban, Mark. *UK Eyes, Alpha*. Faber and Faber Ltd, London, 1996, pp. 174–5.

558 Newsinger: *Dangerous Men*, p. 37.

559 Interview GGG 8 January 2005.

560 *Ibid.*

Chapter 11

561 Thatcher: *Downing Street Years*, p. 384.

562 Internment was introduced under the provisions of the 1922 Civil Authorities (Special Powers) Act (Northern Ireland).

563 Thompson, *Defeating Communist Insurgency*.

564 The IRA mounted a major campaign to have these interrogations banned, and the success of this campaign can be held up as a major milestone in their battle against the British government. Interestingly, the techniques used were no more severe than those used against military trainees in resistance-to-interrogation training. No physical violence was used and no extremes of any sort were applied. In-depth interrogation was ended following Lord Gardiner's minority report condemning the practice in March 1972. It was subsequently alleged that new RUC specialist interrogation centres resorted to abuses in 1977–78, and further safeguards were introduced in March 1979.

565 The MRF included former terrorists known as 'Freds'. It established the 'Four Square Laundry', which examined washing from West Belfast for traces of explosives. However, its cover was blown and its operators murdered by the IRA in October 1972.

566 14 Int personnel operated in plain clothes. They were selected by the SAS from all three services and trained by them. The IRA tendency has always been to blame the SAS for the activities of 14 Int.

567 An abbreviation of 'The Detachment'.

568 'The security service had already learnt its lesson on combined operations with the Regiment. This was during the famous Operation CUFF when criminal activities such as post offices robberies, unofficial beatings and sectarian activities were committed by operational [SAS] members.' Interview FFF 7 January 2005.

569 Interview BBB 20 October 2004.

570 In 1974, Patrol Company 3 PARA (including the author) was deployed to Bessbrook Mill in South Armagh to cope with an upsurge in IRA violence. This deployment was the first by 'special forces' to South Armagh following the deployment of the British Army in 1969.

571 Interview HHH 21 January 2005.

572 ZZ. Former CO of 22 SAS and Commander Land Forces (CLF) in Northern Ireland. *Mars and Minerva*. August 1994.

573 'The original purpose in having every weapon tested was to be able to repudiate quickly any propaganda claims by the Provisionals. E.g. that a dumped body was the work of the SAS'. PRO WO/296/95. D/DS10/44/16/2. DB Omand. DS10. 20 May 1976.

574 PRO WO/296/95 HQNI 1020/37/G Maj PJC JME. 19 May 1976.

575 Captain Robert Nairac was one of the Special Branch liaison officers. The SAS, with whom Nairac worked at Bessbrook Mill, considered him a dangerous maverick.

576 PRO WO/296/95. D/DS10/44/16/2. DB Omand. DS10. 20 May 1976.

577 PRO WO/296/95. D/DS10/44/16/2. Statement of Supplementary Questions. CE Johnson. Head of DS10. 11 May 1976.

578 Interview GGG 8 January 2005.

579 The Gardai took the SAS soldiers to the police station in Dundalk and then to Dublin, where the men had to appear in court charged with firearms offences. Released into British Army custody on bail, the eight, one of whom was a Fijian, were formally tried a year later.

580 See PRO WO/296/95. D/DS10/44/12/1. 11 May 1976.

581 PRO WO2/296/95. Draft letter from Mr C.E. Johnson to Mr J.N. Hartland-Swann, Republic of Ireland, FCO. Date obscured.

582 DLB: *Looking For Trouble*, p.316.

583 PRO WO/296/95. GW Harding. Republic of Ireland Department, FCO. 18 May 1976.

584 PRO WO/296/95. D/DS10/44/16/2. Statement of Supplementary Questions. CE Johnson. Head of DS10. 11 May 1976.

585 The fact that these soldiers had been arrested caused great angst among the SAS, who were understandably concerned about their legal status in this and possible future incidents in which there may be casualties caused to civilians.

586 Four unarmed IRA members hijacked a car and set out to firebomb a post office depot in the Ballysillan area of Belfast. A mixed force of SAS and members of the RUC's Special Patrol Group waited in ambush, having received information about the raid. As the terrorists walked towards their intended target three of them were shot and killed by the soldiers. The fourth member of the IRA group fled. A civilian who was walking home from the pub, with a friend, walked into the ambush and was also shot dead.

587 John Boyle, son of a farmer in Dunloy, County Antrim, had discovered an IRA rifle (M16 Armalite) under a fallen headstone in the local cemetery. He told his father who, unusually, telephoned the police (the public, as a result of terrorist 'punishments', rarely passed information to the security forces). On receiving this information, a four-man SAS team was sent to observe and ambush the site. They split into two pairs and concealed themselves to wait for someone to arrive to claim the weapon. The following day John Boyle inexplicably returned to the scene of his find. He stooped and picked up the rifle and was shot dead by the SAS soldiers. See also, DLB: *Looking For Trouble*, p.316.

588 In a vast surveillance operation a close watch was kept on the plotters while the SAS presence was increased by a group sent over from Hereford. The code name was Operation JUDY. One party of SAS was inside the police station and the main group was hidden in undergrowth and trees opposite the police station, with a football field behind them. The villagers had not been informed of the operation and no attempt had been made to evacuate anyone, as this could have compromised secrecy. In the late afternoon and early evening of Friday 8 May, when the Loughgall police station had ostensibly shut down for the weekend, masked IRA men stole a Toyota van in Dungannon, and shortly afterwards a JCB was taken from a farmyard in the area. The IRA attack went as planned but the attackers were ambushed by the SAS and all eight were killed. Unfortunately, just before the explosion of the bomb in the JCBs, two brothers, called H, drove innocently into the village wearing blue overalls, similar to those worn by the terrorists. On hearing the initial shooting the two men attempted to reverse away from the scene. The soldiers thought they were part of the IRA support group and opened fire on them, killing one brother and severely wounding the other. The government paid compensation to the widow of AH, and to OH for the injuries he sustained.

589 Operation FLAVIUS.

590 See the following publications: 'Loughall and the British SAS at Gibraltar'. *Counterterrorism and Security Reports*. Volume 9, Number 1, 2000, pp. 4–6;

Scott, M. 'SAS in Gibraltar', *New Statesman*. 9 March 1990, pp. 13–15; Jack, I. SAS in Gibraltar. *Observer*. 2 October 1988, p. 14; Campbell, D. SAS in Gibraltar. *New Statesman*. 13 May 1988, pp. 10–11.; Campbell D. 'SAS in Gibraltar'. *New Statesman*, 17 June 1988, p. 11; McGuire, A. 'IRA losses in Tyrone'. *Irish Times*. 18 February 1992, p. 5.

591 Thatcher: *Downing Street Years*, p. 407.

592 The facts of the case were relatively simple. A well-known IRA man and suspected bomb-maker, SS, had been located in Spain in the autumn of 1987, as had DMc, an accomplished terrorist. An extensive intelligence-gathering operation then got under way, and at the beginning of 1988 an MI5 team was sent to Gibraltar. By that time, the British government was fairly certain that the target was to be the resident Army band, which performed the ceremony of changing the guard outside the Governor's residence in the colony. There were concerns about the fact that the IRA had perfected a remote-controlled detonating device that could be activated by pushing a button in a coat pocket. On 4 March, SS and DMc arrived at Malaga Airport where they were joined by a woman, Mairead Farrell, who had a long record of terrorist offences. This was a team of very experienced IRA terrorists who, presumably, were to carry out a major operation in response to the successful SAS operation at Loughgall. The Joint Operations Command in London assessed the situation and authorised the deployment of a troop-sized (16-man) SAS team. The operation was given the code name FLAVIUS. In a thorough briefing to all concerned, the police officer in charge, Canepa, stated that the object was to arrest the terrorists, disarm them and make the bomb safe. In the event, when the soldiers challenged the IRA operatives they believed that they were going to pull weapons or activate the explosive device, and so killed them. It is now known that the three were unarmed; that the bomb was still in a car park in Marbella; and that they intended to use a timing device to detonate it. A two-week inquest into the shootings ended on 30 September 1988 and, by a majority of nine to two, the jury brought in a verdict of lawful killing. This result satisfied the government as well as a large section of British public opinion.

593 The bomb was discovered the following day in a car in a car park in Marbella, Spain.

594 Thatcher: *Downing Street Years*, p. 411. Stated in a television interview immediately after the IRA bombing of the Conservative Party Conference at the Grand Hotel in Brighton at 0245 hrs on 15 October 1984.

595 Newsinger: *Dangerous Men*, p. 36.

596 Interview BBB 20 October 2004.

Chapter 12

597 *US Department of Defense Dictionary*. Joint Publication 1-02. US DoD, Washington, 12 April 2001. As amended through 30 November 2004.

598 Attributed to Adolf Hitler in *Mein Kampf*.

599 DLB: *Looking For Trouble*, p. 274.

600 Brigadier LO MBE, a former Royal Corps of Transport officer, commanded 22 SAS in 1982–85. On leaving the Army he worked for a PMC, DSL Limited, in London. In 1998 he was found dead in his swimming pool.

601 DLB: *Looking For Trouble*, p. 280.

602 *Ibid.*, p. 281.

603 Similar processes in France and Germany caused the establishment of, respectively, the Groupe d'Intervention de la Gendarmerie Nationale and Grenzschutzgruppe 9 (GSG9), which formed part of the Bundesgren-schutz or Federal Border Protection Service, and, somewhat later, Special Forces Operational Detachment – Delta in the United States.

604 Interview BBB 20 October 2004.

605 Referred to in 22 SAS as the PAGODA or 'SP teams'.

606 Delta Force was established in direct and conscious imitation of 22 SAS under Colonel YH, a very experienced Vietnam veteran who had served, on exchange, with 22 SAS in the 1960s. The contribution of the SAS to Delta Force was not always considered a good thing – in their book *Rogue Warrior* Marcinko and Weisman state: 'I believed Delta had been overly influenced by the formal and administrative and training structures of the British SAS.'

607 In a demonstration of SAS versatility, Staff-Sergeant PP was one of a four-man team that parachuted into the Atlantic on 18 May 1972 in response to a bomb scare on board the liner Queen Elizabeth II. The team leader was an army bomb disposal expert.

608 A facility that has since become known as 'the killing house' was constructed to assist the shooting training. In the beginning this was simply a suitably protected room in which paper targets representing a VIP and potential attackers were placed. The aim was to teach men to identify and eliminate would-be assassins or kidnappers. Constantly changing terrorist situations meant that more complicated scenarios had to be considered. A group of terrorists could take hostages and hold them in an aircraft, a train, a building or even on a ship. Such a situation could be created by British nationals either as a criminal enterprise or for political ends, or by foreigners applying pressure on the British government or a foreign power. Finally, the situation could take place in the British Isles or abroad – on British territory or in a foreign country.

609 The hijacker demanded to be flown to Paris and the pilot agreed to comply. The SP Team had been alerted, and it headed for Stansted Airport to set up a reception committee. The hijacker genuinely believed that he had arrived at Paris, and when the SAS stormed the aircraft the man gave himself up. His weapon turned out to be a replica.

610 The police had cornered a four-man Provisional IRA team who had entered a flat in Balcombe Street in London after a car chase and a gun battle and were holding a husband and wife hostage. The police were able to eavesdrop on what was happening inside the flat, and patient negotiation was carried out by telephone. The SAS had arrived on the scene and the police asked the BBC to insert into a news bulletin the information that they were considering handing over conduct of the operation to the military. The terrorists, who were known to be listening regularly to the radio, promptly decided to give themselves up. This happened before the first full deployment of the SAS into Ulster and indicated that the provisional IRA was already aware of the SAS capabilities.

611 On 13 October 1977 a Lufthansa Boeing 737 en route from Palma to Frankfurt with 86 passengers on board was hijacked by four terrorists, who demanded a ransom of £9 million and the release of members of the Red Army

Faction from prison in Germany. A request was made to the British government for SAS assistance for GSG9. This was granted, and two men were selected – Major *OL*, who had led G Squadron to the relief of Mirbat, and Sergeant *FH*. They went to Dubai, where the airliner had landed, with a supply of stun grenades, which the Germans did not have. The grenades were used by the GSG9 team during their successful assault on the airliner.

612 The caller was *MM*, an ex-SAS NCO who was now a dog- handler for the Metropolitan Police. *MM* was outside the Embassy when it was stormed by the terrorists.

613 DLB: *Looking For Trouble*, p. 320.

614 At that time, Brigadier DLB was the Director SAS, an appointment that pre- ceded the current Director Special Forces (DSF). He had a seat on an organ- isation known as the Joint Operations Centre (JOC) of the Ministry of Defence, which also included representatives of the Foreign and Home Offices as well as the intelligence services. The JOC is responsible for acti- vating the SAS, but in the case of a terrorist incident with political connota- tions the final say rests with a group known as COBRA – Cabinet Office Briefing Room – which is chaired by the Home Secretary and reports directly to the Prime Minister.

615 The SAS felt that the numbers of Intelligence Corps support personnel seem to be always increasing. They are disparagingly called 'green slime' because of this knack of 'oozing' everywhere – and they wear green berets.

616 Interview CCC 2 November 2004.

617 Interview FFF 7 January 2005.

618 'The SAS trained Pol Pot's killers in Thailand.' Interview FFF 5 January 2005.

619 The first generation of RWW let the Regiment down and virtually closed the door [on its activities]. At least two books had been written by ex-RWW mem- bers that mentioned this very sensitive department and their secret involve- ment with the Afghani fighters. The next discredit [sic] was when a member of the RWW Khmer Rouge training team was found dead in a toilet, the cause a suspected drug overdose.' Interview FFF 7 January 2005.

620 The Gambian president, Sir Dawda Jawara, was in the UK as a guest at the wedding of the Prince of Wales.

621 See PR: *Eye of the Storm*, pp. 225–35; and Connor: *Ghost Force*, pp. 266–7.

622 See Kemp: *The SAS at War*, p. 155; and Connor: *Ghost Force*, pp. 267–8.

623 As told to John Strawson by David Stirling. Strawson: *A History of the SAS*, p. 245.

624 Interview DDD 4 November 2004.

625 Interview BBB 20 October 2004.

626 Interview CCC 2 November 2004.

627 Those engaged in such operations were discharged from military service and had a civilian contract. Two such operations were the deployment into Yemen in 1962 to search for evidence of Egyptian bombing villages with chemical weapons. This was followed by mercenary support of Royalist forces in the Yemen. When the soldiers returned one or two years later they were automat- ically recruited into one of the territorial units and given rapid promotion back to their former rank. They then went back to regular service. For further details on these operations see: DS: *Arabian Assignment*; DS: *Irregular Regular*; and JC: *One of the Originals*.

628 Interview EEE 17 December 2004.
629 Interview CCC 2 November 2004.
630 Interview EEE 17 December 2004.
631 Interview DDD 4 November 2004.

Chapter 13

632 In 1995, to the chagrin of the SAS, Brigadier RP in his role as Director
     Special Forces and his SAS bodyguards, all in civilian clothes, while visiting
     Sarajevo, were stopped at a Serb roadblock in the suburb of Ilidza. The Serb
     troops disarmed RP and his bodyguards, stripped them of most of their
     clothes, took their weapons, computers and confidential documents and com-
     mandeered RP's Range Rover.
633 On Monday, 17 June 2002, in an unusual utilisation of SAS skills, an SAS
     team helped end a mafia money-laundering racket by taking part in a raid on
     a Bosnian bank. Deputy Commander of the NATO-led Stabilisation Force (S-
     For), Major General Richard Dannatt, called upon the SAS in order to get
     evidence of racketeering claims. Demolitions specialists blew open three safes
     without destroying 3.5 million marks and documents stored inside. It was
     believed that the money-laundering operation was funding a plot to set up
     a breakaway Bosnian Croat state. French and German S-For troops guarded
     the town during the operation. Internet BBC News World Edition, 17 June
     2002.
634 'Albanian rebels, trained by the SAS are gaining ground in Macedonia, aiming
     for the key city of Tetovo.' *The Sunday Times*, 18 March 2001.
635 The first arrest operation was in early summer 1997 – Operation TANGO, an
     SAS operation aimed at seizing Karadzic and two other alleged war criminals,
     Simo Drljaca and Milan Kovacevic. All escaped. Drljaca later died resisting
     arrest by SAS troops in Prijedor, while Kovacevic was captured and sent to
     The Hague, where he died of a heart attack. The other two attempts by the
     SAS collapsed after Karadzic was tipped off. There is a widespread belief that
     the information came from French S-For sources and that the former Bosnian
     Serb leader never left the French-controlled territory between Foca and Pale.
636 The gang actually called themselves the 'West Side Niggers', but in order not
     to offend Western sensibilities the media unilaterally changed the name to the
     West Side Boys.
637 26-year-old Trooper BD from 22 SAS was killed in the operation.
638 The one British fatal casualty was a member of the SAS assault group.
639 Interview GGG 13 January 2005.
640 1 Para is now located in St Athan in Wales.

Chapter 14

641 Correspondence with General Sir OM KCB CBE – former CO 22 SAS – 29
     September 1999.
642 Interview AAA 24 August 2004.
643 *Ibid.*

644 The Borneo campaign did encourage the interoperability of UK/Australian and NZ SAS operations and was a good learning experience for the latter two organisations prior to Vietnam service. A situation similar to that involving the British SAS in Borneo occurred with the use of Australian and NZ SAS in Vietnam. The SAS deployment there was purely tactical and received criticism at the highest ANZAC [Australian and New Zealand Army Corps – a widely used anachronistic acronym dating back to the operations of the NZ and Australian troops in Gallipoli in the First World War] level. This was due to their high-maintenance requirements as well as the high level of resources required, particularly air assets, against the value of their contribution to the success of ANZAC operations.

645 Members of the SAS also learned the Thai language in the event that, following the 'domino' theory, the Vietnam War would spill over into Thailand and down the Malay Peninsular.

646 McManners: *Scars of War*, p. 231.

647 This matter is dealt in some detail, but very subjectively, by PR, who was the RSM concerned. Ratcliffe: *Eye of the Storm*, pp. 281–4.

648 Cohen: *Commandoes*, p. 93.

649 Brian Robinson, one of the longest serving commanding officers of the Rhodesian SAS had this to say about whether the British SAS and the Rhodesian SAS would have actually fought each other if the British Government had deployed them into Rhodesia: 'It was always convenient to believe that the British Armed Forces would never have fought against their own kith and kin. ... but let me assure you that during my attachment to 22 SAS Regiment in 1965, many of the officers and men stated that they would certainly follow orders and put down any colonial UDI if called upon to do so. The SAS was composed of professionals who would probably have been initially reluctant until the first SAS blood was spilt and then it would have just become another war.' Pittaway, J. and Fourie, Craig. *SAS Rhodesia*. Dandy Agencies (Pty) Ltd, Musgrave, 2003, p. 287.

650 Cole: *The Elite*, p. 431.

651 Attributable to Professor Martin Edmonds.

652 The author commanded a training team that established the bodyguard for an East African president. The cost of SAS teams was borne by the FCO, and the MoD was not averse to ensuring that all possible costs involved in using SAS troops, including marriage allowances and pension contributions, were passed on to the Foreign Office. This caused a certain amount of aggrievement among diplomats; the author, on arriving to commence this particular training task, was greeted at the airport by the British Embassy's First Secretary, who sarcastically asked 'How long has the British Army been employing mercenaries?' See Note 582 for a further example of the limited financial rapprochement between these two 'departments'.

653 See Bennett, Philip. 'The Case for Special Forces', *The Australian Army Journal*, 1964.

654 Gray, C.S. *Another Bloody Century*. Wiedenfeld and Nicolson, London, 2005, p. 208.

655 Woodward: *One Hundred Days*, p. 199.

656 Interview GGG 13 January 2005.

657 Curtis, Mark. *The Ambiguities of Power – British Foreign Policy Since 1945*. Zed Books Ltd, London, 1995, p. 18.

658 These were two counter-terrorist actions carried out by the Egyptian special *Saiqa* (Lightning) unit. In March 1978 in Lanarca, Egyptian would-be rescuers attempting to storm a hijacked Egyptian aircraft were mistakenly identified as terrorists by Cypriot security forces and 15 Egyptians were killed. In Malta, September 1985, a rescue attempt on a hijacked Egyptian airliner by Egyptian special forces became a major disaster when the Egyptian demolitions specialists used too much explosive trying to blow an entry into the aircraft collapsing the rear of the aircraft and killing a number of passengers. In the following panic as the remaining passengers tried to flee, a number were shot by the Egyptian sniper cordon and many were killed. A total of 57 passengers died as a result of the operation.

659 Gray: *Another Bloody Century*, p. 215.

660 The arrival in January 1994 of Lieutenant General Sir NX, who had commanded 22 SAS in the Falklands, as commander of UNPROFOR (the UN Protection Force) marked a distinct increase in the regiment's deployment and involved an entire Sabre squadron, continuing the task of observation around besieged Sarajevo and designating targets for air strikes. NX, unfortunately, found his desire to get tough was often at variance with UN policy, in the person of Mr Akashi, the UN representative on the spot who constantly refused to authorise air strikes. SAS patrols also became involved in escorting aid convoys through the mountainous countryside into the various Bosnian Muslim enclaves being besieged by Serb militias. These convoys, manned by civilians from various aid agencies, were particularly vulnerable, especially as the UN was often unwilling to use force to bring them through enemy territory. The first member of the regiment to die in Bosnia was Corporal ZW, who was driving in a vehicle accompanied by an officer and an interpreter in the area around the encircled enclave of Gorazde. They were shot at by Serbs, the officer was wounded and ZW was hit in the head. His wound proved fatal and he was buried in the regimental plot at Hereford with full military honours. The SAS has been supplemented by members of 14 Int. During the Kosovo conflict the SAS supplied vital intelligence to indicate targets for the NATO air forces.

661 Gray: *Explorations in Strategy*, p. 169.

662 Harding, Thomas. 'Secret work of SAS in Iraq exposed', *The Daily Telegraph*. 11 August 2008.

663 Jackson, Mike. 'The Future of Land Warfare'. *RUSI Journal*. Defence and International Security. August 2003, pp. 55–7.

664 Interview GGG 13 January 2005.

665 David Stirling finally received a long overdue knighthood in the 1990 New Year Honours List. He died in November 1990, just missing the fiftieth anniversary of the regiment he had founded.

666 See MCLEOD 1/10 – Memorandum of the origins of the Special Air Service (SAS) by Lt Col David Stirling – 8 November 1948.

667 Woodward: *One Hundred Days*, p. 199.

668 Interview GGG 13 January 2005.

669 Harding: 'Secret work'.

670 Excerpt from the 50th anniversary speech by the 22 SAS Commanding Officer on 27 July 2002.

BIBLIOGRAPHY

Primary References

Akehurst, John. *We Won a War*. Michael Russell Publishing Ltd, Wiltshire, UK. 1982.

Asher, Michael. *The Real Bravo Two Zero*. Cassell, London. 2002.

Beckwith, Charlie A. *Delta Force. The Army's Elite Counter-terrorist Unit*. Harper Collins Publishers, New York. 1983.

Breytenbach, Jan. *Forged in Battle*. Saayman and Weber (Pty) Ltd, Capetown, SA. 1986.

Breytenbach, Jan. *They Live by the Sword*. Lemur Books Pty, Alberton, SA. 1990.

Breytenbach, Jan. *Eden's Exiles*. Queillerie Publishers, Cape Town, SA. 1997.

Butt, Ronald. (ed.) *Margaret Thatcher. In Defence of Freedom*. Aurum Press, London. 1986.

Calvert, Michael. *Prisoners of Hope*. Leo Cooper, London. 1952.

Calvert, Michael. *Fighting Mad*. Airlife Publishing Ltd, Shrewsbury. 1996. (2nd Ed.)

Campbell, Arthur. *Jungle Green*. George Allan and Unwin Ltd, London. 1953.

Camsell, Don. *Black Water, By Strength and by Guile*. Virgin Publishing Ltd, London. 2000.

Churchill, Winston, S. *The Second World War. Vol. 1. The Gathering Storm*. Bantam Books, New York. 1962.

Churchill, Winston, S. *The Second World War. Vol. 2. Their Finest Hour*. Bantam Books, New York. 1962.

Churchill, Winston, S. *The Second World War. Vol. 3. The Grand Alliance*. Bantam Books, New York. 1962.

Churchill, Winston, S. *The Second World War. Vol. 4. The Hinge of Fate*. Bantam Books, New York. 1962.

Churchill, Winston, S. *The Second World War. Vol. 5. Closing the Ring*. Bantam Books, New York. 1962.

Churchill, Winston, S. *The Second World War. Vol. 6. Triumph and Tradegy*. Bantam Books, New York. 1962.

Clark, Wesley K. *Waging Modern War*. Perseus Books Group, New York. 2001/2002.

Clarke, Dudley. *Seven Assignments*. Alden Press, Oxford. 1949.

Clutterbuck, Richard. *The Long, Long War – The Emergency in Malaya 1948–1960*. Cassell and Company, London. 1966.

Coburn, Mike. *Soldier Five*. Mainstream Publishing Company, Edinburgh. 2004.

Connor, K. *Ghost Force*. Weidenfeld and Nicolson, London. 1998.

Connor, K. *Ghosts – An Illustrated History of the SAS*. Cassell and Co. London. 2000.

Cooper, Johnny. *One of the Originals. The Story of a Founder Member of the SAS*. Pan Books Ltd, London. 1991.

Crosland, Peter. *Victor Two*. Bloomsbury, London. 1996.

Cross, Colin. *Fall of the British Empire*. Hodder and Stoughton, London. 1968.

Cross, J.P. *A Face Like a Chicken's Backside*. Arms and Armour Press, London. 1996.

Deane-Drummond, A.J. *Arrows of Fortune*. Leo Cooper Ltd, London. 1997.

de la Billiere, P. *Storm Command*. Harper Collins, London. 1992.

de la Billiere, P. *Looking For Trouble*. Harper Collins, London. 1994.

Devereaux, Steve. *Terminal Velocity*. Smith Gryphen Ltd, London. 1997.

Dorril, Stephen. *MI6*. The Free Press, New York. 2000.

Els, Paul. *Forged in Battle*. Kovos Day Books, Johannesburg. 2000.

Els, Paul. *We Fear Naught But God. The Story of the South African Recces*. Kovos Day Books, Johannesburg. 2000.

Falconer, Duncan. *First into Action*. Little Brown and Company, London. 1998.

Farran, Roy. *Winged Dagger*. Collins, London. 1948.

Farran, Roy. *Operation Tombola*. Collins, London. 1960.

Fergusson, Bernard. *The Trumpet in the Hall*. Collins Books, London. 1970.

Fergusson, Bernard. *Beyond the Chidwin*. Anthony Mott Ltd, London. 1983. (Reprint of 1945 version.)

Follows, Roy. *The Jungle Beat*. Travellers' Eye Ltd, Shropshire. 1999.

Foot, M.R.D. *The 4th Dimension of War, Volume 1. Intelligence, Subversion, Resistance*. Manchester University Press, Manchester. 1970.

Foot, M.R.D. *SOE in France*. HMSO, London. 1966.

George, Jackie and Ottaway, Susan. *She Who Dared*. Leo Cooper, South Yorkshire. 1999.

Gray, C.S. *Strategic Studies – A Critical Assessment*. Greenwood Press, CT. 1982.

Gray, C.S. *Special Operations – What Succeeds and Why?* National Institute for Public Policy, Washington, DC. 1991.

Gray, C.S. *Explorations in Strategy*, Greenwood Press, CT. 1996.

Gray, C.S. *Modern Strategy*. Oxford University Press, Oxford. 1999.

Gray, C.S. *Another Bloody Century*. Weidenfeld and Nicolson, London. 2005.

Heimann, J.M. *The Most Offending Soul Alive – Tom Harrison and his Remarkable Life*. Aurum Press Ltd, London. 2002.

Hoe, A. *David Stirling, Authorised Biography*. Little, Brown and Company, London. 1992.

Hoe, A. and Morris. E. *Re-enter the SAS*, Leo Cooper, London. 1994.

Horner, D.M. *Phantoms of the Jungle*, Allen and Unwin, Sydney. 1989.

Horner, D.M. *Phantoms of War – A History of the Australian Special Air Service*, Allen and Unwin, Sydney. 2002.

Hunter, Gaz. *Shooting Gallery*. Cassell Group, UK. 1998.

Jeapes, A. *SAS Operation Oman*. William Kimber and Co Ltd, London. 1980.

Jennings, Christian. *Midnight in Some Burning Town – British Special Forces Operations from Belgrade to Baghdad*. Weidenfeld and Nicolson, London. 2004.

Kennedy, Michael Paul. *He Who Dares*. Simon and Schuster, New York. 1989.

Kitson, F. *Bunch of Five*. Faber and Faber Ltd, London. 1977.

Laing, Margaret. *Edward Heath. Prime Minister*. Sidgwick and Jackson Ltd, London. 1972.

Large, Lofty. *Soldier Against the Odds*. Mainstream Publishing Company, Edinburgh. 1999.

Leary, John D. *Violence and the Dream People*. Ohio University Press, Ohio. 1995.

Lees, David Sir. *Flight from the Middle East*. HMSO, London. 1980.

Lloyd Owen, D. *Providence Their Guide*. George G. Harrap and Co. Ltd, London. 1980.

Major, John. *The Autobiography*. Harper Collins Publishers, London. 1999.

Marcinko, R. and Weisman, J. *Rogue Warrior*, Pocket Books, New York. 1992.

McAleese, Peter and Bles, Mark. *No Mean Soldier*. Orion Books Ltd, London. 1993.

McCallion, Harry. *Killing Zone*. Bloomsbury Publishing Ltd, London. 1995.

McManners, Hugh. *Falklands Commando*. William Kimber, London. 1964.

McManners, Hugh. *Scars of War*. Harper Collins Publishers, London. 1993.

McNab, Andy. *Bravo Two Zero*. Bantam Press, London. 1993.

McNab, Andy. *Immediate Action*. Bantam Press, London. 1996.

Pittaway, J. and Fourie, Craig. *SAS Rhodesia*. Dandy Agencies (Pty) Ltd, Musgrave. 2003.

Pocock, Tom. *Fighting General, The Public and Private Campaigns of General Sir Walter Walker*. William Collins and Sons Co Ltd, London. 1973.

Ramsay, Jack. *SAS. The Soldiers' Story*. Macmillan Publishing Ltd, London. 1996.

Ratcliffe, Peter. *Eye of the Storm*. Michael O'Mara Books Ltd, London. 2001.

Reid-Daly, R.F. and Stiff, Peter. *Selous Scouts – Top Secret War*. Galago Publishing (Pty), Alberton. 1982.

Reid-Daly, R.F. *Pamwe Chete*. Kovos Day Books, Johannesburg. 1999.

Rooney, David. *Mad Mike. The Life of Brigadier Mike Calvert*. Leo Cooper, London. 1997.

Rose, Michael. *Fighting for Peace*. The Harvill Press, London. 1998.

Royle, Trevor. *Orde Wingate, Irregular Soldier*. Weidenfeld and Nicholson, London. 1995.

Ryan, Chris. *The One That Got Away*. Brassey, London. 1997.

Scholey, Peter. *The Joker. 20 Years Inside the SAS*. Andre Deutsch Ltd, London. 1999.

Schwarzkopf, Norman. *It Doesn't Take a Hero*. Bantam, London. 1992.

Skorzeny, O. *Skorzeny's Special Missions*. Greenhill Books, London. 1997. (1957 reprint.)

Slim, F.M. *Retreat into Victory*. Cassell and Co, London. 1956.

Smiley, David. *Arabian Assignment*. Leo Cooper, London. 1975.

Smiley, David. *Irregular Regular*. Michael Russell (Publishing) Ltd, Norwich. 1994.

Smith, E.D. *East of Katmandu. The Story of the 7th Duke of Edinburgh's Own Gurka Rifles. Vol. 2. 1948–1973*. Leo Cooper, London. 1971.

Smith, E.D. (Birdy). *Counter Insurgency Operations in Malaya and Borneo*. Ian Allan Ltd, Surrey. 1985.

Southeby-Tailyour. *Reasons in Writing. A Commando's View of the Falklands War*. Leo Cooper, South Yorkshire. 1993.

Spence, Cameron. *Sabre Squadron*. Michael Joseph, London. 1997.

Spencer-Chapman, F. *The Jungle is Neutral*. Times Books International, Singapore. 1997.

Spicer, Leonard. *The Suffolks in Malaya*. Lawson Phelps Publishing, Cambridgeshire. 1998.

Starling, Joe. *Soldier On. Testament of a Tom*. Spellmount Ltd, Kent. 1992.

Stiff, Peter. *See You in November*. Galago Publishing (Pty) Ltd, South Africa. 1985.

Strawson, J. *A History of the SAS Regiment*. Guild Publishing, London. 1985.

Swift, Keith D. *Swifty's War – A First Hand Account of the Malayan War*. Cremer Press, Blackburn. 2003.

Thatcher, Margaret. *The Downing Street Years*. Harper Collins Publishers, London. 1993.

Thompson, Julian. *No Picnic*. Cassell and Co., London. 1995. (2nd Ed.)

Thompson, Robert. *Defeating Communist Insurgency. Experiences from Malaya and Borneo*. Chatto and Windus Ltd, London. 1966.

Thompson, Robert. *Make for the Hills. Memories of Far Eastern Wars*. Leo Cooper Ltd, London. 1989.

Urban, Mark. *Big Boys' Rules – The Story of the SAS and the Secret Struggle Against the IRA*. Faber and Faber Ltd, London. 1983.

Van der Bijl, Nicholas and Aldea, David. *5th Infantry Brigade in the Falklands*. Leo Cooper, South Yorkshire. 2003.

Villers, Richard. *Knife Edge – Life as a Special Forces Surgeon*. Michael Joseph Ltd, London. 1977.

Walker, W. *Fighting On*. Morgan Technical Books, Gloucester. 1997.

Warner, P. *The SAS: The Official History*. Sphere Books Ltd, London, 1983.

Wood, J.R.T. *War Diaries of Andre Dennison*. Ashanti Publishing Ltd, Gibraltar. 1989.

Woodward, Sandy. *One Hundred Days. The Memoirs of the Falklands Battle Group Commander*. Harper Collins Publishers, London. 1992.

Wynter, H.W. *Special Forces in the Desert War 1940–1943*. Public Record Office, Kew. 2001.

Zeigler, Philip. *Wilson. The Authorised Life*. Weidenfeld and Nicolson, London. 1993.

Journals

Anon. 'Loughgall and the British SAS at Gibraltar'. *Counterterrorism and Security Reports*. Volume 9, Number 1. 2000, pp. 4–6.

Anon. 'South Africa: Genesis of the Third Force'. *Africa Confidential*. Volume 32, Number 19. 27 September 1991, pp. 1–3.

Clutterbuck, R. 'Sir Robert Thompson', *Army Quarterly and Defence Journal* (April 1990), pp. 140–5.

Deane-Drummond, A.J. 'Operations in Oman'. *The British Army Review*. September 1959, pp. 7–14.

Gray, Colin S. 'Handfuls of Heroes on Desperate Ventures: When do Special Operations Succeed?' *Parameters*. Spring 1999, pp. 1–24

Head, P. ''O' Field Troop – 1st Singapore Regiment Royal Artillery Malaya 1953–1955. Part 2'. *Journal of the Royal Artillery*. Spring 2002.

Jackson, Mike. 'The Future of Land Warfare'. *RUSI Journal*. Defence and International Security. August 2003, pp. 55–7.

Jeapes, J.S. 'The Stay Behind Battle'. *The British Army Review*. August 1967, pp. 81–2.

Kennedy, Harold. 'Forces under stress'. *National Defense*. October 2004, pp. 34–5.

Leary, J.D. 'Searching for a Role – The Special Air Service (SAS) Regiment in the Malayan Emergency'. *Journal for the Society of Historical Research*. Number 296. Winter 1995.

Litt, David. 'Special Ops Forces are a "Tool of Choice"'. *National Defense*. February 2003, pp. 20–3.

Lyon, R. 'Borneo Reflections'. *The British Army Review*. August 1966, pp. 72–9.

Newell, C.L.D. 'The Special Air Service'. *The British Army Review*. September 1955, pp. 40–2.

Newell, C.L.D. 'Special Forces'. *The British Army Review*. October 1961, pp. 29–31.

Price, D.L. 'Oman: Insurgency and Development'. *Conflict Studies*. Number 53. January 1975.

Purdon, C.W.B. 'The Sultan's Armed Forces'. *The British Army Review*. August 1969, pp. 78–9.

Rose, H.M. 'Towards an Ending of the Falklands War; June 1982'. *Conflict*. Volume 7, Number 1. 1987, pp. 1–13.

Shapter, I.R.D. 'The Border Scouts'. *The British Army Review*. August 1967, pp. 36–42.

Smiley, D. 'Muscat and Oman'. *Journal of the Royal United Service Institution*. February 1960.

Thompson, J. 'The Special Air Service'. *Officer*. March/April 1998, pp. 28–9.

Walker, Walter. 'Borneo'. *The British Army Review*. August 1969, pp. 7–15.

Waller, P.J.R. 'Special Operations in Malaya'. *The British Army Review*. October 1962, pp. 22–31.

Watson, C.M.G. 'Field Intelligence Officers in the Aden Protectorate'. *The British Army Review*. September 1959, pp. 59–64.

Newspaper Articles

Connor, K. 'SAS Role'. *Sunday Telegraph*. 18 October 1998, pp. 24–5.

Geraghty, T and Norton-Taylor, R. 'SAS Memoirs'. *Guardian*. 18 March 2003, p. 14.

Gilligan, A. '14 Int Company'. *Sunday Telegraph*. 29 September 1996, p. 20.

Harding, Thomas. 'Secret work of SAS in Iraq exposed.' *Daily Telegraph*. 11 August 2008.

Norton-Taylor, R. 'SAS Man quits in protest at illegal Iraq war'. *Guardian*. 13 March 2006.

Rayment, S. 'SAS Chiefs launch biggest shake-up in regiment's history'. *Sunday Telegraph*. 28 September 2003.

Rayment, S. 'The day the SAS decided "someone else could do it better"'. *Sunday Telegraph*. 28 September 2003, p. 12.

Unpublished Documents (Author's Collection)

Memorandum by Col David Stirling DSO, OBE on the Origins of the Special Air Service Regiment November 1948.

22 *Special Air Service Regiment – Rules for War – 1970*. 5th Ed. 1972.
Briefing to SAS troop commanders by the Commanding Officer on 11 November 1975.
SAS Northern Ireland Standard Operational Procedures (SOP) – 1976.
Counter-Terrorist Team – Visitor Briefing Notes – 1979.
22 SAS Commanding Officer's Speech Notes – 27 July 2002.

Defence Publications

The Application of Force. An Introduction to Army Doctrine and the Conduct of Military Operations. The Stationery Office, London. 2002.
US Department of Defence Dictionary. Joint Publication 1-02. US DoD, Washington, 12 April 2001. As amended through 30 November 2004.

Reports

The Falklands Island Review (*The Franks Report*) Pimlico Publishing, London. Crown Copyright. 1983.

Theses

Bowman, D.K.L. March 1981 *The Insurgency in Dhufar 1965–1975*. University College of Wales, Aberystwyth.
Kiras, James Drew. July 2004. *Rendering the Mortal Blow Easier: Special Operations and the Nature of Strategy*. The Graduate Institute of Political and International Studies, University of Reading.

Public Records Office – Kew

Malaya 1950–59
CO717/202/2 – Rhodesians in Malayan Scouts, SAS.
WO216/494 – Report on Malayan Scouts, SAS, by HQ FARELF.
WO219/1670 – A Comparative Study of the Counter-insurgency operations in Malaya and Kenya.
WO279/241 – Anti-terrorist Operations in Malaya.
CO 1022/48 SEA 10/172/01 'Official Designation of the Communist Forces'.

Kenya 1954–55
WO276/431 – SF (Pseudo-gang) operations against the Mau Mau 1954–56.
WO216/887 – Tactical appreciation by Lt Gen Sir GW Lathbury – Aug 1955. Includes assessment of SF operations.
WO276/411 – Operations against Mau Mau.

Borneo 1962–66
WO219/2407 – Lessons learned from Borneo Operations.
WO32/19269 – Borneo Territories – situation reports and supply of equipment – 1963–64.
WO305/3326 –Borneo operations – Quarterly report – Jan–May 1966.

Radfan/Aden 1964–67
WO386/22 – Report on operations 14 April – 30 June 1964.
WO32/18518 – Aden. Half-yearly security reports.
DEFE 13/68 – Aden – threat to the security of the Protectorate.

Oman – 1958–59; 1970–76
FO1016/656 – SAF operations against Jabel [sic] Akhdar in 1958.
WO337/9 – Operations in Muscat and Oman – 1952–1959.
WO305/976 – 22SAS Official History – operations in Oman 18 Nov 1958 – 28 Feb 1959.
WO305/977/ 978 – 22 SAS Training.
WO337/8 Jebel Akhdar Reconnaissance Report Feb 1959.
DEFE25/187 – Operations in Muscat and Oman 1971.

Northern Ireland 1976–2000
WO296/95 – SAS incursion into the Republic of Ireland. 7 May 1976.

Kings College London – Liddell Hart Centre for Military Archives: Papers of Gen Sir Roderick McLeod GBE KCB (1905–1980)

MCLEOD: *1 Papers relating to operations of the Special Air Service (SAS) during World War Two, and to its formation, 1944–1948*
MCLEOD: 1/1 1944 – Summary of casualties inflicted on the enemy by Special Air Service (SAS) troops during operations in 1944.
MCLEOD: 1/2 [1944] – Operations of the 4th French Parabattalion, relating to operations of 4 French Parachute Bn, Special Air Service (SAS) Bde, in Brittany, France, 5–30 Jun 1944.
MCLEOD: 1/3 [1944] – List of arms, ammunition, equipment and provisions sent to the Special Air Service (SAS) Bde in the field overseas (theatres of operation unspecified).
MCLEOD: 1/4 1944 – List of Special Air Service (SAS) Bde operations in France, 5 Jun 1944–27 Sep 1944.
MCLEOD: 1/5 1944 – List of Special Air Service (SAS) Bde operations in France, Jun 1944–Sep 1944.
MCLEOD: 1/6 1944 Sep 12 – Letter to McLeod from Lt Col Morice, commanding FFI (Forces Françaises de l'Intérieur) in the department of Morbihan, France.
MCLEOD: 1/7 1944 Oct 27 – Memorandum [by Major Eric Barkworth, intelligence officer, 2 Special Air Service?], giving an anecdotal account of the retrieval by an old man of the French Resistance of containers parachuted into the Pontivy area, France.

MCLEOD: 1/8 [1946–1959] – Narrative entitled 'Looking back to the French
    Special Air Service (SAS) in Brittany, 1944' by Lt Col Oswald Aloysius Joseph
    Cary-Elwes, 20 Liaison Headquarters, SAS Bde.
MCLEOD: 1/10 1948 Nov 8 – Memorandum on the origins of the Special Air
    Service (SAS) by Col (Archibald) David Stirling.

MCLEOD: 2 *Papers relating to the SAS following operations in Northern Europe,
    World War Two, 1945–1958*
MCLEOD: 2/1 [1945 May] – Memorandum entitled 'Notes on the organisation,
    history and employment of Special Air Service troops' [by Lieutenant Colonel
    Ian G Collins, General Staff Officer 1 (SAS), 1 Airborne British Corps], con-
    taining review of SAS operations in North West Europe, Jun 1944–May 1945.
MCLEOD: 2/2 1945 May 7 – Memorandum entitled 'Notes on future of SAS' by
    Lt Col Ian G Collins, General Staff Officer 1 Special Air Service (SAS), 1
    Airborne British Corps, containing proposals for SAS role in China, Indo-
    China and Siam under South East Asia Command (SEAC).
MCLEOD: 2/3 [1945] – Memorandum (author not given) on the future organisa-
    tion of the Special Air Service (SAS), particularly relating to lessons learned
    from World War Two in communications, resupply, research and integration
    with the secret services, and to the formation of a proposed SAS Territorial
    Army unit.
MCLEOD: 2/4 1948 Oct 31 – Report by Lt Col Brian F M Franks, Commanding
    Officer, 21 Special Air Service Regt (Artists Rifles), Territorial Army, on his
    unit's first year of existence.
MCLEOD: 2/5 [1958] – 'The Special Air Service', undated typescript paper by Lt
    Col Lemon Evelyn Oliver Turton (Pat) Hart, SAS, reviewing previous duties of
    the SAS and proposing its future role.

MCLEOD: 3 *Papers relating to lectures given by McLeod, 1944–1962*
MCLEOD: 3/1 1944 Nov – Lecture on the Special Air Service (SAS) by McLeod
    [to 6 Airborne Division], mainly comprising summary of SAS operations in
    France following operation OVERLORD.
MCLEOD: 3/2 1948 Aug 4 – Notes for a lecture by McLeod to the Staff College,
    Camberley, Surrey.
MCLEOD: 3/5 [1949] Jul 29 – Notes by McLeod for a lecture [to the Staff
    College, Camberley, Surrey?] entitled 'Small scale airborne operations in
    enemy occupied territories', mainly relating to lessons learned from operations
    of special forces in World War Two and relevance to the planning of similar
    operations in a future war.
MCLEOD: 3/6 [1962] – Lecture on 'Special forces in the British Army' by McLeod
    to the US Army.

MCLEOD: 4 *Maps and diagram relating to SAS operations in France, 1944*
MCLEOD: 4/2 [1944] – Printed map of France and Belgium, showing sites of
    Special Air Service Bde (SAS) operation bases, Jun–Sep 1944.
MCLEOD: 4/3 1944 – Map of Northern France and Belgium, showing sites of
    Special Air Service Bde (SAS) operation bases, 1944 (allocated by 1 and 2 SAS
    Regt, 3 and 4 French Parachute Bn, Belgian 2 Parachute Coy and Phantom
    SAS Signals Section).
MCLEOD: 4/4 1944 – Special Air Service (SAS) troops signal lay-out, operations
    North West Europe, 1944.

<h2 align="center">Interviewees</h2>

AAA Former Troop Commander in Malayan Scouts/22 SAS, and 22 SAS Commander in Borneo during the 'Confrontation'.

BBB Former 22 SAS Troop Commander in Malaya and Jebel Akhdar; Squadron Commander in Radfan, Aden and Borneo.

CCC Served in 22 SAS from trooper to sergeant major; served in Oman and Northern Ireland; commanded an assault team at Princes Gate; and served in the Falklands War.

DDD Served in 22 SAS from trooper to sergeant major; served in Borneo, Northern Ireland and Oman.

EEE Served in 22 SAS from trooper to staff sergeant; served in Aden, Oman (was at the battle of Mirbat), Northern Ireland, in the assault team at Princes Gate, and in the Falklands War.

FFF Served in 22 SAS from trooper to staff sergeant; served in Aden, Oman, Northern Ireland, in the assault team at Princes Gate, and in the B Squadron patrol that landed in Argentina in the Falklands War.

GGG 22 SAS Troop Commander, Squadron Commander and Training Officer. Served in Oman, Northern Ireland, and in the Falklands War.

HHH Served as a private soldier to Warrant Officer 1st Class and was the Senior NCO in the Parachute Regiment. Served in Northern Ireland with a Para Patrol Company, and was a Para Operations Sergeant-Major in the Falklands War.

<h2 align="center">Secondary References</h2>

Adams, J. *Secret Armies The Full Story of the* SAS, *Delta Force and Spetnaz.* Hutchinson and Co Ltd, London, 1988. (Revised Ed. 1989 by Pan Books.)

Adams, J., Morgan, Robin, and Bambridge, Tony. *Ambush – The War Between the SAS and the IRA.* Pan Books, London. 1984.

Addison, P. and Calder, A. *Time to Kill – Experiences of War 1939–45,* Random House Ltd, London. 1997.

Allen, Charles. *Savage Wars of Peace, Soldiers' Voices. 1945–1989.* Michael Joseph Ltd, London. 1990.

Anderson, Duncan. *Military Elite.* Magna Books, Leicester. 1994.

Applegate, R. *Kill or Get Killed,* Paladin Press, Boulder, CO. 1976.

Arastegui, Martin C. *Inside the World's Special Forces.* Bloomsbury Publishing, London. 1995.

Arthur, Max. *Men of the Red Beret. Airborne Forces. 1940–1990.* Hutchinson, London. 1990.

Balfour-Paul, Glen. *The End of Empire in the Middle East: Britain's Relinquishment of Power in her Last Three Arab Dependencies.* Cambridge University Press, Cambridge. 1994.

Barber, N. *The War of the Running Dogs.* Williams Collins Sons and Co Ltd, London. 1971.

Bartlett, C.J. *The Long Retreat. A Short History of British Defence Policy 1945–1970.* Macmillan Press Ltd, London. 1972.

Bateman, M. Elliot. *Fourth Dimension of Warfare. Vol 1.* Manchester University Press, Manchester. 1970.

Beaumont, Roger. *Military Elites*. Robert Hale and Company, London. 1974.

Beckett, Ian F. *Modern Insurgencies and Counter-insurgencies – Guerrillas and their Opponents since 1750*. Routledge, London. 2001.

Bermudez, J.S. *North Korean Special Forces*. Naval Institute Press, Maryland. 1998.

Best, G. *War and Law Since 1945*. Oxford University Press, Oxford. 1994.

Bullock, Christopher. *Journeys Hazardous*. Square One Publications, Worcester. 1994.

Burgess, H. *Inside Spetznaz*. Presidio Press, California. 1990.

Chichester, Michael and Wilkinson, John. *The Uncertain Ally – British Defence Policy 1960 – 1990*. Gower Publishing Company Ltd, Aldershot. 1982.

Clutterbuck. Richard. *Protest and the Urban Guerrilla*. Cassell and Co. Ltd, London. 1973.

Clutterbuck. Richard. *Living with Terrorism*. Faber and Faber Ltd, London. 1975.

Clutterbuck, Richard. *The Future of Political Violence*. The Macmillan Press Ltd, Hampshire. 1986.

Cocks, Chris. *Fireforce*. Covos Books, Roodeport. 1988.

Constable, T.J. *Hidden Heroes*. Willmer Brothers, Liverpool. 1971.

Cohen, Elliot A. *Commandoes and Politicians – Elite Military Units in Modern Democracies*. Harvard University, Cambridge, MA. 1978.

Cole, Barbara. *The Elite – The Story of the Rhodesian Special Air Service*. Three Knights Publishing, Transkei. 1984.

Cole, Roger and Belfield, Richard. *SAS Operation STORM*. Hodder and Stoughton, London. 2011.

Cowles, Virginia. *The Phantom Major*. Oldhams Press Ltd, Hertfordshire. 1958.

Cradock, Percy. *In Pursuit of British Interests – Reflections on the Foreign Policy under Margaret Thatcher and John Major*. John Murray (Publishers) Ltd, London. 1997.

Crawford, Steve. *The SAS Encyclopaedia*. Simon and Schuster Ltd, London. 1996.

Creveld, Martin van. *Command in War*. Harvard University Press, Cambridge, MA. 1985.

Creveld, Martin van. *The Transformation of War*. Free Press, New York. 1991.

Creveld, Martin van. *The Art of War*. Cassell, London. 2002.

Curtis, Mark. *The Ambiguities of Power – British Foreign Policy Since 1945*. Zed Books Ltd, London. 1995.

Davies, Barry. *SAS Rescue*. Sidgwick and Jackson, London. 1996.

Davies, Barry. *Heroes of the SAS*. Virgin Publishing Ltd, London. 2000.

Davies, Barry. *The Complete Encyclopaedia of the SAS*. Virgin Publishing Ltd, London. 2001.

Dennis, Peter and Grey, Jeffrey. *Emergency and Confrontation – Australian Military Operation in Malaya and Borneo 1950–1966*. Allen and Unwin Pty Ltd, New South Wales. 1996.

De Nooy, Gert. *The Clausewitzian Dictum and the Future of Western Military Strategy*. Kluwer International, The Hague. 1997.

Dickens, P. *SAS, The Jungle Frontier*. Arms and Armour Press, London. 1983.

Dickens, P. *SAS, Secret War in South East Asia*. Ballantine Books, London. 1992. (Reprint of 1983 edition: *SAS, The Jungle Frontier*).

Dobson, C. and Payne, R. *War Without End – The Terrorist*. Harrap Ltd, London. 1986.

Elliot-Bateman, M. *Fourth Dimension of Warfare*, Volume 1, Manchester University Press, Manchester. 1990.

Fairburn, W.E. *Get Tough*. Paladin Press, Boulder, CO, 1979. (Reprint of original US military training publication, 1942.)

Finlan, Alastair. *The Gulf War – 1991*. Osprey Publishing, Oxford. 2003.

Fowler, William. *SAS Behind Enemy Lines – Covert Operations 1941 – to the Present Day*. Harper Collins Publishers, London. 1997.

Geraghty, Tony. *Who Dares Wins. The Story of the Special Air Service 1950–1980*. Arms and Armour Press, London, 1980.

Geraghty, Tony. *This is the SAS – A Pictorial History of the Special Air Service*. Arms and Armour Press, London. 1982.

Hamish, Ian A. and Neilson, K. *Elite Military Formations in War and Peace*. Praeger Publishing, Westport, CT. 1996.

Harrison, D. *These Men are Dangerous*. Cassell and Company, London. 1957.

Heilbrunn, Otto. *Conventional Warfare in the Nuclear Age*. George Allen and Unwin Ltd, London. 1965.

Hennessy, Peter. *The Prime Ministers. The Office and its Holders Since 1945*. Penguin Group, London. 2000.

Herclerode, Peter. *Para!* Arms and Armour Press, London. 1992.

Herclerode, Peter. *Fighting Dirty – The Inside Story of Covert Operations*. Cassell and Co, London. 2001.

Holmes, R. *Acts of War – The Behaviour of Men in Battle*. The Free Press – Simon and Schuster Inc., New York. 1985.

Holmes, R. *Firing Line*. Jonathan Cape Ltd, London. 1985.

Hopkinson, William. *The Making of British Defence Policy*. The Stationery Office Ltd, Norwich. 2000.

Hughes-Wilson, John. *Military Intelligence Blunders and Cover-ups*. Constable and Robinson Ltd, London. 1999.

Hunter, Robin. *True Stories of the SBS*. Virgin Publishing Ltd, London. 1998.

James, Harold and Sheil-Small, Denis. *The Undeclared War*. Leo Cooper Ltd, London. 1971.

James, Harold and Sheil-Small, Denis. *A Pride of Gurkhas*. Leo Cooper Ltd, London. 1975.

Janke, P. *Guerrilla and Terrorist Organisations*. The Harvester Press Ltd, Brighton. 1983.

Jonas, G. *Vengeance. The True Story of a CT Mission*. Williams Collins and Co Ltd, London. 1984.

Jones, Tim. *Post War Insurgency and the SAS. 1945–1952. A Special Type of Warfare*. Frank Cass Publishers, London. 2001.

Jones, Tim. *SAS. The First Secret Wars*. I.B. Tauris and Co. Ltd, London. 2005

Kelly, R.S. *Special Operations and National Purpose*. Lexington Books, Lexington. 1989.

Kemp, Anthony. *The Secret Hunters*. Michael O'Mara Books, London. 1986.

Kemp, Anthony. *The SAS at War. 1941–1945*. Penguin Books Ltd, London. 1991.

Kemp, Anthony. *The SAS – Savage Wars of Peace. 1947 – Present*. Penguin Books Ltd, London. 1994.

Kitson, F. *Gangs and Counter Gangs*. Barrie and Rockcliff, London. 1960.

Kitson, F. *Low Intensity Operations. Subversion, Insurgency and Peacekeeping*. Faber and Faber Ltd, London. 1971.

Kyle, Keith. *Suez*. Weidenfeld and Nicolson, London. 1991.

Ladd, J.A. *SBS, The Invisible Raiders*. Arms and Armour Press Ltd, London. 1983.

Ladd, J.A. *SAS Operations*, Robert Hale Ltd, London. 1989.

Lapping, Brian. *End of an Empire*. Granada Publishing, London. 1985.

Larteguy, J.P. and Fielding. X. (Translated) *The Centurions*. Arrow Books, London. 1961.

Larteguy, J.P. and Fielding. X. (Translated) *The Praetorians*. Hutchinson and Co Ltd, London. 1963.

Lloyd, Mark. *Special Forces – the Changing Face of Warfare*. Arms and Armour Press, London. 1995.

Luttwak, Edward. *A Dictionary of Modern War*. The Penguin Press, London. 1971.

Marquis, Susan, L. *Unconventional Warfare: Rebuilding US Special Operations Forces*. The Brookings Institution, Washington, DC. 1997.

McRaven, W.H. *Spec. Ops*. Presidio Press. 1996.

Middlebrook, Martin. *The Falklands War. 1982*. Penguin Books, London. 2001.

Mockaitis, Thomas R. *British Counterinsurgency in the Post-imperial Era*. Manchester University Press, Manchester. 1995.

Morgan, Kenneth O. *The People's Peace. British History 1945–1985*. Oxford University Press, Oxford. 1990.

Morris, James. *Farewell the Trumpets*. Faber and Faber Ltd, London. 1978.

Nadel, J. and Wright, J.R. *Special Men and Special Missions*. Greenhill Books, London. 1994.

Nagel, John A. *Learning to Eat Soup with a Knife: Counterinsurgency Lessons from Malaya and Vietnam*. Praeger Publishers, Westport, CT. 2002. (University of Chicago Press, Chicago. 2005.)

Neillands, Robin. *A Fighting Retreat. The British Empire. 1947–1997*. Hodder and Stoughton. London. 1996.

Neillands, Robin. *In the Combat Zone – Special Forces since 1945*. Weidenfeld and Nicolson, London. 1997.

Newman, Bob. *Guerrillas in the Mist*. Paladin Press, Boulder, CO. 1997.

Newsinger, J. *Dangerous Men*. Pluto Press, London. 1997.

Paget, J. *Last Post – Aden 1964–67*. Faber and Faber Ltd, London. 1965.

Paget. J. *Counter Insurgency Campaigning*. Faber and Faber Ltd, London. 1967.

Parker, John. *SBS – The Inside Story of the Special Boat Service*. Headline Book Publishing, London. 1998.

Paschel, Rad. *Low Intensity Conflict, 2010*. Brasseys (US) Inc. and Macmillan Publishing, New York. 1990.

Pearce, Malcolm and Stewart, Geoffrey. *British Political History. 1867–2001*. Routledge, London. 1992.

Pocock, Tom. *East and West of Suez. The Retreat from Empire*. Bodley Head, London. 1986.

Pugsley, Christopher. *From Emergency to Confrontation – The New Zealand Armed Forces in Malaya and Borneo 1949–66*. Oxford University Press, Melbourne. 2003.

Roberts, James Rhys. *Scapegoat*. Columbia Publishing, Wales Ltd, Wales. 2002.

Rooney, David. *Burma Victory*. Cassell and Co, London. 1992.

Rooney, David. *Military Mavericks*. Cassell and Co, London. 1999.

Short, Anthony. *In Pursuit of Mountain Rats. The Communist Insurrection in Malaya*. Cultured Lotus, Singapore. 2000.

Short, James G. and McBride, Angus. *Men at Arms Series – The Special Air Service*. Osprey, London. 1981.

Smith, Rupert. *The Utility of Force*. Penguin Group, London. 2005.

Stubbs, Richard. *Hearts and Minds in Guerrilla Warfare – The Malayan Emergency 1948–1960*. Oxford University Press, Oxford. 1989.

Sykes, Christopher. *Orde Wingate*. Collins, London. 1959.

Taber, Robert. *The War of the Flea. Guerrilla Warfare – Theory and Practice*. Granada Publishing Ltd, London. 1970.

Taylor, Peter. *The Brits – The War Against the IRA*. Bloomsbury Publishing, London. 2001.

Thompson, J. and Imperial War Museum. *War Behind Enemy Lines*. Macmillan Publishers, London. 1998.

Thompson, J. *The Royal Marines. From Sea Soldiers to Special Forces*. Pan Macmillan Ltd, London. 2001.

Thompson, J. *The Imperial War Museum Book of Modern Warfare*. Pan Macmillan Ltd, London. 2003.

Thompson, L. *The Rescuers*. Paladin Press, Boulder, CO. 1986.

Tinnin, D. *The Hit Team*. Weidenfeld and Nicolson, London. 1976.

Tugwell, Maurice and Charters, David. *Special Operations and the Threats to United States Interests in the 1980s*. National Defense University Press, Washington, DC. 1984.

Tzu, Sun. *The Art of War*. Oxford University Press, Oxford. 1963.

Urban, Mark. *UK Eyes Alpha*. Faber and Faber Ltd, London. 1996.

Urban, Mark. *Task Force BLACK*. Abacus, London. 2011.

Verney, John. *Going to the Wars*. Collins, London. 1955.

Vital, David. *The Making of British Foreign Policy*. George Allen and Unwin Ltd, London. 1968.

Warner, P. *The Special Air Service*. William Kimber and Co Ltd, London. 1971.

Warner, P. *The SBS – Special Boat Squadron*. Sphere Books Ltd, London. 1983.

Weale, Adrian. *Secret Warfare*. Hodder and Stoughton, London. 1997.

Weale, Adrian. *The Real SAS*. Sedgwick and Jackson, London. 1998.

West, N. *The Secret War – The Story of the SOE*. Hodder and Stoughton Ltd, London. 1992.

West, N. *The Secret War for the Falklands*. Little, Brown and Company, London. 1997.

White, Nicholas. J. *Decolonisation – The British Empire Since 1945*. Addison, Wesley Longman Ltd, Essex. 1945.

Wilkinson, P. *Terrorism and the Liberal State*. Macmillan Press Ltd, London. 1977.

Wilson, Dare. *Tempting the Fates*. Pen and Sword Books Ltd, South Yorkshire. 2006.

Wood, J.R.T. *War Diaries of Andre Dennison*. Ashanti Publishing Ltd, Gibraltar. 1989.

Journals

'Acorn'. 'Argentinean Accounts of the landings at Port San Carlos on 21 May 1982'. *The British Army Review*. August 1987, pp. 77–80.

Banks, Tony. 'Low Intensity Conflict (LIC). Planning for a New Kind Of War'. *Jane's Defence Weekly*. 12 May 1990, pp. 903–21.

Bartholomew, H.J. 'The Trucial Oman Scouts'. *The British Army Review*. October 1963, pp. 21–9.

Bennett, Philip. 'The Case for Special Forces'. *The Australian Army Journal*. 1964.

Book, Elizabeth G. 'War on Terror Re-affirming Role of Special Operators'. *National Defense*. February 2003, pp. 32–3.

Bull, S. 'Scud Hunters'. *Military Illustrated*. November 2000, pp. 41–4.

Bull, S. 'SAS in Action'. *Military Illustrated*. October 2001, pp. 50–5.

Bull, S. 'A Review of SAS Operations in Oman and Malaysia'. *Military Illustrated*. January 2002, pp. 48–55.

'Cavalier'. 'From the Sands to the Mountains'. *The British Army Review*. April 1960, pp. 24–9.

Challis, Daniel S. 'Counter-Insurgency Success in Malaya'. *Military Review*. February 1987, pp. 56–69.

Crumplin, W.C.D. 'Operation Blick'. *The British Army Review*. March 1957, pp. 54–9.

De Butts, F.M. 'The Aden Protectorate Levies'. *The British Army Review*. April 1961, pp. 16–24.

Dobson, C. 'Oman – Why we are there'. *Officer*. May/June 1998, pp. 42–4.

Easter, David. 'British Intelligence and Propaganda During the "Confrontation", 1963–1966'. *Intelligence and National Security*, Volume 16, Number 2. Summer 2001, pp. 83–102.

Erwin, Sandra. 'Elite War Fighters Brace For "Asymmetric" Combat'. *National Defense*. February 1999, pp. 18–19.

Eshel, D. 'Special Forces in counter-terrorism'. *NATO's Nations*. Volume 4. 2002, pp. 154–9.

Estes, Kenneth W. 'First to the Fray'. *International Defense Review*. Volume 9. 1995, pp. 34–41.

Finlan, Alastair. 'British Special Forces and the Falklands Conflict: Twenty Years On'. *Defense and Security Analysis*, Volume 18, Number 4. 2002, pp. 319–32.

Finlan, Alastair. 'British Special Forces in the Falklands War of 1982'. *Small Wars and Insurgencies*. Volume 13, Number 3. Autumn 2002, pp. 75–96.

Finlan, Alastair. 'Warfare by Other Means: Special Forces, Terrorism and the Grand Strategy.' *Small Wars and Insurgencies*. Spring 2003, pp. 92–108.

Fitzsimmons, M. 'The Importance of Being Special: Planning for the Future of US Special Operations Forces'. *Defence and Security Analysis*. Volume 19, Number 3. September 2003, pp. 203–18.

Flavin, William. 'Special Operations Forces and Peace Operations in Greater Europe'. *Small Wars and Insurgencies* (special issue), Volume 7, Number 1. Spring 1996, pp. 55–64.

Gaines, Mike and Lowe, Janice. 'Special Forces'. *Flight International*. 10 September 1988, pp. 41–8.

Gibson, T.A. 'Special Forces – to be or not to be'. *The British Army Review*. April 1961, pp. 27–32.

Gourley, Scott R. 'Forging the New Tools for Special Operations'. *Army*. April 1994, pp. 40–3.

Gregorian, Ruffi. 'CLARET Operations and Confrontation, 1964–66'. *Conflict Quarterly*. Volume 6, Number 1. Winter 1991, pp. 48–62.

Gutteridge, W.F. 'The Significance of Aden'. *The British Army Review*. September 1959, pp. 4–6.

Hack, Karl. 'British Intelligence and Counter-Insurgency in the Era of Decolonisation: The Example of Malaya'. *Intelligence and National Security*. Volume 14, Number 2. Summer 1999, pp. 124–55.

Harper, Frank. 'Malayan Emergency 1948–1960. Lessons in Counter-Terrorism'. *Journal of Counter-terrorism and Homeland Security International*. Volume 9, Number 3, pp. 49–55.

Hewish, Mark and Pengally, Rupert. 'Special Solutions for Special Forces'. *International Defense Review*. Volume 5. 1995, pp. 41–9.

Hunter, Thomas B. 'Needles in a Haystack – The Role of Special Forces in Hunting Tactical Ballistic Missiles During Operation Desert Storm'. *Journal of Counter-terrorism and Security International*. Volume 6, Number 2.

'James Hope'. 'TAG or a Tale of Confrontation'. *The British Army Review*. August 1967, pp. 43–53.

Jeffrey, Keith. 'Intelligence and Counter Insurgency Operations: Some Reflections on the British Experience'. *The British Army Review*. January 1987, pp. 118–49.

Kibbe, Jennifer D. 'The Rise of the Shadow Warriors'. *Foreign Affairs Journal*. March/April 2004. Volume 83, Number 2, pp. 102–15.

King, David E. 'Intelligence Failures and the Falklands War: A Reassessment'. *Intelligence and National Security*. Volume 2, Number 2. April 1987, pp. 336–40.

Kutner, Joshua A. 'Special Operations Clout hinges on Modernization'. *National Defense*. April 1998, pp. 23–8.

Manton, L. 'TA SAS'. *Soldier Magazine*. 22 January 1996, pp. 14–15.

Margelletti, Andrea. 'Special Operations in the Desert'. *Military Technology*. Volume 4. 1991, pp. 62–5.

Marley, Anthony D. 'Special Operations in Conflict Resolution: Operational Capabilities Versus Political Constraints'. *Small Wars and Insurgencies* (special issue). Volume 7, Number 1. Spring 1996, pp. 35–40.

Miller, Sergio. 'Special Forces – A Future?' *RUSI Journal*. August 1993, pp. 70–4.

Newsinger, J. 'SAS Assessment'. *History Today*. December 1998, pp. 40–1.

Norell, Magnus and Stroberg, Karin. 'Special Forces in International Operations – Challenge for the Future.' *FOI, Swedish Defence Research Agency*. 14 December 2001.

Nott, C. 'Cock-up in the Falklands?' *Military Illustrated*. April 1997, pp. 18–21.

Paget, J.T. 'Emergency in Aden'. *The British Army Review*. April 1966, pp. 14–21.

Peat, John. 'The Chindits and Special Forces Manpower'. *The British Army Review*. Number 128. Winter 2001–02, pp. 53–61.

Prince, Stephen. 'British Command and Control in the Falklands Campaign'. *Defence and Security Analysis*. Volume 18, Number 4. 2002, pp. 333–49.

Pugh, N.M. 'Special Forces'. *The British Army Review*. April 1970, pp. 35–41.

Ryder, Stuart. 'The Evolution of Posthumous Gallantry Awards'. *RUSI Journal*. February/March 1998, pp. 75–9.

Scot, M. 'SAS in Gibraltar'. *New Statesman*. 9 March 1990, pp. 13–15.

Schoomaker, P. 'Special Operations: Shaping the Future Force'. *Army*. April 1997, pp. 12–29.

Schoomaker, P. 'US Special Operations Forces Prepare for Undefined Future'. *National Defense*. February 1998, pp. 18–23.

Simons, A. and Tucker, D. 'United States Special Operations Forces and the War on Terrorism'. *Small Wars and Insurgencies*. Spring 2003, pp. 77–91.

Steinmann, David. 'An Inside Look at the Most Elite Covert Ops Forces in the World'. *Journal of Counter-terrorism and Security International*, Volume 6, Number 3, pp. 55–9.

Stewart-Cox, A.G.E. 'Operation Tiger'. *The British Army Review*. September 1959, pp. 31–9.

Stoffa, Adam P. 'Special Forces, Counter-terrorism, and the Law of Armed Conflict'. *Studies in Conflict and Terrorism*. Volume 18, pp. 47–65.

Trant, R.B. 'Operation Consul. An Internal Security Operation in the Western Aden Protectorate – 9 August 1963'. *The British Army Review*. April 1964, pp. 22–9.

Tuck, Christopher. 'Borneo 1963–66: Counter-insurgency Operations and War Termination'. *Small Wars and Insurgencies*. Volume 15, Number 3. Winter 2004, pp. 89–111.

Wettern, David. 'Lessons Learned from the Falklands Conflict'. *Janes Defence Weekly*. 1 August 1987, pp. 194–6.

Wilkinson, Paul. 'The Role of the Military in Combating Terrorism in a Democratic Society'. *Terrorism and Political Violence*. Volume 8, Number 3. Autumn 1996, pp. 1–11.

Williams, Paul. 'Who's making UK foreign policy?' *International Affairs*. Number 5. 2004, pp. 911–29.

Newspaper Articles

Adams, J. 'SAS against terrorism'. *Sunday Times*. 2 October 1988, p. B6.

Adams, J. 'Shoot to Kill – Part 1'. *Sunday Times*. 27 November 1988.

Adams, J. 'Shoot to Kill – Part 2'. *Sunday Times*. 4 December 1988.

'Albanian rebels, trained by the SAS are gaining ground in Macedonia, aiming for the key city of Tetovo'. *Sunday Times*. 18 March 2001.

Borger, J. 'Operation Tango – SAS raid for war criminals in Bosnia'. *Guardian*. 12 July 1997, pp. 1–2.

Cameron, N. 'Srebrenica 1995'. *Sunday Times Review*. 7 July 2002, pp. 1–2.

Campbell, D. 'SAS in Gibraltar'. *New Statesman*. 13 May 1988, pp. 10–11.

Campbell, D. 'SAS in Gibraltar'. *New Statesman*. 17 June 1988, p. 11.

Clark, J. 'SAS on recce in Balkans'. *Sunday Times*. 19 August 2001, p. 2.

Colvin, M. and Clark, J. 'Sierra Leone Rescue Operation'. *Sunday Times*. 17 September 2000, pp. 26–7.

Fairhall, D. 'SAS activities in Bosnia since 1990'. *Guardian*. 11 July 1997, p. 14.

Fairhall, D. 'SAS Hype'. *Guardian*. 14 July 1997, pp. 8–9.

Gorman, E. 'IRA Casualties in Northern Ireland'. *The Times*. 4 June 1991.

Hall, M. 'Army magazine gagged over SAS jungle raid'. *Sunday Telegraph*. 29 October 2000, p. 6.

'Intelligence Services in Northern Ireland.' *Sunday Times*. 7 November 1993.

Jack, I. 'SAS in Gibraltar'. *Observer*. 2 October 1988, p. 14.

Knowsley, Jo. 'Day of Reckoning for Special Forces who Ran Away'. *Courier Mail* (Australia). 5 May 2003.

Llewellyn Smith, J and McQueen, A. '14 Int Company'. *Sunday Telegraph*. 18 January 1998, p. 20.

McGuire, A. 'IRA losses in Tyrone'. *Irish Times*. 18 February 1992, p. 5.

McManners, H. 'Paras and SAS to be merged'. *Sunday Times*. 25 January 1998, p. 9.

McManners, H. 'SBS Takeover by SAS'. *Sunday Times*. 23 August 1999, p. 5.

McNab, A. 'Gulf War'. *Sunday Times Review*. 14 January 2001, p. 4.

Moss, A. 'Mission Improbable'. *Guardian* G2. 24 April 2002, p. 4.

Norton-Taylor, R. 'SAS Soldiers left to Die'. *Guardian*. 8 February 2002, p. 9.

Oliver, T. and McQueen, A. 'Death of Capt Westmacott'. *Sunday Telegraph*. 9 January 2000, p. 19.

Smith, M. 'No Medal for SAS man killed in hostage rescue'. *Daily Telegraph*. 6 April 2001, p. 7.

Smith, M. 'Mission to wipe out Exocets'. *Daily Telegraph*. 8 March 2002, p. 9.

Van Straubenzee, A. 'Death of Capt Nairac'. *Spectator*. 13 March 1999,p. 40.

Walker, T. 'SAS Bosnia Raid'. *The Times*. 11 November 1998, p. 15.